The Case of the Indian Trader

THE CASE OF THE INDIAN TRADER

Billy Malone
and the
National
Park Service
Investigation
at Hubbell
Trading Post

PAUL D. BERKOWITZ

UNIVERSITY OF NEW MEXICO PRESS
ALBUQUERQUE

© 2011 by Paul D. Berkowitz
All rights reserved. Published 2011
Printed in the United States of America

First paperbound printing, 2011
Paperbound ISBN: 978-0-8263-4860-9

Library of Congress Cataloging-in-Publication Data

Berkowitz, Paul (Paul D.)
  The case of the Indian trader : Billy Malone and the National Park Service investigation at Hubbell
Trading Post / Paul D. Berkowitz.
    p. cm.
  Includes bibliographical references and index.
  ISBN 978-0-8263-4859-3 (cloth : alk. paper)
  1. Malone, Billy Gene. 2. Hubbell Trading Post National Historic Site (Ganado, Ariz.)—
History—20th century. 3. Indian traders—Arizona—Biography. 4. Berkowitz, Paul (Paul D.)
5. Criminal investigations—Arizona—Case studies. 6. False arrest—Arizona—Case studies.
7. United States. National Park Service—History—20th century. 8. Western National Parks
Association—History—20th century. 9. Navajo Indian Reservation—History—20th century.
10. Navajo Indians—Arizona—Social life and customs—20th century. I. Title.
  F819.G36B37 2011
  979.1′37—dc22

                          2010051227

Design and Composition: Melissa Tandysh
Text is Minion Pro 10.25/14

For Billy Malone and his family
To help set things right

and

For Susan Morton
Who wanted this story to be told

Contents

Illustrations

Foreword

THIS BOOK WILL shatter many illusions about the National Park Service.

This is not another book written by a retired park ranger about his or her exploits in the service. You will not find any romantic or humorous accounts of life as a ranger spent in the great outdoors, engaging tourists, protecting wildlife, or saving lives. And this is certainly not a story told in any of the popular public television documentaries about the unique system of national parks that author and historian Wallace Stegner famously referred to as "America's best idea."

This book tells a different story, providing a rare and intimate glimpse into the inner workings and the culture—warts and all—of America's most beloved federal agency. That is all the more reason why this is an important book—a book that needed to be written and a book that should be read and studied by anyone who has visited and fallen in love with America's national parks. This is the disturbing and all-too-real "story behind the scenery" of the NPS that uses its 2004 criminal investigation at Hubbell Trading Post as a case study to shed light on the dark side of how the agency operates behind the scenes, often self-destructively and at the expense of its very mission.

"The Indian trader" in this story is Billy Malone, by most accounts a gentle and generous soul who spent almost his entire life living among the Navajo Indians in far northeastern Arizona, working as a real, old-time Indian trader in the most remote regions of the reservation. Malone was the last of a breed: the last genuine Indian trader to work at Hubbell Trading Post NHS. Billy Malone is the focal point in this story, the unfortunate individual around whom the investigation spun out of control. But while Billy Malone is at the center of the story, a bigger picture unfolds in the detailed account of how Malone was falsely accused of a host of crimes and then recklessly pursued and nearly railroaded to destruction through a criminal investigation undertaken by the NPS in "partnership" with the nonprofit, cooperating association known as the Western National Parks Association. Along the way, officials from a number of other government agencies jumped into the fray, contributing to the damage and destruction by attempting to cover up what had happened and by trying to strip Malone of what few rights had not already been trampled. It is this account that will shatter your illusions and expose the myths about not only the NPS but the other agencies and organizations with which it is allied.

As a retired NPS special agent, Paul Berkowitz is uniquely qualified to tell this story. There was probably no one else in the NPS who would have dared to tell it. With more than thirty-three years of law enforcement experience under his belt, most of it working in the field as a supervisory special agent, Berkowitz has seen more than his fair share of conflict and corruption in the NPS. He spent a career as one of a small group whose sole responsibility is the investigation of serious crimes committed in the national parks. His integrity and his commitment to his constitutional oath of office long ago earned him a reputation as a trouble-maker in the agency, a brand he wears as a badge of honor. It was only through his efforts, his resolve, and his bold intervention in the Hubbell investigation that a light was shed on the egregious mishandling that had occurred in the early stages of the investigation and the misconduct that had taken place at the highest levels of his agency. Those efforts put Berkowitz on a collision course with his own supervisors and other senior officials in the agency who, after spending nearly a million dollars and nearly two years targeting the Indian trader, simply wanted to see Malone arrested for something—for *anything*—and then have the matter go away. But that was not something Berkowitz could abide. After finishing his own investigation, he turned everything around by handing off the case to internal investigators from the Office of the Inspector General. It is Berkowitz, more than any other person, who knows the details of this story and the disturbing, misguided manner in which the NPS at times operates. Were it not for his actions, this story would have had a different and far more tragic ending. That is all the more reason this is Berkowitz's story to tell.

Berkowitz and I met in the early 1980s at a seminar I was conducting for the NPS. At that time, I was the supervisor of the Behavioral Sciences Unit and

Hostage Negotiations Team for the second largest sheriff's department in Arizona. After my own retirement I went into private practice, consulting and providing training and crisis services as a contract police psychologist for state, local, provincial, and federal law enforcement agencies across the United States, Canada, and Europe. The NPS was one of my clients for much of that time. Years spent providing training and counseling services to NPS emergency services personnel gave me the opportunity to observe firsthand what an unusual and often conflicted organization it really is, particularly in its ambivalent approach to law enforcement, having its own unique way of doing business beyond public view.

Berkowitz describes the culture of the agency and takes the reader through the history of how the NPS has evolved into an atypical bureaucracy, unique in all of government for both its idealistic mission and for the image it has cultivated with the American public. But that culture and public image has left the agency vulnerable to abuse by ambitious and unscrupulous employees, supervisors, and managers—including law enforcement personnel—whose own influence and raw political power has enabled them to operate with alarming levels of autonomy and freedom from meaningful oversight and accountability.

Most Americans have grown accustomed to hearing about scandal and corruption in government. But few people are aware or would even consider the extent to which those same types of problems exist in the NPS. In his account, Berkowitz for the first time exposes, probes, and discusses the unique culture of the service—how it operates, and how it "thinks." In telling that part of the story, Berkowitz is breaking new ground, exploring new territory, and distinguishing himself as a thoughtful, analytical writer. Berkowitz has done an extraordinary job of describing and explaining many of the strange characteristics I personally witnessed as a consultant to the NPS but had not fully understood. In so doing, Berkowitz has done more than simply write an exposé and tell a fascinating story. He has made a significant contribution to the literature dealing with organizational psychology and corruption.

But this book is far more than an academic piece. It is more than a story about the Southwest, Navajos, Indian traders, the NPS, law enforcement, crime, and corruption. It is a complex but real-life mystery with a plot and a series of twists and turns that defy imagination. No one could make up a story as bizarre as this, with one bad judgment leading to another, in a cascade of incompetence, greed, and corruption culminating in a perfect storm of bad government behavior, unfolding step by step, page by page. *The Case of the Indian Trader* is a page turner and a fascinating read. But it most certainly is not just another book about the NPS. It is a story that will entertain and inform you at the very same time that it shatters your illusions. It is a disturbing account told with courage and conviction, in the hope that "America's best idea" can be made even better.

— Kevin Gilmartin

Kevin Gilmartin, PhD, is a behavioral scientist specializing in police ethics and crisis management. He spent twenty years in law enforcement before retiring and entering into private practice. He is retained as a consultant to law enforcement agencies throughout the United States, Canada, and Europe. He is a regular guest instructor at the FBI Academy in Quantico, Virginia, and a frequent instructor for the Royal Canadian Mounted Police. His numerous publications on law enforcement ethics and "emotional survival" are used by law enforcement agencies throughout North America, Europe, and Australia.

Acknowledgments

Heartfelt thanks to the following people for their generous assistance.

For reviewing and commenting on all or a portion of the manuscript:
Elijah and Claudia Blair
Jeff Burnham
David Cuillier
Kevin Gilmartin
Laura Graves
Peter Iverson
Polly Liggett
Carol Moses
Betty M. and Joe Ray
Molina Suer
Steve Sykes

For graciously contributing photographs and other images:
Hank and Vicky Blair
Russ Finley Photography
Steve and Gail Getzwiller
Cindy Jacka and Jerry Jacka Photography
Billy Malone and family
Susan Morton

For legal advice, and persistence in their efforts to secure the public release of reports and other documents related to the Hubbell Trading Post Investigations:

Jeff Ruch

Christine Erickson

Paula Dinerstein

And all the other heroes at PEER

For sharing so freely and making me feel welcome those many years ago:

Dorothy Lameman Fulton

Mona Polacca

Special thanks to:

William Yazzie, my trusted source for the word on the street as well as for Navajo translations and spelling.

Clark Whitehorn, for incredible support from the very beginning.

Billy Malone and the rest of the Indian traders of the Four Corners region, who trusted me to listen, and the many other good people who played a part in this story, who graciously assisted by participating in follow-up interviews and sharing their own thoughts and recollections.

And most of all, my amazing wife, EFL, for love, friendship, and understanding. Your integrity, hard work, and commitment to national parks and the preservation of our natural and cultural heritage is an inspiration. May your own NPS career not suffer for the stand that I have taken in writing this book.

Abbreviations

AAM	American Association of Museums
AUSA	assistant U.S. attorney
AZAG	Arizona State Attorney General's Office
DOI	Department of the Interior
EMS	emergency medical services
FBI	Federal Bureau of Investigation
FOIA	Freedom of Information Act
FTC	Federal Trade Commission
GAO	Government Accounting Office (renamed Government Accountability Office in 2004)
HIDTA	High Intensity Drug Trafficking Area
HTP	Hubbell Trading Post
HUTR	Hubbell Trading Post National Historic Site
IACB	Indian Arts and Crafts Board
IMR	Intermountain Region
IMRO	Intermountain Regional Office
IRS	Internal Revenue Service
ISA	interpretive support account
MNA	Museum of Northern Arizona
NAAUSA	National Association of Assistant United States Attorneys
NHS	national historic site
NGO	nongovernmental organization
NPS	National Park Service
NSAC	national special agent-in-charge

NRA	national recreation area
OIG	Office of the Inspector General
OPR	Office of Professional Responsibility
PEER	Public Employees for Environmental Responsibility
PL	public law
RSAC	regional special agent-in-charge
SA	special agent
SSA	supervisory special agent
SPMA	Southwest Parks and Monuments Association
UITA	United Indian Traders Association
USDC	U.S. District Court
WNPA	Western National Parks Association

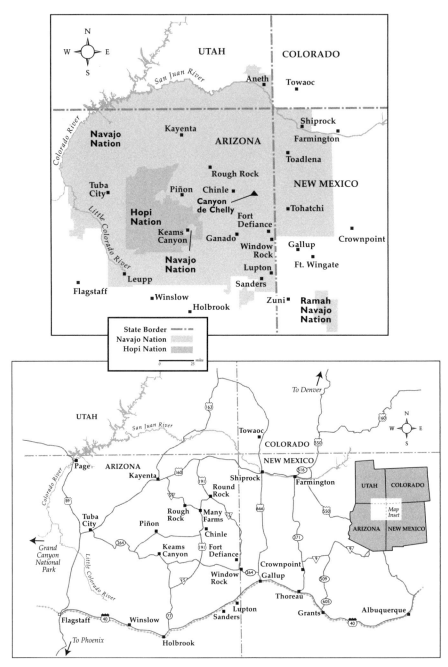

Map: The Navajo Nation and Four Corners region.

Introduction

(Kodóó hane' háá t'i')

B ILLY GENE MALONE had been an Indian trader on the Navajo Reservation for thirty-eight years when he was interviewed by researchers from Northern Arizona University's Cline Library as part of the United Indian Traders Association (UITA) Oral History Project. By then, in 1998, Malone, the last in a line of successors to John Lorenzo Hubbell, had been running the Hubbell Trading Post for the National Park Service (NPS) for eighteen years as an employee of the nonprofit cooperating organization known as the Western National Parks Association (WNPA):

> [John Lorenzo Hubbell] was one of the first. Most of your traders all
> float into the country when the Navajos come back from signing their
> peace treaty. They had been acclimated to coffee beans, sugar, flour, yard
> goods, canned goods, and here came the trader—just like anywhere else.
> I'm not sure how many traders were here previous. There doesn't seem
> to be too much said about the traders here previous to the peace treaty
> thing. I don't think there were too many around, because this was Indian
> country. You could get an arrow stuck in your back or anything like that.
> And really, it was, you might say, the "settlers" coming through the coun-
> try that complained that "the Navajos are stealing our horses, or oxen, or
> sheep," or whatever, that got the ball rollin' for the Army to go pick up

the Navajos. . . . And in those days, the government wasn't very nice to Indian people. I mean, it was pretty rough on 'em. . . .

Lorenzo Hubbell was workin' kind of as a cavalry scout, and he dropped out of that and he hung out around Fort Defiance quite a bit. And he went into the trading business. He was twenty-three years old at that time when he started. . . . He'd already roamed through the country. He'd been up into Utah and whatnot, and this must have been the site he liked, was the Ganado area. . . .

. . . I hope to do this for ten more years. I feel like I got another ten years in me. I want to be here 'till I die with my boots on, so to speak.[1]

That last wish would not come true. Instead, just six years after that 1998 interview, Billy Malone, one of the most well known and respected Indian traders of the twentieth century, would find himself out of a job owing to a series of disturbing events and involuntarily catapulted into the history books, right alongside John Lorenzo Hubbell, as the very *last* Indian trader in the line of succession at Hubbell Trading Post.

Hubbell Trading Post *was* the oldest continuously operating Indian trading post in the West. It lies deep in the heart of the Navajo Indian Reservation in northeastern Arizona, in the community known as Ganado.

In 1965 Congress authorized the NPS to purchase Hubbell Trading Post in recognition of its historic significance with the explicit understanding that the newly designated national historic site would *not* become "just another museum" but would continue to serve the Navajo community as a genuine working trading post and would be run by a real Indian trader.

For the next four decades the legacy of John Lorenzo Hubbell was kept alive by the NPS through employment of a succession of three honest-to-God Indian traders recruited from other trading posts across the Navajo Reservation to run Hubbell's.

However, the legacy of John Lorenzo Hubbell came to an end during the summer of 2004 when Billy Malone was simultaneously fired from his job at the WNPA and subjected to an early morning raid at his home during which federal agents seized what amounted to his life savings: his treasured possessions, including hundreds of rugs and thousands of pieces of jewelry he had collected over his nearly fifty-year career. These events brought to an end a 130-year tradition of genuine Indian trading at the oldest and most authentic place of its kind in America.

For the next two and a half years, with his job lost, his reputation destroyed, and his spirit crushed, Billy Malone was forced to wait as the NPS conducted its criminal investigation into an amazing series of allegations leveled against him, allegations that literally equated him with the likes of Al Capone.

But when all was said and done, the case against Malone was dropped. Charges were never filed and all of Malone's property was eventually returned to him. By this time, however, after realizing the investigation had not gone as they'd planned, most of Malone's accusers were retaining their own attorneys and invoking their own right to remain silent, as they found themselves the subject of an internal investigation undertaken by the Office of the Inspector General at the Department of the Interior regarding the false charges and statements made against Malone and the manner in which the case against him had been conducted.

▲▼▲

This is a story about Billy Malone and the end of an era in the Old West. Malone is the central figure in that story. He is the character on whom all attention initially focused in the NPS's Hubbell investigation. And because Billy Malone lived almost his entire life on the Navajo Reservation working as a genuine Indian trader, a great deal of *his* story is a story about reservation life, Navajos, and old-time trading posts.

But more than a story about Billy Malone, this is a story about the NPS, federal law enforcement activities, politics, corruption, and whistle-blowing. In this case, the backdrop is the Navajo Reservation and Indian traders. The investigation targeting Billy Malone merely serves as a fascinating but tragic example of what can happen when adequate safeguards are not in place to assure honesty, integrity, and accountability in government. And to the extent that I was involved in that investigation and since I ultimately "blew the whistle," this is also *my* story, offering a glimpse into a contentious and controversial career as a federal law enforcement officer and certified troublemaker.

Unless otherwise indicated, the account of events presented is based on official reports, court records, internal memorandums, calendar entries, supplemental interviews, and other documented communications related to the government investigation(s) initiated by the NPS in May 2004 and closed more than three and a half years later under the assumed jurisdiction of the OIG. Portions of those reports and the text of e-mails and memos are extensively quoted and annotated to tell this story, both in the name of accuracy and to provide context.

I assumed responsibility for the NPS investigation in December 2005, after that case had already been underway for more than a year and a half and associated costs were approaching a million dollars. I was assigned the case only after a bizarre series of political maneuvers that began with threats and were followed by promises and then ultimately pressure to reach a predetermined outcome. My instructions were to close the case and arrest Billy Malone without further expense or delay.

But soon after beginning my assignment, during which time I obtained briefings and reviewed the case, I detected a number of extremely serious problems. My findings and the information that came to light about the manner in which the NPS investigation had been previously conducted, as well as my growing concerns about the honesty and integrity of my own colleagues and supervisors, not to mention high-level managers overseeing the investigation from both the NPS *and* the WNPA, led me to deliberately circumvent my own chain of command. I handed off the investigation directly to the Office of the Inspector General (OIG) immediately after filing my completed criminal case report with the U.S. attorney for the district of Arizona in late October 2006.[2]

Contained within that report and accompanying transmittal memorandum was documentation implicating as many as five other federal agents, two government attorneys (one of whom had since been appointed to the federal bench), the current and former directors of the NPS's Intermountain Region (IMR), and both the executive director and board chairman of the WNPA. Whether Billy Malone had committed any crimes or not (and it was certain he had *not* committed most of the crimes of which he'd been accused), the evidence of the government's and WNPA's own misconduct would have made prosecution of Billy Malone impossible.

By then, recognizing the implications of these findings and acknowledging the repercussions of the decision to file my report outside normal channels, my wife and I knew that I would need to retire and that she, also an NPS employee, would need to find a new job. My own supervisors never saw my report. NPS and WNPA managers did not become aware of the extent to which the case had changed course until they found themselves being interviewed by investigators from the OIG. The OIG's internal investigation into the conduct of—and the relationship between—NPS and WNPA officials continued for another full year. Its report, which fully incorporated and then augmented my own report, was filed as DOI-OIG case no. PI-PI-07–0054-I and was finalized and approved in January 2008.

Much of the background information provided in this book, including both historical accounts and illuminating details of behind-the-scenes activities and politics, is based on my own experiences working with the NPS for over thirty-three years and working with—as well as living among—the Navajo and neighboring Native American community for a significant portion of that time. As such, this background material, particularly chapters 1 and 3, reflect my own perspective and opinion. More than a mere academic or editorial exercise, it is intended to help the reader detect cultural influences at work and understand *why* events in this story unfolded as they did, putting particular emphasis on principal players from two very distinct and different worlds, about which the general public has a great many misconceptions.

Unfortunate stereotypes, both good and bad, attach to the old-time Indian traders on the Navajo Reservation, where they live with "the People" (*Diné*). Literally volumes have been written by political scientists, cultural anthropologists, and sociologists about the world of the Navajo. Navajo society is one of the most studied on the planet. And if this book helps satisfy or pique further interest in Navajo history and culture, that is all the better. The interested reader is encouraged to scour bookstores and libraries for academic works in those areas. I don't claim to be an anthropologist or an academic of any sort. But I did live and work in and around the Navajo Nation for a number of years and can attest to what a very different world that place truly is. My crude dissertation on the subject is intended only to offer a brief history of traders and trading and to help the reader understand to at least a small degree how dramatically different some aspects of Navajo life and culture can be, and that there we are "not in Kansas anymore."

The NPS is likewise a world unto its own. In contrast to the Navajo, however, there has been very little research and very little written about its culture and organizational psychology. As John Freemuth has noted: "There is surprisingly little information available on the internal culture of the NPS."[3] Freemuth is more correct than even he may realize, in that what both the public and academia know of the NPS has been carefully orchestrated in the staged images of park rangers periodically splashed on the television or in park brochures. To at least a small extent, I hope this effort will begin to fill that gap. And while my account of the agency is not an academic or sociological study like those that have been done on the Navajo, it is what I believe to be an accurate, if somewhat sobering, insider's view, based on living and working in that equally unique world for more than three decades. In many respects this story exemplifies the unfortunate collision of two competing worlds and distinct cultures, with associated myths, stereotypes, cultural influences and biases figuring prominently in how conclusions were drawn and decisions were made in the investigation.

Over the course of time, several other individuals and organizations took on key roles, none more so than managers from the nonprofit WNPA, which for decades served as the business link between the NPS and the various Indian traders employed to run Hubbell Trading Post. Later, lawyers from the U.S. Attorney's Office and the Department of the Interior's (DOI's) Solicitor's Office, and then investigators from the OIG, took on increasingly important roles. As such, I devote considerable time in the following chapters to explaining the history of each of these organizations. And in the case of the NPS itself, I cite a number of past incidents not only to provide a measure of insight into its inner workings but to also reveal the fascinating web of influence and favor that extends between most of these same players and to demonstrate that the manner in which *this* case—this story—unfolded was regrettably predictable and symptomatic of a much larger problem.

I am no more a lawyer than I am an anthropologist or sociologist. But because legal as well as ethical technicalities, violations, and blunders factor so critically into this story, I also spend time considering matters of law and jurisdiction affecting federal investigations, police conduct, and crimes committed within Indian reservations. Selected statutes as well as court cases and opinions relevant to a particular issue or legal matter are cited throughout the text as reference for the interested reader. Any errors in those citations, however unintentional, are my own.

When all is said and done, as much as anything else this is a story about cultural ignorance, about not asking, not listening, and not wanting to know the whole truth. It is about a rush to judgment and about failing to understand that there are still a handful of places in the United States in the most remote regions of Indian country where time has virtually stood still for decades and, in many respects, where things are still done the way they were done fifty or even a hundred years ago. Ultimately, it is the regrettable and tragic story about the last real Indian trader at Hubbell Trading Post, and how his life, his reputation, and his livelihood were very nearly destroyed by the corrupt partnership between the NPS and the WNPA.

The Trading Post

(Naalyéhé bá hooghan)

IT'S NOT ALL that hard to tell when you've stumbled onto a real trading post, particularly if you're traveling through the Four Corners region of the United States. It's just that most people have never really had the experience, so they can't always tell the genuine article when they see it.

One can find shops calling themselves "trading post" lining the streets of cities like Scottsdale, Sedona, Albuquerque, Santa Fe, Taos, and even Durango, Vail, and Aspen, or most any other town even remotely nearby the region or within a hundred miles of a national park entrance, and even truck stops along the interstate highways, all advertising Indian rugs, baskets, and jewelry for sale. Most of these establishments assume the name "trading post" in an attempt to lure tourists with the promise of genuine Indian arts and crafts, typically at dramatically reduced (but perpetually) half-off prices.

A rare few of these establishments come by their names honestly, tracing roots back to genuine Indian trading posts and genuine Indian traders. Historic family names still tied to daily operations figure prominently on a list of such posts:

- McGee's Indian Art Gallery on the Hopi Reservation at Keams Canyon
- The Leighton family's Notah-Dineh Trading Company in Cortez, Colorado
- Elijah and Claudia Blair's Dinnebito Trading Post in Page, Arizona

- Cameron (formerly the Richardson family's) Trading Post east of Grand Canyon National Park
- Foutz's Shiprock Trading Post and Joe Tanner's Fifth Generation Trading in Farmington, New Mexico
- Richardson's Trading Post, Ellis Tanner Trading, Tanner's Shush Yaz Trading Company, Tobe Turpen's (now Perry Null's) Trading Post, and Turney's Inc. General Trading, all in Gallup, New Mexico
- The Simpson brothers' (along with Jana Kennedy Simpson's) Twin Rocks Trading Post in Bluff, Utah

The legitimacy of these establishments as a naturally evolving incarnation of the old trading posts is evidenced not just by their family ties but by both the quality of their merchandise and the volume of Indian traffic and trade they still receive in the form, for example, of the pawn they take in, the cash loans they provide, the checks they cash, the works of art they purchase, and the weaving and jewelry supplies they maintain for this special clientele. But these establishments are now the exceptions. Most have had to move to (or have been enveloped by) the city and have been forced to abandon many traditional trading practices and commodities to survive changing economic times. Regrettably, some of the old and established trading families have altogether abandoned their interests in the old trading posts and even in off-reservation pawn in favor of less risky and more lucrative business and political endeavors. Others have sold out both their businesses and their family names to foreign or corporate interests, which adds confusion to the mix and compromises the integrity of the Indian arts and crafts industry.

Still, a handful of genuine, old-time trading posts do survive, run by real Indian traders in much the same way they have been for over a century. This is particularly the case on the immense Navajo Reservation that dominates the northeastern corner of Arizona and reaches well into New Mexico as well as southern Utah, which is the setting of this story. These unique establishments typically lie deep within the more remote regions of Indian country, far off the beaten path and often at the end of some deeply rutted dirt road, about as far from any real town as you can get.[1] It is in part their remote location and their isolation from the rest of the outside world that allows them to survive, albeit in a humble way. They are not there to cater to tourists or serve as retail rug or jewelry outlets.

Instead, they are there to serve the needs of the extremely remote Indian communities in which they reside. They provide access to basic necessities where no one else does and frequently provide the only reliable source of income or economic development for the people who live there. The piñon nuts, wool, hides, rugs, baskets, jewelry, and other pieces of fine Indian art they take in trade for food, clothing, gasoline, and other basic supplies or cash are just a part of the currency in which they often deal. These trading posts continue to operate because no one else will live or do business "way out there," and few others are willing or able to tolerate such austere conditions or exercise the flexible and unconventional business practices that are required to make things work in this different world—both for the trader and for the community residents. Most of the people who do run them—the traders—do so because they have made a lifestyle choice, and they generally feel a deep sense of commitment to their adopted community and a desire to live and try to make a living well off the beaten path.

The cultivation of this special currency—particularly the collectable rugs, jewelry, and other items we've come to consider highly desirable Indian arts and crafts—in large part owes to partnerships developed between local residents and the traditional trading posts scattered across the remote regions of Indian

1. Panoramic view of a Navajo home near Round Rock, Navajo Nation, 1978 (*photograph courtesy of Jerry Jacka photography*).

2. Navajo woman
weaving a rug
inside her
home, Navajo
Nation, 1977
(*photograph
courtesy of
Jerry Jacka
photography*).

country. It was the trader's challenge to identify marketable goods that his Navajo neighbors could collect or produce for him in exchange for basic supplies and other commodities carried at the trading post.

Burnt Water, Wide Ruins, Klagetoh, Ganado, Chinle, Crystal, Two Grey Hills, Teec Nos Pos, and more recently Newlands have become famous as names associated with special designs of highly desirable Navajo rugs. In reality, these are the names of communities, or chapters, on the Navajo Reservation, within which trading posts are situated.[2] Old-time traders like John Lorenzo Hubbell, as well as more contemporary but no less legitimate traders like Bruce Burnham, working in concert with their communities, encouraged local weavers to special-ize their designs and improve their craft in order to better market their unique art to the outside world. Among the most recognized of these designs is the Ganado Red, characterized by black borders and contrasting use of brilliant red, black, and grey geometric patterns. Hubbell first promoted this style in the late 1800s and early 1900s at the famous Ganado trading post that bears his name. More recently, in the latter portion of the twentieth century, the term Newlands was adopted to reflect the special design encouraged by Burnham Trading Post for use by weavers relocated from the Coal Mine Mesa area to the Newlands portion of the reservation near Sanders, AZ. Over time the strict geographic distinction between styles of rugs has become blurred, as talented weavers from across the reservation have borrowed aspects of other regional designs or woven entire tapestries in a style associated with another distant chapter because it was in greater demand and would command a better price.

So how *do* you know when you've found a genuine trading post, the real deal?

First, you probably drove more than a fair distance over an unmaintained stretch of highway or on dirt roads just to get there. When you pulled up you likely got tossed around in your seat, since the parking lot is potholed and strains the shock absorbers of your vehicle. There are probably as many stray dogs hanging around and begging for food or sleeping in the shade of the building or a nearby cottonwood tree as there are pickup trucks and other "rez rockets" parked out front. There may also be a few stray cows and horses grazing on the shrubs alongside the building or feeding on the weeds growing through the cracks of whatever pavement is still present at the gas pumps. The raggedy stray dogs provide a welcome relief from the dead ones you saw lying on the highway coming in. The slow moving cows and horses that block your way into the parking lot are still a preferable sight to the bloated dead one you may have passed along the side of the highway, where it was pulled off the road by the Navajo Police Department after being hit the night before.

The only real sign announcing that you've arrived at the trading post is probably a faded wooden one, hand carved or painted, that's easy to miss if you're not looking closely. You may have actually driven past the establishment the first time, unsure as to whether this was really the right place, especially since it bears so little resemblance to all the other "trading posts" you've seen in town.

Walking in, you may be surprised by the absence of rugs, jewelry, baskets, kachina dolls, or tourist stuff. Instead, most of what you see reminds you of something between a modern convenience store and an old-time rural grocery store your great-grandparents told you about. The shelves are stocked with basic (very basic) grocery items and hardware. Heavy-duty pots, pans, and other kitchen utensils may hang from the ceiling, while bags of flour may be stacked in a corner. There may be a refrigerated meat counter and someone working as a butcher, slicing up a locally slaughtered cow or sheep. There are probably several display cases stocked with yarn and weaving supplies and perhaps shelves full of brightly colored velveteen cloth. Mixed in with all these old-time supplies you'll probably also see racks of DVDs to rent, as well as prepaid telephone calling cards for sale. It's likely only when you go to the far back of the store or ask to see the back room (which may be a walk-in vault) that you will discover that rugs, jewelry, baskets, or kachinas are available there for sale.

If you see anyone at all when you first walk in it's probably a couple of local Indians talking or just laughing at a joke told in their native Navajo, because English is still a second language for most of the people who live there. Some of the older people may not speak English at all. The older women will be splendidly attired in some form of traditional garment—a brightly colored blouse and velvet skirt—and adorned with a mix of heavy turquoise and silver jewelry hanging from their neck, on their wrists, or around their waist. All this is set off on the other end by tennis shoes and bobby socks. The older men are probably dressed western style in worn jeans, button-tab shirts, and cowboy boots, perhaps with a cap that proudly commemorates their military service or with their hair rolled and tied back into a traditional bun. In contrast, the younger people, if present, are probably dressed just like younger people anywhere else in America in the latest fashions from town, complete with makeup and styled hair.

The store counter is probably staffed by a couple of relatively modern (as opposed to traditional) Navajo women, chatting with customers or talking between themselves about the local gossip. It's possible that one of them is the wife or daughter of the trader who runs the place. If he's there, he's probably the middle-aged or older white man, plainly but neatly dressed in jeans and a flannel or western shirt. If he's not out front or in the office, he's probably outside at someone's truck or out back at his own house or trailer, talking in broken Navajo ("trader Navajo") with a local weaver or silversmith about the rug, basket, or jewelry he or she brought in to trade. Otherwise, the trader's probably on a road trip to town to get supplies or sell or consign the rugs and jewelry he took in over the past month or so.

The characteristic location, facade, and all the other visible trappings aside, what really makes an Indian trading post genuine is the trader himself and the comfortable social atmosphere he creates in his store for the community. Without him (and it is almost always him) it's just another out-of-the-way convenience store or gift shop. It is the trader who, by living and working as a part of a remote community not otherwise fully integrated into the modern economic world and filling whatever community need or void might otherwise exist—from providing postal or emergency medical services to serving as courier, translator, or mediator—makes a store a real trading post and in many respects bridges the gap between two distinct worlds. During World War II, trading posts even served as military enlistment stations, to which the Navajos turned out in droves. All of this is accomplished not only by living and breathing his job 24–7 and interacting with the community day-in and day-out but also by accepting business practices that would cause panic in any other modern establishment. As fourth-generation trader Bruce Burnham says, "Running a trading post is *not* Business 101."[3]

The old-time trading post is not strictly a profit-driven enterprise, and traders will sometimes sacrifice the bottom line in order to serve the more pressing needs of the community. This translates into a number of unique practices not seen elsewhere in American society for over a century including the issuance of completely unsecured credit, outright loans of cash, and cash advances or credit issued on the mere promise of a new rug or a piece of jewelry to be delivered the following year—secured only by a handshake or a note scribbled on a piece of paper with the customer's mark or thumbprint and then filed away in the trader's shirt pocket.[4] It may also mean purchasing a rug, bracelet, hide, or basket for which the trader has absolutely no use and will never sell (and will likely be tossed into a pile in a back room or shed at home, perhaps because it is of inferior quality or is damaged or perhaps because he already has too much inventory), solely because the client needs the money now. Or the trader may create chores for someone to do—perhaps asking them to stack firewood or move a stack of feed or flour from one location to another (which the trader will then move back to its original location the next day)—in order to give them a way to work off a loan or pay for some food or gas. Equally common is the practice of simply handing out a little cash from the till or his own pocket, giving away a six-pack of soda to a child, or giving food or a Pendleton blanket to a needy client, with no prospect of repayment, at all.

Among the more novel practices seen in trading posts is the trader helping his Navajo clients endorse their checks or affix their mark or thumbprint to other documents. This is a more common practice than many people realize and occurs to this day in many of the remaining trading posts on the reservation. Many of the trader's older Navajo clients may not read, write, or even speak English and so will apply their thumbprint to the back of a check or make their mark in lieu of a signature and then have the trader witness the mark or thumbprint with his signature. And in the not-too-distant past it wasn't just traders acting on behalf of Navajo customers who engaged in this and even more unconventional practices.

Wilford J. W. Ashcroft was a deputy U.S. marshal who worked on the Navajo Reservation near Ramah, New Mexico, and simultaneously worked for the Indian Service during the period of the 1930s when land allotments were being assigned to some Navajos, giving them title to checkerboard parcels near the route of the Santa Fe Railroad. Much of this land was historically occupied by the Navajos but had been excluded from the boundaries of the reservation established by the government after the signing of the 1868 Navajo treaty. For many Navajo families this was a mere technicality; they did not let it stop them from taking up residence on the ancestral homelands they understood had been promised under the treaty. In an attempt to address this problem, the federal government applied new legal authority to assign allotments of sections of this (now public) land to individual Navajos.[5] The concept of an individual owning the land on which he or she relied to live and survive was foreign to most Navajos. Still, most of the Navajos identified as prospective recipients were eager enough to be relieved of the ongoing harassment and trespass by settlers and ranchers who increasingly attempted to encroach on and graze their own livestock on the same tracts of land. However, completion of the process was jeopardized when many Navajos, already distrustful of white men and particularly government officials, refused to sign or make their mark on any of the required documents. That posture was not at all surprising given their past experiences dealing with both federal bureaucrats and with the state governments of Arizona and New Mexico.

While Ashcroft understood their apprehension, he also recognized the long-term repercussions their refusal to sign the documents would have. Many Navajos would miss out on a one-time opportunity to own their own land under legal authority recognized by the government, and the looming alternative was that these "surplus" lands would be sold to settlers. In search of a solution, and understanding that many of the government's rules just did not work or fit life on the reservation, Ashcroft had various members of his own family, including all of his sons and daughters, affix their thumbprints to the necessary documents and then had others sign as witnesses. The Navajos who received their allotments never knew that Ashcroft and his family had forged their thumbprints for them, but they were ultimately granted ownership of their land, all the same.[6] Unconventional measures like this certainly cross the line by modern standards, but they were common enough on the reservation even in the mid-twentieth century.

Perhaps more than anything else, the genuine, successful trading post is a place where the local Navajo residents, and particularly the elders, feel comfortable just hanging around, visiting with friends, telling stories, leaving messages, cashing their checks, selling or trading their rugs and jewelry, picking up mail, or buying groceries and other supplies in a store run by this unique *bilagáana* (white man or non-Indian) who has taken the time to earn the trust and respect of his chosen neighbors by living among them, doing business with them, learning their language and their customs, and becoming a part of their community.

These very traits—the things that truly define and distinguish a real old-time trading post—are, however, among the most difficult things to see. You can't just walk into a trading post for the first time and expect to see how business is being conducted or understand what's really going on. You have to be patient, take your time, and stay for a while. Wait, watch, and listen.

In spite (or perhaps because) of this very real component of trading post life, over the years traders as a group have been maligned and subjected to more than their share of negative stereotyping; particularly in the mass media in the form of images burned into the American psyche through western movies and television shows. Much like their Indian neighbors, traders as a group have been rudely portrayed in movies and TV shows as the bad guy, the cheat, and the antagonist in service to the oversimplified and heavily stereotyped story line, all of which furthers our false image of the Old West and, in particular, of American Indians and their communities.

It is undeniable that over time there have been traders who were bad men and took unfair advantage of the Indian population, especially throughout the eighteenth century up until the middle of the nineteenth century. Such exploitation was generally more common before the first trading posts were established as bases from which to operate. In those times, for a number of years, commerce and trading with the Navajos was in fact prohibited by the government as a form of an embargo intended to pressure them into submission. But the regulation of trading activities prior to the signing of the treaty of 1868 was extremely difficult, especially in the case of traders who roamed the countryside, operating out of wagons. It is widely acknowledged that among these traders were individuals who dealt in whiskey and guns, no doubt contributing to the negative stereotype invoked to this day. However, that practice had largely subsided by the time the first trading posts were approved for operation on the Navajo Reservation, and most of those itinerate and opportunistic traders would not have lasted long in the more stable, community-based establishments.

Many of the very early traders who did effectively survive the transition from trading out of the back of their wagons to the establishment of fixed trading posts within the Navajo communities were affiliated with various missionary efforts. Their presence was encouraged under the administration of President Ulysses S. Grant, which believed that turning the Navajos into Christians would help to pacify them and so showed them preference when it came to issuing licenses to operate trading posts. Under this program, Indian reservations across the United States were assigned "various religious denominations on a regional basis," reflecting the personal church affiliations of Grant and his own cabinet members. The Presbyterian Church was initially "given" the Navajo Reservation. Notably, during this same period Mormon settlers, sent by their church to establish missions and open avenues of commerce with the Native American people of the region, were among the religious groups who faced overt government discrimination and were generally denied such licenses (and were certainly not represented in Grant's cabinet).[7]

Mormon teachings hold that many Native Americans are descended from a group of Israelites, referred to as Lamanites, who journeyed to North America around 600 B.C. In sending its members to settle and establish trade in and around the reservation, the Church of Latter Day Saints hoped to restore faith among the Navajos. The Grant administration viewed Mormons with suspicion not only because of their religious beliefs and practices but also because they were deemed to be not sufficiently loyal to the administration. The government believed the Mormons might be overly sympathetic to the plight of the Navajos as a subjugated people for whom they had a special empathy and with whom they felt a kinship. Consequently, many of the trading posts initially established by Mormon families (as well as by others unable to obtain licenses) were located on islands of private land within or just beyond the regulated boundaries of the reservation. Among these were the Bisti, Tuba City, Cameron, and Marble Canyon trading posts. It was not until Rutherford Hayes became president in 1877 that Mormon traders were able to obtain licenses to operate on the reservation itself. After that, they established themselves as a significant presence in the Navajo trading community, particularly throughout the northeastern corner of the reservation around Four Corners. Establishments handed down through the families of these early settlers, including the Burnham, Foutz, Hatch, and Tanner families, account for a sizeable portion of the genuine trading posts still operating in and around the Navajo Reservation today.

In more recent times the image of Indian traders was tarnished through a series of high-profile and arguably one-sided chapter house hearings convened in 1972 by the Federal Trade Commission (FTC). Those hearings attempted to address concerns over pawning and the issuance of credit on the reservation, focusing on claims of inflated prices and high interest rates applied against saturation credit.

Cited as evidence of the paternalistic practices imposed on Navajo clients was the use of metal tokens referred to as *seco* or *bééshkági* and due bills as the form of negotiable credit, redeemable only at the trading post from which they were issued. The tokens (also called tin money) were issued in place of U.S. currency and carried their own stamped denomination, along with the name of the trading post from which they came. Due bills were similar to the credit slips issued by stores that receive returned merchandise but apply credit toward the purchase of other items from the same store or chain instead of giving a cash refund. Both of these practices, according to complaints, were designed to tether Navajo customers to a particular trading post and to secure and limit the otherwise unsecured debt that an individual could accrue. From the traders' perspective, with no mechanism to pursue a lien or attachment, this was often the only way to protect themselves against defaulted loans.

The bad publicity from the hearings resulted in imposition of regulations that eliminated most of the profit potential for traders who made loans. The regulations simultaneously buried prospective brokers in paperwork. But the new regulations ultimately did little to improve the situation for the Navajos. Pawning certainly did not cease but merely moved off the reservation and into the border towns where the Indian population was increasingly forced to travel to shop and conduct its business. Most of the old trading posts stripped of the tools they had relied on to function and make a profit in the unique world of the reservation, simply closed their doors.

Bill Donovan is a senior reporter for the *Navajo Times* as well as the *Gallup Independent*. He wrote extensively about the FTC hearings in a long-running series of articles syndicated across the country during the 1970s. Decades later, he commented about how the FTC hearings and attendant negative publicity damaged the reputation of the old Indian traders. Speaking before a group attending a series of lectures and discussions on the impact of trading posts in the Southwest in 2007, Donovan acknowledged that most of the media coverage of the FTC hearings, including most of his own articles, had been unfairly slanted against the traders.[8] Even the *CBS Evening News* jumped on the bandwagon with a story highlighting abuses identified at some trading posts.[9]

In a remarkably bold and candid presentation, Donovan acknowledged that almost no effort was made during that period to seek out the traders' perspective. Little effort was made to evaluate the credibility of claims made against the trading posts. The news coverage was largely one sided. Donovan admitted that this editorial slant was strongly supported by both local business owners and even his own newspaper editors. Bad publicity for the Indian traders and the imposition of restrictive regulations on the old trading posts drove more money and more business to Gallup business owners.

Donovan also acknowledged that the imposition of pawn and credit regulations on reservation trading posts ultimately hurt the Navajo citizens far more than the traders themselves. Many traders simply closed up shop and moved away. That left a vacuum in many remote regions of the reservation where essential services had once been provided. This made life much harder for the Navajo residents of those communities, who were then forced to travel sometimes hundreds of miles to distant border towns like Farmington, Gallup, and Flagstaff to pawn their treasured jewelry and other possessions so that they could purchase food and supplies. And there, brokers were not restricted by the new FTC rules. Most were far less accommodating in their extension of credit and less concerned with the safekeeping of pawn than the local Indian traders had been. Generations-old collections of family pawn were subsequently lost, hastily sold off as soon as they went dead.[10] This, according to Donovan, led to an outcry from many Navajo citizens who called for the old system to be brought back to the reservation. But that system was gone forever, and with it, one of the principal mechanisms that had allowed trading posts to survive.[11]

Pawn has long figured prominently in and around the Navajo Reservation. For many traditional Navajos it serves as the primary means by which to secure loans for cash or store credit needed to acquire basic supplies and services. To this day many older Navajos lack the required identification, not to mention credit history, necessary to apply for and obtain a loan from a modern financial institution. And not many banks would even entertain an application for a loan of only a few hundred dollars, an amount typical of the subsistence loans made against items taken in pawn.

Another hidden attraction of pawn is that it enables the owner to deposit treasured pieces of jewelry, guns, and other items with the trader in his vault. This provides many older Navajos with a site where they can safely store and secure their valuable possessions, yet readily withdraw them when needed (during hunting season or for an important ceremony), in exchange for interest payments made on a relatively small loan taken against the items. However, this unique approach to pawn works only when the trader has a personal relationship with the Navajo client and his use of the system and is willing to adjust business practices by relaxing or extending due dates for payments and working with the client to assure possessions entrusted to the trading post are not hastily sold off should the loans expire and the items go dead.

In these unique circumstances, the very same rug, rifle, saddle, or piece of jewelry may repeatedly go in and out of pawn over many, many years, back and forth between the same client and trader, in an ongoing financial relationship built on trust. A trader might even allow a trusted Navajo client to borrow an item back out of pawn without payment, for use in an important ceremony. And so to this day, pawn remains a viable and commonly used mechanism of finance for many older Navajos, who would much prefer to take off a bracelet and pawn it with a trusted trader than attempt to navigate the maze of paperwork for a loan with a modern bank or risk the loss or theft of treasured jewelry or other items left precariously stored at home. Still, for the general public, the historic association of Indian traders with pawning on the reservation undoubtedly contributes to already prevalent misconceptions and negative stereotypes.

Amid all of this history, it is certain that fundamental cultural conflicts and misunderstandings have contributed significantly to the negative characterizations of Indian traders that abound inside and outside of Indian communities.

Most societies experience conflicts between the haves and the have-nots, particularly societies in which the economic gap is characterized by extremes. Life on the Navajo Nation can be very hard. Unemployment as well as poverty run extremely high—some estimates putting the figure between 50–70% or higher, depending on the particular segment of the community one is considering.[12] Statistics relating to other socioeconomic issues and indicators are equally disturbing. Many people still live without electricity, running water, or indoor plumbing. This is particularly the case in those remote areas of the reservation where trading posts are most common. The people living under these conditions could easily be counted among the "have-nots" of American society.

In contrast, the trader undoubtedly lives in comparative wealth in the middle of these communities in what at least passes for a real house or trailer with plumbing and electricity. He has a reliable car or pickup truck, a stable income, and the ability to live in relative comfort and economic security the year round operating his unique business that is wholly dependent on trade with his Navajo clients and neighbors. Along with just being Anglo, this comparative wealth causes the trader to stand out conspicuously within the community, which is an undesirable trait in traditional Navajo society. This alone makes the trader an easy target for criticism.

3. A Navajo home (traditional hogan), northwest of Kayenta, Navajo Nation, 1979 (*photograph courtesy of Jerry Jacka photography*).

From both a historical and a practical standpoint, it is probably no coincidence that most, if not all, of the successful and enduring, old-time Indian traders have been non-Indian, or *bilagáana*. The very first traders were patent outsiders, pioneers and settlers who came to the reservation to establish commerce with the Navajos. They became the critical link between two worlds, bridging cultures by exposing local residents to the things and ways of the outside world while simultaneously learning about and, in many respects, assimilating into the Navajo world, though never completely. In creating ties and building relationships with the Navajos inevitably came the potential for conflicts that could arise from a clash of cultural values or quite simply from the individual trader's personality and attitude, which might compromise relations. Still, while exposing him to greater suspicion and criticism, *being bilagáana*, and *not* born into his adopted Navajo community has also provided most Indian traders with a distinct advantage in running a successful business and working as a trader on the reservation. Being *bilagáana* provides a measure of insulation, making traders far less susceptible to family-like social pressure than a local Navajo, especially one related to his clients by clan.[13]

How traditional Navajos regard trade and property contributes to further conflict and misunderstanding. Survival in Navajo society has historically been based on a significant degree of interdependence and the mutual sharing of needed resources. Life on the Navajo Reservation reflects several very real communal or socialistic elements, the most conspicuous of which is that most of the land belongs to the collective Navajo Nation and not to individuals. While families certainly have their own homes, be it a hogan, a trailer, or even a modern, permanent structure, with few exceptions (e.g., allotments) the property on which the family may for generations have resided and possibly raised their livestock or grown their crops is held under a long-term permit or lease issued by the tribal government. Even use of that land is regulated by highly coveted and aggressively protected nontransferable grazing permits assigned to the head of the family. This unique aspect of Navajo society is but one more factor that has over time prevented many Navajos from establishing their own businesses (including trading posts); they are limited in their ability to acquire and then mortgage their homes or other real property or even use grazing rights as collateral to raise the levels of capital necessary to start a successful business.

These difficulties were compounded in the 1930s when the federal government, under authority of the Taylor Grazing Act, initiated its infamous livestock reduction program.[14] The population of domestic sheep raised by the Navajos, including the Spanish-introduced Churro breed prized by weavers, had swollen to over a million, which far exceeded the carrying capacity of Navajo sage and grasslands and led to widespread soil erosion. The federal government responded with a compulsory program of livestock reduction, the result of which was that as much as 80% of the overall herd was sold off or exterminated. That had the simultaneous effect of aggravating poverty by reducing one of the few forms of personal property and wealth recognized within Navajo society. The concept of personal property is not entirely foreign to traditional Navajo culture, and individuals have historically owned sheep and other livestock, as well as blankets and jewelry, all of which contributed prominently to status and wealth within the community. What is now known as the Navajo Livestock Reduction Program, sometimes referred to as the Second Long Walk, had a devastating effect on the few Navajo entrepreneurs who *had* entered into the trading business, stripping them of the one source of collateral that had been available to establish and maintain their businesses.

As in most societies, trading for the Navajos is based on the concept of fair exchange, on the idea of getting value for value and not on the idea of one side or the other making a profit. This, of course, stands in direct conflict with the very premise on which any business relies, including a trading post. So when a trader buys or takes an item in trade—say an animal hide—for which he pays a certain amount and then displays it for sale at a greater price, there may be among traditional, and even some modern, Navajos, a tendency to conclude that they have been cheated and should have been paid more when they first sold it to the trading post. The same conclusion may be reached when a trader sells an item (retail) such as a bag of feed for more than he paid (wholesale) from his supplier in town.

A well-known and variously told story coming out of Toadlena Trading Post helps illustrate this very point. The trader, George Bloomfield, was talking with his long-time clerk, a Navajo named Sam Teller. Out of the blue, Teller asked Bloomfield why all Indian traders were crooks. Surprised by the question, Bloomfield asked Teller why he thought all traders were crooked. The clerk replied, "When you guys buy something you always sell it for more money than it costs you." Bloomfield tried to explain that the difference in price, the profit, was how he paid the bills, paid the clerk's wages, and even paid himself. In astonishment, the clerk gestured at all the goods around the store and asked, "But why do you need to be paid? You already have everything." Change the names and locations and that same story could be told about virtually every trader and trading post across the reservation.

Misunderstandings like this are easily compounded when translations from Navajo to English are attempted without benefit of a contextual or cultural understanding. A Navajo weaver might label a trader a crook or a cheat (*bina´adló´*), or complain that "he cheated me" (*shi´deez lo´*), only because the trader paid the weaver less for a rug than she thought it was worth or sold a rug for more than he paid the weaver. This situation was often exacerbated back in the days when most trading posts were still dealing in sheep or wool, since transportation costs would often prevent the trader from paying as much as a competing establishment in town. It is certain that more than one old-time trader was labeled a cheat (*bina´adló´*) because he paid five or ten cents a pound less for sheep than a competitor in Gallup. This same predicament contributed to the perception among occasional tourists who, on seeing groceries and other items in the trading post sold for sometimes double their cost in town, concluded the trader was gouging the Indians, giving little or no consideration to the enormous costs associated with stocking the shelves of the post at a site so far off the beaten path and away from established supply routes.

Traditional Navajo society has more fully embraced the concept of "take what you need and leave the rest" than has Western society, which is more inclined to hoarding and stockpiling. The idea of taking only what you need is accompanied by a sense of entitlement to those things you genuinely require, as well as an approach to life that is more focused on immediate needs rather than future ones. "Don't plan ahead, and don't fret over yesterday." If you already have everything you really need, you don't need stockpiles of goods or even money. By this reasoning, someone who has more than he or she needs and does not share it with others is greedy, or *bił hatsoh*. And so the trader, whose business it is to stockpile goods, has often been seen as someone who keeps for himself things that exceed his immediate needs and is *bił hatsoh*, because he does not share the things he has as freely as might be expected by his neighbors.

In their 1946 work *The Navaho*, Clyde Kluckhohn and Dorothea Leighton outline the complexities of traditional Navajo perspectives on wealth and property:

> Possessions are valued both as providing security and as affording opportunities for mild ostentation. But to take attainment of riches as the chief aim of life is universally condemned. This is a typical pronouncement by a Navaho leader:
>
> "The Navaho way is just to want enough to have enough to eat for our family and nice things to wear sometimes. We don't like it when nowadays some of these young men marry rich girls for their money and waste it all right away. The old people say this is wrong. You can't get rich if you look after your relatives right. You can't get rich without cheating some people. Cheating people is the wrong way. That way gets you into trouble. Men should be honest to get along."[15]

There is within Navajo society the understanding that when called on, everyone is expected to share much of whatever property or resources they possess to help family, clan members, and other neighbors. Strong social sanctions exist to encourage sharing and cooperation, and the Navajo language contains terms that distinguish between the different kinds of "my" or "mine." The alliterative term *shí shi'* (high-tone "í" in the first "*shí*," low-tone "i" in the second) is used to refer to "private" personal property, things that are "mine alone" or "my very own," such as *shí shichidí* ("my very own car") or *shí shiłíį́* ("my very own horse"), which one can decline to share without being perceived as selfish or greedy (*bił hatsoh*). Words for other types of property or things may be prefaced or conjoined with the single term *shi*, referring to things that are "mine" but not exclusively so; such as *shich'iiyáán* for "my food" or even *shi dine'é*, meaning "my people." These are among the things or services that one is expected to share with others when one is called on to do so, though a speaker can exercise a measure of discretion in the level of ownership asserted through their words.

That said, and particularly given the levels of poverty and scarcity of jobs and economic opportunities, there is nothing about reservation life that precludes the existence of the same types of jealousies, rivalries, and competition found anywhere else.

Cultural anthropologists refer to the "image of limited good," the theory that societies or communities plagued by poverty often see good, be it in the form of resources, wealth, or even luck and good fortune, as a finite commodity.[16] Those who possess more or better things than others necessarily do so at the expense of others. One person's luck or success is another's misfortune. Elements of this can be seen on the Navajo Reservation, where poverty and the scarcity of jobs of any kind, much less good-paying ones, are an everyday reality. Romantic notions of utopian tranquility or harmonious coexistence are quickly dispelled, particularly in the workplace, where invidious maneuvering, and jockeying for position can be carried out with a level of skill and persistence rivaling that which you'd find in the most formidable corporate environment a la *The Apprentice*. The only difference here is that this competition is situated within the broader context of rules, appearances, and expectations prescribed by Navajo society, and motivation is more likely a struggle for basic survival rather than greed.

A number of other cultural factors distinguish life and business on the Navajo Reservation and figure into how Indian traders were perceived and whether they were successful in adapting to the community and in running their establishments.

Most Navajos freely acknowledge and even joke about what is referred to as "Navajo time." The term does not refer to the Navajo Nation practice of setting clocks out of step with the rest of the state of Arizona for half of the year. Rather, it refers to what could conservatively be characterized as a less-than-obsessive concern with constraints imposed by the clock or the calendar. Things tend to move at a slower and less compulsive pace. This is not unlike the slower pace urbanites observe when they visit a rural community, but Navajo time is even more profound. Few things happen quickly, reflecting what is not only a slower pace of life but also a more patient and even ritualized approach to daily tasks. Routine tasks and interactions usually just take longer to accomplish, especially business and conversation.

Formalities and courtesy play a major role here. In many situations, especially formal or business settings, one simply does not rush into a conversation without considerable overture. Unlike conversations in the outside world, which frequently involve rapid-fire banter and exchange, punctuated with interruptions and interjections from one side or the other, formal conversations on the reservation typically exhibit long monologues from one side, to which the other party is expected to patiently listen until it's finished before offering a response. When one speaks, he or she gives birth to a thought that floats and lingers long after the conversation is over. Those words and thoughts must be chosen carefully, and in return the listener must show them appropriate respect. Unknowing outsiders who interrupt that process and expect to function according to their own sense of time and at their own hurried pace often experience great frustration and are perceived by traditional Navajos as extremely rude.

This frustration may be amplified for authority figures such as supervisors or even investigators who expect to meet a deadline or who hope to quickly accomplish their business or obtain answers to their questions so they can move on to something else. Those who fail to adapt and insist on proceeding at their own demanding pace can expect one of two unsatisfactory responses or a combination of both. One is a lack of eye contact, mistakenly perceived by the outsider as disinterest, lack of engagement, or even stupidity. In reality, however, this is probably a reflection of the listener's own bewilderment or even disgust with the arrogance and lack of manners being displayed. The listener may be thinking *Bilagáana doo biłééhózin da* ("This white person is clueless/ignorant") or *Bilagáana t'óó diigis* ("This white person is stupid!").

Worse yet, in an effort to end the conversation altogether, the person being questioned may passively nod their head in apparent agreement or simply respond with whatever answer they think the other person wants to hear, in the hope that the questioner will just go away, get out of their face, and leave them alone to get on with their *own* business. This reaction is more likely in group settings, where it is particularly undesirable to be seen as loud or outspoken. Critical information or opinions, and even genuine pearls of insight and wisdom, have been completely missed by outsiders who have failed to invest the time and demonstrate the patience necessary to tactfully elicit input from someone quietly awaiting their time to speak.

A tendency to offer a benign or passive verbal response in the face of conflict or confrontation, especially in the presence of an authority figure, is a common trait on the reservation. Friends of mine in the Navajo law enforcement community have acknowledged this behavior, speculating that on a societal level it derives from years of subjugation under the government, compounded for many by growing up in a boarding school environment. In law enforcement settings it is seen in an extraordinarily high number of confessions obtained during suspect interviews, accompanied by remarkably simple and unembellished explanations as to motivation, such as "I wanted it" or "I needed the money" in accounting for a theft or "He made me mad" in explaining an assault or murder. On a broader level, it is a reflection of resignation and acceptance of bad circumstances or fate, not protesting or speaking up but emotionally shrugging, letting go, making do, and just moving on.

Indian traders who could not accept Navajo culture or adapt to it were often seen as arrogant and rude, contributing to negative stereotypes about traders *and bilagáana* generally. In the long run these individuals did not fare well in their businesses and did not typically last on the reservation. But most of the successful Indian traders who stood the test of time came to understand and appreciate these cultural traits and changed their own behavior and business practices to accommodate the ways of their Navajo neighbors. Some traders, especially those who married into Navajo families, came over the course of time to adopt many of these traits and values as their own, incorporating many Navajo ways into their own thinking, behavior, and lifestyle. In these instances the trader also benefited from the matrilineal nature of Navajo society. He earned a new identity and legitimacy as a Navajo woman's husband and the father of her Navajo children and so came to be seen as an acceptable person with whom to do business.

Certainly the passage of time and integration with the outside world and economic system has affected cultural values and changed the way in which modern Navajos view property and wealth and the way in which they communicate. Also, as in any society, wide variations in attitudes exist among Navajos, both regionally and personally, with respect to acceptance of and adherence to these "traditional" values and cultural traits. There is most certainly not one simple, static personality or temperament that can be ascribed to Navajos or any other group of people. And the traditional cultural values effecting attitudes toward property and sharing are merely a backdrop against which individual Navajos develop their own personal values and character; good or bad, mean or kind, wise or foolish, generous or greedy.

Nevertheless, the focus on immediate (rather than future) needs and events, and the expectation that one will cooperate and share one's things with others, is quite real and observable and figures prominently even in contemporary Navajo society. Old-time trader Bruce Burnham has repeatedly noted that "It's very hard to say 'no' [*doodah*] in the Navajo language," explaining that the use of certain Navajo words roughly equivalent to the English term "please," such as *t'ááshǫǫdí*, more accurately convey an imperative to the listener to provide whatever he or she is being asked for. Burnham acknowledged that he sometimes avoids speaking in Navajo with a client, or hides his ability to understand the Navajo language, because if he is asked for a favor in Navajo he is under far more social pressure to give the person what they have asked for.[17]

Cultural clashes have arisen time and again on the reservation, as illustrated in the following account provided by long-time trader Russell Foutz, describing his own efforts to rebuild the Teec Nos Pos Trading Post after the original building burned down in the 1960s:

> It burned down, and it burned down all the pawn. . . . [I]t caused some problems. . . . I bought beads, jewelry and stuff from all over the country to replace that pawn with. I still have a drawer full of wrinkled up [burned] pawn. After that store burned down, they were starting to build the road out there where the Teec Nos Pos store is now. Every time I'd stake out a place to build the store, they'd move the road. But before I could build it, I had to get permission from the community to rebuild that store there. So Indians, they always like to have long meetings, so they had to have a big meeting to decide whether they were going to let me rebuild the store out there or whether I was going to replace their pawn and all that. So they had this meeting and everybody got up and talked. And finally old Fred Todachini got up and he said, "We all know the white men cheat us. But this man we know. He just cheats us a little bit. I think we better keep him." This was all in Navajo. Then he sat down and laughed. So they all voted they would keep me, "because he just cheated them a little bit."[18]

At the same time that this account demonstrates the kind of conflict that can color the relationship between Navajos and Anglos, it also helps to debunk the stereotype of the trader as crook. Most trading posts on the reservation are not owned by the trader himself but by the tribe, that is, the Navajo Nation. The trader (or his employer or predecessor) likely paid to construct the building(s) on the site (which was likely tribal land) but had to secure a lease from the tribe to operate the business. Issuance of that lease would have had to have been approved by the chapter where the trading post was (to be) located. A trader with a track record of dishonest or abusive practices ran the risk of having his lease terminated by the tribe and of simultaneously losing his significant investment in the building and other trading post infrastructure. He would certainly not have his lease renewed if he had established a record of bad relations with the community. Even in those rare circumstances in which the trading post was situated on privately owned land or in which geographic monopoly translated into excessive power, given the isolated nature of the communities where trading posts are located, along with the unconventional manner by which disputes are sometimes resolved on the far reaches of the reservation (colorfully characterized by some in law enforcement as "positively western"), it might not be long before a dishonest and disagreeable trader was either threatened or physically run out of town. Finally, most of the remaining established traders today are too closely tied to the community by marriage and other relations to risk alienating their relatives and neighbors through an end run or a crooked deal.

The first trading posts on the Navajo Reservation were established in the 1870s, following the signing of the treaty of 1868 and the subsequent return of the Navajo people to their native lands after their expulsion and captivity just a few years earlier. In 1864 the Navajos were defeated by Colonel Kit Carson. Under orders, Carson and his troops implemented the scorched earth policy of General George Carleton, intended to quell conflicts between Navajos and the many other tribes in the region as well as those between Indians and Anglo-Americans who were beginning to settle in the same area. Afterward, more than eight thousand captured Navajo men, women, and children were relocated through a series of forced and sometimes fatal marches to Fort Sumner at Bosque Redondo, New Mexico, more than three hundred miles from their homeland. There, they were held captive for nearly four years. The collective march of various groups of captured Navajos under military guard and escort has since come to be known as the Long Walk. The entire period was originally referred to by the Navajo people as *Hwééldi*, describing "the fearing time," imprisonment, or an overwhelming state of dread. Not surprisingly, the term *Hwééldi* also evolved into the Navajo name for Fort Sumner, referring to a place of suffering.

That period of captivity was devastating for the Navajos and expensive for the federal government. The Navajos suffered through repeated crop failures, disease, and raids by the Utes and Comanches. The cost of keeping the Navajos captive and the government's unsuccessful attempts to alter their lifestyle led to negotiations between the government and tribal leaders to end their captivity. The treaty of 1868 was signed on June 1, and the surviving Navajo captives were permitted to return home to live on the newly defined reservation, comprised of a percentage of the original territory they once occupied. That journey back is sometimes referred to as the Long Walk Home.

While living in captivity at Fort Sumner, the Navajo people were introduced to a variety of new practices, materials, and foods to which they became accustomed. This opened the door to relations with traders and soon thereafter to the establishment of trading posts from which the Navajo people could obtain these supplies in exchange for the sheep they raised as well as for their already valued weavings (initially in the form of blankets and later rugs) and the increasingly desirable jewelry they made.

The Navajo word for trader is *naalyéhé yá sidáhí*; however, the term more accurately translates into something roughly equivalent to "one who sits on the treasure" or "guardian of the treasure" (*naalyéhé* referring to something of value, *yá* meaning "for him," and *sidáhí* referring to one who sits on or cares for). It is typically a term of respect, carrying the paternal implication that the person (i.e., the trader) is there to protect and look out for the interests of another. Application to Indian traders evolved out of use of the term to refer to the quartermaster(s) at Fort Sumner who dispensed needed supplies to the Navajo during their internment. Following the journey back to their homeland the Navajo started to use the word to describe and refer to the Indian traders who took on the role of stocking and dispensing supplies at the trading post in exchange for sheep and wool, rugs and jewelry, and other items.

By the 1890s nearly a dozen traders licensed by the federal government had established posts on the Navajo Reservation. Traders usually chose sites that were near both water as well as established routes on which the people of the area were known to travel. Among the very first of these was the store at Ganado, Arizona, built in 1870. It was sold to John Lorenzo Hubbell in 1878 and became known as Hubbell's Trading Post. Other traders established operations at locations in both Arizona and New Mexico, including Two Grey Hills, Lukachukai, Chinle, Piñon, Red Lake, Tuba City, the Gap, and Lee's Ferry. By the turn of the twentieth century, nearly thirty trading posts had been established in the region, and more than one hundred were licensed to operate on the Navajo Reservation by the time of a 1948 survey.[19]

As a young man, anthropologist Edward T. Hall spent much of the 1930s living on the Navajo and Hopi reservations and working as a laborer alongside the Indians. Hall observed that over time there evolved three distinct and often competing groups of trading posts in the Four Corners region. These were, respectively, those trading posts bankrolled by the wealthy and politically powerful Babbitt family of Arizona; posts run by the Lee outfit and other allied and often related Mormons; and trading posts owned and/or operated by the Hubbell family. According to Hall, each of these groups had their own characteristic methods of operation. The Babbitt sites were "run from the point of view of a white man's business world," usually employing others as traders to run the many posts they owned. The Mormons were "aggressively in search of a niche." Hubbell's establishments were "geared more to the culture and buying habits of the Navajos." Along with these formal alliances were also occasional individuals or families, such as the Wetherills, Haldermans, and Lippincotts, who established successful independent trading posts respectively at Kayenta, Keams, and Wide Ruins.[20] Sites owned or operated by all of these groups or individuals account for a substantial portion of the hundreds of trading posts that sprung up on or around the Navajo Reservation during the first fifty to seventy-five years following the signing of the treaty.

In the years since then, and particularly during 1960s and 1970s, there has been a dramatic decline in the number of trading posts operating on and around the Navajo Reservation. Political issues affecting the exercise of sovereignty by the tribal government led to an expanded capacity to both regulate and promote commercial activities. Economic factors also had a big impact, as modern practices such as the use of credit cards and bank or credit union checks found their way into Navajo society. Comparatively modern shopping establishments from the outside world gradually found their way into the more developed areas of the reservation, and so the population did not have to rely as much on the old trading posts for basic food items and supplies. But more significant than anything else was the mobility Navajos realized through the growing use of automobiles, dramatically reducing reliance on nearby trading posts for supplies as well as for social and other needs. As an inevitable consequence, only a comparative handful of real trading posts still exist on the Navajo Nation. These are generally found only in the most remote and least developed areas of the reservation. More often than not they are being run by the very same old-time, on-the-ground traders or their descendents who have arguably, through the generations, assimilated the most into Navajo life and culture and exhibited the most loyalty to their Navajo clients and neighbors.

Among the places like this that survive today are little gems such as Hank and Vicky Blair's Totsoh Trading Post in Lukachukai, Arizona; Shonto Trading Post in Arizona run by trader Al and Margaret Grieve; R. B. Burnham Trading Post in Sanders, Arizona, run by Bruce, Virginia, and daughter Sheri Burnham; Hatch Brothers Trading Post in Fruitland, New Mexico; Al Townsend's Inscription House Trading Post in Tonalea, Arizona; Les Wilson's Two Grey Hills Trading Post near Tohatchi, New Mexico; Mark Winter's Toadlena Trading Post near Newcomb, New Mexico; Cousins Brothers Trading Post near Vanderwagen, New Mexico; and John McCullough's (formerly Russell Foutz's) Teec Nos Pos Trading Post just five miles from the most northeastern corner of Arizona at Four Corners. Only a few of these (e.g., Teec Nos Pos, Toadlena, and Inscription House) still take in sheep and wool, and only those located on private land (such as Burnham's) can now legally accept pawn. But otherwise, walking into any one of these unique establishments is very much like stepping back in time to another century, notwithstanding that newer products line their shelves and that there's evidence of other modern trappings such as equipment to accept credit or debit cards.[21]

Of all the remaining old-time trading posts perhaps the most well known and respected, and arguably the most historically authentic, was Hubbell Trading Post. It is now operated by the NPS as a national historic site via a unique cooperative agreement with the nonprofit WNPA (formerly the Southwest Parks and Monuments Association). And of all the remaining old-time traders, one of the most well known and respected (by both outsiders and the Navajo community) was Billy Gene Malone. A nearly fifty-year veteran Indian trader on the Navajo Reservation, Malone ran the Hubbell Trading Post for the SPMA/WNPA and the NPS from 1981 to 2004.

The story of Hubbell Trading Post begins in the nineteenth century, when the northern portions of New Mexico and Arizona were being settled at the end of the region's Indian Wars. John Lorenzo Hubbell was born in Pajarito, New Mexico, in 1853. He was the son of James Hubbell, a soldier in the U.S. Army, and Juliana Gutierrez, a direct descendant of one of the first governors of New Mexico under Mexican rule. No doubt benefiting from his father's military connections and status, a young John Lorenzo secured a series of jobs that put him in regular contact with the local Navajo Indians. He learned their language and became acquainted with their ways.

The young Hubbell eventually purchased interest in one of the very first trading posts on the Navajo Reservation, located at Ganado Lake. But he was forced to move from that original site when a man suspected of being a witch, or *'adiłgąshii*, was killed in the doorway to the trading post. According to Navajo beliefs this left the building cursed or possessed by evil spirits referred to as *ch'įįdii*. The Navajos would no longer enter the building or handle its contents. To salvage his business, Hubbell bought out a nearby competitor, William Leonard, who owned a store a few miles downstream on a privately held section of land at the current site of Hubbell Trading Post. Hubbell opened the doors to that now-famous establishment in 1878.

In the years that followed, the Hubbell family expanded its business into a virtual trading empire, establishing or buying out trading posts at sites across the reservation, including Keams Canyon, Chinle, Black Mountain, Nazlini, Oraibi, Cedar Springs, Piñon, Big Mountain, Dinnebito, Na-ah-tee, Sand Springs, and Marble Canyon. Over time, owing to changes in the economy and particularly to changes affecting life and business on the reservation, trading posts at many of these sites were variously sold off or closed. However, from the time it was acquired by John Lorenzo in 1878 until 1967, both the home and the trading post located at Ganado remained in the Hubbell family and the post was in continuous operation.

By the late 1950s the Hubbell family was contemplating the sale of their famous trading post. Patriarch John Lorenzo died in 1930. His son Roman along with his wife, Dorothy, carried on the family business for the next twenty years. But Roman became ill and suffered a stroke, leaving him confined to a wheelchair. Dorothy Hubbell assumed responsibility for keeping the post running. That task took its toll and, along with caring for her husband, became more than she could handle. Hubbell Trading Post was put up for sale in 1957.

Dorothy Hubbell received offers from a number of people, but all indicated their intention to liquidate the significant collection of antiques and other valuable artifacts attached to property. Dorothy Hubbell held out. She approached officials at the Museum of Northern Arizona (MNA), in Flagstaff, hoping they would buy her out, sustain her father-in-law's legacy, and preserve the entire site in its historic condition. Museum director Harold Colton and assistant director Ned Danson (father of actor Ted Danson) reluctantly rejected Dorothy's offer but came up with the alternative proposal of approaching the NPS. Their idea was that the government agency could purchase the famous trading post from the Hubbell family and preserve it as a national historic site.

Danson took the lead, soliciting support from several prominent Arizona politicians, including then senators Carl Hayden and Barry Goldwater and congressman Stewart Udall. The response was enthusiastic. Senator Goldwater, in particular, supported the idea. As a child, in 1916, he had met John Lorenzo Hubbell and been a playmate of his children. Representative Udall and Senator Hayden had likewise both visited the trading post in their youth. Both had fond memories of the elder Mr. Hubbell; they recalled a kindly person and an old-time trader whose activities they found fascinating. All considered the trading post to be of national significance and believed that incorporating it into the national park system was a worthy goal and a way to preserve a unique aspect of our American and Native American heritage.

On May 7, 1959, Senator Carl Hayden introduced legislation to authorize the establishment of the trading post as a national historic site. Udall introduced similar legislation in the House of Representatives on May 20 that same year. The Senate bill (S. 1871) was passed, but the House measure was defeated. Opponents argued the proposed $300,000 purchase price of the property was excessive. They labeled the legislation "pork" and temporarily killed the prospects for the national historic site.

The concept languished for a full five years before being resurrected through the introduction of new legislation before both the House and the Senate. This time, however, a new idea was emphasized during the hearings before the House Committee on Interior and Insular Affairs. Instead of merely preserving and providing curatorial and interpretive services at the historic site, the NPS said it wanted to operate the facility as a living trading post in the tradition of John Lorenzo Hubbell, employing a genuine Indian trader to carry on trading with the Navajo community.

Excerpts from these hearings help to illustrate the critical role this commitment played in obtaining congressional approval to establish Hubbell Trading Post as a national historic site. The following is part of the exchange between committee chairman Leon O'Brien and NPS Director George Hartzog:

O'BRIEN (to Hartzog): I would like to ask one question. Throughout all the statements, including yours, you emphasize the uniqueness of this particular place. We are all aware, however, that there are other trading posts scattered around, some going to pot. Would it be the idea of the Department this would be selected not only because it is a good layout and historical but as a sort of symbol of the trading post? We will not be having in the years ahead a whole string of former trading posts coming into being as historical sites? I do not want to close any doors in the future but I can see where sometimes there is a chain reaction. This would be a symbol of the trading post and a good one. [Are] [t]here are plans that you know of in the future for setting up other places in that area?

HARTZOG: Sir, this is what we consider to be, after surveying all of them, the best existing operating trading post. We would hope in our management to maintain it as an operating trading post. The operating trading post is fast becoming a thing of the past. Our study indicates that within a relatively few years there will be no more of them because of the competition from supermarkets, improved modes of transportation, changing tastes and what not. So that we believe that as an operating trading post—this will be the only one.

However, . . . the very next bill that is before this Committee for consideration . . . involves Fort Union as a trading post to commemorate a somewhat different aspect of the interpretation of westward history. This is the one near the confluence of the Missouri and the Yellowstone Rivers. There are no buildings there. This is a site and we would not propose an operating trading post there.

This, Mr. Chairman, as I have mentioned in my appearances before this Committee, I believe is perhaps one of the more neglected aspects of our American history and its interpretation by the NPS in telling the story of the great midcontinent and what happened in terms of its settlement in this period prior to the passage of the frontier in 1890.

O'BRIEN: Mr. Hartzog, I was not attempting to throw a roadblock in the way of the next bill or establishment, where desirable, of some other part of the country for historic site. I was thinking mainly in terms of let us say Arizona. We are not going to have every trading post set up?

HARTZOG: No.

O'BRIEN: You are going to maintain it and operate the trading post?

HARTZOG: That is what we hope to do.[22]

The measure passed and President Lyndon Johnson signed the legislation into law on August 28, 1965. Public Law 89–148 authorized the NPS to purchase and establish Hubbell Trading Post NHS. That purchase was finalized in 1967. The Hubbell family turned legal title over to the NPS, with the binding stipulation that the site would not only be preserved but would also be run as a genuine working trading post under its new status as a national historic site, commemorating the important role of Indian traders and trading posts in the American West.

Perhaps the biggest challenge facing the NPS was how to honor its commitment to Congress to operate the historic site as living trading post and not just a

4. Entrance to Hubbell Trading Post NHS (*photograph courtesy of Russ Finley*).

5. Panoramic view of Hubbell Trading Post (*photograph courtesy of Russ Finley*).

6. North entrance to Hubbell Trading Post (*photograph courtesy of Russ Finley*).

museum. The NPS could not undertake the operation of a commercial enterprise of its own, historic or otherwise. Efforts were initiated to identify a surrogate individual or organization that could do so on the government's behalf.

First consideration was given to the prominent Babbitt brothers of Arizona fame, who were already involved in any number of successful retail operations throughout the state. They declined the offer and in fact were beginning to close down a number of their own trading post businesses across the reservation. The Fred Harvey Company was approached next. It operated the lucrative concession at Grand Canyon National Park. When approached, however, company officials said that if they accepted the offer they would liquidate most of the inventory from the old trading post and use the site as an arts and crafts outlet and purchasing point for products that would be distributed to other Harvey stores. The NPS recoiled at this prospect, noting that "What the Fred Harvey Company had planned for the trading post would kill the atmosphere of a true trading post. . . . The place would be an embarrassment, the trading post, as a bona fide trading post, ruined forever." Then the NPS came up with another idea of trying "to get Southwest Parks and Monuments Association to take over the operation of the trading post." And the NPS already had an old-time trader in mind that the SPMA could hire for the job.[23]

The SPMA was founded in 1938 as a nonprofit organization committed to helping the NPS with educational, scientific, historical, and interpretive activities.

The SPMA, like other cooperating associations (several other such organizations exist throughout the country) provides support to the NPS by publishing and selling books related to national parks. It donates a portion of those funds to NPS research projects, land acquisitions, interpretive and educational facilities, and historic preservation/restoration projects. Most of these funds are acquired through the sale of books at any number of facilities authorized to operate within the national parks, through Internet sales, and through memberships and donations. The idea the NPS advanced in 1967 was for the SPMA to establish itself at Hubbell Trading Post and expand the scope of its operations there, "to assume the responsibility of operating the trading post. It would be necessary . . . for SPMA to take over the store when the NPS assumed responsibility for the care of the land and buildings. *It would be important to hire a good Indian trader*; an inexperienced concessioner would soon 'make a shambles of the operation.'" The SPMA would be required to assume this new role "as a contribution to the Service and not as a money maker."[24]

After much discussion and negotiation, the deal was struck. The SPMA (which in 2002 became the WNPA) agreed to the proposal and in 1967 undertook its new role on "an indefinite basis."[25]

The first trader selected by the NPS and hired by the SPMA for the new historic site was Bill Young, born in 1902 in Winslow, Arizona. He'd worked as a trader for the Richardson family back in 1921, at their trading post in Leupp, near the southwest corner of the reservation. Then he moved to Cameron Trading Post, also owned by the Richardson family, where he eventually married one of Richardson's daughters. By this time an experienced trader in his own right and fluent in Navajo, he struck out on his own in 1928, purchasing the Red Lake Trading Post at Tolani Lakes. He traded there for the next fourteen years. After a few brief detours he ended up in Chinle next to Canyon de Chelly where he ran the Thunderbird Lodge Trading Post until 1967. It was there that he was recruited by the new NPS superintendent at Hubbell Trading Post to become the first trader for the newly created national historic site in Ganado. Bill Young remained at Hubbell Trading Post until 1978 when he retired at the age of seventy-six.

Al Grieve was the next trader to run Hubbell Trading Post. He was born into a New Mexico ranching family in 1946. Grieve was only nineteen years old when he moved to Standing Rock, New Mexico, on the Navajo Reservation, to marry Margaret Etcitty, a Navajo girl he'd met in school. In those first years he earned a meager living working as a cowboy and in sheep camps. He supplemented his income buying and selling Navajo arts and crafts. He spent summers working part time for a local trader and eventually established his own business back at the Standing Rock Trading Post. He ran that trading post from 1971 to 1977. By 1978 Grieve, fluent in Navajo and intimately familiar with the Navajo culture and community, had established a reputation as an experienced trader. He was approached by the NPS with an offer to take over as the trader at Hubbell Trading Post. Grieve accepted the job and was put on the SPMA payroll. His instructions from SPMA board member Ned Danson were to run the trading post and serve the Navajo community exactly as Hubbell had. Grieve did exactly that, serving in that capacity until 1981. He expanded the variety of arts and crafts to be found at Hubbell Trading Post and helped increase sales by reducing prices. More importantly, he paid higher prices to the artists for their work in order to gain their loyalty and promote their continuing interest in the Indian arts and crafts business. That strategy led to an increase of over $250,000 in sales at the trading post in just the first two years that Grieve was the trader.[26] Grieve left Hubbell Trading Post in 1981 to start his own ranch near Chaco Canyon, New Mexico. But he kept his hand in the trading business, running a number of other trading posts across the reservation, including Rough Rock Trading Post (1985–88), Tuba City Trading Post (1989–90), and Shonto Trading Post (1991–92). Grieve and his wife returned to Shonto in 2007 as the resident traders to work in silent partnership with several other old-time traders committed to reestablishing the facility and restoring it to its traditional condition.

The search to replace Al Grieve at Hubbell Trading Post did not take long. A notice was distributed across the reservation soliciting applications. One trader, Billy Malone, was personally approached by officials from the NPS and asked to apply. Malone was initially not interested. He and his Navajo family were then very comfortably established at the Piñon Trading Post, one of the very most remote regions of the reservation, nearly fifty miles west of Chinle, where they had lived for nearly twenty years. Malone's wife, Minnie, had her own career in Piñon as both a successful weaver and silversmith and as the local postmaster (she was one of the first Navajo postmasters in the country). But Malone talked it over with his family and they decided there was no harm in applying. He drove down to Hubbell's to take a look and submit an application. When he arrived, there were already eight or ten other applicants on hand for interviews. All were told that a selection would be made within a few weeks. But only fifteen minutes after his interview, Malone was called back in and enthusiastically offered the job.

Malone accepted. His new employers were thrilled.[27] Malone's reputation as one of the most experienced, respected, and trusted traders on the reservation made him the clear choice for the job. The NPS and SPMA considered it a major victory for the trading post.

During the twenty-four years Malone ran the Hubbell Trading Post he was featured in numerous publications and documentaries. He is widely credited with assuring the survival of the trading post as a treasured institution and social center in and around Ganado, drawing in artisans and residents from across and beyond the reservation, who came in to trade and just visit. He is also credited with elevating Indian arts, crafts, and artisans to previously unimagined levels of prominence, motivating artists to expand their skills and actively promoting new artists and their work, entering their rugs and jewelry in national competitions, generating interest with traveling exhibits, and attracting new clients for fine Indian arts and crafts from around the world.

The administrative history of Hubbell Trading Post provides one more noteworthy observation about the significance of Hubbell as working trading post:

> [Former NPS chief historian and noted author] Bob Utley has stated that [former NPS director] George Hartzog had been thinking about the "living history" concept for some time and that Hubbell Trading Post gave him a chance to create a place that was not just a "dead embalmed historic site." Utley thinks, too, that Hubbell Trading Post may have given the impetus to the living history program throughout the Park Service. The idea appeared to work so well at Hubbell Trading Post that "[Hartzog] plunged the Park Service into quagmires of living history." . . . To that extent, Hubbell Trading Post National Historic Site has historic significance within the Park Service itself. As for Bob Utley, he fought back against much of the living history program, feeling that " . . . it perpetuated all manner of inappropriate excesses on our interpretation of historic properties. [But] I have to concede that Hubbell Trading Post is the one place where it has really worked perfectly."[28]

Presumably the reason it worked so well at Hubbell Trading Post was because it was the one national historic site that did *not* use "reenactors" to tell its story but rather a succession of three genuine, old-time Indian traders who didn't need to act, put on a costume, or assume a persona.

And so the NPS maintained its commitment to operating Hubbell Trading Post as a genuine, living trading post all the way into the beginning of the twenty-first century. According to at least one former Hubbell Trading Post superintendent, the "continuity of experienced traders" who worked there was "responsible for the success of Hubbell Trading Post" after the NPS and WNPA took over.[29]

The Trader

(Naalyéhé yá sidáhí)

BILLY GENE MALONE was born in 1939 in Gallup, New Mexico, the son of a railroad man and a waitress.

Gallup has long been known as a border town, or a "rez" town, with a significant Native American population, situated smack-dab in the middle of Indian country and just a few miles from the boundary of the Navajo Nation. Gallup is also known as a crossroads for commerce and social interaction between the outside world and the many Indian tribes whose lands surround the city. The house in which Billy Malone was raised as a young child sat on a hill overlooking the old Intertribal Ceremonial Armory Building and was shaped like a hogan: the traditional hexagonal or circular-shaped Navajo houses found scattered across the Navajo Reservation. In Malone's own words, "Maybe that's where I got the 'I want to live with the Navajos' in me."[1]

Malone's family left Gallup around 1950 and moved to Texas. His parents eventually divorced, and Malone's mother packed her things, took her four young children, and headed to Durango, Colorado, to make a fresh start. Malone finished high school and one year of college in Durango before joining the army in 1958.

While living in Durango, Malone's mother met Hugh Lee, an old-time trader from Ganado, Arizona.[2] By the time Malone was discharged in 1961, his mother and Hugh had married and were back living in Indian country. Malone returned

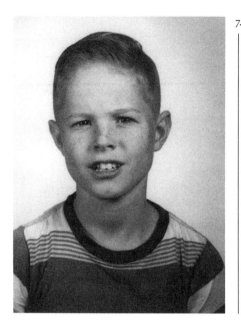

7. Billy Malone, approximately ten years old (*photograph courtesy of Billy Malone and family*).

8. Paratrooper Billy Malone, approximately twenty years old (1959), in the U.S. Army 82nd Airborne Signal Corps, Fort Bragg, North Carolina (*photograph courtesy of Billy Malone and family*).

9. Minnie Goodluck
(Malone), approximately
eighteen years old
(1955?) at Fort Defiance,
before she and Billy met
(*photograph courtesy of
Billy Malone and family*).

10. Piñon Trading
Post, thawing
after a winter
snowstorm,
mid-1970s
(*photograph
courtesy of Billy
Malone and
family*).

to Gallup and tried to use his veteran status and military training in radar tech-nology and electronics to get a job. No luck. With the assistance of his new stepfather, Malone found a job working as a trader's assistant for Al Frick at the Lupton Trading Post, just across the Arizona state line. There, Malone met his future wife, a beautiful Navajo girl named Minnie Goodluck.

Billy and Minnie were married in 1962. They moved to Keams Canyon Trading Post on the Hopi Reservation, enveloped by the Navajo Nation, where Malone's stepfather was already working for trader Cliff McGee. Within just a few months McGee offered Malone the chance to help run the Piñon Trading Post (also owned by the McGee family), across the reservation line on the Navajo side. Billy and Minnie packed their belongings into a stake-bed truck and made the move to Piñon over the bumpy dirt road that stretched between Keams Canyon and their new home.

Malone spent the next eighteen years working at Piñon, first as McGee's assis-tant and then as the head Indian trader. Minnie got a job as the local postmaster, one of the first Navajos to receive such an appointment. She divided her time between running the local post office, developing her own skills and reputation as a silversmith and weaver, and looking after a growing family. Billy and Minnie raised all of their five children there, four girls and one boy. In all the years they lived there, Piñon was accessible only by the dirt road from Keams Canyon or by a fifty-mile newly paved road to Chinle; there were no other communities nearby or in between. The only school was an elementary boarding school (kindergarten through third grade) run by the Bureau of Indian Affairs. Billy and Minnie's chil-dren attended school there along with all the other Navajo children from around the region. Later, for high school, they made the hundred-mile round trip to Chinle, five days a week. One grew up to become a high school teacher, another a postal worker (and later postmaster in Gallup, NM), and still another a policeman, and two became housewives. One of the girls married a Pentecostal minister, Perry Shorty, who with Billy's support developed a reputation as one of the most talented Navajo silversmiths in the country. All of Malone's children eventually married other Navajos and together gave Billy and Minnie twenty-three grandchildren.

Conditions in Piñon were primitive even by reservation standards. During the years that Malone worked there, many people still traveled by horse or wagon or on foot. Throughout almost all of Malone's working life he lived in trailers of various conditions and configurations. At Piñon he and Minnie had to continu-ally add on to the trailer they called their home, fabricating makeshift rooms and then attaching wherever there was a space to punch a hole for a new doorway, to

11. Billy and Minnie Malone posing with four of their five children (Oscar, Karen, Thelma, and Carol) in the late 1960s, before heading to the Navajo Nation Fair. The family is posing in front of the trailer where Malone's stepfather, Hugh Lee, lived in Gallup. Daughter B.J. had not yet arrived on the scene (*photograph courtesy of Billy Malone and family*).

accommodate their growing family. The trading post was the only store in Piñon, and it was the center of the community. Billy and Minnie established themselves as respected citizens and became central figures in Piñon. Billy gained a reputation across the reservation as a generous and experienced trader. And it was living here within a traditional Navajo community, married to a Navajo woman and raising his children as Navajo, that seems to have shaped many of Malone's own worldviews, beliefs, and practices.

That point was reinforced by Malone in 1998:

I remember another instance of one of our daughters getting sick—our oldest daughter—and my wife took her to the hospital, and she was gone and back. I didn't put a time on it, but I knew it was awful quick to go to Keams Canyon and come back. About two days later the daughter cleared up and was real well. I stuck my foot in my mouth, "See what the white man doctor can do for you?" And she said, "Well, I hate to tell you, but I took her to a medicine woman." So the Indian healers do have some knowledge of how to heal a lot of sickness out here and can really do some neat things with people. I suppose most of 'em, after they have a ceremony or something, will tell you, "After my ceremony is done, why

12. Local clientele at Piñon Trading Post, early 1970s (*photograph courtesy of Billy Malone and family*).

don't you go see the white man doctor now, and see if you can get a sec-ond opinion," so to speak. But I was really surprised. My daughter was deathly sick, and she cleared up that quick. And it was just some herbs that a lady knew what to use for. And they worked real fine. It's things like that, that people out here [in town] wouldn't expect that to happen. They might associate a medicine man with a witch doctor or something like that, but not true. They have fantastic healing capabilities.[3]

There were no banks in Piñon. Like most of his Navajo neighbors, Malone did not have a savings or checking account. What money he had was kept in a strong box. Otherwise, in the Navajo way, Malone kept his "savings" in rugs and jewelry he acquired, believing, as most old-time traders did, that they consti-tuted a better investment and were more secure than money in a bank. Often as not, Malone was paid by his employer, as well as customers, in rugs and jewelry instead of cash or a check.

Malone shared his perspective on collecting rugs and on Navajo "economics" and currency in the same 1998 interview:

I think one of my most favorite memories about rugs was when I was leaving Piñon, a grandma by the name of Helen Bly wove me a chief wedding blanket style rug and gave it to me as a going away gift. And that was very dear to me. I mean, it still is. I still have the rug, it's stored away somewhere. But I don't know too many traders that when they left town, somebody gave 'em a $1,500 to $2,000 rug and said, "Here's a gift, take this with you as you leave." And I bought a lot of rugs from her even after I came here [Hubbell Trading Post]. She died a while back of cancer, and it was very sad. But that's one of my most favorite times of buying a rug. And I buy a lot of rugs. I buy rugs from weavers here.... You buy rugs, and then you buy rugs that are, "Oh, gosh, this is really nice. This is something I'd like to own." But you can't own all the nice rugs that you see comin' down the trail, because you'd have to be a millionaire to do it. So you could just say, "That's mine, that's mine." But I do buy a lot of nice rugs that really make me feel good inside when I buy 'em. And I hope I make the weaver feel good, too, when she sells 'em....

... In 1963 I could buy a rug that would fill the floor of this house; I'm talking something that would have been a twelve by eighteen or something like that. They were only $350, $500 dollars in those days. Today, to buy a rug like that, they could run anywhere from $15,000 to $20,000 — a big rug. So things have changed. And little rugs, I know weavers that get $2,500 for a small tapestry rug, $4,000, $5,000. Nobody ever dreamed that rugs were gonna cost that much in those days....

... The older generation, like my mother-in-law, in fact, they know about getting their check on the first of the month, and there's a belief around among the Anglo community, I think, that every Indian gets a check. The only checks the Navajo get are the ones that are deserved of — whether they're on retirement, Social Security, disability, something like that — they just don't go in and pick up a check every month. It's like in the Anglo world: if we deserve a check for something, we get a check for it. But the ones that do, the older ones, during the month they might run short on cash, so they go to town with their nice jewelry and pawn it at a pawn shop. Then during the next month, they either go in and take it out, or they pay on the pawn. So they kind of have a different thing about money than we do. Their money, you might say, is tied up in their jewelry. We got our money tied up in a checkbook, so to speak. So they have a different sense of what money is. They would probably rather go out and buy a nice bracelet or a belt or some old beads, and consider that their money, so that they know they can always go somewhere and get a quick loan on it. Where us, if we've gotta go get a quick loan, it's gonna take ten pages and three weeks of work before the bank's gonna okay it for us. We can't just walk in a bank and borrow $300 that easy anymore. A Navajo can take a nice concho belt to a pawn dealer and pick up $300 without any trouble. So they probably tried the bank thing, some of 'em, and they're not impressed with how much time it takes and the trouble it is, so they'd just rather go to a pawn shop and get their money when they need it, that way.[4]

Malone expanded on the way in which the old trading post was run and financed:

It was mostly a barter system. I think when you started out the year, you counted the money in the cigar box, and it was essentially about that way when the year ended. It was how much money was in the cigar box. Of course rugs and things like that, they would have had to been inexpensive, but money was at an all-time high in those days, too. I mean, $300 in those days is probably like gone to heaven, probably like $30,000 today. So most of the trading posts, even when I worked at Piñon, we ran tabs with our wholesalers. We got our Coke for six months at a time. We paid bills off twice a year. We paid it in the spring when we bought wool and sold it, and then we paid it in the fall when we bought sheep and sold 'em. If you had a good year with piñons or something, that was just extra. But I guess I would say when I first started trading, it was mostly running up a tab on both sides—the store would run a tab with its dealers, and the same way as Hubbell would have done with C. N. Cotton or Gallup Mercantile or any of those people that supplied things.[5]

Later, Malone described the type of services he provided as a trader at Piñon:

Oh, I guess I've done all the things that traders did in that time—make their phone calls, write letters, go to funerals. I've even shot horses at funerals when asked by the family to do so. I had a hard time shooting a horse, too, sometimes, because it's kind of hard just to shoot a horse, but it's part of their belief in doin' the funeral. It's kind of an honor to be asked to do something like that, and I've done that. I can remember one family, I think I went to 'em three times with death messages, because the police department in Chinle couldn't get out, it was muddy, rainy, or

13. Billy Malone at
    Hubbell Trading
    Post, early 1980s
    (*photograph
    courtesy of
    Billy Malone
    and family*).

what. And I can remember one daughter said, "Please don't come see us anymore, because we know when you're comin', it's something bad, bad news is comin'." So that was probably the last time I had to do that for 'em. But I think it was three times I'd been up to their house for something like that, and it was terrible.

Other than that, I guess I did just the usual things: went to squaw dances and fire dances and yéiibicheiis and things like that—which is fun. The healing ceremonies they have are very powerful. They have a strong belief in 'em.[6]

Malone's former employer at the Piñon Trading Post, Cliff McGee, affirmed Malone's penchant for acquiring rugs and jewelry and offered other insights about the young trader who first came to work for him in the early 1960s. McGee recalled that from the very beginning at Piñon, Malone would personally take in pawn at his house to help out the local Navajos with loans. He continued to do that even after FTC rules were imposed on traders in the 1970s restricting pawn operations. Malone felt it was alright since he was married to a Navajo woman, and he didn't usually charge interest, anyway. McGee also speculated that Malone seldom if ever sold any pawn that went dead but instead just held onto it as more of a caretaker or custodian than as the new owner. That way, if an Indian came back one day, it would still be there for them or their family to claim. Malone had a reputation for making sure his clients didn't lose their family treasures just because they'd run on hard times or weren't able to get back in time to claim their property. A lot of loans Malone made to local Navajos against pawn items went on indefinitely, without ever being paid back. Consequently, over the years, Malone acquired a lot of rugs, jewelry, and other items taken in on pawn but never claimed.

Numerous other accounts from fellow traders as well as residents throughout the reservation reinforce the image of Billy Malone as an inveterate collector and even pack rat who was extremely devoted and loyal to his Navajo friends and neighbors. Several of these accounts going back to the 1960s reveal that Malone would purchase handfuls of dead pawn from other traders across the reservation.[7] He was enamored with the old jewelry both for its historic character and because it could be purchased for literally cents on the dollar, since the other traders only needed to recoup the cost of the loans they had made against the pawn rather than get their intrinsic retail value (which, in later years, would increase dramatically). Also, in acquiring these pieces Malone was able to prevent those collections from being sold off in commercial markets off the reservation. Over the decades, Malone amassed an enormous quantity of old jewelry—thousands of pieces—along with hundreds of rugs and other items, many bearing their original tags, left in place to help identify their provenance. That collection was made all the more impressive by the rugs and jewelry his wife and other family members contributed to it.

McGee believed that Malone also just bought and accumulated a lot of rugs and jewelry for himself, never trading them out with or consigning them to other traders and seldom if ever selling things from his collection. When Malone bought a rug or piece of jewelry, he always bartered or paid the Navajos in cash, since neither he nor the Navajos had a bank or checking account. Malone got in trouble once when McGee found out that he was doing his own personal business, buying and trading rugs and jewelry for his own collection, inside the trading post. McGee scolded Malone and told him to go outside the trading post or to his own house if he wanted to conduct personal trades. That, according to McGee, was the only time he ever had a problem with Malone.

McGee felt that Malone had earned enormous trust and respect from the local Navajos over the years he worked at Piñon. The Navajos trusted Malone to write and translate their letters and messages, sign their welfare or Social Security checks for them, witness their mark or thumbprint, and count out their money, knowing that he would never shortchange or cheat them. When Malone became the trader at Hubbell Trading Post in 1981, business at the Piñon Trading Post fell off dramatically. People started going to Hubbell Trading Post instead of Piñon, out of loyalty to Malone.

McGee described Malone as generous to a fault and as "a happy-go-lucky guy." There wasn't anything Malone wouldn't do to help the local Navajos. Also, according to McGee, Malone didn't associate with white people very much and lived "more of a Navajo lifestyle than a white lifestyle."[8]

McGee's son, Bruce, is now the buyer/manager of the gift shop at the famous Heard Museum in Phoenix. The younger McGee expressed many of the same sentiments as his father about Malone when he was interviewed in 2006, noting that "Bill has a soft heart." McGee confirmed his father's observation that Malone often accepted pawn from the local Navajos with absolutely no intention of selling it when it went dead or of trying to realize a profit through interest. If the owner or a member of the owner's family didn't come back to claim it, then Malone just figured it would be good for when he eventually needed to retire.

McGee also cited his father's prohibition against conducting personal business in the trading post. He recalled that during the time Malone worked at Piñon, his father told both Malone and him that as the owner, he retained the right of first refusal when a rug or piece of jewelry came in for trade. But if his father turned it down, he or Malone was free to buy it for their own collection, but they were supposed to go outside or to their own house to complete the deal. When he helped Malone and his wife pack their things for the 1981 move to Ganado, he saw firsthand that Malone had hundreds of rugs and dozens of boxes and cans full of jewelry he had taken in pawn or acquired through trade, had purchased, or had received as gifts.[9]

A number of NPS and SPMA employees and supervisors who had observed Malone work at Hubbell Trading Post or gone into his home corroborated these claims about Malone's character and business practices as well as about his penchant for collecting volumes of rugs and jewelry.

Nancy Stone was the NPS superintendent of Hubbell Trading Post National Historic Site from 1995 until her retirement in January 2006. In a 2006 interview, she said Malone had so much property stored at the trading post warehouse that it was a fire hazard. There were boxes of "personal stuff" mixed in with things from the trading post, including old calendars and a lot of "junk," stuff Malone had purchased and collected over the years. Stone explained that "a real trader is part junk collector." But she also observed that in Malone "there was that benevolence. . . . He was a sort of patron in this town." Stone described Malone's business practices as "shirt-pocket accountability . . . a note in his pocket, a handshake." She added that she had "loved to watch Billy do business" because it was like taking a step back in time and watching a real Indian trader from the Old West. Stone considered it a real privilege to have worked at Hubbell Trading Post during the time Malone was there.[10]

Kris Medina was employed in Tucson as the SPMA's full-time accountant from 1987 to 1994. She was responsible for conducting audits and inventories of the trading post. In her 2006 interview she acknowledged that the SPMA was fully aware of the comingling of property at Hubbell and knew that Malone kept many of his own personal items in the storage room of the trading post. Medina and the rest of the SPMA management team also knew that Malone regularly bought, sold, and traded items for his personal collection, on the side, just as he had back at Piñon. The SPMA had tried for years to get Malone to stop storing his own things at the trading post. But according to Medina, "Getting Bill to accept change was difficult. He'd do it for a couple of months, then go back."

Medina added that Malone just had "a lot of stuff." He simply didn't have enough storage space to keep all of his personal rugs and jewelry in the trailer where he and his family lived on the grounds of the trading post. That situation improved several years later when he finally moved into a real house with its own garage within the government compound. Still, according to Medina, during the audits and inventories she conducted, Malone would have to point out items that were his personal property as opposed to consignment or SPMA property. And while this made conducting audits and inventories difficult, she and the other officials were always able to account for all of the Hubbell Trading Post property and funds and distinguish them from Malone's own property and property taken in on consignment.

Medina recalled a time back in the late 1980s or early 1990s when she went into Malone's home and was "floored" by the size of his collection. "When I went into the man's house, you could not walk through the trailer. It was packed." Medina observed "stacks of rugs up to the waist . . . at least four piles high" and estimated that there were enough rugs and jewelry there to completely fill a twelve-foot by twelve-foot room. But Medina knew that Malone had been a trader and a collector for decades and that Malone's wife, Minnie, also made her own jewelry and rugs in their home. This easily explained how Malone could have collected so many rugs, pieces of jewelry, and other unusual and collectable things. She also knew that Malone often purchased rugs, jewelry, and other items from people in the community just to help them out. "Bill is a man with a big heart." When people came in that needed help, "Bill would pull money out of his pocket. . . . He loved being the trader at Hubbell Trading Post."[11]

In his 2006 interview, the SPMA's former chief financial and operations officer John Pearson observed that Malone "lived his job." He spoke Navajo, didn't drink alcohol, and was one of the last real traders on the Navajo Reservation. Malone "had an incredible knowledge of life on the rez and of the weavers." Pearson added, "We never had any reason to suspect Bill's honesty," even though the SPMA's managers were frequently surprised by some of the strange ways he did business.

Pearson had never been inside Malone's house, but he said he would not have been at all surprised if Malone had stacks of rugs and jewelry there. "Bill's house was reputed to be like a museum, full of treasures and handcrafts." It was also common knowledge that after hours when the trading post was closed, weavers, silversmiths, and other traders would go directly to Malone's house to conduct their business, make their trades, and drop off or pick up consignment merchandise. Malone's house was as much an extension of the trading post as the trading post was an extension of Malone's home.

Pearson recalled an incident in the late 1980s or early 1990s when he received a complaint from another employee that Malone was doing his own trading "on the side" at the trading post. According to the report, Malone even had his own cash box that he carried around to keep the money from his personal business transactions in. When confronted with this allegation, Malone nonchalantly replied, "Oh yeah. That's true." It was then that Pearson realized Malone wasn't trying to hide anything and saw nothing wrong or out of the ordinary in conducting his own business and trades at the trading post. This incident helped to reinforce Pearson's understanding that "Bill wasn't just a trader, 8 to 5. It was his life. It's what he did. He was always ready to trade. . . . He was a trader, and he was a collector." Pearson also acknowledged that there were no rules against

Malone freelancing and conducting his own trades on the job, and "there was never anything that said he couldn't." Pearson told Malone he could continue his freelance trading so long as he would continue to keep his own business transactions separate from those of the SPMA.[12]

Former SPMA executive director Tim Priehs echoed many of these observations, remarking like others on the strange ways that Malone conducted business. "Half the time Billy never even cashed his paycheck. . . . It finally got to the point where we started paying cashier's checks for paychecks." To keep their own books straight, SPMA managers started taking Malone's paycheck to the bank for conversion into a cashier's check before they mailed it to Malone. That way, the SPMA's internal accounts would show his paycheck had been "cashed." Priehs also confirmed that Malone was allowed to conduct his own (personal) trades at the trading post. Priehs acknowledged, "I don't believe there's any prohibition against that. . . . There was no policy that restricted him."

Priehs described Malone as a very good trader who had a real connection with the local artisans. He felt that Malone was indispensable as a trader, that there was no one better. He knew that Malone was raised as an old-time trader and had come recommended to the SPMA as someone with a very good ear for how to do business on the reservation. At the same time, Priehs acknowledged that the way Malone did business did not mesh with what officials at SPMA/WNPA headquarters in downtown Tucson wanted. But Priehs was adamant that he and the SPMA never had any reason to believe that Malone ever did anything improper at the trading post. "That guy lived for the place. . . . You had to prod the guy to take a vacation. . . . He loved it. He loved the artisans. . . . He loved the trading post business."

Priehs explained that "part of Navajo trading is people wanting cash." In 1981 when Malone was hired "there were a lot of weavers at that point that didn't have checking accounts." But the SPMA eventually insisted that Malone write a check, instead of paying cash, to every artist from whom a rug and piece of jewelry was purchased. So when Malone wrote a check to a weaver or silversmith "they would endorse it and cash it [at the very same time]. Especially the elderly weavers who were illiterate; they would at least make a mark."

Priehs acknowledged the frustration that both he and John Pearson experienced in their attempts to supervise Malone and bring him into the twentieth century. But Priehs added, "Bill was dedicated and honest. He wasn't living the high life. He fought hard for the weavers. . . . He always wanted to buy young weavers' stuff, . . . to bring along young weavers, to perpetuate the craft." Malone's insistence on purchasing less-than-desirable rugs from young Navajo weavers led to a number of arguments between him and Priehs. Priehs challenged those questionable expenditures, but Malone would fight and advocate for the young artists, citing the long-term benefits of keeping them employed and encouraging the development of their craft.[13]

Billy Malone spent twenty-four years working as the trader at Hubbell Trading Post. That is longer than any other trader since John Lorenzo Hubbell himself. Throughout that time, Malone almost always worked long hours, seven days a week. He seldom if ever took a vacation or sick leave. Malone's name became synonymous with Hubbell Trading Post. To this day, many people are unaware that he was not the owner of the trading post that he ran from 1981 all the way into the twenty-first century. All told, Malone spent nearly half a century working and living as a genuine Indian trader. He earned his own place in history as a key figure on the Navajo Reservation.

14. Billy Malone waiting on clients at Hubbell Trading Post (*photograph courtesy of Russ Finley*).

15. Billy Malone at Hubbell Trading Post, examining a bracelet brought in by one of his Navajo customers, Maude Slivers, in the late 1980s (*photograph courtesy of Jerry Jacka photography*).

16. Billy Malone at Hubbell Trading Post, examining a rug brought in by Ason Buckinghorse in the late 1980s. Buckinghorse was one of Malone's longtime clients from the Piñon Trading Post, going back to the 1960s. She continued to bring her rugs to "her trader" (Malone) long after he moved to Hubbell Trading Post (*photograph courtesy of Steve Getzwiller*).

In, *Diné*, a landmark piece of scholarship on Navajo history and culture, Peter Iverson, a noted scholar of twentieth-century American Indian history, talks about Billy Malone and his commitment to trading with the Navajo people: "Friends said he was limited by policies that restricted his options and reduced his maneuvering room, yet he maintained his reputation as someone who cared deeply about quality and fairness in his dealings with weavers."[14]

Living in the remote regions of the reservation for all those years and marrying into a Navajo family, Malone came to adopt many of the practices and beliefs held within traditional Navajo society. In the words of long-time friend and fellow-trader, Bruce Burnham: "You live with these people for thirty to fifty years and you become more Navajo than white."[15] By almost all accounts that seems to describe what happened to Billy Malone.

17. "The trader": Billy Malone in the rug room at Hubbell Trading Post, late 1980s. This image was widely circulated as a popular postcard sold throughout the Southwest (*photograph courtesy of Russ Finley*). ⸻

The Agency

(Wáshindoon bá na´ anish bił haz ánígíí)

The [National Park] Service thus established shall promote and regulate the use of federal areas known as national parks, monuments and reservations by such means and measures as conform to the fundamental purpose of said parks, monuments, and reservations, which purpose is to conserve the scenery and the natural and historic objects and the wild life therein and to provide for the enjoyment of the same in such manner and by such means as will leave them unimpaired for the enjoyment of future generations.

NPS Organic Act (AKA, "The NPS Mission Statement")

Do not let the Service become just another executive government bureau; keep it youthful, vigorous, clean and strong.

Horace M. Albright, second director of the NPS

L IKE ANY AGENCY or institution, the NPS undoubtedly has its share of problems. However, most people would probably agree that its public image is not one of them.

Americans love their national parks, and they seem to be equally enamored with the agency that runs them. The NPS *does* enjoy the best image and reputation of just about any agency in the federal government. What child with their family has not at least once gazed with admiration at the iconic park ranger greeting them at an entrance station, leading a campfire program or nature walk, directing traffic on a crowded park road, or conducting a daring rescue on some snow-capped mountaintop or the face of a sheer cliff? And every summer the television networks are filled with seasonal stories about the millions of tourists who will flock to the parks, in which reporters interview uniformed park employees offering safety and travel tips, talking about park overcrowding, dilapidated roads and buildings, the alarming rise in crime, and the disturbing budget cuts that reflect this or that administration's neglect. There are literally dozens, if not hundreds, of books written by retired NPS rangers recalling their experiences living and working in the national parks and telling their tales of humor and heroism. All of this serves to reinforce our love affair with our parks and with the NPS itself. Certainly, most Americans look quite kindly on the people who work for and run that agency. Really, what's not to love?

There is a case to be made, however, that its wonderful public image has also served to insulate the NPS from substantial criticism and, more importantly, to inoculate the agency against outside pressure to change, even where there might be some very compelling reasons to do so.

With its uniquely appealing mission and characteristically idyllic and isolated work environments, a very distinct culture and psychology has evolved within the NPS. NPS employees tend to think of themselves as separate and apart, special and elite within the government. They are not merely loyal civil servants in the employ of a unique federal agency. They are lucky and privileged members of a workforce internally characterized as a family, and its good and loyal members demonstrate in both their work *and* their personal lives that they have green blood flowing through their veins and are "green and grey" through and through.[1] Employees are indoctrinated into this culture and encouraged through a system of very real social and professional incentives and sanctions to commit themselves fully to the agency whose mission and traditions they embrace.

An example of how extreme this indoctrination can be is that both new and transferring employees in many park areas have been required to swear a distinct oath of allegiance (". . . So help me God") to the NPS itself at the very same time they swear to support and defend the U.S. Constitution (the effect of which is to literally merge the NPS mission statement into and thereby modify the statutorily prescribed language of the oath of office).[2] For many, pressures like this serve to blur the distinction between the two ideals, creating real confusion over expectations in the performance of their duties.

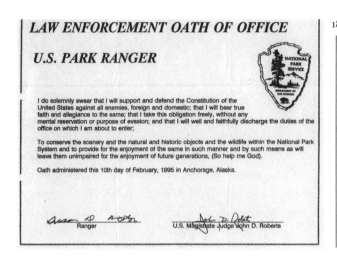

LAW ENFORCEMENT OATH OF OFFICE

U.S. PARK RANGER

I do solemnly swear that I will support and defend the Constitution of the United States against all enemies, foreign and domestic; that I will bear true faith and allegiance to the same; that I take this obligation freely, without any mental reservation or purpose of evasion; and that I will well and faithfully discharge the duties of the office on which I am about to enter;

To conserve the scenery and the natural and historic objects and the wildlife within the National Park System and to provide for the enjoyment of the same in such manner and by such means as will leave them unimpaired for the enjoyment of future generations, (So help me God).

Oath administered this 10th day of February, 1995 in Anchorage, Alaska.

Ranger   U.S. Magistrate Judge John D. Roberts

18. NPS Oath of Office (*author's collection*).

The extent of the confusion within the organization over whether employees owed allegiance first to the NPS or the U.S. Constitution was highlighted in the late 1990s during heated internal debates related to national law enforcement policies. One proposal was voiced to formally list employee obligation to defense of constitutional rights and principles ahead of allegiance to the NPS mission. So contentious was the ensuing committee debate that the topic and the policy section were dropped altogether. The employee who advanced the original proposal was left ostracized and stunned, having mistakenly thought it a simple matter that employees be reminded of their primary obligation to behave in a constitutional manner in the exercise of their secondary responsibilities to the NPS and its mission. The experience served as a graphic example of the institutional disconnect produced by a confused set of values at the highest levels of the agency, more than hinting at the potential for abuse that can result from the mentality that the ends may well justify the means when it comes to satisfying their personal vision for the NPS. Most employees, at least initially, accept this commitment with great passion and devotion, reflecting their own idealistic attitudes that drew them to the NPS in the first place.

It's not at all easy to secure a permanent position within the NPS unless you already know someone in the agency who is willing to do you a favor. Unlike most other agencies, uniform standards and qualifications for position applicants and candidates do not exist, and one does not simply take a standard test, receive a score, and wait in line for a position as a ranger. You generally have to obtain help from the inside to even learn about a job opening, and then you will need to get tips on how to ace the application.

Selection criteria for a given position are usually crafted by that position's direct or second-level supervisors, who can construct and manipulate those standards to reach the person they have very likely preselected for the job, again underscoring the importance of having an inside track and friends in the right places. Most experienced supervisors are well versed in techniques and loopholes that can be used to circumvent or defeat the Office of Personnel Management "merit system" process and regulations, allowing them to reject qualified applicants they may not want in favor of friends they are trying to recruit or promote. Many senior managers openly sanction this process, brazenly filling key positions by altering or altogether ignoring hiring standards prescribed by regulations or policies in the name of recruiting people they believe are the best for the agency. Simultaneously, they leave behind a long trail of discouraged applicants who mistakenly thought they might have a fair chance to compete.

Likewise, a disturbingly high percentage of leaders in the NPS, especially park superintendents, have been selected not for their experience or qualifications per se so much as for their demonstrated loyalty and friendship to even more senior officials in a particular regional or Washington office. This helps to explain the appointment of superintendents who may never have even worked in a park before or the shuffling of superintendents and others who have messed up in very significant ways from one park to another or their promotion to even more senior regional positions. Also, of course, there is a distinct advantage to being a second-, third-, or even fourth-generation Park Service employee, with your career path into a leadership position virtually assured and, in some instances, quite literally scripted from a very early age.

This is not to say that an outsider can never penetrate the system. But individuals who do so are frequently confronted by harsh organizational realities soon after they enter on duty, including the reminder that they are lucky to be working for the NPS and if they're dissatisfied they should go elsewhere. More than one established professional from the outside has found themselves confronted with the humbling realities of the NPS after being required to swallow their self-esteem along with their bachelors, masters, or even doctoral degrees and often decades of prior experience with other agencies or organizations by first accepting an entry-level job as an entrance station attendant or perhaps a seasonal clerk, at the very bottom of the food chain, so as to prove their worth and loyalty to officials already established and indoctrinated within the NPS.

It's surprising how many people actually do accept this challenge out of a sense of environmental and civic idealism as well as a desire to "live the dream." Some go their entire careers holding onto that dream and showing an almost irrational loyalty to the NPS and its leadership, as they overinvest in the agency itself in the formation of their personal identity. But for many others the dream soon fades into the harsh reality of low pay, less-than-ideal living conditions, and the realization that the honesty, hard work, and new ideas they brought with them are not particularly welcome.[3] The NPS has turned the practice of feeding on its own young (particularly volunteers and seasonal employees) into a virtual art form. And so in addition to the distinction of having the best image in federal government, the NPS arguably also holds the distinction of having lost more genuinely talented employees, through transfers and even outright resignations, than any other agency.[4]

One simply does not challenge the NPS culture or its leadership or mention problems and make complaints outside of the internal agency structure. The image of the agency is paramount, and that's one reason why it so successfully garners public and political support. Do nothing to compromise the image or damage the reputation of the agency, which certainly precludes airing a problem in public.

In practice, this mantra is not so much directed at preventing acts of misconduct that might cause embarrassment to the agency as it is at preventing the *exposing* of such acts to the outside world. Likewise, concerns about liability arising from agency or employee misconduct or negligence are addressed not so much through the establishment of systems to guard against misconduct, negligence, or incompetence as through systems to prevent the documentation of such acts. An act of misconduct itself, however egregious, is not as serious a transgression as is publicly exposing it, especially if it was committed by a senior manager or favored employee. And for park superintendents or other managers facing dissent within their domain, the worst offense is not having allowed conditions to deteriorate or breed discontent so much as having failed to control the situation by suppressing the public voicing of dissent.

To allow a problem to surface into the public arena is an unforgivable act that could embarrass the agency and tarnish the image of the green and grey. As a consequence, there is a pervasive reluctance to openly discuss or even learn from the mistakes or transgressions of others. Embarrassing details about incidents ranging from employee-on-employee molestations to Anti-Deficiency Act violations to bad "officer-involved shootings" have been kept under wraps in the name of "privacy concerns." To openly cite or even discuss such incidents as examples of unacceptable behavior would require the acknowledgment of problems and deficiencies and would elevate the visibility of acts or incidents damaging to the image of the agency. This de facto code of silence also allows a rather large segment of the workforce to remain simultaneously content and naïve, oblivious to the magnitude of serious misconduct occurring beyond immediate view and often tolerated behind the scenes. Many employees are thereby able to cling to their own idealized view of the NPS and are merely bewildered by the vague and bureaucratic ethics memos periodically handed down reactively from the Washington or regional offices in lieu of a real discussion or explanation. The divergent experiences of different segments of the workforce, often delineated by rank or grade level, also account for the genuine disconnect between what employees in these various segments passionately believe and the truth about the real extent to which problems, up to and including serious corruption, exist within the agency.[5]

Agency loyalty is valued above almost any other attribute, and, in return for loyalty, employees benefit from a conspicuous system of rewards, which frequently includes protection from substantial accountability in both their performance and their conduct. To be considered a trusted employee in the NPS is often more a statement about loyalty to one's peers and allegiance to the agency than it is about individual honesty and integrity. This has been repeatedly demonstrated over time within the NPS, with the result that many individuals whose integrity has been seriously compromised have been placed in senior positions in the agency. In the aftermath of even the most serious of misconduct, there is frequently the expectation that an institutionalized system of alliances and presumptive quid pro quo will protect insiders, because, after all, everybody knows about everybody else's skeletons. And in those instances when a leader is forced from power by outside forces and can no longer be protected, there is very likely to be some protégé or progeny waiting in line and prepositioned to take their place. And only then, after a leader has fallen, will former colleagues predictably share their own accounts or suspicions about past misconduct they had known about all along.

Among the more well-known and accepted alliances within the NPS is a group referred to as the Yosemite mafia comprised of "employees with formative experiences in law enforcement gained at Yosemite who are now in positions of influence throughout the agency."[6] Members of the Yosemite mafia are widely credited with leading the agency and implementing many service-wide reforms and initiatives throughout the latter part of the twentieth century.

Amid the social turmoil of the early 1970s, the NPS was confronted with a series of events that elevated the visibility of its law enforcement problems and, more importantly, its widespread failure to keep up with the times by instituting a professional law enforcement program. The first of these was a riot that erupted in 1970 over the Fourth of July holiday in Yosemite Valley. The NPS had to call on emergency resources from neighboring state jurisdictions to assist it in dispersing and arresting hundreds of reveling youths, leaving the public with the distinct impression that the agency was ill equipped to deal with modern law enforcement challenges.

Next, in the summer of 1973, was the high-profile murder of NPS ranger Ken Patrick at Pt. Reyes National Seashore. This incident sent shock waves through the agency, as it was inaccurately represented by both the media and the NPS itself as the first time a ranger had been murdered in the line of duty.[7] Both of these incidents—the Yosemite riots and the murder of Ken Patrick—made national news, at least temporarily exposing a long-hidden reality about national parks. National parks, like any other tourist destination occupied by tens of thousands of care-free visitors along with a transient workforce staffing hotels and restaurants, are subject to the same types and levels of crimes as tourist towns and small cities throughout America.[8]

The revelation sent the NPS running for cover. It began devising a plan to respond to glaring deficiencies in its law enforcement program, all the while struggling to retain control and maintain its broader "ranger image." The agency initiated a "comprehensive law enforcement training program, to include 225 entry-level rangers and selected management personnel" and also established a Washington-based law enforcement office. "With the rangers bureaucratically allied with park superintendents (and solidly within the main feeder group for superintendency positions) the law enforcement programs, or 'visitor protection and safety' programs, as they would become known, were virtually assured of continued strong support from Service leadership."[9]

It was this effort that gave rise to the Yosemite mafia, comprised of loyal up-and-coming rangers: its members were cultivated and trained from *within* the agency, as part of an effort to create a special proprietary brand of "NPS law enforcement." In the process, many of these same individuals, internally identified as loosely defined "law enforcement specialists," developed a reputation for leadership, rising to positions of power and significantly influencing the manner in which the law enforcement program of the NPS would unfold.

Among the members of the Yosemite mafia are many good individuals who have undoubtedly made legitimate contributions to the advancement of the NPS law enforcement program. However, in a grim irony, the humorous title proudly

invoked by the group belies a darker side exhibited by many of its more powerful and influential members, lending altogether different meaning to the much-
touted image of the NPS as a "family." Over time several of these powerful figures
have variously been implicated in illegal activities ranging from trespassing and
molestation, electronic eavesdropping and attempted blackmail, the use of government funds to pay off extortion attempts, the theft of government firearms, to
even kidnapping and rape.[10] These and other activities have been exposed almost
exclusively through outside investigations, leading in most cases (but not all) to
the untimely yet nevertheless celebrated retirement of the guilty party but never
to an NPS-initiated prosecution.

The familial—or at least fraternal—quality suggested by their name has
added to the mystique of the Yosemite mafia, as many members, including those
forced out of their positions, have successfully used their power, influence, and
connections to assure the placement of their own children or friends—perhaps
better educated, more sophisticated, and even more skilled in agency politics
than their fathers or mentors—into key NPS positions. This power and influence doesn't just permit sons to follow in the footsteps of their fathers but also
frequently affords them preferential placement into government-sponsored
management development programs and even garners them congressional fel-
lowships. Bold pronouncements issue from *within* inner circles, years ahead
of the fact, about the career path charted out for heirs. This system of favored
recruitment and treatment, and the raw political power and influence held by key
figures within the NPS, is somehow accepted as part of the rules of NPS culture,
as other employees looking on from *outside* of the inner circle observe with resignation, "Oh, it's so-and-so's son."

Given its system of recruitment, rewards, and sanctions, it's not all that surprising that the NPS has evolved into a very insulated, provincial, and sometimes
cult-like organization. Many of its more powerful and charismatic leaders are
genuinely revered—and frequently feared—figures within the agency, demanding enormous loyalty from their followers, and suspicious of outsiders and outside opinions.

The cult-like character of the NPS is realized through the almost completely
government-controlled environment in which many employees live and work.
National parks are, in many instances, federal reservations and small federal
towns or communities. They are islands unto themselves, separate and apart
from other communities, and often extremely remote. The infrastructure within
is often completely controlled by the NPS manager—the superintendent—who

has been placed in charge based in large measure on their relationship with and loyalty to progressively more senior managers.

It's not unlike living on a military base or in a company town, such as existed in the late nineteenth and early twentieth centuries.[11] The NPS controls not only an employee's duty station, work schedule, and work assignment but also many aspects of personal daily life, such as housing assignments (including where and with whom they live), how much rent they pay, and rates charged by the stores that operate within the park. For couples, who are frequently both NPS employees, the situation is even more difficult and challenging—discretion over dual-career assignments (management discretion in allowing the couple to live and work at the same park or duty station) is often selectively used as both reward and punishment, depending on the couple's standing and stature within the organization. Under extraordinarily dictatorial superintendents or supervisors, employees have quite literally been told whom they should and should not socialize with, what types of hobbies and activities to undertake in their personal time, and in some extreme cases even directed about what types of food to eat, all in the name of team building and the demonstration of loyalty to the NPS.

The demand for loyalty insinuates itself into virtually every aspect of NPS employees' professional and personal lives, as reflected in the following statement from an official memorandum distributed by one regional director, pressuring employees to join a prominent employee association:

Why should NPS employees belong . . . ? My first answer is commitment, responsibility, loyalty to the total NPS. A person should be so dedicated that when they sign up to work for the NPS, they should want to automatically sign up for membership . . . If this commitment is not total, the people might just as well work for Sears Roebuck or Bell Telephone, because the loyalty for NPS is not there.[12]

I was first confronted with this mentality early in my own career, when a supervisor called me in for a counseling session. I had properly submitted a request for overtime pay after having been scheduled to work on my day off to cover for another employee who was sick. The supervisor berated me for my lack of devotion, expressing disappointment that I expected to be paid extra for working scheduled overtime. To emphasize his point, he noted that he had "married the NPS" long before he had married his wife and that he would leave his own wife before ever leaving the agency. Over his desk, this same supervisor had a picture of his infant son dressed in a full (albeit miniature) NPS uniform that his wife made for their baby.

NPS employees hear this message time and again, both officially and otherwise, throughout their careers and even into retirement. As one politically active retiree association proudly proclaims in their logo, "The green blood still runs deep," a sentiment that reflects impassioned agency loyalty more than a consistent environmental ethic.

Because the parks are federal enclaves and often extremely remote, information about what goes on inside can be tightly controlled, and there is typically very little if any on-site media or free press. Instead, information about NPS activities is regulated and restricted through carefully crafted press releases that are designed to suit management needs. These press releases often spin facts and fabricate accounts about embarrassing matters with a level of skill rivaling that of partisan politicians. Meanwhile, both official and de facto restrictions on speech exist, since almost every resident or at least one family member is an employee and can be disciplined for talking or corresponding with outside entities about work or park-related issues. Official gag orders and other agency tactics to restrict employee speech (including whistleblower disclosures, communications to Congress, and even mere off-duty discussion of work-related issues) prompted one employee advocacy group, Public Employees for Environmental Responsibility (PEER), to comment in a 2002 press release that "It's apparent that the NPS needs to be reminded again that its employees are American citizens with First Amendment rights."[13]

The unspoken social pressures and psychological impacts of this type of environment, where employees may literally live next door to or across the street from their own supervisors, produce workers that over time become extremely obedient to and dependent on their employer for virtually every aspect of their lives. The social environment is often rigidly stratified, and the agency is able to exercise a level of control over the resident and even visiting population not seen elsewhere in normal American society.

The strong idealism that attracts many people to the agency combined with the provincial mentality that stresses allegiance and obedience to the NPS itself (rather than the statutory agency mission and the rule of law) helps explain the excesses in how many local NPS programs, including law enforcement, are managed and operated.[14] Over time, these excesses come to affect many employees' sense of what is and is not acceptable behavior, as they assimilate into the culture, often acting with near-blind obedience as they surrender their own better judgment to that prescribed by their employer.

Police administrators and psychologists have coined the term "noble cause corruption" to describe a similar phenomenon often seen in law enforcement organizations.[15] It describes breaches in established constitutional protocols and procedures committed by law enforcement personnel out of a desire to make sure that legal technicalities and case weaknesses do not get in the way of an arrest and prosecution and that "bad guys" don't get away with anything. Lost in the equation is the dominant role of the Constitution as "the law of the land" and the overriding obligation to respect and protect constitutional rights and principles. In the case of the NPS, the phenomenon transcends law enforcement and can be observed in a variety of different program areas where employees, and particularly superintendents and other supervisors, are encouraged through the prevailing culture to bend rules and take shortcuts to achieve the greater good for their own program, park, or employing agency. One senior NPS law enforcement official succinctly verbalized his belief in the noble cause during an interview for a television documentary on NPS law enforcement. Commenting on negative public perceptions about NPS law enforcement activities and personnel, the official echoed the common internal belief: "Don't these people know that I'm a ranger? Therefore I must be good?"[16] An even more graphic example was presented by the superintendent of a famous western park when he explained his illegal use of law enforcement personnel and electronic surveillance equipment to secretly record a conversation with a prominent political adversary. When finally confronted by investigators from the OIG three years after the fact, the superintendent commented that, "this action on my part was a lapse in judgment, but my intentions have always been to further the interests of the NPS."[17]

To a degree far greater than is found in most other agencies, the integrity and success—and sometimes even the very existence—of critical programs in national parks and throughout the NPS is dependent almost entirely on the integrity, skill, and ego of the manager in charge at the time, and it is unlikely that same program will endure in the same form beyond their tenure. There is remarkably little similarity from one park to the next in what should be the same types of programs, evidenced by wildly disparate levels of funding, staffing, expertise, and effectiveness. Some extremely progressive, innovative, and effective programs have been developed, funded, and established under one motivated manager only to be summarily dismantled and destroyed by a successor. Even the best and most critical program(s), including those that are statutorily mandated or funded through special appropriations, can be eviscerated or abolished when a change of the guard occurs, either locally or nationally, and a new superintendent or other manager with a different set of values, different friends, priorities, political motivations, or skills moves in. The prevalence of this purposefully inconsistent method of operation contributes to often poor relations with park neighbors and other NPS constituents who in many instances, over time, learn to distrust the agency and any promises or commitments made by its various managers and other personnel.

Credibility problems are exacerbated through manipulation of the service's own ad hoc workgroups, investigative teams, and "blue ribbon panels" made up of selected colleagues and even handpicked and contracted groups of retirees. The manner in which these teams and workgroups are assembled generally assures a desired finding or outcome or at least obfuscation of facts that might damage the reputation of the agency. Organizational pressures to operate in this manner are virtually without limit and have been applied to everything from routine program reviews to the investigation of employee fatalities and even agency-caused disasters affecting entire communities.[18]

Worse still is active manipulation of the service's internal affairs branch, the Office of Professional Responsibility, which, as we shall see, has on more than one occasion been effectively used to either target or exonerate employees and even entire programs through the selective and even false documentation of evidence, depending on the expressed desires of the manager requesting the investigation.[19] Even more absurd, more than one NPS employee has found themselves the target of the service's search and destroy method of dealing with whistleblowers in which the agency uses official internal investigations and disciplinary actions to punish those who have literally done nothing more than document and report misconduct committed by a supervisor or other favored employee.[20]

The combined effect of these practices—used to preserve the image and reputation of the agency and its senior officials—led at least one high-ranking DOI official to observe that many of the statistics and programmatic reports generated by the NPS were "not worth the paper they were sent in on."[21]

Successful NPS managers are aided in their mission of resisting change and perpetuating the image of the agency (not to mention advancing their own careers) through the cultivation of friendships and alliances with both elected and appointed political figures. Politically savvy NPS managers who learn to "run with the big dogs" are uniquely positioned to ingratiate themselves with powerful people who are all too willing to take advantage of government-funded river rafting trips, catered backcountry trips, private park overflights, exploratory junkets

(AKA family vacations), and other extraordinary favors the NPS manager might offer, often in derogation of the NPS mission itself and "park values." In the bigger parks such as Yosemite, Yellowstone, Grand Teton, and Grand Canyon, homes reserved for the superintendent are often lavishly maintained and appointed at government expense, the justification being that they will host visiting dignitaries, including the president and other heads of state. More than one congressman, senator, or presidential appointee has answered the call from a park superintendent or regional director asking for a favor after that manager found themselves in political or legal hot water or under investigation by an outside agency.

Meanwhile, complaint letters and reports submitted by employees identifying problems within the NPS very often fall on deaf ears, since those same elected and other officials who receive the complaints (including the OIG) frequently refer the matter right back to the NPS for "self-investigation" or to the very same NPS managers about whom the complaints were filed. This virtually assures that very little if anything will be done about the problem and frequently also exposes the source of the complaint, almost certainly assuring some form of reprisal. Over time, most employees, including that vast majority who are honest, well intended, and hard working, learn that it is far wiser to just keep quiet and live with a bad situation rather than waste time filing a complaint or reporting misconduct. Many, if not most, who have attempted to report senior officials for serious misconduct have lived to regret it and pronounced that they would never do it again.

Equally critical to the success of NPS managers is the ability to befriend and ingratiate themselves with various park "partners," who are typically powerful individuals and entities outside of the NPS or DOI establishment. This may include the leaders of neighboring gateway communities comprised of hotel, restaurant, and tour operations, whose economic survival often hinges on park-related tourism. It also includes the corporate management of concession operations licensed to operate hotels, restaurants, and other facilities within park boundaries. These operations have transformed over the decades from what may once have been mom and pop businesses, evolving through buyouts and competitive bids into multinational corporations and conglomerates. These types of organizations learned long ago that there are millions to be made in monopolistic contracts available at places such as Grand Canyon, Yosemite, and Yellowstone national parks. At the same time many NPS managers also figured out it's in their own best interests to balance their governmental responsibilities against the desire to keep corporate interests and other "very powerful people" happy.

Other key partners to be courted are the various nonprofit nongovernmental organizations (NGOs), such as the National Park Foundation, the Eastern National Parks Association, and the WNPA, all created to support the NPS, itself through the creation of educational materials and programs and the contribution of unregulated funds to park activities. Meanwhile, many of these organizations, such as the WNPA, have themselves evolved into extremely powerful, multimillion dollar institutions on which the NPS relies heavily for both financial contributions and political support. The stationary masthead for such organizations are heavily lined with the names of prominent and very powerful political figures as well as former high-level NPS and DOI officials who serve as either board members or advisors and who are thus able to maintain a considerable degree of influence over both the NGO *and* the NPS. Successful NPS managers understand the influence that these organizations wield and strive to maintain extremely close and cordial relations with their respective board members and administrators.

This state of affairs, in which high-ranking superintendents, regional directors, and other senior NPS managers compete for power and influence and successfully broker political alliances, has led to the observation that the NPS functions more as a loose confederation of independent parks, regions, and managers than as a unified federal agency under the meaningful direction of an agency head. This recalls the way the earliest national parks, such as Yellowstone, Yosemite, Sequoia, and others, functioned prior to the establishment of the NPS in 1916, each having been administered separately, independent of a unifying national parks organization. Today, while there is most certainly an agency hierarchy, it does not always translate into—or coincide with—a coherent chain of command. Parks, regions, programs, and their respective managers function with alarming levels of autonomy and little if any real oversight. Decisions made by managers and others are often guided by passions, loyalties, and raw political expedience. The acceptance and even cultivation of this approach as an integral part of the NPS culture has opened the door to serious abuse.

The theory that the NPS in many ways continues to operate the way parks did before the 1916 Organic Act accounts for what seems to be an uncanny ability exhibited by many powerful figures within the agency to openly ignore or defy national policy and direction handed down by the NPS director and even the Office of the Secretary at the DOI, further resisting and obstructing meaningful organizational change or reform.[22] This attitude was graphically apparent in the way several superintendents at a national training session on new service-wide law enforcement policies responded to certain provisions that were introduced; they openly questioned whether use of the term "mandatory" in them really meant they'd be required to comply and implement those policies in "their" parks. Needless to say, no matter what response they received to their question, compliance throughout the country was inconsistent at best.

This same amazing degree of autonomy also helps to explain the frequent restructuring that is seen in the agency: supervisory and management positions are openly created and/or eliminated in response to political maneuvering and alliances, and regional directors, deputy and associate directors, and high-level park superintendents interchangeably swap positions in a manner that belies the existence of a real chain of command.

Because the NPS system of recruitment, retention, and rewards is focused on the top layers of the organization, the integrity of virtually any program area, from administration to budget, from maintenance to fire management and suppression, resource management, and environmental stewardship itself, can be compromised by a single, powerful manager. This is particularly so in the case of a high-profile project or when powerful political, corporate, or NGO figures have a special interest in a park or park issue. Deference to these individuals or entities, often at the expense of legal or policy requirements, is justified in the name of recruiting a political ally, concealing an unflattering reality, or merely protecting the image of the agency or the career of a friend. And while not every park or park program suffers this fate to the same degree or at the same time, virtually *every* park or NPS program is susceptible to this type of manipulation owing, at least in part, to the personality-driven (as opposed to systems-driven) manner in which most NPS programs (and parks) are managed and the almost complete absence of meaningful systems of prioritization, program oversight, and accountability. In combination with the enormous levels of power and autonomy bestowed on park superintendents, the lack of meaningful oversight and accountability has given rise to what is euphemistically referred to as "superintendent personality disorder," or SPD. That term was coined to characterize the management style and swagger exhibited by those managers (superintendents or otherwise) who are afflicted by an overdeveloped sense of self-confidence and entitlement, managers who expect that their judgment will not (and must not) be challenged and who know that they will not be held accountable for their actions and decisions.

The Wahweap Marina case, which later came to be known as the Glen Canyon NRA battery dumping case, serves as a graphic example of how NPS managers are encouraged to act in deference to various partners so that they might benefit from the complex system of protection and rewards that these types of relationships confer.[23]

During the 1980s, concessions operations at Glen Canyon NRA's Wahweap Marina in northern Arizona and up lake in southern Utah were contracted to Del Webb's Marina Operations Corporation. Beginning around 1985 NPS divers and concessions specialists discovered that batteries, engine parts, and other refuse from rental houseboats were being systematically dumped from the docks into the marina by concession employees. The NPS put Del Webb on notice about the problem as early as October 1988, but no criminal enforcement action was taken. That posture was adopted in open acknowledgment of the "double standard" employed by NPS management when it came to taking law enforcement action against "the powerful concessioner."

Late during this same period, Del Webb entered into negotiations to sell its concession contract at the national recreation area to ARA Leisure Services. To assure that a pending sale of the concessions contract from Del Webb to ARA was not jeopardized, the NPS concessions chief and other park managers made a concerted effort to conceal previously detected environmental violations and "keep the matter quiet," because "any adverse publicity regarding debris or batteries would certainly endanger the sale of the concession."

The sale of the Wahweap Marina concession to ARA was completed January 1989. However, even after ARA assumed the NPS concession contract, the practice of dumping batteries and other refuse into the lake did not stop. These continued violations were documented by the NPS in its September 1989 quarterly inspection. However, NPS managers again decided that the "NPS was not going to cite ARA criminally for the dumping, but would handle the matter administratively through the concession contract."

Subsequently, in 1990, the NPS lost control of the entire matter when word of the dumping incidents became public and the Arizona State Attorney General's Office (AZAG) initiated its own criminal and civil investigation. The special investigations section for the AZAG verified the deliberate dumping of toxic waste and other materials, resulting in the filing of environmental charges against both Del Webb and ARA. Del Webb entered a no contest plea to a class 6 felony and paid a $1 million fine.[24] ARA entered a civil consent decree and paid a $225,000 civil penalty. Both companies paid $100,000 in restitution costs to the local sheriff's office and AZAG. Four ARA managers entered the civil consent decree and agreed to complete one hundred hours of environmental community service to resolve their liability in the matter.

Notably, throughout the course of their investigation, state investigators also documented a disturbing series of efforts on the part of NPS officials to obstruct the investigation by lying about their knowledge of the incidents, destroying evidence, and pressuring subordinate NPS staff to lie to state investigators.

Also, when asked why the Del Webb violations had not resulted in unsatisfactory ratings or why the violations had not been formally documented in annual reports, the park's concessions division chief acknowledged it was standard practice to allow concession operators to both review and edit their own annual performance appraisals and that it was also the practice to leave adverse comments out of the written appraisal and instead "give verbal instructions concerning major problems." The concessions chief ultimately admitted to investigators that "it would be political suicide for the superintendent" to document such issues in the written report, adding that "all of the concessions have strong political friends in government."[25] This was not the first and would not be the last time an NPS manager offered this rationale and these types of words to justify misconduct after being caught in a scandal.

In the aftermath of this case, Grant Woods, the attorney general of Arizona, sent a letter directly to Bruce Babbitt, then secretary of the interior, sharing concerns about the numerous incidents of "indiscretion and impropriety" on the part of senior NPS managers. The attorney general specifically cited the Glen Canyon NRA superintendent, who throughout the investigation continually denied any knowledge about the incidents even though there was extensive written documentation on the matter bearing his signature. Also named and cited for misconduct was the chief of concessions, who had omitted documentation about known violations from annual concession evaluations and made a point of instructing others to "keep the matter quiet." Many of these acts could potentially have resulted in criminal prosecution. Instead, the attorney general deferred to the secretary and the NPS, suggesting that appropriate administrative action be taken.

The action taken by Secretary Babbitt and the NPS ultimately included allowing the superintendent to take his authorized retirement, after which he obtained an appointment to the board of directors of the prestigious NPS partner, the WNPA. The action taken against the NPS concessions chief tells the rest of the story. Soon after this incident he was promoted to chief of concessions for the entire IMR and a few years later to deputy regional director.

Disturbing as examples like this are, the most frightening potential for NPS management abuse may well lie in a program area the American public does not normally associate with the NPS.

Law enforcement is probably not the first thing that comes to mind when one thinks about the NPS. But law enforcement has been a responsibility of the NPS and its rangers since establishment of the very first parks. Regrettably, it is also, at best, viewed as a necessary evil within the organization, and senior-level officials make every effort to very tightly control and manipulate it to assure that law enforcement activities strictly support the position of management and do not create embarrassment or tarnish the image of the agency. So seriously is this matter of "image" taken by senior NPS management that in the mid-1970s a full-blown "ranger image task force" was commissioned to confront and contain the growing "problem" of rangers visibly engaging in law enforcement activities.[26]

This internal effort followed on the heels of the Yosemite riots and the murder of Ken Patrick, immediately after and in direct response to congressional actions that reaffirmed statutory NPS law enforcement authorities through the passage of PL 94–458 in 1976. That legislation, codified at 16 USC 1a–6, clarified that designated NPS employees were authorized to carry firearms, make arrests, serve court orders, and conduct investigations into both misdemeanor and felony violations occurring within the national park system. The legislation emphasized that NPS law enforcement responsibilities and authorities were "consistent with the authority exercised by other Federal personnel having law enforcement responsibilities, such as agents of the Federal Bureau of Investigation and United States Marshals, and specifically would not restrict their investigative jurisdiction."[27]

In response, NPS management issued a report and series of internal directives to diminish and dilute the impact of the new legislation and assure that the traditional ranger image would not be compromised. In so doing, management simultaneously assured that law enforcement within the agency would *not* be managed as a legitimate profession and that modern standards and practices as well as safeguards for performance, conduct, and integrity consistent with the greater (outside) law enforcement profession would *not* be implemented. Up until the 1990s this included steadfast resistance to carrying out basic background investigation otherwise mandated by DOI policies. Even thereafter and to the present, compliance has been spotty and only marginally effective in identifying serious character issues, particularly since there are still no psychological screening requirements. Compounding the situation is the success with which both the incumbent subjects of investigations and their supportive supervisors are frequently able to steer background investigators away from credible witnesses who may have observed disturbing behavior and the equally uncanny success with which powerful managers are able use their authority to influence adjudication.

In more than one prominent national park this overall approach has resulted in what has internally been characterized as "the Yellowstone (or Yosemite or Grand Canyon, etc.) exception to the Constitution," referring to observed governmental excesses over the decades. This phenomenon also accounts, at least in part, for what some frustrated employees and former employees have characterized as "one hundred years of tradition, unimpeded by progress" and an extremely sophisticated system of control and resistance to change.

Such statements may seem harsh and extreme to the uninitiated, but they are borne out by the record and by the facts. And it is not just disgruntled former employees who have come to that conclusion.

The OIG investigates serious financial crimes committed within or against DOI agencies and is also responsible for independently conducting audits, investigations, evaluations, and reviews relating to DOI programs and operations. It is charged with reporting its findings to the secretary of the interior and to Congress and for proposing solutions to the most serious management and program challenges, especially those relating to fraud, waste, abuse and mismanagement. Stated another way, it retains authority and responsibility for independently conducting high-level internal investigations into agency programs and personnel and for conducting major program audits and reviews.

In 2001 the DOI-OIG conducted an extensive review of Interior agency law enforcement programs, including that of the NPS. The findings of that review were released January 2002 in a report entitled "A Disquieting State of Disorder: An Assessment of Department of the Interior Law Enforcement." Therein the OIG identified a number of extremely disturbing program deficiencies common to most of DOI agencies, including the U.S. Fish and Wildlife Service, the Bureau of Land Management, the Bureau of Indian Affairs, and the NPS.

In addressing the NPS the OIG cited the inappropriate influence NPS management and political interests exerted over law enforcement generally and particularly over criminal investigations. In support of its findings, the OIG documented literally hundreds of incidents where managers inappropriately and illegally inserted themselves into the domain of law enforcement, obstructing investigations, destroying evidence, ordering the falsification of official reports, and influencing investigations to assure a desired outcome. Also documented were a disturbing number of incidents where NPS managers and employees themselves were found to have engaged in serious criminal activities while on duty, for which they were never officially investigated or prosecuted.

Perhaps the most disturbing pattern the OIG report documented was the almost complete absence of administrative accountability for engaging in misconduct, with many individuals—including senior law enforcement officials—left in place and even promoted after the agency became aware that they had engaged in criminal and other misconduct. The situation is not unlike that of various clergy who have abused children under their care but when caught were merely reassigned and relocated. In one notorious instance, a ranger even obtained a government step (pay) increase while sitting in jail on local charges related to voyeurism.[28] The same employee had repeatedly been caught under similar circumstances in various parks to which he was assigned but was continually moved and promoted through the ranks (including chief park ranger) after each incident until reaching the position of assistant superintendent at a national recreation area, where he continued to oversee law enforcement activities and personnel. Meanwhile, a clear pattern of reprisal was documented against employees who attempted to report these types of activities.

Focusing specifically on NPS investigations operations, the OIG offered the following indictment:

> The NPS . . . suffers from such extreme organizational dysfunction that none of the NPS officials interviewed during the course of this assessment were able to explain just how NPS Special Agents were supervised and managed. . . . The level of discretion granted to local managers is so extreme that, in some instances, it utterly emasculates the law enforcement function entirely. . . . [T]he Assessment Team was troubled by the sheer number of allegations of interference by local managers. . . . The policies governing law enforcement units in the DOI give the managers unrestricted discretion in how, or whether, to pursue investigations into potential criminal violations. However, competing program interests often prevent those managers from exercising independent and objective judgment. Non–law enforcement managers with multiple program responsibilities should not be approving, supervising, or managing criminal investigations. . . .
>
> The Assessment Team heard innumerable anecdotes about incidents involving law enforcement officers that would typically be subject to an internal affairs investigation. The anecdotes ranged from excessive shooting incidents to the chronic loss of law enforcement equipment. Unfortunately, when the Assessment Team attempted to review some of

the most alarming incidents, they were unable to verify the accuracy of the anecdotal reports based on the files available. In fact, in some cases, the files concerning alleged incidents were actually empty. For the matters that had some investigative information available, it appeared that the only concern addressed was the matter of potential criminal liability on the part of the law enforcement professional involved, completely ignoring the applicability of civil or administrative action that might be taken. . . .

There is a common belief among some who were interviewed that non–law enforcement managers have hired individuals for law enforcement positions that were not qualified. Allegations were made that a manager hired "a friend of a friend" or promoted a lower grade employee to a law enforcement position simply for the "raise in pay." . . . Both BLM [Bureau of Land Management] and NPS law enforcement officials stated that Regional or State Directors have often hired applicants without the input or review of their National Law Enforcement Office. In one situation, Departmental requirements for certification were not followed which led to the hiring of a Special Agent-in-Charge that did not have the law enforcement training required for Departmental certification.

Finally, commenting on the entrenched manner in which law enforcement is managed and seems to withstand repeated calls for reform, the OIG remarked:

Remarkably, this assessment of DOI law enforcement programs has not identified any new issues. It has confirmed and validated the findings of all the reviews, evaluations, and assessments that preceded it.

Citing these findings, the inspector general himself, Earl Devaney, reportedly proclaimed his intention to be the one to finally force real reforms on the NPS. Toward that end, he poignantly noted in his cover memorandum to the secretary that

many of the issues uncovered in this assessment have been identified previously in past evaluations, reviews and assessments. In the last three years alone, the Department has spent in excess of $1.5 million to have law enforcement programs assessed by consultants such as the National Academy of Public Administration (NAPA), International Association of Chiefs of Police (IACP) and Booz, Allen & Hamilton. The Department and Bureaus have demonstrated unwillingness, or inability, to recognize and address the thoughtful recommendations advanced by these professional law enforcement and management experts. The reports have been largely ignored and do little more than gather dust on a shelf.[29]

The inspector general closed his memorandum expressing hope "that this report and its recommendations do not simply become one more for the shelf."[30]

Not surprisingly, the NPS reaction to the OIG's report was one of open defiance. A number of high level officials flatly dismissed the OIG's findings and challenged its authority or ability to tell the NPS how to run its affairs. One regional director nationally circulated an e-mail letter stating that the OIG could not possibly understand the complexities of the NPS and encouraging others to ignore its findings. Other NPS officials brazenly stated they would cut off funding for law enforcement programs altogether if any attempt was made to reduce local management's control over law enforcement activities.

Nevertheless, as a result of the OIG's January 2002 report and recommendations to both Congress and the secretary of the interior the NPS (along with the other DOI agencies) was directed in July of that same year to restructure its law enforcement program. Agencies were called on to set up a new chain of command, establish new standards, and implement new systems to prevent outside manipulation of law enforcement activities and criminal investigations and restore a measure of overall integrity to the law enforcement program. All of these program reforms were to have been implemented by certain deadlines, and by 2003 the NPS claimed to have satisfied most of the mandates imposed on it.

However, when it was time for the OIG to audit and evaluate the progress made by the NPS in implementing reforms, it encountered familiar roadblocks. Relying on its favorable public image and many strong political connections, and employing various rationalizations, shell games, delays, and smoke and mirror tactics (largely the shuffling around and re-titling of the same or other trusted personnel), the NPS was found to have quite effectively sidestepped the meaningful implementation of virtually every directive imposed on it by the secretary of the interior. On January 30, 2003, Inspector General Devaney offered the following testimony before Congress, addressing the NPS's observed progress on the implementation of mandated reforms:

Mr. Chairman and members of the committee, I have served in Federal government for a little over 32 years. I have never seen an organization more unwilling to accept constructive criticism or embrace new ideas than the National Park Service. Their culture is fight fiercely to protect the status quo and reject any idea that is not their own. Their strategy to enforce the status quo is to take any new idea, such as law enforcement reform, and study it to death. Thus any IG recommendation or, for that matter, Secretarial directive, falls victim to yet another Park Service work group charged by their National Leadership Council to defend the status quo from those of us who just do not understand the complexities of being a ranger.

Three years later, in April 2006, the OIG released a second progress report. In that document the NPS was identified as having implemented less than 25% of the mandated reforms. The report cited specific failures in both the NPS internal affairs and special agent (i.e., criminal investigations) programs, noting that they "are reported to be managed ineffectively and are described as being in the process of imploding."

On September 13, 2006, in separate congressional hearings, Inspector General Devaney offered the following additional comments:

This brings me to the second matter of concern to the Committee—the culture at the Department of the Interior that sustains manager irresponsibility and a lack of accountability. . . . Simply stated, short of a crime, anything goes at the highest levels of the Department of the Interior.

All things considered, it really should be no surprise that the 2002 secretarial directives imposed upon the NPS would fail and would not lead to meaningful law enforcement program reforms. In all of his best efforts, even Inspector General Devaney failed to understand that the problems within the NPS are more than just structural or the mere reflection of the absence of standards and procedures. The problems identified by the OIG cannot be corrected through simple reorganization or policy changes. They are the result of a deeply rooted mentality and culture, created, nurtured, and handed down through literally generations of individuals committed to the mythology of the agency and its system of recruitment, rewards, and sanctions.

The NPS workforce has become quite accustomed to seeing misconduct openly sanctioned. Many of the most egregious offenders in the agency have been merely relocated and placed, through directed assignments, into increasingly more powerful positions from which they cannot be removed, infecting the higher levels of management. At the same time, the selective enforcement of policies, standards, and ethics rules is often wielded more as a management weapon of control and retaliation than as a legitimate tool to achieve program-matic integrity. And since it is the highest levels of management that are charged with implementing agency policies and directives, the chances for real reform are few without the infusion of new leadership not descended from or indebted to the existing system. Meanwhile, the workforce has also observed many of the agency's more honest and outspoken employees labeled troublemakers and ostracized for not being "team players" and "not thinking outside of the box" when confronted with a violation of law or policy. Many of those who *have* spo-ken up, reported misconduct, or openly advocated for change have found them-selves maligned, marginalized, and effectively precluded from advancement into positions where they could affect real change or altogether driven out of the organization, thus assuring the perpetuation of the culture.

With its idealistic mission and squeaky-clean public image, the NPS may be the very last agency anyone envisions having any serious problems, The public, public officials, and the media thus tend to respond with incredulity at the very notion that anything all that serious could be wrong or that NPS rangers or man-agers would ever intentionally engage in conduct not deserving of the public trust. In truth, however, the NPS is vulnerable to the very same types of problems and system failures common to every organization as well as to corruption. Left to its own devices and free of objective outside scrutiny and real accountability, any organization risks corruption and compromise to program integrity. These risks are enhanced where passions are extreme and there is an underlying sense of institutional elitism, where leaders are literally descended from within the ranks of the organization as heirs to a legacy and are chosen and rewarded for both their allegiance and their indebtedness to the entrenched agency culture.

None of this is to say that the NPS stands alone as the *most* corrupt or dys-functional of federal agencies or that it does not have many honest and hard-working employees within its ranks. Indeed, the NPS continues to attract and somehow retain some of the most honest, talented, and hard-working individu-als in federal government, who do professional work under what are often very difficult and politically tenuous circumstances. It is equally certain that most of the service's supervisors and managers are reasonably competent and well mean-ing. Their continuing presence within the agency is testament of what could be. That said, there is all the more reason to be alarmed over the disproportionate levels of power wielded within the agency by those individuals and groups that truly *are* dishonest and unscrupulous. Their accepted presence and influence within the agency, often at its highest levels, has an intimidating as well as demoralizing effect on the balance of the workforce, signaling for many the futility of trying to do the right thing and play by the rules. The impact of that situation has been compounded over the decades by the failure of both executive and legislative officials from both sides of the aisle, Democratic and Republican, to take the matter seriously and take steps necessary to address the problem.

The Cooperating Association
(Íighah deiyíl nishígíí)

In partnership with the National Park Service
Slogan displayed by Western National Parks
Association on the cover of its publicity folders.

A s one of several federally recognized "cooperating associations," the WNPA operates under unique legal authority "to provide program and financial assistance to the National Park Service for interpretation, education, and research in national parks through the production and sale of educational materials."

The history of cooperating associations like the WNPA goes back to 1920 when the Appropriations Act for the NPS authorized the agency to accept donations of cash, lands, and buildings from private organizations. Later, in 1937, Congress extended formal legal status to cooperating associations as "non-profit, state-chartered entities" authorized to support the interpretative, educational, and research activities of various national park sites.[1] Each association is required to operate under a formal agreement with the NPS, obligating it to abide by NPS management policies and director's orders. Association activities are strictly limited to bolstering interpretation, education, and research. Agency policies specifically address these restrictions, noting that:

Association employees are not authorized to undertake any government function or activity on behalf of the Service beyond routine visitor information services or other activities authorized by the Cooperating Association Agreement, supplements to the agreement, or agreements for voluntary services.[2]

Also, under the terms of their agreements, all associations are required to

comply with all applicable laws and regulations. This Agreement is subject to all laws, regulations and rules governing NPS property, whether now in force of hereafter enacted or promulgated. Nothing in the Agreement shall be construed as in any way impairing the general powers of the NPS for supervision, regulation, and control of its property under such applicable laws, regulations, and rules.[3]

Sixty-four NPS-affiliated cooperating associations have been established across the country. Collectively, they account for nearly $117 million in annual revenue, of which more than $26 million (approximately 22.3% of association revenues) finds its way to the NPS through donations.[4] The sheer magnitude of the financial contributions they make readily explains why most cooperating associations enjoy standing as major NPS partners, playing a significant role in support of NPS activities. Given the revenues their activities generate and the amount of money they donate to the NPS, many cooperating associations are also, in many respects, big business, albeit 501(c)(3) tax exempt.

All funds and other support provided to the NPS by these cooperating associations are clearly identified as donations. That is, they are not funds owed to the government but tax deductible gifts or contributions made to the various parks. In fact, the funds associated with these donations remain in accounts managed solely by the cooperating association, and not the government, until they are expended or earmarked for a purchase or project. It is this well-known and accepted provision that allows the cooperating associations to maintain their nonprofit status.

The WNPA enjoys a place of prominence among the sixty-four cooperating associations affiliated with the NPS. The WNPA maintains operations at sixty-five national park sites throughout eleven western states, generating between $8–9 million in annual revenues. According to its own records and reports, the SPMA/WNPA has donated more than $30 million in aid to the NPS in its more than sixty-five years of operation, averaging more than $2 million each year since 1998.[5] As such, in assuming the position of WNPA executive director in 2003,

LeAnn Simpson moved up several rungs on the ladder to join the ranks of major and influential players in NPS activities and politics.

Simpson came to the WNPA after having served eleven years as executive director for the Glacier Natural History Association and had worked at the Custer Battlefield Historical and Museum Association before that. She assumed her position as WNPA executive director in August 2003, based in the organization's spectacular new sixteen thousand-square foot, multimillion-dollar headquarters facility located in Oro Valley, Arizona, north of Tucson. Simpson replaced Tim Priehs, who left the SPMA (just prior to the name change) nearly a year earlier. Priehs had served as executive director for more than two decades. Simpson came to her new six-figure position with solid credentials and a reputation as a tough and aggressive manager and a competent if somewhat rigid businesswoman.

John Pearson was the fiscal administrator and director of operations for the SPMA prior to Simpson's arrival. He left the organization in May 2001. He played a key role in the development of SPMA programs. During his thirteen-year tenure, Pearson's duties expanded from fiscal administrator to director of operations. Annual revenues for SPMA grew from approximately $2 million to nearly $7 million.

Scott Aldridge was hired by John Pearson in 1999 to serve as the SPMA's marketing director. When Pearson left in 2001, Aldridge was promoted to replace him as the SPMA's director of operations. Later still, with the departure of Tim Priehs in 2002, Aldridge was temporarily designated the SPMA/WNPA's acting executive director.

Consequently, when LeAnn Simpson came into her new position she was handicapped by several factors. Both Tim Priehs and John Pearson had departed the SPMA/WNPA well before Simpson's arrival. Simpson started her new job without the benefit of a meaningful transition period or briefings from Priehs *or* Pearson about finances or operations in general, much less the unique operation and challenges at Hubbell Trading Post. And though Pearson had taken a job with another cooperating association by the time Simpson came to work at the WNPA, and Pearson did actually call Simpson to congratulate her, Simpson made no serious effort to solicit his advice or input or to question him about the manner in which the SPMA/WNPA or Hubbell Trading Post was operated in the past.

Compounding the problem was the rapid turnover of bona fide accountants employed by SPMA in the years immediately preceding Simpson's arrival.

Virtually all of the SPMA/WNPA's professionally trained accountants and controllers had, in succession, resigned or retired in the years following Pearson's departure. That left Simpson dependant on Scott Aldridge and various members of the WNPA's board of directors for financial briefings and guidance. Opportunities to simply call and speak with former accountants were apparently never pursued. Simpson thus had a less-than-clear or comprehensive picture of the WNPA's real financial condition, which apparently was shaky, the organization having reportedly slipped into financial disarray and crisis, unable to distinguish between operating capital and committed resources.

This problem was not uncovered until the independent accounting firm of DeVries, Carpenter, and Associates reviewed the WNPA's books, disclosing that approximately $1.5 million that the WNPA's management thought it had "in the bank" as surplus to operating costs had been previously obligated. Simpson and the WNPA reportedly found themselves in very precarious financial waters, having both before and since Simpson's arrival incurred any number of new expenses via marketing, expansion efforts, and donations to the NPS. All of this occurred while the WNPA was still recovering from expenses related to its new multimillion dollar headquarters. That money crunch was reportedly compounded by a series of financially devastating lawsuits filed against the SPMA/WNPA by former headquarters employees. By many accounts, Simpson had walked into a financial mess: financial records were in a state of chaos, accounting practices were poor or nonexistent, and there was no accurate sense of the WNPA's—much less Hubbell Trading Post's—own overall revenues and expenses, profits and losses.[6]

Jim Babbitt was named chairman of the executive committee of the WNPA's board of directors in 2003, at nearly the same time LeAnn Simpson was hired as executive director. Babbitt was a longtime member of the board of directors. He served as vice chair of the executive committee before assuming the top spot as chairman in the transition from fiscal year 2003 to 2004. Even before that, his appointment to the board of directors had been viewed by the SPMA/WNPA as a coup, both because he and his family were prominent throughout Arizona and the environmental community and also because his family had deeps roots in the state.

Babbitt is from a wealthy and influential Arizona business family. His grandfather was C. J. Babbitt, who came to Flagstaff, Arizona, in 1886 from Cincinnati, Ohio. C. J. Babbitt and his brother established the Babbitt family empire of northern Arizona ranches and businesses, which ultimately included a number of trading posts located across the Navajo and Hopi reservations. Jim Babbitt's father, Paul, was an attorney. Jim Babbitt's brother is Bruce Babbitt, former attorney general and then governor of Arizona and later U.S. Secretary of the Interior for the whole of Bill Clinton's administration.

Jim Babbitt was born and raised in Flagstaff, Arizona, but followed the family tradition of going out of state to obtain his college education in the more worldly and prestigious academic environments of Notre Dame University in Indiana and Stanford University in Palo Alto, California. He remained in California after graduating and went to work for the Bank of America. He returned to Flagstaff in 1979 to take his place in the family business, serving in the "human resource area" of the company. At first, he was only peripherally involved in the Babbitt family's trading post businesses on the Navajo and Hopi reservations, but he later assumed the role of "supervising those trading operations."

Jim Babbitt is known as a leader in the northern Arizona business, arts, and environmental community. His family owns Babbitt's Backcountry Outfitters, based in Flagstaff, Arizona. His wife, Helene, runs the family business known as Babbitt Wholesales. In addition to his numerous business ventures, Babbitt has served on the board of directors and/or as a trustee for several prominent Arizona organizations, including the Grand Canyon Trust and the Grand Canyon Association (another NPS-affiliated cooperating association). Babbitt was also a member of the board of trustees for the Museum of Northern Arizona, where he served as board president for several years. Babbitt's term as chairman of the executive committee of the WPNA expired at the end of 2006, but he remained on the board of directors for another year, resigning at the end of 2007.

Jim Babbitt's family background in the trading business made him particularly valued as a member of the WNPA board and executive committee. He played a key role overseeing and advising on operations at Hubbell Trading Post. But as Edward Hall and others had noted, the Babbitt family's approach to running trading posts "from the point of view of a white man's business world" was not without controversy.[7] Far more than most of the other basic trading operations that served remote communities of the reservation, Babbitt trading posts, such as their establishment at Tuba City, were full-blown business enterprises. The Tuba City Trading Post sat on eighty acres of fee land and included a hotel and restaurant, a mobile home park, and several commercial leases to other businesses. Jim Babbitt acknowledged this distinct approach to his family's trading post operations when he was interviewed in 1999 as part of the UITA Oral History Project. Asked how his family had staffed their stores, Babbitt explained that the most prevalent way was that it would be a little partnership, and our family would really provide the financial resources for generally half, or maybe a little more than half, of the ownership of the trading post. And then there would be a partner who would be the manager—the resident trader, if you will. And so we were partners with a whole bunch of people around the reservation who functioned as the resident trader. We in town then did all the accounting work and all the financing, as well as the wholesale supplying of the goods to the trading post. That's the way it generally worked. Sometimes we owned the trading post outright, and would then just hire a trader on salary to go out there and work. It could be different combinations.

Babbitt went on to offer his perspective on the viability of the trading post business:

By the time I became involved, in the early 1980s, the trading post business had evolved a great deal, and was actually really on the way out. Our stores had been reduced from probably more than twenty down to—I think we had four at the time on Navajo and one at Hopi. . . . I would say, in a large way in the 1970s, the old-time trading posts started to close up, and it became really a dying way of life. So by the time I became involved in our trading operations [in the 1980s], it was already becoming a dying part of our family's business. And from the time I started in the business, we had five trading posts. Today, 1999, we are down to only two—Tuba City and Red Lake. We closed down Cedar Ridge Trading Post, we closed down Cow Springs Trading Post, and we sold the little store at Kykotsmovi to the village there, to the village people, and they continue to operate it. But even with our two remaining stores, I would say we won't be in that business a lot longer.

Finally, Babbitt acknowledged that his family's status and reputation among the larger trading community was not particularly good. When asked how the Babbitt Brothers Company was perceived by other traders around the reservation, Babbitt replied:

I'm sure a lot of people took a pretty dim view of it, and probably said, "They charge too much," and on and on. I don't know any of that, really, firsthand so much, but I just suspect that that was probably true—much in the way that today a lot of people would have bad feelings toward Wal-Mart or the big guy now, you know, whoever that might be.[8]

The difference between the experiences of Billy Malone and Jim Babbitt and their respective attitudes toward Indian traders and the operation of trading posts could not have been greater. Malone lived as a real Indian trader in the most remote regions of the Navajo Reservation for almost his entire life. He demonstrated little concern for the bottom line or standard business practices in his dealings with the Navajo community. In contrast, Jim Babbitt was an acknowledged outsider who adopted the perspective of a modern businessman in his operations of trading posts, viewing the trading post "business" as an investment opportunity to be shrewdly managed or abandoned. It was probably inevitable that these two individuals would not see eye to eye on how Hubbell Trading Post should be managed.

Predictable conflicts between the two men arose almost immediately after Jim Babbitt took his place on the SPMA/WNPA board. The potential for these conflicts to escalate to catastrophic levels for Billy Malone grew exponentially with the appointment of LeAnn Simpson to the position of executive director working directly under the guidance of board chairman Jim Babbitt.

The rivalry and conflict between Babbitt and Malone was likely fueled by the fact that Jim Babbitt was viewed as and reportedly asserted himself to be the SPMA/WNPA's own resident expert in trading. Babbitt enjoyed this stature even though he prided himself on being more of a historian than a trader. By his own admission, he had never worked as a trader at any of his family's trading posts but rather as the bookkeeper and personnel officer who supervised family trading operations across the reservation.[9] Billy Malone, on the other hand, though not formally schooled in business, accounting, or personnel issues, had been highly valued throughout the years for his reputation as "the real deal": a genuine Indian trader from the old school. Nevertheless, Malone was eventually told that Jim Babbitt had been identified as the SPMA/WNPA's in-house expert on trading post operations and that Malone would be required to consult with him in the management of Hubbell Trading Post.

Hints at troubles for Billy Malone with Jim Babbitt and the SPMA/WNPA began to surface as early as 2001. Malone's longtime friend Bruce Burnham recalled an occasion when he and Jim Babbitt were jointly leading a tour of old-time trading posts for patrons of the MNA. Burnham told Babbitt that the SPMA was making it very hard for Malone to do his job as trader. The organization was imposing more and more restrictions on funding to purchase rugs and jewelry from local artisans and interfering generally in how Malone ran the trading post. The SPMA used their on-site bookkeeper as "a sort of mole" to monitor Malone's activities and report to headquarters every time Malone gave a free six-pack of soda to a local family or paid "too much" to a weaver for a rug. Babbitt reportedly acknowledged that the organization had indeed adopted some of these measures but asked Burnham to "tell Billy we're not out to get him." Babbitt told Burnham that he and the rest of the board just wanted to get a tighter handle on operations at the trading post and keep better track of Malone's activities. Ironically, not too long after this conversation, the very same bookkeeper who used to keep tabs on Malone was herself fired by the SPMA and escorted off of the trading post grounds by NPS personnel.

Not long after that, Babbitt intimated to then Hubbell superintendent Nancy Stone that Malone was in trouble. That conversation took place in Flagstaff during a fund-raising event for the park sponsored by the Friends of Hubbell. Malone and several other traders were present to conduct informal appraisals of rugs and jewelry brought in by members and patrons; a la "antiques road show." Babbitt attended both as an author/historian and a representative of the SPMA/WNPA and expressed annoyance with Malone and the other traders at the event for, in his view, overestimating the value of the rugs and jewelry they examined. Stone knew that Malone was almost always in some sort of "trouble" with the SPMA/WNPA management over either his profit margins, inventory levels, or the incessant complaints, backstabbing, and constant bickering between the other trading post employees. But Stone found it both odd and significant on this particular occasion that Jim Babbitt himself brought up the SPMA/WNPA's relationship and problems with Malone. Stone was left to wonder why Babbitt was telling her this, and if there might not be something more to it.

One of the first direct conflicts between Billy Malone and Jim Babbitt reportedly occurred at the trading post in late 2002 or early 2003, during an unannounced visit by Babbitt, who questioned Malone about the wholesale supplier from whom he secured the Pendleton blankets sold at the trading post.

Babbitt Brothers Trading Company had been a wholesale supplier for Pendleton Woolen Mills since the late 1800s. Pendleton blankets have historically played a prominent role in Navajo society, serving as a relatively inexpensive and utilitarian alternative for the now-famous handmade Navajo blankets and rugs. Babbitt discussed the history of Navajo weaving and the historical association of Pendleton blankets with both the Babbitt Brothers Trading Company and the Navajo community in his 1999 interview with Cline Library researchers:

> In the very early days, going way back, the Navajo people learned weaving probably from the Pueblo people, over on the Rio Grande. They had never woven before they met up with the Pueblo people. Well, being so adaptable and doing things so well, as they do, they picked up this weaving art and turned it into something uniquely their own, and wonderful. But in the early days, anyway—and by "the early days," I'm meaning the early or mid-1800s maybe—they were weaving for utilitarian purposes. That is, they were weaving wearing garments. And they did that for a long time, and very well. But at some point or another, they figured out that they could sell those weaving garments to Anglo people for a big price, and then they could go out and buy a machine-made woolen wearing garment, in the early days made by the Pendleton Woolen Mills, or there were two or three other woolen mills that were producing these Indian trade blankets. Very serviceable, very durable, and very cheap. So weaving became something other than what it started out as—that is, a utilitarian wearing garment. I will never forget hearing from some of the real old-time Navajo people about that, and about their complete inability to grasp what happened when they would sell these wearing garments to the Anglo people. They said the Anglo people would take them and do a thing that they never could understand. They said they would throw them on the floor and walk all over them! And I think they had a big joke about that for a long time. Of course they became rugs, and we all know what happened.
>
> But anyway, going back to the Pendleton business, that was a part of our wholesale supply to the trading posts, because the Indians bought those and still do, as both wearing and burial garments. And so in 1989, at the 100th anniversary of our company, we were up on our buying trip to the mill in Portland, the Pendleton Mill. We'd go up there once a year to do our annual buying. And we had mentioned in conversation with them at the time that it was our 100th year anniversary. So they asked us if they couldn't produce a special Pendleton blanket commemorating that 100 years. So we worked together on a design, actually a storm pattern design, of a prevalent type of Navajo weaving that came out of the Red Lake area, and they produced for us a storm pattern interpretation

in that Pendleton blanket, that turned out to be a great success, both with the Navajo people and with sort of the collector's market.[10]

According to Malone, on this particular day when Babbitt stopped in at the trading post, he questioned Malone about why he wasn't using Babbitt's Wholesale Company to purchase Pendleton blankets sold at the trading post. Malone was immediately uncomfortable, fully aware that as an executive on the WNPA's board of directors, Jim Babbitt exercised considerable influence and could apply considerable pressure on Malone in his job. In Malone's mind this made it all the more inappropriate for Babbitt to have even suggested that he transfer the Pendleton blanket account for Hubbell Trading Post to Babbitt's own wholesale company. Malone told Babbitt that he had been using the same supplier, Bolton and Cohen, for over thirty years and would just as soon keep it that way. Nothing more was ever said on the subject between the two men. But Malone felt his relationship with Babbitt cooled immediately after that.

Later, around Veteran's Day in 2003, Malone was attending one of the WNPA's annual board meetings. The topic of finding a replacement for Malone was openly raised and discussed. This caught Malone off guard, and he quickly inserted himself into the discussion. He said he was not ready to retire and wanted to work another five or ten years as the trader at Hubbell's. Members of the board hastily responded with assurances that they were merely engaged in strategic planning and "just looking out for the future."[11] But once again, Malone was left with the impression that the board of directors, and particularly Jim Babbitt, was out to get rid of him.

It was widely acknowledged that Malone did not operate as a modern businessman or supervisor. But when it came to knowledge of trading and running a trading post, he was second to none. People were constantly amazed at his ability to almost immediately locate a specific piece made by a specific artist from among the piles upon piles of rugs or boxes upon boxes of jewelry that everyone else saw as an incomprehensible mess. And when he held a rug or piece of jewelry in his hands, he could relate virtually everything about it with near encyclopedic command, including when, where, and by whom it was made, along with the family history of the piece, going back decades. In many respects Malone was not disorganized at all but simply had a different set of priorities, and these were the things that were important. The same could be said about the baffling system he used to tag consignment items or old rugs and jewelry in his own collection. Many people found it confounding, as if he were using some sort of secret code.

But as often as not, the letters written on a recycled tag were nothing more than the initials of someone's wife or child or the original name of a trading post that had changed hands a dozen times and was now abandoned.

Among those who had supervised him, Malone's reputation as a real Indian trader, and his close connection and ties to the Navajo community, both accounted for and excused his unconventional methods of doing business. While perpetually frustrated in their attempts to supervise Malone and obtain compliance with their standard procedures, previous board members and SPMA/WNPA supervisors, including both Tim Priehs and John Pearson, considered it an acceptable trade-off, justified by their desire to maintain a truly authentic atmosphere in which a real Indian trader stuck to old-time trading practices. After all, Malone had been recruited and hired precisely *because* he was a genuine Indian trader and not just another salesman, businessman, or store manager.[12]

This approach had more than paid off for the SPMA; it realized ever-increasing profits as a direct result of Malone's own character and background and the special relationships he maintained with both the Navajo community and the public. Even former SPMA accountants, who had for years struggled to conduct audits and track accounts at Hubbell Trading Post, understood Malone's unique character and appreciated the integrity with which he ran the operation. Time and again they found that if they took the time and effort to work with Malone and understand his bizarre and baffling "system" of doing business and keeping records, they were always able to reconcile the books. They simultaneously saw just how much Malone contributed to Hubbell as "a trader, not a businessman."[13]

The conflict between modern business practices and old-time trading was formally acknowledged by the NPS in its own record of the administrative history for Hubbell Trading Post NHS:

One day in the spring of 1991 a young Navajo woman approached Bill Malone in the bullpen and exchanged greetings with him. She told Bill that she was taking some children on a field trip. She would need gasoline. She had some craftwork with her that she wanted to exchange for just a bit of credit. If Bill would do that for her, she could make the trip. Bill didn't hesitate.

An old-time trader would often keep a great deal of what was going on at the trading post in his head. Deals were struck suddenly, and maybe it was just too time consuming to make a record of it. Such an operation would drive a modern merchandiser mad. But of course an old-time trading post was absolutely nothing like a modern store where most of the pricing is done half a continent away, where all the sales are recorded by a computerized cash register.

There has always been a lot of give and take at a trading post. Al Grieve mentions that when he would sell an expensive rug, he might include in the deal—for free—a book on how to care for the rug. The trader is always trying to treat his customers fairly and possibly without the interference of computerized pricing and an up-to-the-minute inventory check.

It may well be that it is impossible to run a traditional trading post from downtown. The distant accountant, trying to balance his figures, is going to wonder what happened to a six-pack of Coca Cola that was given away and forgotten, a book that was thrown into a deal, a little cash exchanged for arts and crafts, the transactions not recorded because the trader was too busy to do so. The accountant has a right to know what is going on, but it may be impossible for a trader to deal in the traditional way and still be completely responsible to a distant office where modern technology is trying very efficiently to account for every penny.

This is indeed a conflict for the trader as well as the SPMA. They are working on the problem, but it does seem likely that a trading post cannot be run at long distance and that it must be operated to a great extent on old-fashioned trust if it is to maintain the aura of an old-fashioned trading post. And an old trading post was operated on guesswork, snap decisions, and personal whimsy. If Hubbell Trading Post ever enters the modern merchandising world, it may no longer be a trading post, and SPMA will no longer need a bona fide trader to run it. To what extent should Hubbell Trading Post devote itself to making money, and how much time should be devoted to "interpretation?" Buying and selling wool and mohair is hard work, time consuming, and not particularly profitable. But that's what trading posts did.[14]

The extent to which the WNPA considered these acknowledged challenges remains a point of contention. But in light of the events that would transpire in the first couple of years following the nearly concurrent appointment of Jim Babbitt as board chairman and Simpson as executive director, it's not hard to see why many observers have speculated that this period signaled a critical juncture in time, a time when the WNPA indeed decided it no longer needed or wanted a "bona fide trader"—or Billy Malone.

Many old-time traders as well as interested observers have speculated that one of Simpson's first assignments as executive director was to look into what was happening at Hubbell Trading Post and to find a way to get rid of Billy Malone and replace him with a more malleable personality, schooled and accepting of more conventional business practices. Admittedly, most of the Indian traders advancing this theory are long-time friends and supporters of Malone. But the Four Corners trading community at large seems to have held Malone in very high esteem, both personally and professionally. Even among rival traders (including those who expressed animosity against one another), there seems to have been virtually unanimous affection and support for Malone.

The trading community was not the only one that harbored the suspicion that Simpson was directed to get rid of Malone. Several NPS officials who worked or still work at Hubbell Trading Post have echoed the speculation that someone within the WNPA was out to get Billy Malone and looking for a reason to fire him.

It may well be that Jim Babbitt and the WNPA's board of directors were simply frustrated by their lack of success in changing the way Malone ran the trading post and in getting him to accept more conventional business practices. The difference of opinion between Malone and Babbitt, and particularly the idea that Malone was expected to consult with Babbitt as the WNPA's expert in Indian trading and trading posts, likely added fuel to the fire. Before Simpson, Priehs and Pearson had experienced more than their own share of frustration in attempting to supervise Malone. But they had always viewed him with a measure of affection and considerable respect, and they had always believed that in spite of all his quirks and unconventional ways, he was totally honest, generous to a fault, and fundamentally essential to the ongoing legitimacy and success of Hubbell Trading Post.[15]

With this foundation, many observers advance the theory that in the organizational transition that occurred in 2003 the political dynamics shifted against Malone, allowing Babbitt to now more fully assert himself and his own ideas about how Hubbell Trading Post should be run. Others have speculated that LeAnn Simpson experienced a virtual panic attack when confronted with the financial troubles revealed within SPMA/WNPA after the audit(s) conducted by DeVries, Carpenter. Advocates of this theory suggest that Simpson as well as Babbitt may have been looking for—or at least very eager to accept—a scapegoat who could be blamed for the crisis in which the WNPA found itself. Given their less-than-accurate understanding of the financial state of affairs within the WNPA, particularly at Hubbell Trading Post, Billy Malone and Hubbell Trading Post arguably presented an extremely easy target for them.

Adding to speculation about Babbitt's involvement was the observation made by several of Malone's friends about striking similarities between the financial troubles and events that unfolded at the WNPA and those that only a year earlier had been exposed at another nonprofit association where Babbitt concurrently served on the board of trustees, the MNA.

In the late 1950s MNA directors Harold Colton and Ned Danson had played a key role in helping to establish Hubbell Trading Post NHS. But years after the departure of Colton and Dansen, from 2003 through 2005, the museum experienced a scandal of its own, resulting in the highly publicized loss of accreditation from the Accreditation Commission of the American Association of Museums (AAM). That occurred after an independent investigation revealed that MNA board members had run up a $1 million deficit and then improperly sold items entrusted to the museum's collection, using the proceeds to cover operating expenses. The entire board, including Babbitt, resigned in the wake of a complaint filed with the AAM and a petition drive by the museum's members to remove the entire board of trustees.[16] The board's resignation was further clouded by rumors that the unauthorized sale of the twenty-one items of western art and Navajo weavings from the collection was made to the very same appraiser the board of trustees had contracted to assess its market value. In effect, the board had allowed the buyer to set his own purchase price, which was subsequently exceeded several times over when that individual broke up the collection and resold the same items a short time later.

Among the things for which the MNA board was chided in public hearings were its efforts to keep the museum's financial troubles secret from its members and the public over an entire two-to-three year period and its quiet attempts to make up staggering deficits through methods labeled "unethical" by the AAM. Those activities included selling nearly $1 million in artifacts entrusted to the museum for display and preservation, misinforming members or lying to them about the disposition of that collection, and closing the museum's internationally renowned geology department that had provided "a hard science focus spanning more than seven decades."[17]

▲▼▲

While the exact nature of internal discussions within the WNPA may never be known, it is clear that among LeAnn Simpson's first priorities in her new job was to scrutinize WNPA operations at Hubbell Trading Post. That attention would have been warranted in any event, given the prominent role that Hubbell Trading Post played in the WNPA's overall financial affairs.

Back in 1967, SPMA had committed to run Hubbell Trading Post "as a contribution to the [National Park] Service and not as a money maker."[18] But in the decades that followed, Hubbell Trading Post evolved into a cash cow, the single most profitable site in the vast empire of nonprofit business operations run by the WNPA in more than sixty national parks throughout the West. According to Simpson, profits made through Hubbell Trading Post, alone, historically accounted for a large percentage of the WNPA's overall revenues, far exceeding profits realized through any of its other operations. Of the approximately $8–9 million in revenues generated annually by all of the WNPA's operations, between $1.3 and $1.5 million came from its operations at Hubbell Trading Post.[19]

Simpson soon developed a number of concerns. Alarm was likely compounded by her lack of familiarity with life on the Navajo Reservation and by Malone's idiosyncrasies and unconventional (but traditional) ways of running the trading post. Not having received the benefit of an orientation or briefings from any of her predecessors, Simpson was shocked by what she found, which no doubt reinforced for her the legitimacy of whatever marching orders she may (or may not) have received from Babbitt and the other board members.

Also, Simpson of course knew nothing of the many personalities at Hubbell or the rivalries, conflicts, and long history of backstabbing that existed in that workplace, discontent aggravated by the fact that positions with an organization like WNPA are highly coveted since they pay far better than most. Simpson's predecessor, Tim Priehs, had learned this over his many years at the SPMA. He was forever responding to petty in-fighting that occurred at the trading post. When interviewed in 2006, he bluntly noted that "there was constant crap going down at Hubbell Trading Post. It was a constant." He speculated that it was, at least in part, clan-driven. He added, "We constantly had people accusing people of improprieties," noting that if someone saw an opportunity to advance themselves, they would make an allegation against someone else. And even when employees were caught stealing money, attempts to fire them were sometimes frustrated by formal protests brought by tribal officials.[20]

Former chief financial and operations officer John Pearson observed this same dynamic at Hubbell Trading Post throughout his own tenure with the

SPMA. Reflecting on his experiences during a 2006 interview, Pearson described the working environment at Hubbell as extremely competitive and invidious. Many employees would take every opportunity to stab Billy Malone in the back, just to make him look bad in the hope he would be fired and that they would be able to take over his position, and they would aggressively compete against one another for better or higher paying positions by filing complaints and making allegations. If Malone promoted or showed favor toward the work of an award-winning weaver working at the trading post, it would inevitably alienate and anger other employees and weavers, resulting in "two distinct camps of people there," those who were for Malone, and those who were against Malone. Pearson clarified, however, that membership in these camps was dynamic and would shift back and forth on an almost daily basis depending on who, at any given time, was the perceived favorite.[21]

At the same time, the turnover of Navajo employees at Hubbell Trading Post was high. This is due, at least in part, to cultural, religious, and other issues affecting work attendance as well as conflicting priorities between work and family obligations. The impact of these issues can easily be compounded if an employer or supervisor does not understand, consider, or accommodate the unique attitudes and practices often found on the reservation. Traditional values notwithstanding, one person's loss is still another person's gain, and that dynamic figured prominently in workplace interactions and politics at Hubbell. Compounding this situation at Hubbell was the widely held belief that one long-term employee was actually a witch, or 'adiłgąshii, who used her dubious abilities and reputation to curse, or at least threaten and intimidate, other employees. Outsiders would not understand how real that threat could be. Past managers and supervisors had learned to exercise caution in their acceptance of claims or complaints made by one employee against another, having been stung on more than one occasion after trying to take action based upon those types of claims, only to learn later that the person making the complaint had been doing the very same thing.

It's difficult to say whether on-the-ground briefings on the culture and history of operations at Hubbell Trading Post would have made a significant difference in perspective for Simpson in her new job. It's hard to say if Simpson was properly equipped to take on the challenge of comprehending and managing operations at Hubbell Trading Post. But at least one NPS official expressed frustration over her own failed efforts to orient and explain to Simpson the unique and challenging manner in which Hubbell Trading Post operated.[22]

Consequently, in 2003 when Simpson showed up to inspect operations at the trading post, she was apparently overwhelmed by what she found:

> [Simpson] observed things to be in what she considered a state of disarray, with boxes, "junk," and other personal property of Billy Malone stored in the trading post storeroom, comingled with WNPA property. Simpson noted that also comingled in the storage room with WNPA property was property belonging to friends of Malone and that this condition had apparently existed for years. She described the overall condition at Hubbell Trading Post as being "complete chaos."[23]

In many respects, the chaotic conditions Simpson observed were as much a part of the genuine trading tradition as any aspect of the trading post. Individuals present when Simpson made this visit to Hubbell Trading Post add that she apparently took it on herself to bring order to the chaos she observed by summarily throwing much of what she found, including most of Malone's personal "junk," into a nearby dumpster. Afterward, employees scrambled to recover and claim for themselves many of the items belonging to Malone that Simpson had thrown out, including old saddles, deer heads, antlers, sheep skins, old books, and calendars. Describing this bizarre scene, one former NPS employee said it seemed as if Simpson was making a public statement by throwing away Malone's things; declaring, in effect, that while Malone's former supervisors may have put up with his ways, she would not, and that she had come, both literally and figuratively, "to clean up Hubbell Trading Post."

In yet another demonstration of intolerance for the conditions she found at Hubbell Trading Post, Simpson much later reportedly lashed out in a tirade about the "mess" John Pearson left for her there. On that occasion, apparently under the stress of mounting scrutiny over activities at the post, she reportedly let loose with a string of accusations as well as complaints about the situation she had inherited, remarking on Pearson's failure to "do anything" about Billy Malone.[24]

And so over the course of her first year Simpson devoted considerable effort to reviewing accounts, records, and operations at the trading post. Through that process, she soon concluded that "finance-related irregularities" were occurring at Hubbell. Those concerns were quickly compounded by complaints made by some of the other employees at the trading post about how Malone conducted business. Simpson began to suspect that Malone was involved in a forgery and embezzlement scheme that had been going on for over a decade. On April 10,

2004, Simpson reported her findings and suspicions to members of the WNPA's board of directors. They authorized Simpson to approach NPS IMR director Steve Martin with a very special request.

On April 28, 2004, Simpson and Babbitt met with Martin to share their suspicions and ask for authorization to shut down Hubbell Trading Post to the public so that the WNPA could conduct an unannounced three-day audit of the trading post. The WNPA intended to use DeVries, Carpenter, the WPNA's contracted accounting firm. Billy Malone would not be given advance notice. Martin granted the request, offering NPS assistance in closing the national historic site to facilitate the audit.

Martin arranged for Simpson to speak with one of his associate regional directors, Hal Grovert, as well as regional chief ranger Kevin Fitzgerald and IMR chief budget officer John Wessels. Simpson told the group what she believed was occurring at the trading post. Fitzgerald then arranged for Simpson to speak with newly designated regional special agent-in-charge (RSAC) Jim Reilly. Reilly was requested to initiate a criminal investigation into Billy Malone's "forgery and embezzlement scheme."

The Investigation Begins

(Ní' diilkáá')

In all matters relating to investigative work, the investigative organization must be free, in fact and appearance, from impairments to independence; must be organizationally independent; and must maintain an independent attitude. This standard places upon agencies, investigative organizations, and investigators the responsibility for maintaining independence, so that judgments used in obtaining evidence, conducting interviews, and making recommendations will be impartial and will be viewed as impartial by knowledgeable third parties.

> President's Council on Integrity and Efficiency,
> *Quality Standards for Investigations.*

JIM REILLY WAS a veteran ranger who came into his new RSAC position in a way that could only happen in the NPS.

I'd known Reilly since the early 1980s when we both worked at Yosemite, and we'd remained friends throughout our careers. But where my own career had been narrowly focused on law enforcement and criminal investigations, Reilly was a true "ranger's ranger." He was skilled, competent, and experienced in a wide range of areas that included law enforcement but also the broader and more traditional spectrum of ranger "protection" duties. He had intensive experience in fire fighting, advanced life support, and emergency medicine as a paramedic as well as highly developed skills in search and rescue as a big-wall climber.

Prior to his RSAC assignment, Reilly was the ranger activities branch chief within the IMR. While law enforcement was certainly a program for which Reilly had significant responsibility, his duties also included management of the regional emergency medical services and search and rescue programs. These three program areas were (and continue to be) considered the core duties of uniformed rangers throughout the service.

As one of the IMR's branch chiefs, Reilly was in a staff position under the regional chief ranger and had no line authority over field rangers or programs. In the organization of the NPS those field personnel and programs remained (and still remain) under the direct control and supervision of each local park superintendent. Reilly did have a small staff that included four special agents: one located in his own office in Lakewood, Colorado, one in Tucson, and the other two in Santa Fe. These were Reilly's staff experts in criminal investigations. They provided investigative assistance to parks that did not have their own special agents. The agent in Tucson, Susan Morton, was committed almost entirely to supporting NPS as well as interagency drug enforcement and anti-smuggling efforts along the Mexican border. When not assisting smaller parks with their own investigations, the agents in Lakewood and Santa Fe helped to conduct internal investigations.

Among the reforms the NPS was directed to implement in the wake of the OIG's 2002 report was to "stovepipe" all special agents into a line organization in which they would report through their own autonomous chain of command, separate from the parks and the regions, to a national special agent-in-charge (NSAC) in Washington, D.C. The NPS was also directed to establish a separate, centrally managed internal affairs and investigations organization. Both of these actions were supposed to assure that criminal investigations undertaken would be conducted professionally and objectively, free from the influence and interference of local and regional managers.

But in its own inimitable way, the NPS managed to mitigate the effect of those orders. In its restructuring, the service went to great lengths to handpick individuals for the most senior supervisory special agent and even more senior law enforcement management positions so that park and regional managers could still assert control over investigations and get what they wanted when they wanted it and often prevent altogether investigations they did *not* want from being undertaken. In many instances, senior supervisors and managers for the new agent program were selected by the very same managers from whose pro-grams the agents were removed. The only real difference under the reforms was that if a park and regional manager could not exercise the degree of leverage and control they desired through direct communications with field-level super-visors, they merely went over and around the "obstruction" to their old friends and colleagues now in charge of the new special agent program. Exacerbating this situation were standing orders relayed to all of the special agents that they were to cooperate fully, as partners, with park and regional officials who were now considered their "customers."

In the weeks coinciding with the implementation of reforms, much to the amazement of many people in the field, Patricia "Pat" Buccello was designated the acting NSAC. She had previously served as a nonsupervisory agent. She was later promoted to NPS Medical Standards Program coordinator, respon-sible for overseeing medical and fitness examinations for emergency services personnel and "peer counseling" and mental health services for employees and/or survivors of fallen employees. Buccello remained in her acting NSAC posi-tion for sixteen months. In early 2005 she assumed the NSAC position on a permanent basis.

Buccello's selection as the NSAC was distressing to many field agents and even rangers because of her reputation for ethical abuses. Many agents (myself included) had had numerous confrontations as she skillfully advanced her way up in the organization by playing the system and manipulating supervisors. In light of the number of people familiar with these issues, it was difficult to under-stand how she could have passed the scrutiny of a new background investigation to obtain the necessary clearance for her new position. For many, it validated their worst impressions about the standards and selection process used by the most senior NPS law enforcement officials. Her selection as the new NSAC, followed by an unscheduled pay raise along with thousands of dollars in cash awards, did not bode well at all for many of us individually or for the future of the newly restructured agent program as a whole.

Meanwhile, as we struggled through the first weeks of the restructuring, many existing supervisory special agents located in parks and regional offices across the country were designated as special agent-in-charge for the regions in which they were already located. As the supervisory special agent (SSA) at Grand Canyon National Park and the most senior special agent in the NPS, I was identi-fied in a memorandum to the field as the acting special agent-in-charge for the IMR. But that would not last long.

▲▼▲

I made a number of enemies over the course of my career, including several distinguished chief rangers, "law enforcement specialists," superintendents, and members of the regional and Washington directorate. They viewed me as a troublemaker.

I never properly embraced the "ranger image" advanced by the NPS or the notion of a special proprietary brand of "NPS law enforcement." While the NPS apprehensively viewed law enforcement as just one among a number of combined ranger duties (the others being "interpretation," fire fighting, search and rescue, and EMS), I was interested almost exclusively in law enforcement. I had managed to keep my career focused on law enforcement, largely avoiding assignments encumbered with those other duties. Once, in a documentary widely aired on public television, I flatly rejected the notion of a special kind of NPS law enforcement. More than hinting at deficiencies in the way the NPS managed its program, I defiantly proclaimed in an interview seen across the country that there are really only two kinds of law enforcement; *professional* law enforcement and *unprofessional* law enforcement.[1] My own focus on law enforcement and my outspoken rejection of the traditional ranger image left me exposed to silly internal labels such as "inflexible" and "hard-ass cop."

That reputation was compounded by a long and high-profile record of speaking out publicly about misconduct and corruption within the NPS. That violated the most sacred of the service's unwritten commandments.

My fall from grace began in 1982 after I secured a transfer and promotion into what I initially viewed as my dream assignment—a full-time criminal investigator position in drug enforcement in Yosemite National Park. But far from the dream assignment I had envisioned, that transfer placed me smack-dab in the middle of what turned out to be a completely rogue law enforcement operation under the control of the park's chief law enforcement officer and a supervisory ranger who served as the park's own federal prosecutor. Together, the two gave new meaning to the concept of creative law enforcement, shredding the line between legal and illegal police activities.

I found myself in the unenviable position of witnessing supervisors promote as well as engage in a wide range of illegal conduct, from the falsification of reports and destruction of exculpatory evidence to misuse and misappropriation of government funds and even extortion and attempted blackmail. In his efforts to target one particular drug dealer—a nemesis of sorts—the chief threw away the policy manual, altogether bypassing procedures for the delegation of law

enforcement authorities by secretly recruiting and commissioning street informants—*other* drug users and dealers—as gun-toting, salaried undercover officers. Yosemite, it seems, had its own real-life "mod squad." But unlike the cast of
characters in the 1970s television show, this group had most decidedly *not* gone
straight or turned their lives around. They weren't good looking enough to be TV
stars, and they weren't educated or smart enough to write a coherent sentence,
much less a police report. They were constantly getting into their own trouble, getting into fights, buying, selling, and using their own drugs, and getting
arrested by rangers. Whenever that happened, their own drugs and other evidence were inexplicably thrown out, along with any charges and ranger reports
that might have documented their conduct or compromised their credibility as
"federal agents."

I also learned that the chief had arranged the use of law enforcement personnel and electronic surveillance equipment to secretly monitor and record
the private conversation of a political adversary, a prominent critic of NPS land
acquisition policies. One of the park's more unscrupulous and politically ambitious district rangers had come up with the idea. He suggested it to the superintendent, who in turn approached the law enforcement chief to help carry out
the plan. I unwittingly watched and listened as the park prosecutor planted a
bug in the superintendent's office. The signal was transmitted to a van outside,
where the entire meeting was secretly monitored and recorded. It was only then
that I realized this was not a drug bust but a meeting with a member of the NPS
Advisory Committee, a presidential appointee.[2] When the meeting was over and
the tapes had been turned over to the superintendent for use as political ammu-
nition, the park prosecutor confronted me, warning, "This never happened.
Don't ever tell anybody about this." The law enforcement chief subsequently
privately boasted to friends about the incident and the leverage it gave him over
the superintendent.

On another front, it was widely believed that the very same park prosecutor who planted the bug in the superintendent's office was also a pedophile.
Colleagues claimed to have seen him hitting on boys in the community. Many of
us suspected he was using his position to recruit young men to work for him as
informants and to have sex with him in exchange for suppression of charges for
which *they* had been arrested.

I first shared my concerns with senior law enforcement officials in the regional
office. Receiving absolutely no support there, I took my complaint to officials in
the DOI, and then to the OIG. But those efforts were less than fruitful and even

counterproductive, resulting in a wave of unmitigated reprisals. The OIG did initiate an investigation and spent more than a year on the case. And it substantiated
every one of the allegations that it investigated. Those issues it did not investigate
(or at least did not document) were regrettably corroborated with the passage
of time and the victimization of more innocent bystanders. The damning OIG
report—several hundred pages long—was shared with the most senior NPS,
DOI, and congressional officials.[3] But the report was inexplicably kept secret
and withheld from the public for several more years. Out of sheer frustration, in
October 1985, I surprised the House Subcommittee on National Parks, Forests,
and Public Lands by presenting public testimony about corruption at Yosemite
National Park and elsewhere in the service.[4]

The bold, if naïve, act of voicing my grievances in open congressional hearings precipitated a flurry of defensive maneuvers. The subcommittee chairman,
a strong supporter and friend of the NPS, assigned the Government Accounting
Office (GAO) to conduct its own review of Yosemite law enforcement activities.
That feeble effort amounted to a full-blown cover-up of a long list of illegalities
that had already been documented (but kept secret) by the OIG and a smear
campaign directed my way, questioning my motives and labeling me a "disgruntled employee."

Fortunately, I still had copies of the documents I had turned over to the OIG
and GAO. Better yet, I had copies of consensually made recordings of my own
lengthy interviews and telephone conversations with investigators from both of
those agencies. When the subcommittee chairman issued a press release claiming
the GAO had cleared NPS officials of any wrongdoing, I responded with a letter,
copied to a range of congressmen from both sides of the aisle. I reminded the
subcommittee chairman that I still had tape recordings and documents proving
all of the allegations I had made over the past three years in my previous reports
to both the OIG and the GAO. The same evidence could now *also prove* his own
and the government's cover-up of those same illegal activities. I threatened to
release those materials to the news media, including my recorded conversations
with the OIG and the GAO about the three-year-old bugging incident.[5]

That was more than NPS, OIG, and congressional officials could handle.[6]
To provide their own cover, the OIG was forced to launch a second investigation into the very same bugging incident it (and the GAO) had been told
about but failed to document or investigate more than two years earlier.[7] The
park superintendent became the sacrificial lamb and lost his job. The DOI's
inspector general reportedly also lost his job over the role his own agency had

played in the cover-up. But the NPS did a masterful job of spinning the story to deflect the blame and minimize the damage to its image. The officials who proposed, orchestrated, and implemented the bugging and engaged in other illegal activities cited in my testimony got off free and clear. The House sub-committee chairman proclaimed that the NPS was "one of the most respected professional organizations in the national government."[8] The regional director sent a letter of commendation to the law enforcement chief, thanking him for his service and apologizing for the ordeal he'd been put through.[9] The district ranger who first suggested the illegal monitoring was awarded with a congressional fellowship and then promoted to associate regional director. The park prosecutor remained in his position for another fifteen years. He retired in 1998 after he was finally arrested by local officials in Fresno, California, on multiple counts, ranging from kidnapping to lewd and lascivious acts and oral copulation with juveniles.[10]

My experience in Yosemite was a saga in its own right, an amazing four-year ordeal that shaped many of my own views about the NPS, law enforcement, politics, and corruption. I was predictably ostracized, harassed, and even targeted with death threats for having damaged the image of the NPS by exposing its seedier side and "causing" the superintendent to lose his job. When the story about the bugging made the front page of the California newspapers, one of my new supervisors (who had pressured me to keep the incident quiet) took me aside and scolded me, exclaiming, "This is a sad day for the NPS." I defiantly challenged him, responding that the sad day had been when the bugging occurred, and he and his friends conspired to cover up their activities.

My exposé solidified my reputation as a troublemaker. Ironically, I started receiving unsolicited reports from both identified and anonymous sources documenting other serious acts of misconduct within the agency. Others who had seen the negative repercussions of attempting to report misconduct through official channels came to view me as a trusted surrogate through whom they could safely submit reports. I repackaged and sterilized many of those same reports, passing them along to the OIG while safely storing copies for my own use to defend against any future attempts of retaliation or cover-up.

In openly documenting and reporting misconduct to the OIG, I demonstrated an unacceptable lack of reverence and respect for the NPS hierarchy. I did not heed the warnings of supervisors who told me to keep quiet about the things I saw. I could not be trusted to protect the image of the agency. I was not a "team player."

I aggravated still more people by writing a number of essays and editorials, and even a book, critical of the NPS law enforcement program.[11] I presented lectures in both academic and formal conference settings, citing serious deficiencies in the NPS law enforcement program. Resentment was compounded by my own unlikely career success as a supervisory special agent and my ability to withstand repeated personal (and personnel) attacks through meticulous documentation and submission of an ever-growing list of whistle-blower reports to the OIG. Over time, that resulted in termination of the careers of a number of otherwise popular supervisors, chief rangers, and even a few superintendents. One superintendent at Grand Canyon National Park (who was, himself, pressured into retirement following a multimillion dollar contracting scandal) reportedly accused me of "character assassination by investigation."

But not everyone who was reported, investigated, and found to have engaged in serious misconduct suffered discipline or lost their job. This left a sizeable and fairly vindictive group of people in very high places. Through it all I somehow managed to survive and occasionally even thrive, probably through sheer stubbornness. Over time, my reputation as a whistle-blower actually became an asset, helping me to withstand any number of creative acts of reprisal and retaliation. It also did not hurt that I gained a measure of support from newly appointed officials in the OIG who, on more than one occasion, intervened on my behalf.

Still, when people figured out that I had inadvertently been designated the special agent-in-charge for the IMR, it was quickly and quietly determined that a grave error in judgment had been made. Without any notice or explanation, my name was hastily removed from the next list of new senior supervisors, and Jim Reilly's name was inserted in my place. My own protests and requests for honest answers, formal and informal, written and telephonic, went unanswered.

▲▼▲

Before that, as a ranger, Reilly had not even been incorporated into the newly restructured special agent organization. To effect that move, Jim was quietly reclassified into the GS-1811 criminal investigator series (to which he had never before been assigned) and reassigned into the new special agent organization as the permanent RSAC. The secrecy with which this all took place was highlighted by the fact that Reilly himself was not aware that he'd been reclassified and assigned as my permanent replacement—and therefore my new supervisor—until I called to tell him. Prior to that, he had graciously sent me a series of congratulatory messages offering his assistance in undertaking my new responsibilities throughout the region. He was first incredulous and later apologetic when I had finally convinced him there had been a change in plans and that he was now not only a special agent but the new, permanent special agent-in-charge for the IMR.

As the new RSAC, Reilly was left with the task of reviewing Simpson's complaint and assigning the case to one of the agents now on his staff. Special agent Clyde Yee, conveniently located just down the hall in Reilly's office complex, was assigned to the investigation and identified as the "lead" or "case agent."

The Hubbell Trading Post investigation was opened under the internal designation of NPS case no. IMDE 04–008. Following briefings provided by Kevin Fitzgerald, the regional chief ranger, and preparation of basic background information, Reilly and Yee launched the investigation by jointly conducting two preliminary interviews that would formally document the complaint.

On May 25, 2004, agents Reilly and Yee called LeAnn Simpson to talk with her about Hubbell Trading Post and Billy Malone.

Simpson explained her suspicions, citing an unsigned, undated, handwritten letter she and Scott Aldridge found in an envelope addressed to "John P.," in a drawer in John Pearson's old desk. The writer expressed a loss of interest in their job. That was followed by a series of broad and disjointed allegations against not only Billy Malone but most of the other trading post staff. The writer cited secondhand accounts of several suspicious incidents. According to the writer, cash was reportedly taken out of the register to pay for other people's meals, signatures were forged on checks, other employees were allowed to sell "their rugs on consignment," and purchases were written "for things that weren't there." Even more space in the letter was devoted to complaints about how Malone promoted one person's weaving over another's (the writer's) and how he delegated supervisory responsibilities to one co-worker instead of another more qualified employee (also the writer). The writer also complained about "snobby" comments made by female co-workers against one another. Although Simpson was alarmed by these allegations, she never followed through with a call or letter to John Pearson to inquire about the letter's source or significance.

Based on her review of the financial records for the WNPA and specifically Hubbell Trading Post, Simpson had also concluded that "financial irregularities" were occurring at Hubbell. Simpson again noted that of the roughly $8 million in revenue the WNPA generated every year, Hubbell was supposed to account for between $1.3 and $1.5 million. On closer examination Simpson found that Billy Malone "had complete control" of these Hubbell Trading Post funds, and that there was little if any oversight from her office. Simpson also concluded that the funds generated at Hubbell were "not being managed or tracked very well" and that in spite of all the money to which Malone allegedly had access, the WNPA was transferring funds from the Tucson office to Hubbell. In Simpson's estimation Hubbell was losing money, even though it was supposed to be a self-sustaining operation that generated millions of dollars in revenue for the association. This alone aroused Simpson's suspicions that Malone was stealing money. She became even more suspicious when she found out that two WNPA checking accounts were maintained at the trading post and that Malone did his own purchasing for the trading post and also made the deposits. Simpson apparently found both of these points "unusual from an internal controls standpoint."

Simpson traveled to Hubbell in March 2004 to conduct an audit. It was then that Simpson heard stories from an informant, one of the employees at the trading post, that Malone was forging checks. The informant told Simpson that when Malone sold a rug on consignment, he paid the weaver in cash and then wrote a check out of the consignment account to the name of the weaver for an amount that was more than what the weaver had been paid. Then Malone would take the check to Griswold's, a pawn and check-cashing store located a few miles to the east, off the reservation, just across the New Mexico state line. There, Malone would endorse and cash the check. When he returned Malone would put the same amount of money that had been paid to the weaver back in the trading post funds and pocket the rest.

With this information, Simpson and her accounting manager, Michelle Boden, initiated an examination of endorsement signatures appearing on a number of Hubbell Trading Post checks that had cleared through the bank. They identified approximately fifty checks with signatures that seemed to be in the same or similar handwriting. In Simpson's mind, this corroborated the informant's report of forgery, as well as the allegations contained in the handwritten letter she and Scott Aldridge had found in John Pearson's desk.

Also, according to a September 2003 inventory conducted by Simpson, the value of consignment rugs maintained at the trading post approached $745,000. Malone reportedly handled all consignment inventory, and he alone determined what items would be taken in on consignment at the trading post and from whom. As Simpson continued her review and examination of records for the trading post she found that apparently no one maintained an ongoing inventory of consignment property, and much of the required paperwork associated with consignment sales was either lost or missing. There was some speculation that this paperwork may have been lost by the business manager for the trading post who had recently been fired for "misuse of property" (the same one keeping tabs on Malone for the WNPA). But that alone did not resolve Simpson's concerns. Simpson also heard that Malone maintained a consignment book in which he documented consignment sales, but he had sole control of the book and took it home with him when he left the trading post. Making matters worse, after recently reviewing consignment check stubs, Simpson determined that Malone was "maintaining approximately $84,000 in uncashed consignment WNPA bank checks . . . written in 2002 and 2003." These checks would now be expired and could no longer be cashed but still counted against trading post expenses. According to Simpson, Malone was evasive and uncooperative when questioned about missing sales tickets and his management of the consignment program in general. He explained the uncashed consignment checks by telling Simpson he had written them to different artisans for various amounts but that they either had not yet picked up their checks or else had not cashed them.

Simpson provided Reilly and Yee with additional details about the system used at the trading post to track inventory, consignment property, and sales. Her own review of records from previous audits revealed that Malone often did not even cash his own paychecks and that those checks had expired over the course of time, compelling WNPA to issue cashier's checks to pay him instead. Without the benefit of an explanation, Simpson found this to be a highly suspicious practice. Simpson also learned that Malone was selling telephone calling cards he brought in and was reportedly keeping the profits of those sales. Finally, Simpson told Reilly and Yee that following her March 2004 visit to the trading post, Malone reportedly removed all of the consignment jewelry from the shelves. Simpson didn't know what he had done with the jewelry, but she speculated Malone may have returned it to another trader.[12]

Simpson shared her belief that Malone had been forging checks and stealing money from the WNPA since 1990, which could potentially amount to millions of dollars. If that were the case, it could explain the revenue losses Simpson said were occurring at Hubbell Trading Post.

A few days later Reilly assisted Yee in conducting one more interview.

Michelle Boden had been employed in Tucson with the WNPA for a little over a year, having started in March 2003 as an assistant to the accounting manager. When the accounting manager was fired, Boden moved up to replace her. Boden was present with Simpson in March 2004 when the informant at Hubbell Trading Post told them about Billy Malone.

Boden's May 28, 2004, account of the scheme attributed to Billy Malone was slightly different from Simpson's. Boden's understanding was that when a weaver brought a rug into the trading post, Malone paid that person in cash, up front, from a cash box. According to the informant, the rug should then have become WNPA property and been appropriately tagged and entered into inventory. Instead, Malone treated the rug as consignment, which required far less paperwork and tracking. Then, when the rug finally sold (as opposed to when it was first brought in and purchased from the weaver), Malone would write out a check from the WNPA consignment account to the name of the original weaver.

Boden was less certain about what happened next, merely speculating that Malone may have been "endorsing the check and cashing it at Griswold's." She explained that she'd observed that of the WNPA checks issued at the trading post, approximately one-third were cashed at a bank and the other two-thirds were cashed either at Griswold's or right there at the trading post, but mostly at Griswold's. Boden found it suspicious that a weaver would go all the way to Griswold's with a check from Hubbell instead of cashing it right there at the trading post.

When she was asked why no one at the trading post ever noticed or determined that money used to pay the weavers was missing, Boden acknowledged it was possible that Malone "could be replenishing the cash register after he cashes the check." Boden said she really didn't know what happened to the money, but there was no indication that Malone was stealing or taking money from the register that did not get returned. Still, she agreed with Simpson's very reasonable conclusion that "it looks like someone is forging the checks."[13]

It appears that after this interview the investigation kicked almost immediately into high gear.

Yee set about the task of securing warrants to search Malone's Hubbell Trading Post residence and vehicle. Notably, the trading post employee—the informant—with whom Simpson and Boden had spoken was not interviewed. Simpson's account of missing revenues at the trading post were not corroborated with the WNPA's contracted accounting firm, DeVries, Carpenter. Perhaps more significantly, no attempt was made to interview Billy Malone, his past supervisors, or any former or current SPMA/WNPA accountants.

Yee immediately began contacting federal prosecutors in Flagstaff, Arizona, to obtain their assistance in securing the search warrants. Mark Aspey, an assistant U.S attorney (AUSA), would handle the case.

With that critical contact in place, Yee went to work preparing the affidavit required to obtain those warrants.

The Warrant

(Ánohwii´ ahii binaaltsoos binaji´ na´ alkaahí)

A man's house is his castle; and whilst he is quiet, he is as well guarded as a prince in his castle. This writ, if it should be declared legal, would totally annihilate this privilege.

James Otis, February 1761

SECURING A SEARCH warrant in the federal system is generally a team effort between the case agent and the prosecutor, the AUSA. The agent usually approaches the AUSA with the facts and reasons why a search warrant is desired. Then the AUSA, in the superior role, determines whether to support the agent and authorize submission of an application for a warrant.

The AUSA is in a superior role not only because they control the process and authorize submission of the warrant application but also because the federal courts have ruled that "the individual prosecutor" has responsibilities that cannot be delegated or entrusted to the agent, including "a duty to learn of any favorable evidence [favorable to the accused] known to others acting on the government's behalf in the case," even where the agent is not forthcoming or fails to make a relevant disclosure.[1] Other courts have echoed this sentiment, noting that "'because the prosecution is in a unique position to obtain information known to other agents of the government, it may not be excused from disclosing what it does not know but could have learned.' Under *Brady* a prosecutor's duty necessarily requires the cooperation of other government agents who might possess *Brady* material."[2]

This superior role, as well as the special ethical obligations borne by federal prosecutors, is widely known and acknowledged.

Richard L. Delonis was the president of the National Association of Assistant United States Attorneys. In 2003, speaking on behalf of the NAAUSA membership, Delonis presented testimony before the Senate Subcommittee on Criminal Justice Oversight on the topic of the Federal Prosecutor's Ethics Act. Portions of his testimony specifically addressed the role and responsibilities of federal prosecutors:

> We are the government's front-line litigators, those whose duty it is to investigate and vigorously prosecute the criminals who prey upon American society and the American people. . . .
>
> . . . We embrace the words of Mr. Justice Sutherland in *Berger v. United States*, 295 U.S. 88 (1935), where he wrote that the United States Attorney is "the representative not of an ordinary party to a controversy, but of a sovereignty . . . whose interest, therefore, in a criminal prosecution is . . . that justice shall be done. . . . [As such, he is in a peculiar and very definite sense the servant of the law, the twofold aim of which is that guilt shall not escape or innocence suffer. He may prosecute with earnestness and vigor—indeed, he should do so. But while he may strike hard blows, he is not at liberty to strike foul ones.] It is as much his duty to refrain from improper methods calculated to produce a wrongful conviction as it is to use every legitimate means to bring about a just one." . . .
>
> . . . Typically, an Assistant United States Attorney's first contact with a given criminal case occurs when it is presented to him or her by the case agent, i.e., the investigator to whom the case has been assigned by the federal investigative agency. . . .
>
> . . . Common practice requires the federal agent to have the application for a search warrant reviewed and approved by an Assistant United States Attorney prior to its submission to the court. . . .
>
> . . . In recent years, federal prosecutors have become more active in the investigatory process and have assumed a greater role in the direction and supervision of investigations. . . .
>
> . . . A federal prosecutor's authority and responsibilities are far different from those of an attorney engaged in the private practice of law. As a representative of the people, the duties of the federal prosecutor occupy

a different, if not special, place in the operation of our legal system. The federal prosecutor represents not an individual client, but the people of the United States of America. It is the prosecutor's duty to enforce the law, not to seek a remedy or damage for a client. In proving a case the prosecutor must prove it beyond a reasonable doubt, not to a preponderance of the evidence as the plaintiff's counsel in a civil case. The federal prosecutor may not prosecute a defendant he or she knows to be innocent, yet the defendant's attorney is duty bound to vigorously defend a client known to be guilty.[3]

How a prosecutor responds when they learn of deficiencies in a case and credibility issues with an agent is problematic at best. This is particularly so late in the game, at which point an investigation is well underway and the prosecutor has already made a substantial investment in authorizing search or arrest warrants or a grand jury subpoena and testimony. Beyond the mere embarrassment of not detecting problems sooner through adequate "direction and supervision of investigations," the fallout from newly discovered legal issues may raise the specter of appeals and challenges in other past cases involving the same agent.

In spite of this defined role, it is not all that uncommon to see the cordial relationship between prosecutor and law enforcement officer (including NPS rangers and special agents), along with the shared desire to put bad guys in jail, lead to conflicts that undercut objectivity, compromise checks and balances, and subvert the ideals articulated by Justice Sutherland in *Berger v. United States*. It is undoubtedly the case that the intimidating power of the prosecutor (and the court) has at times been used to leverage a plea agreement from an unsophisticated defendant wrongly targeted, arrested, or charged as a way to cover and insulate a law enforcement officer from liability created through errors or misjudgments made in the course of an investigation or through systemically bad local law enforcement practices promoted by supervisors.[4]

Though acknowledged to be in a subordinate role to the prosecutor, the federal agent seeking a search warrant bears a reciprocal duty to be not only honest and forthcoming in their presentation of facts and related case information but also to verify that the search warrant ultimately submitted and then approved by the court is not flawed by incorrect or inaccurate information or deficient by the absence of information.

The courts have ruled that the warrant must contain on its face or in an incorporated and attached search warrant application sufficient information to instruct both the executing officer *and* the occupant of the place to be searched of the nature of the violation(s) alleged and the description of the items to be seized. The agent who prepares the search warrant and supervises its execution but fails in this responsibility is not entitled to qualified immunity from liability.[5]

These technical requirements are so fundamental and so important that the Internal Revenue Service cites both of the applicable court cases (i.e., *Groh v. Ramirez* and *United States v. Bridges*) in the opening pages of its national policies pertaining to the preparation and execution and search warrants:

> It is the special agent's responsibility to proof all documents prepared by the attorney for the government. . . . It is imperative that the special agent review the prepared search warrant to ensure all the proper information from the Application and Affidavit for Search Warrant is contained in the search warrant issued by the court. The warrant must be sufficient on its face or refer to an affidavit that is sufficiently incorporated therein, and specifically set forth:
>
> - the violations being investigated
> - a description of the person/premises to be searched
> - a description of the items to be seized[6]

A search warrant application summarizes the specifics of the search warrant, addressing the particulars of the person, property, or premises to be searched; the title and employing agency of the special agent; the judicial district where the person or property exists; a description of certain items to be seized; and the nature of the alleged criminal violations. The affidavit for the search warrant that is submitted with the application is supposed to set forth, in a logical fashion, evidence to establish probable cause that a crime was committed, that evidence of the crime exists, and that the evidence is located at a particular location. It is the affidavit that serves as the factual basis on which a judge determines whether or not sufficient evidence exists (i.e., "probable cause") to issue the warrant authorizing the agent to search and seize specific items constituting evidence of a crime from a designated location. The agent submitting the affidavit is required to swear, under penalty of perjury, that the information provided in the affidavit is true and correct to the best of their knowledge.

In the week following the interviews with Simpson and Boden, Yee, working closely with Aspey, prepared an affidavit in support of a search warrant claiming the existence of probable cause to believe that

within the residence of Billy Gene Malone there is evidence in the form
of *financial and business documents, ledgers, records, receipts, including
consignment ledgers, consignment checks, loan index cards and white and
pink sales tickets, for the period 1990 through the present* [June 8, 2004],
reflecting purchases and sales of inventory by Hubbell Trading Post and
Western National Parks Association and goods taken on consignment
and *currency reflecting fruits of the fraud* that reveals a violation of Title
18 United States Code, Sections 641 (Theft of Public Money), 1001 (False
Statements), and 1344 (Bank Fraud) (emphasis added, denoting items
subsequently authorized for seizure in the warrant).

The five-page affidavit submitted by Yee provided general background information about the WNPA and its operations at Hubbell Trading Post and restated
much of the more incriminating information obtained in the interviews with
Simpson and Boden. While it's not necessary to review all of that information
here, it is worth highlighting a few key points that would later create difficulties
in the investigation.

The theory that a theft of federal funds was occurring was based on two key
assumptions:

1) that Simpson reportedly believed that Hubbell Trading Post was inexplicably
   losing money and that its operations were no longer financially self-sufficient,
   requiring the WNPA to regularly transfer funds to maintain operations. That,
   combined with reports that Billy Malone had been seen forging endorsement
   signatures on checks, maintaining exclusive control of consignment operations, and taking cash out of the register (whether he returned that cash or
   not), led to the conclusion that he was stealing and embezzling large sums of
   money ("millions of dollars") from the WNPA.
2) that under the terms of a contract between the WNPA and the NPS, the
   WNPA is obligated to pay 6.5% of its revenues to the NPS (an unattributed
   claim repeated five separate times in the affidavit).

The second assumption was absolutely fundamental to the establishment of
federal jurisdiction. The reasoning advanced under this unusual theory was that
if someone (e.g., Billy Gene Malone) was stealing cash or embezzling funds from
the WNPA, it would concurrently constitute a theft of public money.

A couple of other points bear mentioning but would not be raised as issues of concern in the investigation for nearly a year and a half.

Even though one of the original (and arguably most compelling) allegations presented by Simpson was that Malone was forging endorsement signatures on WNPA bank checks, the crime of "check forgery" (i.e., 18 USC 513) was not even listed on the warrant application or supporting affidavit submitted by Yee and Aspey.

While the search warrant application and the supporting affidavit both listed false statements (18 USC 1001) as one of the three suspected violations that had occurred, the affidavit contained no mention or suggestion whatsoever that Malone had even been interviewed by or made any statements to federal officials (he had not) or that he made false statements (or any other statements) on any federal forms or applications.

Finally, while both the application and the affidavit listed three suspected offenses attributed to Malone, none of those offenses—in fact no offenses at all—were listed or cited on the face of the warrant. In the belief "that to release the contents of the affidavit . . . would jeopardize the ongoing investigation," Aspey specifically asked the court to seal "the Search Warrant Application, Affidavit, and the government's Motion to Seal." This meant that when served with the warrant, Malone not only *would not* know the charges being made against him but *could not* find out even if he asked, because that information would be secret and would remain secret for the next two and a half years.[7]

Yee's supervisor, Reilly, did not believe Yee had evidence rising to the level of probable cause necessary to support a search warrant. Much of the information contained in Yee's affidavit reflected mere beliefs expressed by Simpson that Malone had engaged in "the theft and embezzlement of retail sales proceeds from WNPA and the NPS and the forgery of WNPA bank checks" or that "WNPA business records indicate the Trading Post is regularly losing money and requires sustaining funds." The affidavit relied heavily on other similar conclusions, such as, "Simpson suspects . . . Billy Malone . . . is forging WNPA bank checks and embezzling cash and funds from the trading post" or "Malone is also fraudulently maintaining WNPA's required consignment ledger which details the buying and selling of Indian artisan products which he is stealing cash funds through." Reilly was particularly concerned about the implied conclusion that since the WNPA didn't know what was really occurring with its funds, it must be attributable to Malone, and evidence supporting that conclusion must, for lack of any other explanation, be inside Malone's residence.

These points notwithstanding, on June 8, 2004, the visiting federal magistrate from Tucson to whom the application was submitted (substituting in Flagstaff while the resident magistrate was away) authorized the two search warrants (one for Malone's residence, another for the WNPA-owned vehicle assigned to him and kept at his residence) as well as the motion to seal the warrant application, the affidavit, and the motion to seal, itself. U.S. District Court number 04–4129MB was assigned to the case.[8]

The Raid

(Ánohwii' ahii binaaltsoos binaji' na'askáá')

It is of more importance to community that innocence should be protected than it is that guilt should be punished.

John Adams, October 1770

The Constitution sometimes insulates the criminality of a few in order to
protect the privacy of us all.

Antonin Scalia, 1987

B EYOND A DESIRE to show deference to the WNPA, there was no real urgency
or need to rush the investigation and hastily launch a raid—that is, execute
the warrant on Malone's Hubbell Trading Post residence. But the WNPA wanted
to get on with the audit, and NPS officials had meanwhile made the decision to
execute the warrant during the now-authorized closure of the national historic
site. June 9, 2004, was selected as the target date. That left Yee with barely more
than a week to secure the desired search warrants and prepare for the raid, to be
launched concurrent with the WNPA audit. Whatever the reasoning, this schedule left little time for additional background work or investigation. And once the
warrant was issued, the clock began ticking.

In fact, without telling Simpson or the WNPA, Yee had duly noted the already
scheduled WNPA audit in his affidavit, indicating his intent to utilize accountants

from DeVries, Carpenter as participants in the execution of the warrant, under authority provided in 18 USC 3105.[1] This meant that the WNPA would be handicapped in conducting its own audit, because their contracted auditors would not be available while they were participating in the execution of the search warrant.

In a manner indicative of the extent to which this partnership would characterize the investigation for the next year and a half, on June 8, 2004, members of both the raid and audit team assembled in LeAnn Simpson's hotel room in St. Michaels (west of Window Rock), approximately thirty miles east of Hubbell Trading Post. Despite the NPS's claims that reforms had been made to assure investigative independence, Mike Snyder, deputy regional director, was also present. Plans were discussed and assignments were made. But not everything would go as planned.

At six o'clock in the morning of June 9, 2004, Snyder knocked on the door of Superintendent Nancy Stone's on-site government residence to tell her the national historic site she managed was closed and that search warrants were being executed across the street at the nearby residence of Billy Malone. Simultaneously, the WNPA would be initiating an intensive three-day audit at the trading post.

Stone had been kept completely in the dark out of concerns that she might tip off Malone and in the belief that a forgery and embezzlement scheme of this magnitude could not possibly have gone on for so long without her knowledge. Internal memorandums document speculation that she might have somehow been complicit in the scheme. Simpson, on the other hand, was so intimately involved in the investigation that she was able to corroborate that Steve Martin, the regional director, had "made the decision that HUTR [Hubbell Trading Post] Superintendent Nancy Stone was to be left 'out of the loop' and was not to be given advance notice of either WNPA or NPS activities."[2]

Stone was shocked. She was expecting Snyder that morning but certainly not for this reason. She had been told the deputy regional director was coming for a site visit, his first ever to the famous trading post. In anticipation of Snyder's arrival, employees had been instructed to prepare by tidying up the grounds and to be on their best behavior, while Stone had made arrangements for a tour of the facility and the opportunity for the visiting official to meet her staff. The only indication of a change in plans came the night before (June 8, 2004), when she learned that Rick Frost, the regional public relations officer, was accompanying Snyder and that both men were staying down the road at a hotel in St. Michaels. Stone had assumed Frost was along simply to shadow the deputy regional director and was being groomed for career advancement.

After Snyder told Stone what was happening, she looked out the window and could see several law enforcement vehicles positioned in the front of Billy and Minnie Malone's house. She immediately asked Snyder why she had not been told about this before. He answered, "We wanted to protect you."

The superintendent was not only hurt but also infuriated by Snyder's response. She scoffed but was otherwise in no position to question him or challenge his motives. Snyder was secretive about details of the developing case but indicated that what was occurring was extremely significant, adding that Stone wouldn't believe the magnitude of what Billy Malone had really been up to for years. In his overall vague account, Snyder made clear that the case against Malone (whatever that was) was "an open and shut thing" and that the current crop of WNPA managers were the real heroes for having uncovered Malone's long-running scheme. Later, after the raid, LeAnn Simpson echoed this sentiment, telling Stone that "Bill is a thief; you cannot believe what he has done."[3] Later still, Simpson reportedly told at least one incredulous official from the nonprofit, charitable organization known as Friends of Hubbell Trading Post the same thing, claiming that Malone had stolen "not just one million dollars" but "millions and millions."[4] As Stone observed NPS and WNPA officials parade in and out of Malone's residence throughout the day, she drew an altogether different conclusion, suspecting that the events occurring across the street more likely reflected some sort of collusion between the WNPA and the NPS.

Snyder told Stone that Jim Babbitt would be coming in later that morning for an all-employee meeting to be held at the visitor center. Stone was instructed to place phone calls to community leaders such as the Ganado chapter president and other park "stakeholders," such as the Friends of Hubbell, to let them know what has happening. She was also to pass word along to her staff to make sure they attended the meeting.

Later that morning both NPS and WNPA employees gathered together in the visitor center. Stone was placed in the awkward position of addressing the group and announcing only that Billy Malone was no longer the trader at Hubbell Trading Post. There was little more she could say. Snyder, Simpson, and Babbitt also addressed the group. They confirmed that the trading post would remain closed for the rest of the week, and the staff of the WNPA could go home. No further explanation was provided, except that the reason behind the day's events would become clear in the weeks and months to come.

Earlier, at the very same time that Mike Snyder surprised Stone by showing up at her doorstep, Yee and a team of support personnel were knocking on the door to Billy Malone's residence. Malone got out of bed, put on his pants, and went to see what was going on. When he opened the door he was greeted by Yee who "flashed his badge," identified himself, and demanded entry, explaining he had a warrant to enter and search for evidence. Malone was immediately patted down and handed a copy of the warrant verifying the government's authority to enter and conduct the search. The warrant listed the ledgers, receipts, currency, and other documents to be seized but contained absolutely no indication of *why* the search was being conducted or what crimes the government believed Malone had committed. The officers then escorted Malone back into the house to wake his wife as well as his mother-in-law, who was staying with them while recovering from a recent heart attack.

Malone, along with his wife and mother-in-law, were told they could remain at the residence, under guard, if they desired but that if they left they would not be permitted back in until the search and seizure of evidence was completed. All three remained at the residence through most of the day and evening, as Yee, the other rangers and personnel from the WNPA (including the accountants from DeVries, Carpenter) went through the house and garage in search of evidence. Around 7:00 p.m. Malone's wife and mother-in-law left to attend evening church services. Malone remained in the house for the rest of the night until the search was completed and the search team departed, around midnight. Even then, Malone stayed in the house for the next two full days. He had been instructed by the officers not to leave or go anywhere, so he didn't. Several of Malone's daughters came by to take care of the sixty-five-year-old diabetic, who was now humiliated, distressed, and despondent and refusing to receive outsiders. By the account of Malone's closest friends and relatives, the experience very nearly killed him.

Even while investigators were conducting their search of Malone's residence, several events occurred and were documented by investigators that underscored the extent to which Malone routinely conducted trading post business from his own home. On one occasion around 11:35 a.m., the telephone rang and Malone answered, "Hello, Hubbell's."[5] Later in the day a Pendleton distributor showed up looking for Malone but was turned away.[6]

In the course of their search, both law enforcement officers and the WNPA-contracted accountants from DeVries, Carpenter opened closet doors and inspected the contents of boxes and other containers in search of evidence listed on the warrant. But as the search team made their way through the residence they made a totally unanticipated discovery.

Within the residence and attached garage were old as well as contemporary Navajo rugs numbering in the hundreds, stacked in pile after pile, making it difficult to navigate. The officers and accountants also found boxes upon boxes of both old and contemporary Navajo jewelry, as well as Navajo paintings, baskets, and pots.

The search team was overwhelmed by what they saw, immediately suspecting that no one person could own or otherwise have all of these precious objects in their legitimate possession. Some, if not all, of the items had to be stolen.

Adding to their suspicions was the presence of tags on a number of rugs of the type, style, and marking of those once (formerly) used at Hubbell Trading Post, with pairs of letters and prices suggesting consignment inventory. Even more rugs had tags from other trading posts or just plain tags bearing various initials and codes, apparently indicating their point of origin. Still more rugs had no tags at all. Much of the jewelry had very small, plain stickers attached bearing small handwritten prices as well as letters or numbers, again, apparently indicating their consignment owner or inventory number in some sort of code.

But there was a problem. The search warrant listed only various financial and business documents, such as ledgers, receipts, checks, loan index cards, sales slips, and "currency reflecting fruits of the fraud" as being authorized for seizure. The warrant did not authorize the seizure of rugs, jewelry, baskets, pots, or any other types of personal property, and the supporting affidavit made no reference at all to the suspected theft of rugs, jewelry, or other real property.

The case law surrounding searches (and seizures) conducted in residences is extensive. Two cases figure prominently, known respectively as *Arizona v. Hicks*, and *Horton v. California*.[7] The courts have embraced the age-old axiom that "a person's home is their castle" and recognize a greater "expectation of privacy" in the home than in any other place. Absent consent or a true emergency or "exigency," officers must have a valid warrant authorizing the entry and subsequent seizure of items from the residence. Even when officers are legally in a home under authority of a search warrant, *only* those items listed in the warrant can be seized unless other evidence is observed in "plain view" and "its incriminating character [is] immediately apparent." Also, officers must be able to determine its "incriminating character" and establish probable cause for a seizure without moving it to more closely examine it and without further searching or testing. Otherwise, if officers find items for which they believe probable cause exists to justify a seizure, they must first secure from a judge another warrant or they must amend the initial warrant and then get it approved.

The theft of property such as rugs and jewelry was not among the crimes under investigation when Yee secured the search warrant and subsequently entered Billy Malone's residence, so their suspected theft arguably constituted a new area of investigation. Also, since Malone's residence was within the government compound of the trading post, and he was known to conduct trading post business from his house, particularly after hours, the presence of trading post property within his house might not be illegal at all but a long-standing and accepted practice.

It is for reasons like these that federal prosecutors, including those in the district of Arizona, instruct law enforcement officers that "if you are in a home on a search warrant, and find items not listed, it is best to secure the premises and obtain a search warrant directed at the new area of investigation." They also counsel officers to "make sure that any additional items are reasonably related to the crime investigated. It is best to secure and get another warrant if additional items are discovered or if you must read or examine unlisted items."[8]

With this dilemma staring him straight in the face, Yee placed a number of telephone calls to Aspey to explain what he had found and what he wanted to do. Yee believed he had found even more evidence of criminal activity on a grand scale, and he wanted to seize it. But he didn't want to take the time to call in additional personnel to assist (as many as a dozen or more rangers and special agents were readily available within a range of anywhere from 30–160 miles at various nearby sites including Canyon de Chelly, Petrified Forest, Flagstaff, and Grand Canyon), and he didn't want to take the time to prepare the paperwork necessary to amend the old warrant or secure a new one.

Aspey told Yee that he could seize the rugs and jewelry along with any other property he believed was stolen. But there was a catch. Aspey reportedly told Yee to take only those rugs, pieces of jewelry, baskets, pots, and other items that had some sort of marking or tag indicating they belonged to the WNPA and Hubbell Trading Post. Then, they would be safely back in the government's and the WNPA's hands and Yee would have time to sort things out and, if necessary, return those items to Billy Malone that might really be his.

A full year and half after the fact, on January 11, 2006, I interviewed Aspey about his June 9, 2004, telephone conversations with Yee and the authorization he had reportedly given to seize the rugs, jewelry, and other property. Following that interview I prepared a draft report documenting what I had understood him to say. Some time later, in deference to the federal judge, I provided Aspey with the opportunity to review my draft report of the interview and make any

changes that he saw fit to accurately and fully reflect his thoughts and recollection. Aspey's edited and modified version of my report was the first written
account that he personally prepared (by way of handwritten edits, deletions, and
even additions to my draft) to document what he claimed to have told Yee.[9] His
edited version was cited verbatim in my final report:

> Judge Aspey indicated it had been some time since the event and he had
> no file or notes from which to refresh his memory, but recalled receiving
> several telephone calls from Agent Yee during execution of the search
> warrant. Judge Aspey stated he believes he directed Agent Yee to go ahead
> and seize those items that had indicia as being HTP [Hubbell Trading
> Post] property, such as items bearing tags that could be readily identified
> as HTP property through reference to ledgers or inventories on scene.
> However he did not summarily direct Agent Yee to seize everything or
> any items or property that did not have indicia as belonging to HTP.
> Judge Aspey further noted that he had understood that any items mistak-
> enly seized would be returned to Malone. He was surprised to learn that
> clear ownership of all the property had not yet been established and that
> it was still in evidence.[10]

My own recollection is that Aspey's original (oral) response was not nearly
as specific and formal as the final report suggests and that he expressed more
alarm and concern than is reflected. Also, my original (draft) version referenced
comments Aspey made that Yee might have misunderstood his instructions and
that "items mistakenly seized would be returned to Malone in just a week or
two." Aspey crossed out both of these comments in his edit. Still, the differences
between my original write-up documenting the interview and Judge Aspey's
subsequent edit (used in my final report) are not dramatic. But the devil is in the
details, and over the course of time there would be no less than four different
versions provided by three different people attesting to what Aspey actually said
to Yee when he authorized him to seize at least some of the property. My accommodation to Mark Aspey, allowing him to review and modify my draft report
in his own handwriting, would ultimately prove invaluable in withstanding later
attacks alleging that I had misrepresented the judge's own statement.[11]

Even within the context of his edited account of instructions to Yee, Aspey
conceded that it would be necessary for Yee to conduct further "testing" of
the rugs, jewelry, and other property, through examination of the various tags

From:
To:
Sent: Thursday, June 29, 2006 7:54 AM
Subject: seizure of property

In discussions with Agent Yee about this discrepancy and ultimate seizure of between $5-6,000,000 in personal property from MALONE's residence, Agent Yee has explained that upon entry into MALONE's residence he and his staff were surprised and overwhelmed by enormous quantity of valuable Navajo rugs, jewelry, and other art objects found within the residence and the garage. By its sheer volume as well as the presence of Hubbell Trading Post tags on some of the items, Agent Yee and others concluded that much or all of this property must have been stolen from HTP. Agent Yee indicates that during the course of the search he made several telephone calls to [then] AUSA Aspey to obtain guidance on this property. Agent Yee has stated that AUSA Aspey directed him to seize all of the property that might belong to HTP, and that they could sort it out and verify ownership later. Agent Yee has explained that is what he did, seizing any and all property present in the house and garage that appeared as though it might belong to HTP (including by the presence of a HTP tag or any other tag or marking of any sort), or was located next to or adjacent to property that appeared as though it might belong to HTP.

I subsequently arranged to meet in person with Judge Aspey in his *[handwritten: indicated it had been some time since the event and he had no file or notes to refresh his memory from but]* chambers in Flagstaff, AZ. This meeting took place on January 11, 2006. I explained my reason for wishing to talk with him, and requested that he provide me with any information he could that might shed light on the justification employed to seize the large quantity of property from MALONE's residence. Judge Aspey recalled receiving several telephone calls from Agent Yee during execution of the search warrant, ~~but offered that there must have been a misunderstanding.~~ Judge Aspey stated that he ~~had~~ directed Agent Yee to go ahead and seize ~~only~~ those items that ~~were clearly marked~~ *[handwritten: believes he]* as being HTP property, as ~~well as any~~ items bearing ~~other~~ tags *[handwritten: had indicia]* that could be readily identified as HTP property through reference to ledgers or inventories on scene. However he did not summarily direct Agent Yee *[handwritten: did not have indicia]* to seize everything or any items or property that ~~could not readily~~ ~~and promptly be verified~~ as belonging to HTP. Judge Aspey further noted that he had understood that any items mistakenly seized would be returned to MALONE ~~in just a week or two~~. ~~Judge Aspey expressed surprise when I explained the quantity of items actually seized and that, in fact, the majority of those items did not bear tags~~ identifying them as HTP property. He was ~~also~~ surprised to learn that clear ownership of the property had not yet been established and that it was still in evidence. *[handwritten: all]*

                                                              6/29/2006

19. Author's draft "report of interview" with handwritten edits by AUSA/U.S. magistrate-judge Mark Aspey (*author's collection*). ——————————————

and markings they bore and "reference to ledgers or inventories on scene" to determine if they actually were Hubbell Trading Post property. Aspey further acknowledged that he "understood any items mistakenly seized would be returned to Malone," which in itself makes clear that the "incriminating character" of the property was not "immediately apparent," as required for it to be seized under *Horton v. California*. This exact point would resurface more than a full year later when investigative files were reviewed by another federal prosecutor to whom the case had transferred. That AUSA noted in July 2005 that "items found in Malone's house, which has been valued in the millions of dollars, need to be examined and analyzed as to whether or not they were stolen from the trading post."[12]

Regardless of what he was told by Aspey, what Yee actually did is a matter of record.

When all was said and done, in addition to the ledgers, receipts, sales slips, currency, and other financial records listed on the search warrant, Yee seized more than 550 Navajo rugs and roughly 6,000 pieces of jewelry and other property collected in bulk, in piles of rugs or boxes of jewelry. They would all remain in NPS custody for more than the next two years.

In preparation for the execution of the search warrants, Yee had apparently failed to anticipate the volume of "evidence" located in Malone's residence. The search team was overwhelmed and unprepared, and Yee did not have sufficient staff with him to conduct an inventory of all the property or even load and transport it all away to a storage facility (which had yet to be identified). Consequently, when the search was finally completed and the seized property was loaded into vans outside, the property receipt that Yee was required to provide Malone was not properly itemized. Instead, it listed primarily "boxes," "drawers," and "bags" containing miscellaneous jewelry and baskets and stacks of "10 rugs," "75 rugs," or "340 rugs" from various rooms in the house or garage. The inventory and receipt provided no precise accounting of the number of items seized or their descriptions, and no photographic record was created to document them and the location or condition in which they were found. The extent to which investigators truly did *not* initially know how much property they had seized from Malone's residence was reflected in Yee's July 2004 "Preliminary Case Development Plan." There, he referenced the "tens of thousands of pieces of jewelry ... [that will require] ... documentation, digital photographing, and cataloging."[13]

Yee seized not only those items bearing actual tags from Hubbell Trading Post (however old, obsolete, and recycled those tags might have been) but also any *other* rugs with *different tags* or *no tags* at all found next to or in the same stack with rugs tagged from Hubbell Trading Post. Of the "boxes," "drawers," and "bags" of jewelry seized containing what would eventually be counted at slightly over six thousand pieces (as opposed to "tens of thousands"), none had tags readily associated with Hubbell Trading Post. The only markings evident on some of the pieces were nondescript handwritten letters and numbers or prices applied to the underside of rings, bracelets, necklaces, and earrings. Other pieces bore no markings at all. Two years later, after the case had changed hands, it would be discovered that only 162 rugs (of the 554 rugs seized) bore Hubbell Trading Post consignment tags, and those tags were old and recycled. "None of the thousands of pieces of jewelry bore tags indicating Hubbell Trading Post ownership."[14]

Yee was now faced with yet another challenge. He apparently did not feel he had ready access to sufficient law enforcement or other NPS personnel or vehicles on site to assist in transporting all of the property and evidence away from the scene and to the commercial storage locker expediently rented 150 miles to the west in Flagstaff.

That first night following the raid "the two vehicles that transported the seized items were secured and parked at the St. Michaels, AZ, Days Inn. [Ranger] Foust checked on the security of these two vehicles periodically through the night."[15]

The next morning, in another decision reflecting the truly cooperative nature of the developing investigation, Yee enlisted Simpson to assist in transporting the evidence.

Prior to calling on Simpson, Yee had first asked one of the accountants from DeVries, Carpenter to drive the van full of evidence, but she refused. Inexplicably, no consideration was given to assigning any of the numerous NPS rangers on scene to this task. Instead, "On June 10, 2004, LeAnn Simpson, driving the WNPA van and this Agent [Yee], driving the Government SUV truck departed St. Michaels to Flagstaff. The seized items were secured in the AAA Discount Storage of Arizona."[16]

Simpson would later acknowledge the conflict of interest created by her accepting Yee's request to drive her own WNPA van full of property seized from Malone, especially in light of her (and the WNPA's) role as both the reporting party and the alleged victim in the criminal investigation, not to mention her position as Malone's (soon-to-be former) boss.[17] Simpson was alone in the vehicle she was driving but did follow behind Yee as they proceeded down the highway and interstate freeway to Flagstaff, where they met and unloaded the property.

In driving the van full of evidence from Malone's residence to Flagstaff, Simpson was "in a unique position to observe the quantity and character of items seized from Malone's residence.... She had thought the purpose of the search was primarily to obtain ledgers and other records necessary to conduct an audit and attempt to make sense of records and accounts. While off-loading property in Flagstaff, she questioned Yee about the enormous quantity of rugs, jewelry, and other property agents had seized. Yee reportedly explained that they had taken everything that was even just nearby or next to something that looked like it might belong to Hubbell Trading Post. Where the rugs were concerned, Agent Yee explained that if, within a stack of rugs found in the house or garage, there had been any rugs bearing Hubbell tags, they had seized the entire stack of rugs, including those that did not have identifying tags."[18]

Case files indicate that only one or two people were formally interviewed during the three-day raid, audit, and general closure of the trading post. One of those was the trading post employee—the informant—with whom Simpson and Boden had spoken. That same informant would later be terminated by the WNPA for her own conduct and performance issues. Yee, along with Foust and Marianne DeVries, contacted that individual on the last day of the audit in an effort to confirm or clarify the secondhand accounts cited in the affidavit for the search warrant.

By most accounts at the time, the government raid on the home of Billy Malone had been an overwhelming success. Not only did the agents obtain the documents they were seeking (mostly from the trading post itself rather than Malone's residence), which they hoped would help prove the theft and embezzlement of millions of dollars, but they had also, by good fortune, stumbled onto what they now believed to be millions of dollars worth of stolen rugs, jewelry, baskets, and other property located in the home of their suspect, Billy Gene Malone. Almost all of the players from the WNPA and the NPS believed they were onto something big.

Just one week after the raid at Hubbell and being suspended from his position (concurrent with the public announcement that he was no longer the trader at Hubbell), Billy Malone was presented with a formal notice of termination, along with instructions to vacate his government residence. The letter from Simpson and Babbitt cited five "infractions" justifying his "immediate termination": "improper activity surrounding the consignment program," including "dubious practices," "lack of security surrounding WNPA funds and property," "improper bank deposits," "uncollected NSF (nonsufficient funds) checks," and "perpetuation of negative employee morale." The letter further elaborated on the reasons for termination:

> Due to the volume of information being audited, many other serious issues are still under investigation, including a claim of sexual harassment against you. Other infractions of policy may be discovered/confirmed through this process.
>
> As a result of your gross misconduct, your employment with WNPA is being terminated immediately.[19]

On receipt of his termination notice, the beleaguered Indian trader said a simple "thank you" and left the building.[20]

In all of the events and activities of June 9–11, 2004, there is one point that stands out as particularly ironic. As short staffed, ill equipped, and unprepared as they were to deal with what they would ultimately find and seize from Billy Malone's residence, the one thing for which Yee and his team *did* plan was the presence of media: newspaper, radio, and perhaps television reporters who might be drawn to Hubbell Trading Post by the promise of a big story about the ongoing raid on the home of the world-renowned Indian trader. Frost, the regional public relations officer who had flown in the night before with Snyder, had actually come along to serve as the point of contact and "information officer" responsible for speaking with representatives of the media who might show up to cover the story. But *no one* showed up for the story!

In their assessment of the community and culture of the Navajo Reservation, it seems that Yee and his team had misjudged the way things work. And with the seizure of his life savings in rugs and jewelry, notice that he was being kicked out of his house, termination of his employment with the WNPA, and public notice to the entire Hubbell community that he had been fired from his life-long job as a trader—all in the course of a single day—the only person for whom the raid had really been big news, and very bad news at that, was Billy Malone.

A Life of Its Own

(T'áá bíni'dii deez t'i')

T HE EXTENT TO which Yee viewed the raid on Billy Malone's home a success is reflected in part of his July 2004 case summary and funding request:

Hubbell Trading Post National Historic Site is under the proprietary jurisdiction of the United States within the judicial District of Arizona and the 9th Circuit Court of Appeals. The NPS owns and is responsible for the 160 acre site along with all of the buildings; the Trading Post, the Hubbell House, the Guest House, the barn, the Visitors Center and accompanying Government housing area. The State of Arizona maintains responsibility for investigating crimes covered under State law and the Navajo Nation has responsibility for crimes committed by Navajo people. Malone is not Navajo, but married a Navajo woman. However, crimes that fall under Federal laws are the responsibility of the Federal Government entity responsible for the property, in this case the NPS.

The initial phase of this investigation involves the processing of more than $5 million dollars in property and a [*sic*] several hundred thousand documents. At the time of the seizure, Malone was suspected of a number of Federal crimes; including Bank Fraud, Theft of United States Government Property and providing False Information to the United States Government, all crimes against WNPA and the NPS. Immediately following the execution of the search warrants, additional interviews with WNPA employees working at the trading post were conducted. These interviews uncovered a larger criminal potential of this investigation. It is believed that Malone has been stealing money from hundreds of Navajo patrons of the trading post through a classic Social Security Fraud scheme, Extortion, and money theft through their personal trading post accounts. As a part of the search warrant, financial documents were seized and as we review these documents, we are finding complaints from tourists across the country whom either visited the trading post or contacted the trading post electronically (phone or e-mail) and paid money for merchandise that was promised them through the mail that was never sent. Additionally, many tourists from across the nation have sent to the trading post their personal rugs and jewelry for repair and have never received them back or a monetary settlement for the items claimed loss. These crimes are included under Federal Interstate Theft laws. It is suspected that Malone has not claimed much of his outside financial earnings on his Federal taxes (similar to Al Capone). The investigation of this Tax Fraud or Tax Evasion aspect is important due to its potential use in his defense claim to the other above pending charges.

Even though currently the information contained within the search warrants has been sealed by request of the U.S. Attorney, word of Malone's employment termination is spreading by word of mouth. Some local trading post journals have noticed Malone's replacement as trader and as the investigation progresses regional and national news media will be interested, especially with the Navajo people as victim.[1]

In the year and a half following the NPS raid at Hubbell Trading Post, the investigation took on a life of its own. The focus of attention, and certainly the commitment of resources (i.e., money) in many respects shifted away from suspicions of embezzlement and forgery to the enormous volume of property that had been seized from Billy Malone. Internal notes document that as early as July 2004, NPS officials told the WNPA that the goal of the investigation was now to "'determine the rightful ownership' of the property so that it is not returned to Bill [Malone]."[2]

In the weeks following the raid, arrangements were made to transfer the property out of the temporary storage locker rented in Flagstaff to a far more secure facility in Tucson, the Service's Western Archaeological Conservation Center, or

WACC. The WACC is an impressive facility staffed by archaeologists, librarians, and other specialists skilled in the stabilization, restoration, and cataloging of artifacts and historic objects. Within the facility are enormous, high-security, climate controlled storage areas, which were ideal for the newly identified needs of the investigation.

Susan Morton was already stationed in the Tucson area, assigned to an interagency task force targeting border drug activity.[3] She was directed to assist Yee by securing the services of the WACC to store and process the rugs, jewelry, and other objects seized in the raid. Morton was designated the evidence custodian and would directly receive these items and accept responsibility for them so as to assure their integrity for introduction as evidence in the developing case against Billy Malone. As a part of that process, the locks on the four hundred-square-foot room designated for storage were changed. Morton maintained exclusive keyed access. Yee rejected Morton's suggestion that he be a back-up evidence custodian and keep a duplicate key in the event he needed direct access.

Morton assumed sole custody for all of the rugs, jewelry, baskets, and other objects. The various boxes containing the jewelry, baskets, pots, and other objects (except for the rugs) were still under seal and would not be opened or inventoried until Yee identified the process he wanted Morton to use for examining and cataloging them. It would take nearly three months for that process to begin before they were inventoried. Documents seized in the raid were ultimately transferred to either Santa Fe or Yee's own offices in Lakewood.

Protocols at the WACC called for all of the rugs to undergo a freezing and thawing process before long-term storage to ensure the extermination of any larvae, beetles, or other insects that might cause damage. After that, under Morton's supervision, the WACC staff would begin the long process of cataloging and photographing each of the several thousand items, piece by piece. The inventorying alone was projected to take up to six months and would ultimately cost upward of $200,000.

But even before the cataloguing of the property began, the investigation experienced another in a series of potentially case-damaging irregularities and conflicts.

Morton assumed custody of the property on July 9, 2004. She spent most of the following month moving rugs from the trailer in which they had been transported into the freezer for treatment and then, finally, to the evidence locker. At the same time, discussions took place about the process Yee wanted to use to conduct an initial inventory of the boxes of jewelry (and other property). As Morton later noted, "the contents of the sealed boxes of jewelry were unknown" and the inventory needed to be done before the evidence was officially transferred to the WACC "to assure that the items turned over to WACC personnel were the same items returned."[4]

By late August 2004, Morton had still not received a final decision from Yee about how to inventory the thousands of pieces of evidence. All of the property was still secured and under Morton's exclusive control. Morton took off on approved family leave on August 25, 2004. She was scheduled to return on September 2. Before leaving, Morton provided Yee with her schedule as well as telephone and pager numbers where she could be reached.

As scheduled, Morton returned to her office on September 2, 2004. She went about her other drug enforcement duties. There were no messages from Yee or anyone else about the Hubbell investigation or the evidence from that case. A week or two later, Morton contacted officials at the WACC to see if they had received any update. Morton was not at all pleased with what she learned.

Yee apparently made his decision about how to process evidence while Morton was still on leave. On August 31, just two days before Morton's return, Yee faxed a letter to the WACC authorizing the staff to secure the services of a locksmith to break into the evidence locker and change the locks and to begin inventorying and cataloguing evidence. In his letter, Yee delegated total authority to WACC personnel to "conduct maintenance practices that you see fit that will further the processing of this evidence in a timely manner." None of these personnel were trained, screened, or certified in law enforcement procedures and the handling of evidence, and yet they would be the first people to unseal the yet-to-be inventoried boxes of jewelry.

Also, remarkably, in the same letter Yee stated, "The evidence in this case is part of the larger criminal investigation being conducted by the National Park Service, Office of Criminal Investigations, WASO [Washington Office], and is being supervised by the Intermountain Regional Office-Denver."[5] This statement suggests that, despite mandated reforms and restructuring of the agent program, nothing had changed, and it raises even more questions about just who was really in charge of the investigation and running the show. Yee did not even inform his own supervisor, Jim Reilly, about the custody change.

The locksmith broke into the vault on September 1, 2004, just one day before Morton returned to work. No transfer of custody took place between Morton and personnel from the WACC. Morton was not even aware that she no longer had custody and control of the evidence. She didn't find that out until two weeks later, when she called the WACC to check in.

On October 4, 2004, Morton prepared a memorandum documenting the series of events leading up to what she described as "a break in the chain-of-custody." She distanced herself from the investigation (for the time being), stating, "As a result of the foregoing information, I believe my responsibility as evidence custodian ended on September 1, 2004, when the lock core was replaced and access was gained to the evidence locker without my knowledge or presence."[6]

Initially, Morton's supervisor was as displeased by her detailed documentation of the events affecting the evidence as he was by the break-in itself, believing that Morton's memorandum might create problems for the case. Yee was upset too, reportedly claiming that Morton was "just causing trouble because [she] was jealous of his big case."[7]

Reilly subsequently made a number of phone calls to determine who else knew about the incident. When he called me to explain his concerns and seek my opinion, I argued that Morton had been absolutely right to document the incident. From both a legal and an ethical standpoint, she really had no choice. Reilly seemed to accept this position, acknowledging the need to document all aspects of the investigation, both good and bad.

Thereafter, Reilly would encounter more than his own share of other problems in dealing with Yee and in trying to convince him to appropriately share information. Morton's memorandum, the secret of its existence, and, more importantly, the series of events the memorandum documented would crop up later as one of a series of issues raising questions about the manner in which the case was being handled and the level of integrity with which the investigation was being conducted.

At the same time that discussions and disputes were occurring over evidence, Yee and a team of rangers and other agents were gathering to sweep through the communities of Ganado and Gallup in search of leads in the investigation. By August 2004, OIG special agent Jamie Howard, stationed near Yee in Lakewood, had been assigned to assist in the investigation and serve as a point of contact for the use of other OIG resources. Her participation was authorized based on Yee's report that the case involved a theft of government funds.

Also now assigned to assist in the investigation was NPS special agent "Chip" (Carl) Davis. Davis had long enjoyed the ability to move his own duty station from place to place to follow his wife, also an NPS employee, when she got a new assignment. This extraordinary level of agency accommodation has historically been afforded to only a handful of "dual-career couples" over the years, in this case enabling Davis to flexibly work in the same basic position at duty stations as diverse and distant from each other as Brunswick, Georgia, Missoula, Montana, and now Santa Fe. Davis had worked for Jim Reilly before, when he was still ranger activities branch chief for the IMR. However, in the 2003 restructuring of the service's special agent program, Davis was designated as one of the few agents assigned on a full-time basis to internal investigations in the newly established Office of Professional Responsibility, or OPR.

Internal investigations are among the most critical and sensitive assignments to be had. Both Yee and Davis had periodically conducted internal investigations under the old organization. But Davis was now assigned to that role on a permanent basis, reporting directly from his Santa Fe office to a supervisor in Washington, D.C. Still, in light of the ever-increasing workload associated with the Hubbell Trading Post investigation, Davis was made available to assist Yee, and his office was used to photocopy and store the financial records seized in the raid.

Agents Howard and Davis and eight to ten other officers were detailed to work under Yee on his "Hubbell task force," undertaking various assignments, including interviews of prospective witnesses throughout the reservation and adjacent towns. The first of these deployments took place August 1–15, 2004.

Reports contained in Hubbell case files indicate that the majority of effort during this first sweep was focused on interviews with individuals who had worked at Hubbell Trading Post under Billy Malone. Investigators solicited incriminating information about Malone and the manner in which he ran the trading post. Members of the task force were reportedly instructed by Yee to use "aggressive interviewing techniques." Not surprisingly, a number of witnesses broke down in tears and ran out of their interviews. One witness was reportedly told that she would lose custody of her children if she did not cooperate fully. Another tearful witness was told to expect the same aggressive treatment later on, during cross-examination. Several witnesses, who were either intimidated or insulted or did not trust the investigators, refused to talk altogether. Whatever reliable information investigators may have obtained, it is certain that they simultaneously alienated a sizeable portion of the community in the process.

Concurrent with this first sweep, on August 11 agents executed two more search warrants on commercial storage lockers Malone had rented in Gallup. Malone had moved many of his household belongings into those lockers after he was kicked out of his home at Hubbell Trading Post in the wake of the June 9 raid.

The new warrants authorized seizure of the same types of financial and business documents that were identified in the first warrant. This time, however, the warrants also listed "Navajo rugs, Indian jewelry, and crafts." Receipts prepared after service of the warrants, however, document the seizure of only one Navajo sand painting and three wooden beaded necklaces. Otherwise, the property seized comprised books, paintings, photographs, and "blank sales tags," as well as one Pendleton blanket. Also seized were appraisal, insurance, title, and mortgage documents for the small (975-square-foot) house Malone had purchased from another friend and trader in Gallup back in the 1980s. Malone's youngest daughter, her husband, and their two children had lived there for years. Malone and his wife were forced to move in with them after being fired by the WNPA and evicted from Hubbell Trading Post.

A second sweep was conducted around the middle of November 2004. Those efforts focused on contacting individuals whose signatures appeared to have been forged on WNPA checks. The interviews confirmed that many, but not all, of the endorsement signatures were made by someone other than the person whose name appeared on the checks. Most of these people had sold rugs, jewelry or other items to or through the trading post, but they were always paid cash. No one claimed they had been cheated or were owed money.

Meanwhile, Yee and his team of investigators were also confronted with the tens of thousands of receipts, ledgers, and other documents seized from Malone's house during the raid, and still more from the trading post. The NPS did not have its own accountants to conduct a forensic audit. So Yee proposed that DeVries, Carpenter assume those duties. Although the firm had already assisted in the search of Malone's residence during the raid, while under contract to WNPA, Yee now wanted to use it under a separate contract to conduct the forensic audit for his investigation.

Yee also recruited a questioned document examiner from the Jefferson County (Colorado) Sheriff's Department to assist in the investigation. She compared "believed known samples" of Malone's handwriting against suspected forged signatures. It was her preliminary opinion that at least some of the endorsement signatures had probably been forged by Billy Malone. But a more conclusive opinion could not be rendered until handwriting samples were secured in a controlled setting for use in comparison and analysis.

Throughout his investigation, by Yee's own account, he received as many as "six to ten" calls a week from LeAnn Simpson soliciting case briefings and updates on the investigation. On at least two occasions Yee also called and briefed Jim Babbitt, so that Babbitt could in turn update the rest of the WNPA board members.[8] Simpson and Babbitt were provided with a long list of detailed information about the developing investigation, including the value of property seized from Malone ("their first estimate was $6–7 million"), how many boxes of documents had been seized from Malone and the trading post ("46 boxes to date"), the number of copies made in the investigation ("to date, 40,000 copies"), progress on the processing of seized rugs, the amount of government funds that had been spent on the investigation, and even what charges might be brought against Malone.[9]

However, there must have been increasingly little in the way of genuinely substantive information to pass along to Babbitt and Simpson, or Snyder and Martin, or even Yee's immediate supervisors. In spite of all the efforts and resources that had been committed in the first year and a half of the investigation, not enough progress had been made to present the case to a grand jury or otherwise file charges against Billy Malone.

One other significant event occurred in the year following the raid on Billy Malone's home and his termination from the WNPA.

Eight months after firing Billy Malone, the WNPA announced it had found a replacement for the old Indian trader. The official press release began,

> Stephen Pickle will become the new Trader at Hubbell Trading Post as of February 21, 2005.

Pickle had no real experience working at a trading post or as an Indian trader. But he had been the retail operations manager and buyer at the MNA for the previous eighteen years and had worked several years before that in the Babbitt stores and gift shops at Grand Canyon National Park.

On the occasion of Pickle's departure from the museum, MNA director Robert Breunig said: "Steve Pickle leaves MNA with 18 years of solid accomplishment. His dedication to artistic quality, his warm personality, and his managerial experience will all be very much missed." Pickle himself was quoted in the press release: "For me, this is the ultimate career move and a chance to enter the history books."

The press release closed with the observation that "Jim Babbitt, chairman of the board of directors of WNPA and a past trustee at MNA, feels that Pickle's experience will 'bring a fresh respect for the crafts of the Southwest and the artists who make them.'"

Breunig's sentiment about Steve Pickle's warm personality was widely shared, even by those loyal to Billy Malone. Almost no one seems to have harbored any resentment or ill will toward Pickle. Almost everyone seemed to agree that he was a decent fellow. But he was most certainly not a trader, as touted by the WNPA. He did not even maintain full-time residence at the trading post, instead commuting back and forth on weekends to his home in Flagstaff.

In hiring Pickle to replace Billy Malone, the WNPA fueled even more speculation about its motives in firing Malone and raised more questions about its commitment to the congressional mandate for Hubbell Trading Post.

From the very beginning, recruitment of a genuine Indian trader to run Hubbell Trading Post had been recognized as a key requirement in fulfilling the NPS's promise to Congress. To reiterate the service's statement in its own administrative record:

> *It would be important to hire a good Indian Trader;* [since] an inexperienced concessioner [*sic*] would soon "make a shambles of the operation." . . . It is the continuity of experienced traders who have worked there . . . [that is] responsible for the success of Hubbell Trading Post since the NPS and SPMA [WNPA] took over.[10]

All three of Steve Pickle's predecessors—Bill Young, Al Grieve, and Billy Malone—were long-time Indian traders from the reservation. Each had been personally recruited by the NPS to carry on the trading tradition at the national historic site.

A shift in the balance of power seemed to be occurring at Hubbell. For the very first time, the WNPA and not the NPS had assumed the role of recruiting and selecting someone to run the trading post. Now, it appeared to many that Jim Babbitt and the WNPA no longer wanted a real Indian trader running it.

Cyd Martin, IMR director of Indian affairs and American culture, reportedly acknowledged that the NPS had relinquished its role in the recruitment process to the WNPA and that there were no longer any real trading posts on the reservation.[11]

A report issued jointly by the NPS and WNPA in April 2005 seemed to confirm that the ideal of employing a real Indian trader at Hubbell had been abandoned and that now the trader at the post would be closer to an interpreter. That report spelled out new guidelines for the operation of Hubbell Trading Post, including a requirement that "the Trader/Manager will continue to wear clothing appropriate to the persona of an Indian Trader."[12]

After all was said and done, the circumstances under which Steve Pickle came to Hubbell Trading Post might not have been the ideal way for him "to enter the history books."

The long-term impacts of these changes at Hubbell Trading Post would not go unnoticed by the larger Navajo community or the outside world. The trading post almost immediately suffered significant declines in local trade and traffic. Other long-term employees and Navajo exhibitors subsequently quit their own jobs with the WNPA in the belief that the firing of Billy Malone signaled that Hubbell's was no longer operating as a real trading post where members of the community would be cared for and made welcome.[13]

Officials at the historic site were flooded with protests in response to Malone's termination. Laura Graves, professor of history at South Plains College in Leveland, Texas, submitted a three-page letter to regional director Steve Martin, spelling out the mistake the NPS and WPNA had made in firing Malone:

> One cannot successfully understand the trading post business with its very complex and convoluted human relations (some of which stretch across generations) from the perspective of Accounting 101 or Management 101—the business does not work like any ordinary business and those who try to force it into post-modern business management practices will do two things: suffer from a profound misunderstanding and destroy the business. If you approach the trading business as if it were a grocery store or a Wal-Mart, you will ruin it as a trading post. I have written a good deal about the process of trading—how deals are struck, how important personal integrity and honor are (for both the buyer and seller), and why the conventional business procedures do not work (. . . see my book *Thomas Varker Keam, Indian Trader*, published by the University of Oklahoma Press . . .).
>
> I would also suggest that the history of trading posts on the Navajo Reservation is a history of repeated situations just like this present one between Bill Malone and the board of Hubbell Trading Post National Historic Monument: at issue is a group of well-meaning and very conscientious individuals who have decided that it is "time for an accounting" of the business practices at the trading post and the trader who was

hired because of his very specialized knowledge and expertise. In this instance, Bill Malone was hired to run Hubbell's Trading Post as a functioning post—it was to be a nonprofit adjunct to the monument, but unlike the monument, the post was charged with the mission to give visitors a glimpse into the past by allowing the business to function as it always has. If Hubbell's Trading Post is to function as a real trading post (and not some virtual reality post or a department in a Wal-Mart) then it must function like a trading post—and the board must understand that and learn to appreciate the complexities of the business instead of condemn it for what it is not. If the decision to allow the post to function as a trading post in all its glorious confusion can not be made by the board, then so be it. Get a store manager who can account for every bean and penny and watch an historic and very important part of our history vanish before your eyes. . . . If, on the other hand, you are true to the mandate that created the relationship between the Hubbell family and the National Park Service, recognize and adjust to the reality that the business may be profoundly confusing to you, but rest comfortable in knowing that you had the very best and most honest trader at the helm when you had Bill Malone behind Hubbell's desk.[14]

In her book *Patterns of Exchange*, anthropologist Teresa J. Wilkins likewise commented on the combined negative effects of the series of business decisions made at Hubbell by the SPMA/WNPA beginning in 1994 and culminating in 2004 with the termination of Billy Malone as trader:

Until recently, the Western National Parks Association (WNPA), which manages the store, had employed trader Bill Malone as the manager. Malone is an experienced reservation trader who knows the intricacies of conducting business in the local community. He often conducts transactions in Navajo language, he knows the trading protocols Navajos expect, and he knows respectful ways of trading with Navajo elders. Malone is also an internationally recognized expert in southwestern Native American arts. But in 2004, WNPA and NPS replaced Malone with a store manager whose background lies in retail sales of Native American arts, rather than more traditional trade.

The WNPA also employs an assistant manager, bookkeeper, and numerous sales clerks, usually young Navajo women. All personnel are trained to answer questions for tourists, but few are able to assist elderly Navajo-speaking customers with their transactions. The NPS is charged with operating the trading post in the traditional frontier manner, a situation that sometimes conflicts with contemporary business practices and goals. For example, until 1996, the post gave credit and occasional loans to community members. They regularly donated merchandise or money to community events such as school fundraisers, parties, and funerals. In 1996 a new policy halted loans and limited credit accounts to artists who regularly sell rugs or jewelry. For long-time customers, a ceiling of fifty dollars was placed on credit accounts. Malone then apparently made loans and donations from his personal funds due to a responsibility he felt as a long-standing trader in the Ganado community. But these practices changed when he was replaced. The Navajo language also began to disappear at that time. Many local trading post patrons complain that the employees are not able to converse with them in Navajo. The need to turn a profit is apparently shifting the goal of the trading post from meeting community needs and selling the finest examples of art, toward becoming another tourist souvenir shop.[15]

The Politics of Change

(Ał ̓ąą hoot ̓áłígíí bik ̓ehgo áhoonííł)

B Y SPRING OF 2005, concerns were growing over the escalating costs of the Hubbell investigation and the lack of real progress. The week of March 14, Reilly brought a group of outsiders to Denver to be briefed by Yee on the investigation and then offer comments and suggestions. I was one of a handful of individuals requested to participate. Only limited case information could be shared, since many court records were still under seal. Still, the presentation was impressive and gave a broad overview using PowerPoint displays, graphs, and photographs of the piles of rugs and jewelry seized during the raid and now in NPS custody. But there were obvious gaps in the case. There had still been no determination about who really owned the seized property. There was also no real proof of a theft of property or funds from the WNPA. Several of us suggested that efforts be refocused on the suspected forgeries and embezzlement, through formal handwriting analysis and examination of bank and other financial records. We also suggested that Yee immediately attempt to question both Billy Malone and his former SPMA/WNPA supervisors.

That same month Mark Aspey left his position in the U.S. Attorney's Office to accept an appointment as the new U.S. magistrate-judge in Flagstaff. The Hubbell Trading Post investigation was transferred down to Phoenix, where another AUSA, Howard Sukenic of the white collar crimes section, took over the case.

A couple of other critical staff and organizational changes occurred that would affect the investigation and eventually, through a series of bizarre twists, lead to my own involvement in the case.

In February 2005 IMR director Steve Martin transferred to Washington, D.C., to assume the position of deputy director of the entire NPS, the number two position in the agency. His wife, Cyd Martin, accompanied him on the move to Washington, D.C., retaining her Indian liaison role for the IMRO in Denver. Nearly concurrently, deputy regional director Mike Snyder was promoted to replace Steve Martin as the new director for the IMR.

Finally, back in 2003 Jim Reilly and I had collaborated in filing a whistle-blower complaint with the OIG about then-NPS Medical Standards Program coordinator Pat Buccello. We suspected she was involved in a travel scam costing the government an estimated $40,000 to $50,000 a year. The complaint alleged that Buccello had convinced her supervisors to change her official duty station from Washington, D.C. (where she worked and maintained an office) to Bar Harbor, Maine, where her husband worked as the chief ranger at Acadia National Park. That enabled her to travel back and forth between the two locations on an almost weekly basis at government expense, staying in expensive area hotels during the weeks she spent working in Washington, D.C.

The OIG investigated and corroborated the allegations. Buccello as well as her own supervisors (who were complicit in authorizing the change in duty station) got in trouble. Nobody was seriously disciplined or lost their job, but they were directed to cease and desist. Buccello's duty station was moved back to national headquarters, and she was told to purchase or rent a home in the D.C. area. She would no longer be able to travel back and forth to Maine, at government expense, to be with her husband. Like Chip Davis, Buccello had for years enjoyed the freedom to move across the country as her husband obtained transfers and promotions and she received special dual-career accommodation in her own assigned duty stations. But with this latest scam revealed, that was all purportedly put to an end.

At the time Reilly and I submitted our report to the OIG, Buccello was not our supervisor. She was not even a special agent. But now she was the NPS NSAC, with line authority over both of us. Our role in reporting the scam to the OIG was supposed to have remained confidential. But more than a year later, around the time Buccello's assignment as NSAC was made permanent, she somehow learned that we had turned her in. When that occurred, we both knew there would be trouble. Reilly sent me the following message on January 24, 2005:

Got more information that Pat Buccello has been offered the [permanent] NPS NSAC position. That could put us in a difficult position given our involvement in bringing to the attention of the IG her "travelgate" issues, i.e., $40K spent in a year on travel, duty station questions, etc.

Further, the Washington office made her move to WASO [Washington, D.C.] not too long after we brought those issues to the IG's attention, which I'm told had her extremely upset for an extended period of time. She clearly didn't want to live apart from her husband and wanted the government to continue to pay for her visits. Add to that the fact that she implied to me in one conversation that she knew we were passing information on. How she could have known that I don't know but we could be in for a difficult time. She's not one to let bygones be bygones.

I immediately followed up with an alert to a trusted contact in the OIG:

If rumors are true and Jim's observations are correct, and Pat Buccello either knows or even merely suspects that Jim and I are responsible for reporting improprieties relating to her old duty station and travel extravagance, then both Jim and I are facing a very ugly situation. As Jim notes, and I'm sure you have heard before, Pat Buccello is well known for being not only ethically challenged, but also extremely vindictive and ruthless. Our own past interactions and experiences (and those of numerous others) with Pat on any number of other issues provide ample evidence of the type of acts and behavior she is capable of.

I know there is probably nothing that can be done before the fact, but I hope you and your office will be attentive and responsive to concerns about the inevitable reprisal that awaits us.

Reilly's speculation about bad things to come was nothing if not prophetic. Within just a month or two of Buccello's assignment as the new, permanent NSAC, Reilly found himself shuffled out of his position as RSAC and placed into an unclassified position with no staff, no duties, and no position description. As of April 28, 2005, Reilly no longer exercised any supervisory control over the Hubbell investigation, Yee, or any of the other special agents across the region. That role transferred to the only remaining supervisory special agent in the entire region who was still in good graces with Pat Buccello, Brian Smith at Yellowstone National Park.

Almost immediately after being unceremoniously booted out his RSAC position, Reilly filed a complaint against Buccello alleging, among other things, reprisal for "whistle-blowing."[1] Also, Reilly was approaching the mandatory retirement age of fifty-seven. His inexplicable removal from a senior position so near the end of his career would look suspicious and damage his prospects for postretirement employment opportunities. Reilly suspected that removal from his position as RSAC had, at least in part, been a way for Buccello to finally stick it to him and show him what payback is all about. Considering the stalling tactics and resistance normally employed by the NPS in response to employee grievances, Reilly's claim was resolved with remarkable speed. While he was not reinstated as RSAC, he was given the working title of assistant special agent-in-charge (reporting to Buccello) and authorized to resume work on the Hubbell investigation, albeit no longer as Yee's supervisor.

Buccello's revamping of the program over which she now exercised permanent control had not quite ended with moves made against Reilly. Concurrent with Reilly's reassignment, I was approached with an offer from Buccello for my own unique dual-career opportunity. Buccello directed Reilly to communicate the offer to me because, as he explained it, "Pat knows you don't trust her."

At that time I was stationed on the South Rim of Grand Canyon National Park as the supervisory special agent. Along with a staff of agents in that office, I also supervised agents stationed in both Page and Flagstaff. My staff and I were responsible for conducting criminal investigations for parks located throughout northern Arizona and Utah.

My wife and I met and were married at the Grand Canyon, where she also worked. In the latter portion of our shared tenure on the South Rim, my wife applied for and was selected to become the assistant superintendent at Canyon de Chelly National Monument on the Navajo Reservation, some 160 miles away from what had been our home for nearly ten years. In light of our standing within NPS political circles, the prospect of a special dual-career accommodation had never entered into the equation for us. That meant we would both be doing a lot of driving back and forth on our own time at our own expense to be together on weekends and holidays.

The situation was difficult but not unworkable, especially since I was already responsible for providing investigative support to national parks throughout northern Arizona, including parks on and around the reservation. Going back to 1995, I already had a ten-year history of working cooperatively on the reservation with colleagues in the FBI Indian Country Unit, arguably the most hard-working and unrecognized group of agents in the FBI. My relationship with the Navajo Criminal Investigations Unit and tribal prosecutor's office was at least as close; we had worked together on any number of investigations and had cosponsored training sessions, and I had assisted it with the implementation of a number of initiatives designed to increase the capacity of tribal officials to prosecute non-Indian offenders through the federal courts. The Navajo chief of criminal investigations and I met regularly, and she had actually recruited me to become the first NPS official to join the Indian country section of the International Association of Chiefs of Police. That history of cooperation suggested there would continue to be frequent opportunities to work cases and projects on the reservation and save government time and expense by staying with my wife, in Chinle, instead of hotels in the area, or driving repeatedly back and forth to the South Rim in a single week. What's more, I knew that Canyon de Chelly experienced one of the highest and most violent crime rates in the entire national park system, but that the crime rate had been artificially suppressed by deliberate efforts to prevent the accurate documentation of crime statistics. The park had been largely neglected by the NPS over the decades because it was "just the Rez," and most victims of crimes within the monument, including NPS employees, are local residents instead of tourists. Instead of working with law enforcement officials to address the larger problem, the NPS simply restricted tourist access from areas of the park that experienced too much crime and violence. With my wife now there, I hoped we might at last be able to collaboratively address the issue and turn things around.

That vision for change and continued collaboration was about to be put to the test. Now, with Pat Buccello as the new, permanent NSAC, I was being told that unless I agreed to retire by the end of the year I would be restricted in my ability to work Indian country crimes at all, including those occurring within Canyon de Chelly and the other NPS sites for which I had previously been responsible. But if I did agree to retire by January 2006, I could be detailed to a "temporary" duty station in Chinle to finish the last six to eight months of my career as the sole and solitary member—both supervisor and staff—of the service's own "Indian country unit."

Human resource specialists in the federal government caution supervisors against ever suggesting or pressuring an employee to retire. Doing so is considered improper and a prohibited personnel practice, exposing the supervisor to a legitimate grievance. I knew this when I received Buccello's offer. I also knew that protesting the special conditions of the illegal action would be a waste of time. I was torn.

The prospect of continuing to live in one place with my wife and avoiding the hassles of expensive weekly drives back and forth was extremely appealing. Also, I was tired. Living in the closed government community that exists on the South Rim of Grand Canyon National Park can be a draining experience. Beyond dealing with the usual bizarre politics and interpersonal dynamics that most residents deal with, I was also continually doing battle with senior managers insistent on doing things their own "Park Service" way. Open hostilities existed between me and the most recent superintendent. He took particular exception when I provided the OIG with information related to its ongoing, multiyear investigation of massive contracting fraud at the park involving Pacific General, Inc. (PGI) that had been allowed to occur through neglect and incompetence under the superintendent's watch. The superintendent was further angered when the OIG asked me to assist in conducting interviews with key park staff implicated in the case. That led to a number of heated phone calls from the superintendent and his chief ranger to Buccello and other Washington officials, demanding to have me pulled from the case and prevented from supplying any further assistance to my OIG counterparts.[2] The superintendent certainly wanted me gone. And though I no longer worked for him (because of the reorganization and reforms), he made his feelings abundantly clear through an ongoing series of maneuvers carried out by his staff, designed to make both work and personal life difficult. It also did not help that he and I lived virtually across the street from one another, at minimum forced to drive past each other's house every day going to and from work.

I was not ready to retire either emotionally or financially, and I was still several years away from the mandatory law enforcement retirement age of fifty-seven, but I was eligible.

After considerable reflection and discussion with my wife, I apprehensively accepted Buccello's "offer." By July 2005, my wife and I were back living together under one roof on the Navajo Reservation, in the middle of some of the most spectacular scenery in the entire southwest.

▲▼▲

Meanwhile, more or less back on track and no longer distracted by the combined headaches of battling Pat Buccello and attempting to manage and supervise an increasingly dysfunctional program, Reilly focused his attention on the Hubbell investigation with a renewed sense of interest and enthusiasm. In reviewing the work Yee had done, Reilly started to question some of the legal decisions that had been made related to jurisdiction. The change in prosecutors also signaled an opportunity to reevaluate the case and consider new strategies and leads. The need for a fresh look was reinforced by alarm from both Washington, D.C., and regional officials about the enormous amount of time and money being expended on the investigation.

On June 2, 2005, Buccello sent an e-mail message to Yee in which she revealed her growing frustration and impatience with case progress and put pressure on Yee to surrender some of the control he exercised over the investigation. Her message read:

Clyde,

I understand that you recently briefed Regional Special Agent-in-Charge Brian Smith on the status of the Hubbell case. I hope you know that I respect the complexity this case presents to you and the support staff you have assisting you. While I am certainly not an expert in fraud cases, the few I have been involved in have exposed me to how complex, tiresome, frustrating, and time-intensive they can be. I learned to make friends with my peers in the IRS and that paid off exponentially!

Brian expressed to me your concern that you are not being allowed to manage this case as you would like. You do need to know that the expense of investigating this case is causing concern by my bosses, the region, and by me. Therefore, we are going to have to feel comfortable that we are balancing limited resources, agency needs, and the reasonable prediction of closure with prosecution in a timely manner.

Don [Coelho, NPS chief ranger] and I have assured IMR that you are working with subject matter experts from other agencies, including the U.S. Postal Service, FBI, and IRS in addition to the county. It sounds like you are working well with the AUSA which is vital. Don has requested a concise, to the point briefing on this case status. We don't need a lot of background, the complexities have been explained to us, but we do need an up to date diagnosis and prognosis immediately. It is reasonable that the IMRO [IMR Regional Office] has a stake in how their monies are being spent.

I have directed SSA Jim Reilly to take a more active role in this case and am assigning him as the case agent with you as the co-case agent. This is the scenario we utilized effectively for large cases on the ARPA [Archaeological Resources Protection Act] Task Force. Moving Jim into a more "hands on" role in this case will provide you with more support on a day to day basis. I have also asked Jim to bring SSA [Paul] Berkowitz into the case to utilize Paul's valuable contacts with Indian Country agencies. I understand you will be working with the evidence backlog and connecting again with the AUSA next week; please don't hesitate to call me if you have any questions or concerns.

In the months before Buccello's message to Yee, Reilly shared with me his own growing questions and concerns about the case, including frustrations about the lack of cooperation from Yee and limited amount of information he was sharing. I also learned that back when Reilly was still his supervisor, Yee had disobeyed orders by going on unauthorized travel to attend a training session, after being explicitly told he could not go. Reilly was forced to impose a disciplinary period of time off without pay for insubordination. After that, according to Reilly, Yee became completely uncooperative and uncommunicative. The situation only became worse when Reilly was moved out of his position as RSAC. Since then, he had rarely if ever seen Yee and certainly did not know how his time was being spent.

With the situation deteriorating, Reilly apparently succeeded in convincing Pat Buccello to reduce the level of autonomy enjoyed by Yee. Reilly simultaneously convinced Buccello to bring me in on the investigation to officially consult and assist. That provided Reilly with the freedom he needed to share previously restricted case information with me and solicit my thoughts and opinions.

In early June 2005 while I was moving out of our house on the South Rim, Reilly sent a draft version of a case summary he was preparing for presentation to the new federal prosecutor assigned to the case in Phoenix. Reilly wanted me to review the draft and offer both editing and content suggestions. That gave me the opportunity to get up to speed on basic case activity.

A week or two later, Reilly and Yee traveled to Phoenix to meet with the new case prosecutor, Howard Sukenic. They presented Sukenic with the summary Reilly had prepared and laid out details of the developing case. Yee took the lead in the presentation, but Reilly periodically chimed in with his own apprehensions about jurisdiction as well as the specific charges under consideration. These unresolved issues reportedly worried Sukenic. Otherwise the meeting seemed to proceed reasonably well. That is, until Reilly had to remind Yee to address one additional sensitive issue.

Toward the end of Yee's presentation, Reilly asked Yee if he intended to tell Sukenic about the problem with the evidence and chain of custody. With a measure of annoyance, Yee told Reilly that he didn't want to bring that up right now.

Yee had not intended to tell Sukenic about Morton's memorandum documenting the break in the chain of custody or his own instructions to WACC personnel to change the locks, break into the evidence vault, and begin processing evidence. Now, prodded by Reilly, Yee was compelled to share the sequence of events with Sukenic. Yee speculated that the "break" was not really fatal to the chain of custody but a simple problem that could be overcome through additional interviews and documentation. Yee also didn't think that Morton's memo would need to be shared with the defense. Sukenic corrected him on that legal matter, clarifying for Yee that Morton's memo most certainly would be subject to discovery.[3]

However simple or unimportant the matter may have seemed to Yee, his failure to include the topic in his own presentation created a bigger problem that would dog him throughout the investigation. Yee's explanation notwithstanding, Sukenic made note of his concerns over the level of candor Yee exhibited in his case presentation.

This incident with Sukenic was not the only one creating credibility problems for Yee. While the Hubbell investigation was underway, Yee worked at least one other theft investigation during which he had a similar run-in with another federal prosecutor in Flagstaff.

In that unrelated but concurrent investigation, Yee obtained a tearful confession from an NPS employee at Hubbell Trading Post, who admitted to stealing several hundred dollars in government funds from an envelope temporarily stored in another employee's desk. Yee convinced the prosecutor to file charges for the misdemeanor theft. This was a special accommodation, as such matters were normally handled by simply firing the employee or by applying other administrative remedies instead of by arresting them. But Yee told the prosecutor the NPS wanted to make an example with this case. Filing charges would demonstrate to other employees at the trading post that incidents of this type would be taken very seriously.

A criminal complaint was authorized and the woman was brought in to face charges. She entered a plea of guilty. Sentencing was scheduled for a later date, after preparation of a standard presentence report that would provide the court with background information and recommendations. But the prosecutor became angered when he found out the woman was not even going to be fired by NPS. The superintendent at Hubbell Trading Post was not even aware the woman was being prosecuted and had, in fact, been told that Yee was going to "go light" on the woman. Yee had failed to disclose those important points until challenged by the prosecutor, very late in the game. Claims that the NPS wanted the employee prosecuted to serve as an example for others did not ring true. To make his own point to Yee, the prosecutor filed a motion to vacate the woman's guilty plea, drop all charges, and dismiss the case against the woman altogether. The woman walked away free and clear and returned to work at the park visitor's center. Yee's own supervisor, Reilly, was never told about this incident or the reputation Yee had established with at least one federal prosecutor in Flagstaff.[4]

On July 21, 2005, approximately one month after his meeting with Reilly and Yee, Sukenic followed up with his own memorandum. The memorandum was blunt in its assessment of the investigation:

> From a prosecutorial standpoint, the investigation has many holes that need to be filled before anybody could file this case and be assured of a reasonable likelihood of conviction. For instance, the witness statements alleging theft on the part of Mr. Malone are to [sic] broad and non-specific to prove any allegation of theft. The checks need to have the endorsements reviewed by a handwriting expert. Thereafter, if the endorsement comes back to Malone, in conjunction with the artisan's statement that they did not receive these checks, this would be sufficient to go forward. Therefore, this investigative work needs to be done.
>
> Furthermore, Mr. Malone's bank statements need to be analyzed and reviewed in order to see whether questionable income was deposited. To my knowledge this has not been done. Also, the items found in Malone's house, which has [sic] been valued in the millions of dollars, need to be examined and analyzed as to whether or not they were stolen from the trading post. To my knowledge, this has not been done.
>
> Finally, I realize that Mr. Malone, as your report reflects, is represented by counsel. However, it appears that no one has contacted Mr. Malone's counsel to see if he would be willing to submit to an interview. This is essential, and to my knowledge has not been done.[5]

Sukenic's evaluation, coming more than a full year after the government raid on Billy Malone's Hubbell Trading Post residence and expenditure of between a half million and a million dollars (including dedicated salary costs), signaled trouble and conveyed a new sense of urgency with respect to the investigation. Compounding these pressures was the looming January 2006 retirement of Jim Reilly and the need to either hastily close the case or at least identify a replacement to supervise the investigation.

Stalemate and the Hand Off

(Dahidiiyá)

B Y SEPTEMBER 2005 I was having real regrets over my announced retirement, for two compelling reasons. First, I was experiencing anxiety over the
prospect of a dramatically reduced retirement income. Working for just a few
more years would significantly improve that situation.

Second, we were starting to see real progress in addressing criminal activity
at Canyon de Chelly. I had secured support from the U.S. marshal in Arizona
to participate as a special deputy on the fugitive task force. I was concurrently
expanding my participation in cooperative efforts with the FBI's Indian Country
Unit, Safe Trails task force, and Navajo tribal methamphetamine initiatives, targeting gang, drug, and related activity both within and adjacent to the monument. Both of these ventures enabled me to participate to an even greater extent
in interagency law enforcement activities beyond NPS boundaries. More importantly, in working with both task forces, I was able to draw attention to activities
occurring *within* NPS boundaries and attract personnel from other agencies to
come in and assist. In focusing attention on Canyon de Chelly and the other
NPS sites located on the Navajo Reservation I was able to document one of the
highest murder rates in the entire park system, not to mention rates of nonfatal
shootings, knifings, and beatings. Meanwhile, I also learned that NPS staffing
and funding at Canyon de Chelly was among the lowest in the nation, nearly ten
times less than enjoyed at other NPS sites with equivalent acreage and visitation.

Documenting the level of historical neglect by the NPS was the first step in turning that situation around.

The satisfaction I was feeling at the prospect of making a real difference and improving conditions on the reservation, and particularly within and adjacent to the NPS sites, was invigorating. I was keenly aware of what a unique and challenging experience it was to be living and working as a *bilagáana* law enforcement officer, deep in the heart of the amazing Navajo Reservation. My own satisfaction was compounded by independent efforts successfully initiated by my wife to obtain substantially more funding for the park, with the goal of recruiting from within the Navajo community for not only law enforcement positions but also for fire, EMS, resource management, and other long-neglected program areas. Over time, that could benefit both the park and the community at large. In just the short time she'd been there, she'd secured funding to establish "the *Diné* crew," comprised of nearly thirty talented and incredibly hard-working residents of the greater Chinle community, to work on vegetation and fire-related resource management projects. Several other positions were established and filled with fully credentialed but previously underemployed biologists from the immediate area. It was an exciting time in the community.

There's a huge difference between living *next* to the reservation in the familiar comfort and convenience of tourist towns like Grand Canyon, Flagstaff, and Page, or even modern border towns like Farmington, Gallup, or Grants, and actually living *on* the reservation, day in, day out, especially in a remote community like Chinle. Analogies to third-world countries are not overstated. Over the course of time you just see and experience things, good and bad, you would otherwise never imagine or believe and would certainly be hard pressed to explain to outsiders. I was learning more every day and feeling more fulfilled than I had in years. I didn't want to stop, and on reflection, didn't see any particularly good reason to do so. I had honestly changed my mind.

Buccello was predictably enraged when I sent word of my new decision. She accused me of breaking my word and, ironically, said she should have known better than to trust me. I told her I had changed my mind and rejected the idea of being illegally pressured into an early retirement. We were in a stalemate. And I was gambling.

Having been merely detailed into my self-created Indian country assignment, I still officially occupied my old position based at the Grand Canyon. The worst Buccello could do without another major reorganization and the expense of an official move was force me to return to the South Rim to resume my supervisory duties there. I was betting that the superintendent at Grand Canyon would do almost anything in his power to keep that from happening and that Buccello didn't have the guts or the clout to take him on in her effort to make me pay. I told Buccello I was prepared to move back to the South Rim if she would not allow me to continue my work in Indian country. She told me to prepare to go back to the Grand Canyon.

On Tuesday, November 22, 2005, I received a telephone call from Brian Smith, the newly designated IMR special agent-in-charge (Jim Reilly's recent successor and now Yee's direct supervisor). Smith explained that the Hubbell investigation was floundering. The NPS was running out of money as well as patience. Both Jim Reilly and former regional chief ranger Fitzgerald (who had since been promoted to assistant superintendent at Great Smoky Mountains National Park) had made the case that I should take over the investigation, citing my experience managing complex investigations and my familiarity with the Navajo Reservation and Indian country law enforcement. Smith wanted to know if I'd accept the case. I asked how I was supposed to effectively work the Hubbell investigation if Buccello was going to make me move back to the South Rim at Grand Canyon. Smith replied, "That'll go away."

Smith explained that if I did a good job and arrested Malone without any more expense or delay, Buccello would leave me alone and allow me to remain in my Indian country assignment, indefinitely.

While I didn't have any great confidence in the deal I was being offered, it did seem like a reasonable way to at least extend my time in Indian country. Besides, what little I knew about the case sounded interesting. I have always been fascinated by the history of the American West. This would be a way to immerse myself in a piece of that history while sorting through a case that looked interesting for all of its complex cultural and jurisdictional issues. Frankly, at this stage, I also accepted the likelihood that Billy Malone probably had done most of the things of which he was accused. I was eager to take on the challenge of attempting to make the case at which others had been unsuccessful.

I accepted the offer, breathing a small sigh of relief for the time it bought me and for the at least temporary relief it gave me from the long battles with Pat Buccello.

A conference call took place the following Monday (November 28) in which NPS chief ranger Don Coelho, Pat Buccello, Brian Smith, and I participated. The general tone of the call was amicable enough, and no mention was made of the behind-the-scenes politics. Instead, discussion centered on how to move forward with the Hubbell case and how I would transition into the lead. However, I was certainly cautious throughout the call and sensitive to what was being said. Of particular concern to me were comments I was hearing about expectations as to how the case would evolve to a conclusion justifying the hundreds of thousands of dollars already invested and the assumptions that criminal charges would be filed against Malone. Still very much on my mind were Smith's comments suggesting that my assignment to this case (and relief from threats to move me back to Grand Canyon) was predicated on the expectation that I would "do a good job" and arrest Malone without unnecessary delays or expenses. I didn't challenge anyone on the call, but I did make notes about some of the comments being made, for my own reference and use.

The call ended on a positive note, with everyone expressing satisfaction with the agreed-on transition. The next step was for me to get fully briefed on the case and brought up to date.

Smith suggested that I get hold of Jim Reilly to talk some more after the conference call and that I might want to consider making a trip to Lakewood to meet with Yee for a one-on-one briefing. Reilly and I spoke that same afternoon, and I picked his brain for ideas and solicited his input on issues he felt needed to be addressed. I also obtained the name and phone number of the new (third) AUSA, Rob Long, in Phoenix who had only recently been assigned to the case.

One point Reilly stressed was the need to interview SPMA's former chief financial officer, John Pearson. Reilly had been advocating for this interview for quite some time in the belief that Pearson might be able to shed light on a number of questions still unanswered about Malone's business practices. However, Yee had brushed this recommendation aside. Reilly, no longer able to direct Yee's activities, had been unsuccessful in convincing him to pursue the interview.

The week of December 7 I drove up to Lakewood to meet in person with Reilly and then spend time with Yee to receive a full briefing on the investigation and on his activities. Talking with Reilly provided me with some key insights that would play a role in how I approached the case.

The next day I returned to the Lakewood office to meet with Yee for the briefing he'd been instructed to prepare. Also there, to my surprise, was OIG agent Jamie Howard, who had been brought into the investigation to assist.

Howard had joined the investigation in response to a request for OIG assistance in reviewing financial records. Howard was based in the OIG's Lakewood office, a short distance from NPS headquarters. Since having been assigned to the case, she had apparently been working as a full-blown partner with Yee. She was not merely assisting with financial records but also conducting interviews with a variety of witnesses in the field.

Yee provided me with a large notebook containing written case summaries and copies of the sworn affidavits used to support and the search warrants authorizing the raid of Malone's house, car, and storage lockers. The notebook also contained a list of twenty-one witnesses interviewed in the case and copies of their respective interview reports. Also listed as "targets" and suspects in the investigation but not yet interviewed were "William" Gene Malone and Russ Griswold Jr. (treasurer at Griswold's Trading Post).

Other than the interview reports and rough summaries with which I was presented, there was apparently no form of comprehensive or cohesive report that tracked progress on the investigation. I asked Yee and Howard a series of questions about the current status of the investigation, as well as what activities or interviews they planned for the future.

I specifically asked Yee about the seizure of what was estimated to be millions of dollars worth of rugs, jewelry, and other property from Malone's residence, when none of those items appeared to be authorized for seizure under the search warrant I was now examining. Yee explained that this had been done as a matter of expedience in the belief that the property was probably stolen. Yee gloated that he could even prove Malone had intended to keep the "stolen" property, because throughout the search and seizure Malone had protested to investigators that the items they were taking were his, his wife's, his son-in-law's, or a friend's, and didn't belong to the WNPA or the trading post. This was the first time I heard about the calls Yee made to Aspey, the guidance Aspey had reportedly given about what property to seize, Yee's interpretation of that guidance, and his rationale for seizing entire stacks of rugs and boxes of jewelry, even if only some of those rugs or pieces of jewelry bore tags associated with Hubbell Trading Post. This was but the first of several different (and sometimes conflicting) accounts I would hear in the course of my investigation.

When I later had the chance to review the materials Yee provided, I noticed that he had not included copies of the receipts he was required to leave with Malone following the raid. Later still, when I asked Yee to provide me with copies of those receipts, he was unable to locate them in his files. Instead, I was forced to approach Malone's own attorney, who promptly sent me copies of the documents he had. Those documents revealed the less-than-comprehensive inventory that had been conducted on scene. There was no itemized listing or even quantification of items seized from Malone's residence.

I asked Yee about the allegation of false statements (18 USC 1001) contained in his search warrant application and affidavit, noting that I didn't see anything in the affidavit or other case files suggesting that Malone had ever been interviewed or made statements of any kind, oral or written, to federal officials or their agents or representatives. Yee confirmed that Billy Malone had never been interviewed but justified the insertion of the allegation in the documents with the flip explanation, "That's just something they always throw in."

I also asked Yee why he had used the Jefferson County Sheriff's Department instead of the U.S. Secret Service to conduct the handwriting analysis. He responded that it was a slow and difficult process to secure the services of the Secret Service. It was more convenient for him to use the local sheriff's department.

Because neither Yee nor Howard mentioned it, I inquired about the prospect for an interview with John Pearson at the Grand Canyon, as well as Malone's other former supervisors and friends. As Reilly had predicted, Yee dismissed this as a very low priority if not a complete waste of time, suggesting that the other leads he and Howard wanted to pursue back in New Mexico would be far more productive. Yee and Agent Howard reinforced this point by noting that when they'd approached Malone's close friend and fellow Indian trader Bruce Burnham for an interview, he had refused to speak with them. Yee added, with a chuckle, "I don't think he liked us very much," and Howard echoed the amusement.

I also asked if Yee or anyone else had approached former WNPA executive director Tim Priehs for an interview. Yee again answered no, explaining that according to the people at the WNPA, Priehs dropped out of sight and no one had heard from him in years. Priehs had reportedly moved to Ft. Collins, but no one really knew how to get in touch with him.

I agreed to Yee and Howard's proposal to follow through with their plans for more interviews in New Mexico. However, noting that it had been more than a year and a half since the original allegations of forgery were made, I said I also wanted them to obtain subpoenas to secure controlled handwriting samples from Billy Malone and any other suspects or witnesses for use in formal handwriting analysis. We also needed to determine whether Malone was hiding or laundering money, so I directed Yee to identify banks or other financial institutions from which we should subpoena records. But I told Yee I would personally follow up on both the John Pearson and Tim Priehs interviews. I also planned on driving to Tucson to introduce myself to LeAnn Simpson and talk with her about her initial report and complaint about Billy Malone.

My decision to have Yee and Howard continue pursuing the leads they'd identified was deliberate. I did not want to divert them in the direction I wanted to pursue. Based on the comments they'd made while providing their briefing, I was concerned they might not give the attention I thought was warranted to interviews with John Pearson or others with whom Malone might have had positive relations. I did not want to risk missing out on a chance to uncover critical information by directing agents who were not really interested in eliciting information or hearing what was being said or offered by witnesses to conduct the interviews. Even if the interviews yielded denials of any relevant knowledge, or only statements supportive of Malone and his activities, or even lies intended to shield Malone from culpability, complete documentation of that type of information from prospective defense witnesses would be critical to conducting a thorough investigation, resolving false or conflicting statements, preparing a prosecution, and responding to defense arguments that would inevitably surface during a trial. The lack of effort that had been made on this front would prove to be a major issue affecting the integrity of the investigation. Over time, I would discover that key information and evidence had been overlooked or, worse, altogether omitted from the record. I summarized these observations and concerns nearly a year later in a cover letter submitted October 23, 2006, to AUSA Rob Long along with my own final report:

> Several factors contributed to my decision to personally conduct the subsequent interviews and inquiries in this case, rather than making significant assignments to Agents Yee and Howard, or others who had participated on the investigative task force. First, I was aware that contemporaneous with this investigation, Agent Yee had been disciplined for insubordination by his former supervisor, SSA Reilly. I had concerns over the effect this might have on his credibility as a witness (e.g., Giglio/Henthorn).
>
> Second, the briefings I was provided by Agents Yee and Howard left me with the distinct impression there had been a general disinterest or reluctance to effectively interview potential defense witnesses, or to pursue or document leads that might disclose exculpatory information or provide alternative explanations for observed or suspected conduct. This impression was reinforced by expressions of amusement from both Agents Yee and Howard when relating their contacts with witnesses who responded unfavorably when approached for an interview, were hostile, or uncooperative.

Finally, I had heard anecdotal accounts of "cultural insensitivity" exhibited during early NPS operations related to this case resulting from the manner in which task force participants "swept" into the community in and around HUTR, and reportedly used aggressive or intimidating interviewing techniques; creating considerable tensions and negative feelings within the Navajo community and among HTP staff. . . . While I did not independently verify or investigate any of these accounts, I wanted to make sure none of these concerns compromised progress on this investigation, and wanted to restore a measure of community trust in order to secure productive interviews with previously reluctant or uncooperative witnesses and suspects.[1]

Also, of course, I was already aware of Morton's memorandum documenting problems in the chain of custody for items of evidence stored at the NPS facility in Tucson. I also knew about Yee's run-in with the federal prosecutor who dismissed the case against Yee's other theft suspect, the NPS employee who had admitted to stealing cash from Hubbell Trading Post NHS.

In spite of these issues, at this point I had no particular reason to believe that Billy Malone was not a legitimate suspect or that the investigation would not eventually result in anything other than an arrest and (hopefully) conviction; if not for possessing stolen property, than for at least some of the other offenses Yee had identified in the affidavit or his briefing statements.

The following week, on December 14, I put in a call to Rob Long. The fact that Long was also new to the case and not vested in the investigation suggested to my mind that he could offer a fresh perspective and approach. He might be a good partner with whom to develop a new strategy for the case. We spoke only briefly but shared information about our respective backgrounds. Long had recently transferred to the U.S. Attorney's Office from the Securities Exchange Commission where he had worked as a government attorney. While he did not have an extensive background in criminal prosecutions, he did have considerable experience working on financial schemes and crimes. He had only recently received the Hubbell case file and was in the process of reviewing it. We tentatively scheduled a meeting for sometime after the holidays and agreed to stay in touch in the meanwhile with any thoughts or developments relating to the case.

The holidays passed with no significant activity on the investigation and just a few telephone calls with Reilly and Yee back in Lakewood and with Rob Long. I spent the majority of my free time reviewing the case summaries and reports

Yee had provided me and researching various statutes cited in court documents. I reviewed other statutes that might be applied, as well as court decisions that might have a bearing on previous case activity.

Of particular interest was what appeared to be a major omission in both the sworn affidavit Yee had submitted and the resulting June 2004 search warrant issued by the court. Neither made any mention of suspicions or probable cause relating to stolen rugs, jewelry, pots, baskets, or other Indian arts and crafts. The search warrant authorized the seizure of only financial documents and currency, not rugs or jewelry. Also, while I was no expert on cooperating associations or cooperative agreements, the spin represented in Yee's affidavit about the financial relationship between the NPS and the WNPA did not seem right. I questioned whether a theft or embezzlement of WNPA funds would indeed constitute a concurrent theft of federal funds, and I was becoming increasingly convinced that the seizure of the real property had been inappropriate and illegal, regardless of what Yee claimed had been authorized by the AUSA. The court opinions I was reviewing, and even instructional materials distributed by the U.S. Attorney's Office seemed to support my growing apprehensions.[2] And while I didn't want to be in the position of challenging or disputing the advice and opinion of an AUSA (who was now a federal magistrate-judge), I remained convinced that the millions of dollars in property seized from Malone's residence would only have been legal and admissible as potential evidence if Yee and his agents had prepared a new affidavit citing new or additional probable cause and secured a separate warrant through established procedures.

These were just some of the issues I intended to focus on as I began my own review of the investigation that had been conducted so far and that, for better or worse, I had now inherited.

A Closer Look

(Yéego nánél' įh)

I GREETED 2006 WITH relief, a renewed sense of purpose, and a desire to immerse myself in the investigation I had taken over.

The second week of January I took off on a road trip to meet and talk with several key figures in the investigation, including LeAnn Simpson, Rob Long in Phoenix, and Mark Aspey in Flagstaff. I also made arrangements to meet with Susan Morton and have her coordinate a visit to the WACC in Tucson so I could see for myself the now famous collection of items seized from the home of Billy Malone.

Tuesday morning, January 10, I met with Simpson at her office in WNPA headquarters in Oro Valley, Arizona. I briefly explained the circumstances under which I had assumed supervision of the Hubbell investigation and asked her to indulge me by recounting the observations that had led her to file the report with the NPS.

Simpson was cordial and seemed relieved that I was taking over the investigation. She expressed frustrations that the investigation had taken so long and was not yet resolved. She voiced her own questions about the type and volume of property seized from Malone's residence, noting that she "had thought the purpose of the search was primarily to obtain ledgers and other records necessary to conduct an audit and attempt to make sense of records and accounts." She acknowledged the conflict of interest created not only by her assuming custody of property seized from Malone's residence and assisting in its transport but also in the participation of the WNPA's own contracted accounting firm to assist in the search and investigation.

Simpson shared yet another disturbing piece of information. After the investigation was underway, at the specific request of the NPS, WNPA issued a new and separate contract to have Mari DeVries conduct the forensic audit in support of the criminal investigation. That contract, executed August 2, 2004, obligated the WNPA to pay DeVries, Carpenter as much as $75,000 for six to nine months work (plus an additional $200 per hour for depositions and court appearances) to perform "a forensic examination as a result of certain allegations which have come to the attention of Western National Parks Association . . . working closely with and under the direction at times of the investigators with the National Park Service."[1]

Simpson was telling me that the WNPA helped pay for the NPS criminal investigation targeting Billy Malone. The WPNA had even agreed to pay for testimony that might be presented against Malone by its own accountants, all at the request of the NPS. In this instance, the conflict of interest was amplified since DeVries had performed the WNPA's audits and financial accounting reviews at Hubbell Trading Post for the several preceding years. If Simpson's suspicions about Malone forging checks and embezzling enormous sums of money were correct, it meant that DeVries (and all the other contracted accounting firms before them) had failed to detect those same losses during their prior audits.

By actively participating in the criminal investigation, the WNPA had likely violated NPS policies that strictly limit its role in service activities. Again, those policies clearly state that,

> Association employees are not authorized to undertake any government function or activity on behalf of the Service beyond routine visitor information services or other activities authorized by the Cooperating Association Agreement, supplements to the agreement, or agreements for voluntary services.[2]

Also, in requesting that the WNPA donate funds to support the Hubbell investigation, NPS officials had very likely violated their own policies (and possibly federal laws) regarding contributions from cooperating associations. Under those policies, a regional director has the authority to accept donations only for major research projects, land acquisitions, interpretive/educational facilities, and historic preservation/restoration projects.[3]

Yet another point I wanted to clarify was the financial relationship that existed between the NPS and the WNPA. Simpson confirmed that in the strictest sense of the word no contract even existed between the two entities. Rather, the WNPA maintained a broad cooperative agreement with the NPS, authorizing it to utilize government facilities at a variety of NPS sites for "the production and sale of materials of interpretive, educational, and thematic value and for the presentation of specified and approved programs relating to the interpretive themes or areas." There was a separate supplemental agreement specific to operations at Hubbell Trading Post. But Simpson confirmed that neither agreement obligated the WNPA to pay or even donate any amount of money to the NPS. She denied that she'd ever suggested anything different to Yee or anyone else. In fact, according to Simpson, I was the first person in the entire investigation who had asked to see copies of the agreements.

When I finally received them, I was able to confirm that neither document obligated the WNPA to provide the NPS with funds or financial support of any kind, at any level or amount. There was certainly no reference to figures such as "6%" or "6.5%" of revenues that WNPA was obligated to pay the government. In fact, the only mention of contributions to the NPS in either of the agreements is in clause 22 of the general agreement. It states only that the NPS agrees to "determine jointly with the association the appropriate level of *aid* to the Service based upon the nature and extent of the association's activities and the need of the Service" (emphasis added). Clause 2 of the Hubbell Trading Post agreement clarifies that "all net profits from the trading operation will, directly or indirectly, support the educational, interpretive, and scientific research programs of the National Park Service." The clear distinction maintained between WNPA and NPS funds is emphasized with the additional notation that "revenue that the Association receives in excess of expenses will be deposited in the Association's general account and will, directly or indirectly, support educational, interpretive, and scientific research programs of the National Park Service for the benefit of park visitors."

While Simpson did not provide it, there is, in fact, a third document that addresses the amount or percentage of funds deposited in WNPA's various "Interpretive Donation Accounts." That document is not a part of any contract or signed agreement between the NPS and the WNPA. Instead, it is a statement of internal WNPA policy contained within that organization's *Area Handbook*. It is this internal WNPA policy alone that references a "grant" to each park where WNPA operates, "equal to 6.5% of its prior year sales or $2,000, whichever is greater," and it reiterates that WNPA funds may be expended as "donations" in support of a park's interpretive or other operations, but only upon the written request submitted by a park superintendent, and approval by the Executive Director of WNPA.[4]

These discoveries confirmed my original suspicions that a major error had occurred early in the investigation. The statements provided by Simpson and verified in the cooperative agreements suggested that the warrant authorizing seizure of property from Malone's residence was plagued with problems far beyond mere technicalities. Those warrants were at minimum based on incorrect information, if not patently false statements, contained in the supporting sworn affidavit submitted by Yee.

Equally perplexing was the apparent failure to even attempt an examination of the agreements earlier in the investigation. Even if Yee had been reluctant or simply embarrassed to ask for copies from Simpson, he could easily have obtained the documents back at his own office. Copies of every agreement with every cooperating association throughout the entire IMR were just across the hall, next door to Yee's office, in files maintained by the regional coordinator for cooperating associations.

As for the hundreds of rugs and thousands of pieces of jewelry seized during the raid, Simpson claimed that "no one could ever track or make sense out of the paper trail or accounting practices that had existed at HTP during Billy Malone's tenure . . . [and] . . . that they would never be able to account for property ownership, particularly with respect to consignment property."[5]

Later that afternoon I drove back down to Tucson to meet with Morton at the WACC. This was my first time at the center. Since Morton knew the site managers and had helped arrange use of the facility for the investigation, she seemed like the logical person to show me around.

Appropriate security appeared to be in place, as we signed in to the building and were escorted through a series of locked and alarmed passageways to the large vault where the evidence was being stored. The climate-controlled room was filled with enormous rolling shelves that moved on metal tracks embedded in the floor, allowing a single individual to easily roll each massive shelf or rack back and forth to access property. Both Morton and the site manager explained the process that had been used to sterilize the property when it was originally brought in to protect against insect infestation. Then I was shown the volumes of rugs, jewelry, baskets, and other items neatly stacked in piles on shelves or stored in sealed plastic or cardboard boxes. Every one of the rugs was now labeled with its own individual cardboard evidence tag that had been affixed by NPS officials during the extensive inventory process. The dozens of plastic and cardboard boxes containing jewelry, baskets, and other items were each sealed with evidence tape.

The collection of property was impressive, but it did not seem to me that its value would rise to the $5 million or more figure estimated by Yee. Still, the volume was considerable, and it wasn't necessary for me to go through each box of jewelry or stack of rugs, one by one, to get a general picture of just how much property had been seized. I did, however, get a chance to examine the sign-in book. Most of the names and signatures of visitors to the room appeared to be WACC staff assigned to the inventory process. However the names and signatures of at least a few regional officials (including Steve Martin, Hal Grovert, and Dave Mihalec) who were not directly involved in the investigation also appeared,

20. Inside the evidence vault at the WACC. Some of the rugs seized from Malone by NPS agents. Most of the visible tags were applied by the NPS during the inventory process in the months following the raid (*author's collection*).

21. Tubs and boxes of jewelry, baskets, and other items seized from Malone by NPS agents shown inside the evidence vault at the WACC (*author's collection*).

indicating that a certain amount of "show and tell" and grandstanding had taken place to show off the spoils of the investigation.

The next day, Wednesday, January 11, I drove to Phoenix to meet with Rob Long for the first time. He was a relatively young lawyer whose appearance was typically clean cut, especially compared to my own long-haired, mustached, and casual (if not outright disheveled) appearance. His friendliness, enthusiasm, and lack of pretense betrayed his inexperience as a prosecutor. But he readily acknowledged that he was new to the role of an AUSA and welcomed any and all thoughts and suggestions on how to approach the case. This was a refreshing trait that I thought would help us both in taking a new look at what was now becoming an old and stale investigation.

Long had reviewed most of the case materials Yee had provided. He had also been briefed by Sukenic. He immediately shared many of my own concerns. It was clear to us both that it was long past time to attempt an interview with Billy

Malone. Long said he would contact Malone's attorney, Michael Kimerer (whose services were being paid for by Malone's friends). I planned on reaching out to Malone's known friends and colleagues, both for new interviews and to convey our desire to speak directly with the Indian trader.

I shared my thoughts about the many legal problems I saw in how the case had been handled, emphasizing both the fact that the seizure of property went well beyond the scope authorized by the search warrant, as well as the revelations about false statements contained in Yee's affidavit for the search warrant. If I was correct in this assessment, we needed to consider returning the property, something that would not please Yee or my own supervisors at all. I expanded on this point, noting that in assigning me this case, my supervisors had applied more than a little pressure to quickly arrest Billy Malone and just charge him with "something" to justify the time and money already expended on the investigation.

Long told me about Sukenic's experience when Yee had to be prodded into sharing information about problems related to the chain of custody and Morton's memorandum. That was just one reason his office had been less than enthusiastic about the case, along with all the other deficiencies already noted by Sukenic in his July 2005 memorandum and what Long now characterized as the collection of "Keystone Kops" who had previously been assigned to the investigation.

Long and I also discussed the need to critically reevaluate jurisdiction as well as prospective charges. We agreed that application of statutes related to theft of public funds and false statements was problematic at best and that more attention should be focused on the check forgeries. I told Long that I'd let him know what else I learned in upcoming meetings with Aspey and in interviews I hoped to conduct with Malone's friends and former supervisors and colleagues.

Before leaving, Long took me down the hallway to introduce me to his supervisor, former case prosecutor Howard Sukenic. We shook hands and exchanged greetings. Long and I explained that I had been assigned to take over the Hubbell investigation. Sukenic's unsolicited response provided me with all the insight I needed about the impression the NPS had already made with this investigation. He bluntly exclaimed, "Has our Mr. Yee created another fine mess for us?" As Long escorted me out of the office complex, we both acknowledged it was probably a very good thing we were each new to the case and in agreement about the need to take a fresh and critical look.

I drove up to Flagstaff that same afternoon for a meeting I'd already scheduled with Aspey. I arrived at his chambers around 3:00 p.m. In scheduling the meeting, I had mentioned my desire to talk about the Hubbell investigation but did not elaborate. There was, however, one particular topic on which I wanted to focus, namely the instructions Aspey had given Yee about what rugs, jewelry, and other property he could seize from Malone's residence.

Aspey seemed a little surprised and taken aback when I explained the reason for our meeting. Given his standing as a federal judge, my approach to him was certainly not as a regular witness. But I was keenly interested in what his reaction would be to concerns that the seizure might not have been proper. He seemed surprised when I told him that all of the reported $5 million in property was still in NPS custody and that no determination had been made yet that any of it was actually stolen. He had expected that any items not confirmed stolen would have been returned to Malone within a matter of a week or two. He also made clear that while he'd authorized Yee to seize property that had tags indicating it belonged to WNPA, he had certainly not authorized the seizure of untagged items or items that did not clearly belong to the trading post. He seemed surprised to learn of the broad rationale applied by Yee in seizing not only tagged items but other untagged items located in the same piles or simply nearby. Over the course of our conversation Aspey seemed to become a little defensive, both personally and on Yee's behalf, offering the explanation that Yee may simply have misunderstood his instructions. He expressed confidence, however, that Yee would not have done anything improper. He felt that Yee had taken all reasonable measures under the circumstances and pressures of the moment to act lawfully and in good faith.

I thanked Aspey for his time and assistance and headed to my hotel room to reflect on the day's developments and begin drafting reports to document the day's activities. The next morning I drove the 160 or so miles back to Chinle to catch up on paperwork, e-mail correspondence, and telephone calls.

Even the very preliminary information I had obtained from Simpson and Aspey, not to mention the editorials offered by Sukenic, made me very apprehensive in the light of my own supervisors' expectations for an arrest. I wanted to make sure Long was fully aware of the political climate surrounding the investigation and the pressure I felt was being applied by my own supervisors to quickly charge Malone. I made a follow-up phone call to Long to reiterate my concerns and elaborate on the manner in which I had been assigned the case. I subsequently documented this conversation in a message to the OIG:

As far back as January 12, 2006, I called AUSA Rob Long to advise him of comments made to me during a series of recent conference calls with my

D.C.-level supervisors (specifically including Don Coelho, Pat Buccello, and Brian Smith) about expectations for this investigation. On that occasion I told AUSA Long about statements made to me such as or similar to "I just want this guy arrested," and "I don't care what we charge him with," leaving the distinct impression that I was expected to arrest Malone and charge him; even though the investigation was not completed and, in my judgment, no clear determination had been made regarding the accuracy of the allegations. The context for these comments was discussion about the large amount of time and money already invested in this case, and the desire to justify that time and expense and wrap up the investigation without further expense, delay or embarrassment for the NPS.

I clarified for AUSA Long that I was never overtly directed to reach a predetermined conclusion in the investigation; but given the expressions of general expectations I was hearing, I did feel as though I was being pressured. On one particular occasion I was specifically told that if I "did a good job," and quickly wrapped up this case and arrested Bill Malone, I'd be permitted to continue my assignment in Indian Country, and pressures to return to Grand Canyon would "go away." I noted for AUSA Long my own suspicions that some of the assumptions and conclusions already reached by investigators in this case (and, apparently by senior NPS management) might reflect a lack of familiarity and understanding of the unique social, cultural, and living conditions on the reservation and within the traditional trading community. At the time I had no idea of the ulterior motives that might exist for this type of pressure.

As an example, I questioned the conclusion that the mere presence of large quantities of Navajo rugs and jewelry within Malone's house was clear evidence of theft; given his long history as a trader and a collector, and the likelihood that he (like many employees at NPS sites) might often take his work home. I assured AUSA Long that I intended to conduct this investigation objectively and thoroughly, but wanted him to be aware of the internal discussions occurring within my chain-of-command, and the prospect of negative repercussions for me should my findings not fully support all of the allegations (conclusions?) already made by the NPS (or WNPA).[6]

At the end of this conversation Long assured me that when he was hired, his standing orders from U.S. attorney Paul Charleton were to "do the right thing" and that facts disclosed in the investigation would be the sole basis on which a prosecutorial determination would be made. Knowing what I did about Charleton, that gave me all the assurance I needed that the case I presented would be handled fairly.

Later that same day I made another call to Rob Eaton, assigned to the Santa Fe Office of the Field Solicitor for the DOI. This office serves as legal counsel for the various agencies and officials throughout the DOI. It is typically consulted on matters involving potential liability for the government. It is also directly involved in handling and defending civil or "tort" claims filed by individuals or organizations against the various DOI agencies and their employees.

I wanted to give Eaton a heads-up about the problems we (Long and I) were seeing in the Hubbell investigation and to notify him of the very real prospect that we might be returning the millions of dollars in property seized from Billy Malone during execution of the search warrant. Implied in that prospect, given the growing number of errors being identified in the investigation, was the potential for a lawsuit against the NPS. Eaton seemed to appreciate the call and asked that I simply keep him abreast of developments in the case.

January 16 and 17, 2006, was spent meeting with detectives from both the Gallup Police Department and McKinley County Sheriff's Office, inquiring about Russell Griswold and his family. Griswold's Trading Post (which is more accurately now a pawn and check-cashing operation just across the reservation line in Tse Bonito, New Mexico) was cited by Yee as the probable location where Malone co-conspired with the owners in his alleged embezzlement scheme against the WNPA. Criminal records checks had revealed that one of the owners' sons had a history of problems principally related to drug use. Based solely on that record, he had been identified as Malone's likely partner in crime. I was skeptical of this conclusion because the elder Russell Griswold was Malone's contemporary and friend. Russ Griswold Sr. was old enough to have known and visited the Hubbell family when they were still operating the famous trading post. It was Russell Griswold Sr. with whom Malone had maintained a long relationship, not his son. I thought it unlikely Malone would be in a complex partnership with a troubled man so many years his junior.

Local detectives confirmed that the son identified as a suspect by Yee was not known to even work at Griswold's Trading Post. By the same token, those same detectives believed that the elder Griswold was an honest man who ran an honest business and merely suffered as a parent through problems associated with his oldest son's drug use. Not surprisingly, case files indicated that neither the elder Griswold nor *any* of his sons had ever been contacted for an interview. Instead, all NPS investigators had done was go into the storefront, anonymously, to observe the operation and assess its business practices and the character of its employees and patrons.[7]

Later that same morning (Tuesday, January 17) I drove to the South Rim of Grand Canyon National Park to meet with John Pearson. Pearson's office was located at the far end of the long, historic wooden building that is headquarters for the Grand Canyon Association. He came to work as chief financial officer for that organization after leaving the SPMA in 2001.

Almost immediately after exchanging greetings, Pearson expressed surprise at how long it had taken for someone from the NPS to contact him. He first heard about the raid at Hubbell and Malone's firing way back in the summer of 2004. Given his long employment history with the SPMA and his own experiences supervising Malone, he expected that he would have been one of the first people approached for an interview.

I apologized for that oversight, explaining that I had only recently taken over the investigation. I assured him that I wanted to learn all I could about his interactions with Malone, and how the SPMA had managed Hubbell Trading Post. Pearson was more than willing to share what he knew. We talked through the afternoon and met again the next day to continue our conversation. The information he shared would prove every bit as valuable as Jim Reilly had speculated it might.

Pearson had supervised Malone for nearly thirteen years. He knew how proud the SPMA was about having Malone as the resident trader at Hubbell Trading Post. Pearson told me that "Tim Priehs was thrilled to death to get Bill . . . because of his background." Malone ran Hubbell Trading Post as if it was his own, like the rest of the old-time traders who traditionally owned and ran their own trading posts. According to Pearson, "Bill grew up in that mold."

Pearson spoke at length about how honest Malone was. Even when audits and inventories appeared to indicate a loss in profits at the trading post, according to Pearson these discrepancies were usually attributable to overlooking inventory that Malone stored off-site for perfectly legitimate reasons.

Pearson and the other SPMA managers knew that Malone used consignment sales as a way to circumvent corporate rules that limited the funds he could apply toward the purchase of inventory. This, too, was considered acceptable since it enabled Malone to maintain a large inventory and keep Hubbell Trading Post in the forefront of the trading, rug, and jewelry community without spending the

SPMA's own money. Pearson even acknowledged that SPMA knew Malone often paid artists an advance or purchased rugs or jewelry "out of his own pocket as a way to keep the artist coming back to Hubbell with more rugs or jewelry."

The SPMA also knew that Malone frequently stored at lot of consignment inventory at his own house. He consigned Hubbell merchandise to other trading posts around the reservation. He hauled inventory to auctions held across the Southwest. Most of those items were selected, tagged, and loaded at Malone's residence. Pearson speculated that Malone probably also kept special items at his house to keep them from inadvertently being sold at the trading post, including items promised to a client or another trader or items with the potential to win a ribbon or prize at a scheduled show or competition.

Pearson was not at all surprised to learn about the allegations that Malone had forged endorsement signatures on checks issued at the trading post. He suggested that I check to see if any of those checks corresponded to other records bearing the thumbprint of an artist, explaining that many of Malone's Navajo clients could not speak, read, or write English or sign their own names. Pearson suggested it would not have been unusual for Malone to sign endorsement signatures on checks without the artist knowing: "I have no doubt that he might have done that . . . It makes perfect sense." Pearson also suggested I explore whether any excess amounts for which checks were issued might have settled some other cash advance, credit, or other past, present, or even future deal or trade with a Navajo artist or resident.

Many of the financial transactions between the trading post and Malone's Navajo clients incorporated a multitude of deals or agreements spanning a significant period of time. A single transaction might reflect a client paying off a past loan, receiving a new loan, receiving an advance on artwork promised for delivery to the trading post the next season or year or reconcile a past or present trade or barter of artwork in exchange for food, gasoline, or other supplies. Pearson doubted that Malone ever forged checks with the intent to defraud or that Malone had ever embezzled funds or stolen items from the trading post.

All of the seeming eccentricities of Malone's way of doing business had been viewed as acceptable trade-offs for having one of the last real traders to run Hubbell Trading Post, which allowed the post to maintain a genuine historical atmosphere. In keeping with that tradition, Tim Priehs had hired Malone "on a handshake" alone, since "Tim was adamantly opposed to contracts." And so when Priehs hired Malone, he told him, "I'll pay you this much a year. Bill said OK, and that was it."

Pearson acknowledged that he and the SPMA struggled constantly to find a balance between their desire for sound business practices and the NPS mandate to run Hubbell as a real, old-time trading post. That sometimes led to conflicts between Priehs and Hubbell superintendent Nancy Stone. Stone, for example, took issue with the SPMA's conspicuous use of newer techniques or equipment at the trading post.

Pearson recalled the time when the SPMA abandoned the traditional cardboard tags that had been used for decades to mark Navajo rugs sold at the trading post. They were replaced with new, glossy, foldout tags containing an attached photograph of the weaver. Stone objected to the change and wanted the SPMA to go back to the more traditional, historically authentic tags. But Priehs flexed his own political muscle by calling John Cook, the NPS regional director at the time. Cook overruled Stone and told her to keep her nose out of SPMA business. The SPMA won the argument and got to use the newer design. Boxes full of old cardboard tags were tossed out to the dusty storage room where Malone kept the rest of his old junk, in case any of it might ever come in handy.

Pearson also explained the history behind the SPMA's practice of taking Malone's paychecks directly to the bank to be cashed and converted to cashier's checks before they were even sent to Malone. His account raised questions about the very notion that Malone even cared enough about money to ever steal from SPMA/WNPA or anyone else. According to Pearson, Malone was simply eccentric about the way he operated; he was paternalistic both in the way he operated Hubbell Trading Post as well as in his relationship with the Navajo community. Malone frequently just gave things away, including his paycheck. When the SPMA figured out how much he was giving away, it set up an entirely separate account for Malone to use for this purpose, just to help keep their records straight.

My final questions for Pearson were about the handwritten letter Simpson and Aldridge had found in his old desk. In many respects, that's what had first triggered suspicions about Billy Malone. Pearson immediately recognized the letter when I showed it to him. It was a complaint letter against Malone, written by one of the other Hubbell employees. Pearson explained, "We got these notes all the time. It's a 'let's get Bill' memo."

As he reread the letter, Pearson acknowledged that there were probably elements of truth in some of the allegations. But he cautioned that most of the conclusions and characterizations it contained were inaccurate. Pearson didn't doubt that events described in the letter had occurred. Rather, he questioned the motives attributed to Malone by the writer. As an example, Pearson cited a section of the letter alleging that Malone had been "stealing" cash out of the register and giving it to another favored employee. Instead, Pearson speculated this was more likely one of the many occasions where Malone simply took cash out of the register to provide a legitimate travel advance or compensation to an employee who probably didn't have a bank account through which they could cash a check.

As the second day of our interview came to a close, Pearson again acknowledged how difficult it had been to supervise Billy Malone. But that was true of the entire trading post and all its employees. Managing that operation was the single biggest challenge Pearson had faced in his many years with the SPMA. It didn't help that Malone was not the most organized supervisor or manager. But the SPMA also knew Malone was quite possibly the best of the old-time traders still around. That's why it was proud to have Malone as the trader at Hubbell Trading Post.[8]

My two-day conversation with John Pearson left me with a lot to consider. The things he told me could explain a great deal of what had really occurred at the trading post. Most striking, of course, was the fact that no one—not LeAnn Simpson or Jim Babbitt and not Yee or any of the members of his task force—had taken the time to speak with Pearson and solicit his insights into Billy Malone or the operation at Hubbell Trading Post. The magnitude of that oversight, and the potential harm caused by the simple failure to seek an explanation by asking basic questions, was disturbing, to say the least. As Pearson himself had observed when we first met, it was hard to understand why it had taken nearly two years for anyone to ask him about Hubbell Trading Post and Billy Malone.

That same afternoon I drove back to Flagstaff to meet with AUSA Joe Lodge. Lodge was considered the resident expert on Indian country jurisdiction, and I had arranged for a conference call with him and Long so Lodge could explain the unique criminal jurisdiction at Hubbell Trading Post. I wanted to clarify for Long how the failure to comprehend those jurisdictional issues had contributed to a lot of wasted time and effort in the investigation.

Contrary to Yee's rather imprecise declaration that Hubbell Trading Post is an area of simple "proprietary federal jurisdiction," the site is in fact subject to the broader authorities of Indian country jurisdiction that prevail across the Navajo Reservation. An understanding of this topic was essential in determining whether crimes committed at the national historic site were under federal versus state or even tribal jurisdiction. More to the point, if Billy Malone, a non-Indian, had merely committed a theft of WNPA funds or property at the trading post but those funds and property did not really, by linkage, belong to the federal government, then a state rather than federal crime would have been committed. Meanwhile, since a forgery of state or private securities (e.g., bank checks) is a prospective federal offense no matter where it occurs, that matter would remain under federal jurisdiction, whether committed by an Indian or non-Indian, on or off the reservation.[9]

The following week (January 23–26, 2006) I drove back to Lakewood to examine more files and share my recent findings with Yee and Howard. I later documented that meeting in a memorandum to the U.S. Attorney's Office:

> I briefed both agents on what I had heard from Mr. Pearson, including potential explanations for both the suspected forged checks as well as the vast quantities of property located in Malone's residence. Also in that meeting I cited potential problems detected with the search warrant and related affidavit. In response, Agent Yee exclaimed, "Man, I hope we can charge him with *something*."[10]

Déjà Vu
(Ánáá nádzaa)

T HURSDAY, FEBRUARY 2, 2006, I drove the forty miles from Chinle to Hubbell Trading Post to meet with former superintendent Nancy Stone. Stone had retired in early January and was still packing and moving out of her government housing. I was anxious to speak with her, if for no other reason than to obtain her perspective on the investigation and what had taken place at the trading post. I also wanted to ask her assistance in contacting Billy Malone and convincing him to meet with me for an interview.

I already knew the investigation had created tensions at Hubbell's and throughout the Ganado area. That word spread quickly throughout much of the reservation, as members of the investigative task force swept through the community clumsily pressuring employees and other residents to talk and asking if they knew about any crimes in which Malone might be involved. Stone seemed frustrated by the manner in which the investigation had been handled but was otherwise reserved in her comments or criticisms. She was adamant, however, that there had been "a rush to judgment" and that neither the investigators in the case or the WNPA really understood how an old-time trading post like Hubbell's operated.

Stone explained that Malone and his predecessors at Hubbell Trading Post had established a national and even worldwide name for maintaining top quality items in their inventory. Malone, in particular, accomplished this by taking in consignment from other traders and brokers like Bruce Burnham (Burnham Trading Post) and Steve Getzwiller (Nizhoni Ranch Gallery), as well as prominent artisans who relied on the traffic generated by Malone's reputation at Hubbell to move much of their own inventory.

Stone conceded that Hubbell was always a headache and a problem for the managers at the SPMA/WNPA. Malone was probably not the easiest person to supervise. But she added that "a trader is usually very autonomous, and doesn't respond to the rules from the home office. . . . No new trader would likely submit to the constraints of WNPA." Stone explained that trading is done opportunistically, not on a schedule or according to a business plan, observing that "You buy things when you can. . . . WNPA was always complaining that he had too much inventory." But again, according to Stone, it was because of Malone and the way he ran the trading post (in spite of mandates from Tucson) that "Hubbell was the first place good artists came [to sell or consign their goods]."

Stone echoed many of the insights Pearson had shared with me about the politics and interpersonal dynamics and relationships in the trading post. There was "constant cliqueyness" that was "mostly personally driven. . . . There were people that were Bill's favorites and people that were not Bill's favorites."

Like Pearson, Stone observed that money was "not a big thing" or a motivation for Malone. Acquiring and holding onto "stuff" to have available to trade was more important to him. As far as Stone knew, Malone did not even have a bank account until very recently, instead living in a strictly cash and barter world.

Describing the politics of the Hubbell workplace and interacting with the SPMA/WNPA, Stone brought up one of the incidents that Pearson had to illustrate how the management of the SPMA/WNPA was frequently able to assert its will over hers in the operation of the trading post.

The topic came up inadvertently when I asked Stone how consignment sales were managed at the trading post. With a tone of resentment, she said she really didn't know how consignment and other business activities were handled at Hubbell. She explained that on those occasions that she tried to influence visible business activities to maintain the historic character of the trading post, SPMA/WNPA management in Tucson would do an "end run" and go directly to the IMR director to have her overruled.

Stone shared her own account of the incident in which the SPMA abandoned the old-fashioned tags used to mark rugs and switched to slick, glossy, folder-style tags with a photo of the artist. Stone was not pleased and felt it detracted from the historic character of the trading post. She independently corroborated what Pearson had already told me—that when she challenged Priehs, he called Cook, who told her not to interfere with trading post business.

Pearson and Stone did not know it, but their recollection of this incident would later serve as a critical point of corroboration for the explanation offered by both Billy Malone and at least one other witness for why so many of the rugs found in his house bore these same old-style, abandoned cardboard tags.

My last questions focused on the financial relationship that existed between the NPS and the WNPA. Stone's explanation received special attention in my own final report:

> Ms. Stone explained that approximately 6% of sales/profits from WNPA at HTP went into an "Interpretive Services Account" maintained by WNPA, and controlled by WNPA. The National Park Service (usually she, the superintendent) would submit requests to spend money out of the account for specific items or projects, but the money remained WNPA's to obligate and WNPA retained ultimate discretion over expenditures. Stone clarified that the NPS is not able to claim those funds as their money.

Toward the end of our conversation Stone noted, with apparent frustration, that she'd offered many of these same comments and explanations when she was interviewed the first time. She had hoped the other investigators would have done more of their own research to help resolve what she believed were false accusations against Malone.

This last comment caught me off guard. With more than a little embarrassment, I told Stone that I was not aware she'd already been interviewed. Her name was not included in the list of witnesses I'd been provided by Yee, and I had certainly not been provided with a copy of any reports documenting an interview. Stone seemed more than a little annoyed to hear this.

Finally, Stone suggested I interview at least two other individuals to obtain more information and perspective on Billy Malone. She again named both Steve Getzwiller and Bruce Burnham. She offered to contact both of these individuals, as well as Billy Malone, to urge them to meet with me for an interview.[1]

It is interesting, in retrospect, that during this first conversation Stone did not talk about her own experiences the morning of the raid on Malone's residence. It wasn't till much later, after she and I had spoken several more times, that she elaborated on that disturbing experience. Only then did she really open up and concede that her own decision to retire was precipitated, or at least accelerated, by strained interactions with Mike Snyder, and her impression that the investigation against Malone had been driven by NPS and WNPA politics. During my first conversation with her, Stone, apprehensive and suspicious, was sizing me up.

The following week I drove back down to Phoenix to attend an advanced homicide investigation class sponsored by the FBI for tribal investigators as well as their own agents assigned to Indian country. In the evenings, I took the opportunity to contact and interview more of Malone's past supervisors and colleagues, including his former boss at the Piñon Trading Post, Cliff McGee, as well as son Bruce McGee, with whom Malone had worked for many years.

Both men spoke affectionately of Malone, acknowledging many of the same strengths and weaknesses observed by others and recounting a host of fascinating stories of life on the reservation to emphasize various points. Much to my surprise, Cliff McGee's home was comparatively void of the Navajo rugs and other artwork I'd expected to see. But he did proudly identify a number of historic artifacts, such as an elaborately decorated cane, as well as a pristine handmade chair given to him years ago by the Hubbell family.

McGee's recollections and perspectives were those of an employer and sometime father figure to a then twenty- and thirty-something Billy Malone. McGee discussed the Federal Trade Commission rules imposed on pawn activities during the 1970s and 1980s. Those rules had had a serious impact on his trading post operation. He also recalled that throughout that period Billy Malone carried on his own pawning and loaning with the local Navajos, separate from the trading post. Malone ignored the rules because he didn't charge interest at all and simply loaned his own money to people who just needed enough cash to get by for another week or month. McGee explained that Malone "would just advance money to local Navajos, expecting that they would someday pay him back or bring in a rug or jewelry." He added that Malone "didn't put down his transactions and deals on paper or receipts, but instead probably just kept everything in his head."

McGee seemed to acknowledge that his own approach to trading and conducting business with the Navajos was considerably different from Malone's. While affectionate and respectful in his characterizations, he seemed to view Malone's approach to living and trading with the Navajos as overly generous and charitable and perhaps even foolish from the standpoint of operating a successful business. He speculated that Malone's family background may have influenced his character, observing that Malone's mother married Huey Lee, son of Albert

Lee who had been owner of the Ganado Trading Post. Malone had essentially grown up on and around the Navajo Reservation.[2]

The next day I met with son Bruce McGee at the Heard Museum in downtown Phoenix. The younger Mr. McGee seemed to view Billy Malone as more of an older brother figure who had "taught him more than just the money and merchandise aspects of the business, but also the importance of community relationships." He credited Malone with helping him obtain his position as buyer and manager of the Heard Museum Gift Shop and teaching him about Navajo weaving, jewelry and doing business with Navajo artists. McGee also credited Malone with teaching him that "banks aren't always the safest place to put your money," convincing him to "keep his money in rugs and jewelry instead of a bank." McGee confirmed that over the decades these artworks had proven to be a far more prudent investment than a savings or bank account. He observed that Malone "lived his own life and finances that way" and for most of the time he knew him, Malone didn't have a checking or savings account. "Instead, Malone had his account in rugs and jewelry."

McGee confirmed his father's characterization about Malone's philanthropic approach to living and trading with the Navajos but did so in a far more sympathetic and supportive manner. McGee expressed admiration for Malone's ability to conduct business and trade with the locals, noting that "his memory was his thing. He never worried about paperwork." At the same time, McGee acknowledged that "Bill's only downfall is his lack of record keeping. . . . If you trusted Bill, it was OK. If you were suspicious, there was no way to satisfy." He added, "Bill's strongest strength is his integrity and his loyalty. . . . At Piñon he always thought of the store first . . . [and] . . . treated the store like it was his own in terms of care."

Aside from the occasion when the elder McGee scolded both the younger McGee and Malone for conducting their own trades inside Piñon Trading Post, McGee recalled only one other occasion when Malone had an argument with his father. During a particularly bad winter storm when National Guard helicopters and volunteer airplanes were being used to drop emergency food and supplies to the Navajos, the elder Mr. McGee wanted to hastily raise the price of the red cloth the Navajos were using to mark emergency drop sites. Malone took great exception to that idea and forcefully protested in the belief that it was unfair to take advantage of the Navajos that way.

Bruce McGee continued his close friendship with Malone well after Malone moved to Ganado to run Hubbell Trading Post. McGee continued to do business with him and even took his own merchandise to Malone to place on consignment at Hubbell's. In these deals, "Hubbell Trading Post would generally get around 20% commission; but . . . there was seldom any paperwork done to document the deal." Throughout this time, until around 1998 when McGee moved off the reservation, he saw his share of interactions and politics at Hubbell Trading Post. Malone generally had a one-on-one relationship with the locals, and "a lot of the 'Navajo gals' who worked for Malone got jealous . . . because a lot of the weavers would go straight to him instead of speaking with the staff." McGee added that Malone would often give money to older Navajo people who needed the money, but not to the local staff, and that created further jealousies. McGee explained that "if you did a favor for one person, you would anger another."

At the conclusion of our discussion McGee gave me a personal tour of the magnificent museum grounds and facilities, during which he broke away on one or two occasions to examine and then purchase a rug, kachina, or piece of jewelry brought into the store by an Indian artist. Before leaving I thanked McGee and asked him to see if Malone would consider contacting me for his own interview.[3]

The following weekend I was back in Chinle, relaxing at home and catching up on reports when I received a telephone call from Steve Getzwiller. Getzwiller said he'd obtained my name and telephone number from Stone, along with a recommendation that he call to arrange an interview. Getzwiller was in town and staying just down the road at the Thunderbird Lodge. He wanted to know if I could come over to talk. I said I could be there in just a few minutes.

The rest of that entire evening (Sunday, February 12, 2006) was spent talking with Getzwiller about what he thought was really going on at Hubbell Trading Post. That would be the first of a series of conversations with Getzwiller that would, over time, shed considerable light on the NPS raid and associated investigation at Hubbell and their impact.

Unknown to me at the time was Steve Getzwiller's standing as one of the leading authorities and dealers in Navajo rugs and textiles in the world.[4] He developed his unique business over more than thirty-five years traveling across the reservation and commissioning weavers to make custom Navajo rugs, frequently to his own specifications. These rugs, with large and intricate designs, are of the highest and often award-winning quality. Getzwiller has played a key role in reintroducing a registered herd of Churro sheep as a source of wool for the weavers. That coveted breed was nearly exterminated from the reservation, first during the Long Walk, and later in the 1930s during the Navajo Livestock

Reduction Program. Success in his approach has allowed Getzwiller to augment his inventory of custom rugs and tapestries with highly collectible antique
Navajo rugs and blankets. Getzwiller and his wife, Gail, operate their Nizhoni
Ranch Gallery out of their hacienda-style home on their ranch near Sonoita,
Arizona. In the world of old-time traders, Getzwiller is something of an anomaly,
having achieved an unusual level of prosperity and success by roaming tens of
thousands of miles every year back and forth across the reservation and conducting business with weavers at their own homes, or hogans, rather than setting up
shop at his own trading post or store. This sets Getzwiller apart from most of
the old-time traders, some of whom may view him as an unfair competitor or, at
least, an extremely successful rival.

That said, Getzwiller knew Billy Malone well, having been an extremely close
friend of his for more than thirty years.

Getzwiller credited Malone with the dramatic increase in profits realized for
the SPMA within just the first few years of his coming to work as the trader at
Hubbell Trading Post. But then, according to Getzwiller, the SPMA/WNPA got
greedy, seeking ever greater profits. The relationship between Malone and the
SPMA/WNPA suffered even further when board member Jim Babbitt tried to
tell Malone how to run the trading post. As an example, Getzwiller shared with
me his own version of what happened when Babbitt came to Hubbell's and pressured Malone to buy Pendleton blankets for the trading post from Babbitt's own
wholesale company.

Getzwiller explained that "Billy lived like somebody fifty years ago. . . . He
lived in that store" and conducted business like someone from another era.
Placing his hand on his own shirt pocket to emphasize the point that Malone
held to the old ways of conducting business, Getzwiller observed that "his filing cabinets were right here." He echoed what Nancy Stone and both of the
McGees had told me, proclaiming that "Bill's more Navajo than he is Anglo," and
"Money's not the commodity he used. . . . Bill had every dime he had in jewelry
and rugs."

Getzwiller also told me about an incident that reminded me of what both
John Pearson and Nancy Stone had told me.

Several years earlier, Getzwiller had pressured Malone to organize the hundreds of rugs from his own collection that were scattered across the floor of the
new garage attached to his trading post residence. Malone finally agreed, and the
two men spent three full days sorting, tagging, and stacking the rugs. Malone had
even more rugs piled inside his house, along with boxes and boxes of jewelry made

by his wife and his son-in-law or that he had just purchased and collected as pawn over the years. The two men were able to sort through just a portion of the rugs stored in the garage. They applied tags to some pieces, those worthy of display or whose history Malone could readily recall. The tags the two men used were from the boxes that had been abandoned and discarded at the trading post when the SMPA introduced the newer, slicker tags. According to Getzwiller, he and Malone simply used the old, abandoned cardboard tags to label Malone's own rugs.

This remarkable account, if true, would explain yet another piece of the mystery surrounding the volume of rugs and jewelry found in Malone's house and seized by federal agents during the raid. I queried Getzwiller repeatedly about his recollection, seeking details of the process he and Malone used to sort and tag the rugs. I also reminded Getzwiller about the importance in being absolutely honest and complete in what he told me, not only because of the significance of his account but also because of the legal repercussions for him if he was being less than truthful. Getzwiller acknowledged both points and assured me that what he was telling me was the complete truth. To reinforce the need for complete honesty and candor, I asked Getzwiller if he would be willing to submit to a polygraph examination. Without the slightest hesitation, Getzwiller answered with one simple word: "Absolutely."

Getzwiller told me that he frequently brought in his own rug stock to place on consignment at Hubbell Trading Post. He recalled that in April 2004 alone, he brought in fifty rugs and then another twenty-five or so the next month. That was common practice for him because like many other traders in the area, he knew he could sell the rugs on consignment through Hubbell and still make a decent profit for himself (and the WNPA would make their normal profit, too) because of the reputation Malone and his predecessors had established at Hubbell Trading Post. Getzwiller recalled at least one occasion in the late 1990s when several of his rugs sold in one single transaction at the trading post, totaling nearly $120,000.

I asked Getzwiller to speculate about why profits from Hubbell Trading Post might have gone down dramatically in recent years. He doubted that was necessarily true. But he was extremely critical of the WNPA's recent efforts to limit consignment sales and restrict Malone in amassing inventory for the trading post. That was the main reason the organization might have seen a reduction in its profits.

In the past, Malone frequently provided volume discounts to good customers. In those instances, the WNPA might not have realized its usual consignment profit of between 50 and 100%. Then WNPA would claim that Malone caused it to lose money, because it "only made 30% profit on the consignment sale." But according to Getzwiller, it was Malone's reputation for keeping the best merchandise and being flexible with customers from around the world that provided the SPMA/WNPA with huge profits through high-volume sales of high-quality merchandise in which it had absolutely no capital outlay. Getzwiller added that "WNPA has known for years that 80% of its inventory was consignment," and when it tried to make Malone reduce his inventory, it caused its own profits to decline.

Getzwiller added that visitation, and therefore business, throughout the entire Four Corners region had been dramatically affected by the events of September 11, 2001. The situation was aggravated by sky-rocketing gasoline prices and the devastating fires experienced throughout the area the following year. The financial impact of these events put more pressure on the WNPA to reduce its outlay of capital, which it, in turn, imposed on Hubbell Trading Post by restricting Malone's ability to acquire inventory and donate gifts to members of the community. But Getzwiller also speculated that the constant turnover in the WNPA accounting staff might have contributed to confusion about what its actual profits and losses really were.

Getzwiller was very suspicious of the motives behind the WNPA's firing of Malone and the NPS raid of his house. He stated, "They took away his life savings." Getzwiller's suspicions were compounded after he learned who was hired to replace Malone, observing that "Steve Pickle used to work for Jim Babbitt."

Getzwiller pointed out that he'd shared virtually all of this information when he was interviewed by NPS special agent Chip Davis in Santa Fe, back in August 2004. He seemed disappointed that I was unfamiliar with so much of what he had to say.

With embarrassing recollections of my interview with Nancy Stone, I told Getzwiller I was not aware that he'd been interviewed before and that his name had not even appeared on the list of witnesses provided to me by Yee. I had certainly not seen any reports by Davis or anyone else documenting an earlier interview.

Getzwiller was not particularly surprised to hear this. He said he'd gotten the clear impression that Davis was not really interested in anything he had to say during that interview, explaining "I don't think it was going where he wanted to go. . . . He was getting way more information than he wanted." Getzwiller noted that when he tried to tell Davis about helping Malone organize his own rug collection by using surplus Hubbell Trading Post tags, "he quit taking notes. . . . He put his pen down."

Getzwiller later told me in frustration that he'd gone to great lengths to share this same information with other NPS officials, including Steve Martin, the regional director at the time. Following his failed efforts to convince Davis that there was a problem, Getzwiller even contacted the NPS in Denver to schedule a meeting with the regional director and anybody else involved in the investigation that would see and listen to him. The third week of September 2004 Getzwiller traveled to Denver to meet in person with the regional director, to try to convince him that the NPS had made a serious error in its assessment of Billy Malone and had acted on bad information. But when Getzwiller arrived, he was told the Martin was not available. Instead, the meeting would take place with Martin's wife, Cyd.

Cyd Martin was (and is) the IMR's director of Indian affairs and American culture. Like a handful of others in the NPS, she has enjoyed special dual-career status. She has been able to maintain her position and perform her role without regard to duty station, co-locating throughout the country (even beyond the IMR) at whatever duty station to which her husband is assigned. Also, because of her unique position and influence over virtually all NPS activities within Indian country, she had participated in meetings related to the investigation at Hubbell Trading Post and in other meetings concerning the changes made to trading post operations in the wake of the investigation.[5] Now, for this September 2004 meeting, Getzwiller was told that Cyd Martin would be acting on behalf of her own husband to hear what Getzwiller had to say.

The meeting lasted for an hour or more, as Getzwiller spelled out the reasons he believed the NPS investigation was based on bad information provided by WNPA and thus misdirected. Getzwiller stated time and again that Malone had not stolen the rugs and jewelry law enforcement personnel seized from his home and that Malone was not a thief. He again explained how years earlier he had helped apply obsolete Hubbell Trading Post tags to the private collection of rugs that Malone kept in his garage.

Getzwiller described Cyd Martin as "stone faced, but cordial." But she reportedly told him there was nothing more that could be done since the matter was already under investigation.

Later still, Getzwiller drew my attention to new guidelines for the operation of Hubbell Trading Post, crafted by Cyd Martin's office shortly after Malone was fired by the WNPA. Those guidelines went through a series of revisions, eventually reflecting a dramatic relaxation of standards imposed on the WNPA for maintaining traditional trading practices.

As one example, language in an August 2004 draft acknowledged a recent decline in "traditional hospitality." That was seen by many people as alluding to conditions resulting from WNPA firing Billy Malone in June 2004. The section originally read,

> This tradition of hospitality continued until just recently. Its disappearance has been noted and is a source of discomfort for local residents and members of the close-knit trading community, making them feel that they are no longer welcome at the post.

But that language was removed from subsequent draft-versions of the guidelines.

Instead, for the very first time, the revised guidelines allowed the museum-like "display" of materials traditionally traded with the Navajos. The new guidelines also permitted the outright elimination of consignment sales, displacing original guidelines that recognized consignment as "necessary" and "indispensable" to trading post operations. The final guidelines also limited the trader's ability to negotiate with clients over prices. Radical restrictions were imposed on the issuance of credit and loans. Consequently, the trading post altogether stopped giving significant discounts and cash advances, and it no longer cashed social security and welfare checks. It also no longer accepted mail addressed to local residents care of the trading post.

Finally, although Lorenzo Hubbell had once observed that "the trader who would be successful with the Indians must speak their language as well," for the first time in history the resident trader would no longer speak or understand the Navajo language.

In drawing my attention to all of these revisions, Getzwiller speculated that the abandonment of traditional trading practices had been made in direct accommodation to the will of the WNPA.[6]

As our conversation neared an end that winter evening, I promised Getzwiller that I would look into why his name had not appeared on the list of witnesses interviewed in the investigation. Before leaving, I also asked him to pass along word to Billy Malone that I was extremely interested in meeting, personally, for an interview with him.[7]

By this point I was more than a little troubled to have discovered that both Nancy Stone and Steve Getzwiller had been omitted from the list provided to me by Yee that named witnesses that had been interviewed. My concerns were compounded by the fact that both of these individuals, and Steve Getzwiller in particular, had provided critical information that, if true, could explain a great deal about what agents found during the raid on Malone's house. Even if we could not verify the accuracy of those accounts, they would certainly be raised as defense arguments for which the prosecution would need to prepare. As "exculpatory information," we (the government) were legally obligated to document those types of statements and include them in our reports. It was difficult to understand what legitimate reason might exist for Yee having altogether failed to include Stone's and Getzwiller's names and interview reports in the briefing materials I'd been provided.

The next morning (February 13, 2006) I drove down to R. B. Burnham and Co. Trading Post in Sanders, Arizona, to meet with Billy Malone's old friend Bruce Burnham.

The Burnham family has a long history of trading on the Navajo Reservation, going back five generations to the 1870s. Burnham's great-grandfather, George Franklin Burnham, traded as a freighter operating out of the back of a wagon as he traversed the reservation to visit each of his three wives who respectively lived in Mancos, Colorado, Kirtland, New Mexico, and Ramah, New Mexico. In the years following the presidency of Ulysses S. Grant, grandfather Roy Burton Burnham secured a license to establish Burnham Trading Post at Burnham, New Mexico, near Toadlena and Two Grey Hills. That trading post is now abandoned, but the Burnham chapter house still exists in the community, now renamed Tiis Tsoh Sikaad. Bruce Burnham's own father, Roy Barton Burnham, also worked in Burnham, New Mexico, and then the Bisti Trading Post several miles to the southeast. Bruce worked at a number of trading posts in his early years, starting in 1961 at the Red Rock Trading Post in Red Valley, Arizona, then moving to Aneth Trading Post in Utah and after that to Dinebitoh Trading Post, the Gap Trading Post, and Cedar Point Trading Post, all in Arizona. Finally, in 1976, he and his Navajo wife, Virginia, established their own Burnham Trading Post in Sanders, Arizona, which remains in operation today under the management of their daughter Sheri Burnham.

Bruce Burnham's folksy manner masks an incredible wealth of knowledge about Navajo and trader culture. His command of even the most subtle aspects of Four Corners and, particularly, Navajo history is astonishing, as is his familiarity with both academic and popular literature on the subject. Over the years, Burnham has earned his own reputation as a respected historian and authority on Native American culture. He has guest lectured at universities and museums throughout the West, has been the subject of magazine articles, and has appeared on public television.

Burnham shared much of this knowledge over the course of our three-to-four hour meeting as he attempted to explain to me the significant role of both Hubbell Trading Post and Billy Malone in the Navajo community.

Burnham acknowledged that shortly after the raid at Hubbell Trading Post two federal agents, Clyde Yee and Jamie Howard, did indeed call on him for an interview. Burnham turned both of the agents away, finding their approach insulting and their attitude disrespectful.

Burnham explained that he had been friends with Malone since high school days in Durango, Colorado. He knew Malone as an honest and trusting individual. And while Malone probably didn't run the trading post the way the WPNA wanted him to, Burnham was confident that Malone would never "cook the books" or "out and out do something that was illegal." Instead, Burnham explained, "he'd give away a six-pack of pop to a weaver when she'd sell a rug." All Malone was guilty of, he said, was "giving a little advance[,] . . . of giving a sack of groceries [to the local Navajos]."

Burnham justified Malone's trading practices, explaining "a trading post is not a tourist oriented operation. . . . A trading post is in the business of serving the community. . . . We're not here just to make money on a rug. We're here feeding people."

Then, criticizing the WNPA, Burnham said, "They're trying to turn it into a museum gift shop . . . You got free enterprise conflicting with a socialist system. . . . When someone needs something, they're entitled to the solution. . . . I've bought rugs from four generations of families. I've been the solution to their problems. Everybody in the Navajo culture has this interdependency on each other. So your friends become the answer to your problem. If someone places a demand on another's resources, you're obligated to do it. It becomes very hard to say 'no' in Navajo." It was in this context that Burnham observed about Malone, "You live with these people for thirty to fifty years and you become more Navajo than white."

Burnham said it was Billy Malone that made Hubbell Trading Post a center for the Navajo community and a focal point for trading and dealing in Indian art. Burnham frequently brought items from his own trading post to place on consignment through Hubbell's. He could still make more money consigning through Malone than he could selling the same items in Sanders, even with a commission taken out by the WNPA. Burnham echoed a now-familiar sentiment, explaining that he once told his own daughter that if you "buy a rug and consign it to Hubbell and you'll make more money than in the bank." Burnham's own consignments placed through Hubbell Trading Post were seldom, if ever, documented on paper. Instead, the deals were based entirely on trust. But now, he added, since the WNPA had fired Malone, neither he nor anyone else he knew took rugs or jewelry to Hubbell. Referring to the resulting decline in business throughout the area, he observed, "This is hurting the community."

Burnham felt that the WNPA made some very bad business decisions when it saw fluctuating profit margins and then tried to force a profit by limiting Malone's ability to purchase inventory out of WNPA funds. "WNPA doesn't want to maintain a million dollar inventory there. You need a million dollar inventory to run Hubbell." Burnham explained that when the WNPA cut back on funding to purchase rugs and jewelry from the local artists, Malone was forced rely upon consignment from dealers like himself and Steve Getzwiller to maintain his inventory. He recalled the time Malone complained about this, telling him, "They took my checkbook away from me."

According to Burnham, "Business 101 just doesn't apply to running a trading post. . . . It wasn't a book business." He explained that Malone and the other real traders would often buy artwork that they didn't even want or need for their shelves, just to help support the artists and their families. "He bought grandma's rugs there out of respect." He also acknowledged that "when you're a trader, you want to own it all," explaining that collecting and acquiring things is just a part of the lifestyle. "[Billy] bought lots of old jewelry and rugs and saddle-blankets . . . The stuff they confiscated from him . . . 80% of it was his before he got there [to Hubbell]. He had it from Piñon."

Burnham speculated on the interpersonal dynamics and rivalries at the trading post that might have contributed to allegations made against Malone. Various employees were always jockeying for position in an attempt to sabotage one another's chances for promotion.

Burnham also speculated that there was probably some ulterior motive that would explain both the raid and the firing of Malone. He cited the Babbitt family's influence within the DOI and Jim Babbitt's own reputation for abandoning business ventures, particularly his family's own trading posts. He also pointed out similarities between what occurred at Hubbell Trading Post and the million-dollar scandal at the MNA, both while Babbitt was a member of their respective boards. Burnham believed that the WNPA was using Malone as a scapegoat for its own bad business practices. He said that Babbitt was reportedly spreading rumors in Flagstaff that Malone had stolen millions of dollars from the WNPA and Hubbell Trading Post.

As our conversation came to a close, Burnham provided me with a long list of recommended reading to become acquainted with the history of trading on the Navajo Reservation. He also urged me to visit the Cline Library at Northern Arizona University to review its extensive collection of oral history interviews of old-time traders and to learn more about the history of Indian trading. The oral history interviews, in particular, he said, would shed light on the different attitudes of and rivalries that existed between various groups and families of traders. Finally, as I had done before with Nancy Stone, Bruce McGee, and Steve Getzwiller, I asked Burnham to tell Billy Malone that I wanted to meet with him for an interview and listen to his own account of what really happened at Hubbell Trading Post.[8]

The very next day I sent the following e-mail message to Yee:

Clyde,

Can you put together the following documents/information for me:

- Clean copies of all the checks (and other documents, front and back as appropriate) that have been identified as bearing possible forged signatures by Malone or others. I imagine these would be the same documents as are now undergoing examination, but I'd like to have a copy as well.
- Were you able to determine if any of the suspected forged checks were cashed in Arizona. . . . I gather these would be among the documents being examined . . . If these are separate, can you please include copies as appropriate.
- Copy of report(s) documenting interviews with Steve Getzwiller, Nancy Stone, and Bruce Burnham (attempt?).

I'm going to try to get to Denver later this week (Thursday) and will get with you then if I make it (weather's not looking good at the moment so it may end up being next week).

Three days later (February 17, 2006), Yee answered back:

Hey Paul:

I have made copies, front and back, of all checks that went to the examiner for you.

Here are e-copies of the Getzwiller and Stone interviews. . . .

I will type up the Burnham attempt and send soon, nothing there, said friends since high school and refused interview.

I will FedEx the check copies to you at Chinle.

Clyde

By this point, I was hopeful that Malone might soon agree to an interview. But I was leaning against including Yee, out of concerns that his participation might be counterproductive. I didn't tell him why, but I wanted to make sure I had copies of the checks for use during questioning.

Of course, I was keenly interested to see if Yee would now acknowledge the existence of interview reports with both Nancy Stone and Steve Getzwiller. He had not known about my own interviews with either of them, and I didn't make an issue out of their names not being included on the list of witnesses already interviewed. It was also interesting to find that even now, a full year and a half after the fact, no report had been prepared to document the interview attempt with Bruce Burnham. As I later learned, Burnham's "interview" by Yee and Howard was not the only one not properly documented, and Burnham was not the only witness to cut off an interview after being offended. At least one other merchant in Gallup, Keith Wallace of Turney's, Inc. General Trading, had also been approached by investigators, only to throw them out of his store.

Keith Wallace comes from an extremely distinguished family on the Navajo Reservation. He is the son of old-time trader Stephen P. Wallace, the only non-native member of the famous Navajo code talkers of World War II. The elder Mr. Wallace was raised and attended school on the Navajo Reservation, where his own father was an Indian Service agent in the late 1920s. It was son Keith who spearheaded efforts to make sure his bilingual father was included among the otherwise exclusively Navajo group of WWII heroes honored for their service with the Congressional Silver Medal.[9]

The younger Wallace was reportedly approached by two investigators shortly after the raid at Hubbell Trading Post. They came into his store to ask about Malone's consignment activities and to inquire if Wallace knew about any illegal activities involving Malone. Wallace was incredulous and angered by the very suggestion that Malone was dishonest and might be a crook. Citing examples, he argued that Malone was one of the most honest and trustworthy people he knew. But Wallace felt insulted and became so angered by the manner in which he was approached that he, like Burnham, stopped the interview and told the two investigators to leave his store before he punched them in the face.[10] Wallace's interview was another about which I had been provided no documentation.

Meanwhile, the reports now in my possession documenting both the Stone and Getzwiller interviews were revealing not so much for the facts they contained as for the conspicuous omission of information reportedly provided during the interviews, as well as the inaccurate and mischaracterized representation of statements offered by the witnesses. These omissions and inaccuracies were later verified when both Stone and Getzwiller were asked to review and comment on the reports documenting their own interviews.[11]

The report documenting an August 2, 2004, interview of Nancy Stone was written by Jamie Howard under her (OIG) case no. OI-CO-04–0453-I, incorporated into the case file. The report itself was dated August 4, 2004.[12]

That report began with a short case history documenting the complaint received by the NPS from LeAnn Simpson alleging "possible theft and embezzlement at the Hubbell Trading Post National Historic Site [by Billy Malone]." That same paragraph contained a brief history of trading post operations, as well as repetition of the claim that, "through a contract, the WNPA pays 6.5% of the net proceeds from the HTP to the NPS."

After a short paragraph describing Nancy Stone's personal background, Howard separately addressed what Stone knew about Hubbell Trading Post's financial and consignment procedures, her relationship with Malone, and the matter of the numerous items she had observed in Malone's garage. In her report Howard claimed Stone had told her that "the NPS receives 6.5% of the net proceeds that are earned by HTP." On reviewing Howard's report, Stone cited this as a misstatement and noted that it was incorrect.

Stone reiterated that she had tried to explain to Howard that the WNPA and Hubbell Trading Post funds are never transferred to the NPS and *never* become NPS funds but are simply made available through the WNPA interpretive support account. Under the cooperative agreement with the WNPA, these funds are made available for the use of the individual park, on request from the NPS and on approval of the WNPA.

Stone also took exception to Howard's claim that "Stone noticed that the HTP income was decreasing yearly when in 2003 HTP's net income was in the negative." Instead, according to Stone, she had told Howard she was disappointed in 2003 when the WNPA made only $2,000 (the minimum amount awarded to a park) available for park use through the ISA fund. That reflected a dramatic reduction in what the park had received in past years, which was typically on the order of $12,000 to $18,000. Stone was adamant that she never told Howard that income for the trading post was "in the negative." Stone pointed out that she was usually not even told what the Hubbell Trading Post's income levels were. The WNPA had merely claimed that the radical reduction in ISA funds owed to its own reduced income. Stone also pointed out that ISA funds made available as contributions to the NPS by the WNPA in any given year (e.g., 2003) typically reflected WNPA income from Hubbell Trading Post for the previous year (e.g., 2002). Stone's observation about reduced funding had specifically referred to the nearly 90% reduction in WNPA's ISA contribution to the park for 2003 rather than to a decrease in revenues from Hubbell Trading Post.

Howard apparently got other things wrong, too. During the interview, Stone had referenced one particular employee, noting that he was a Hubbell descendant. In her report, Howard interpreted that to mean that the man had been "an employee at the HTP for a very long time." But Stone had literally meant the employee was a genetic descendant of John Lorenzo Hubbell, emphasizing the point that Lorenzo Hubbell was known for his own gregarious relations with local Navajo women.

Although Stone did state that "Malone played a predominant position at the HTP," it did not appear to Stone that Howard had grasped or conveyed the full impact Malone's termination had had on Hubbell Trading Post.

Stone said she had tried to explain to Howard that because of Malone's standing and reputation, Hubbell Trading Post was a regional gathering point for all the artists and traders across the reservation and throughout the Four Corners. Malone didn't need to travel the reservation to buy goods for the trading post because everyone came to him at Hubbell's. This also meant that the trading post was constantly filled with artists and other traders who came there to both trade and socialize, to talk about various artists, rugs, and jewelry, as well as the history of the area. According to Stone, this gathering of characters was a spectacle in itself and a major part of what made Hubbell Trading Post so special. But when the WNPA fired Malone, that special component and atmosphere of the trading post was completely lost. This was the point she had attempted to convey to Agent Howard in the hope her report would accurately reflect the important role Billy Malone had played in the trading community and the damage that had been done by the manner in which the NPS and the WNPA had conducted their investigation.

Most disturbing to Stone was Howard's misrepresentation of her relationship with Billy Malone. While the report did accurately contain Stone's description of Malone as "kind" and "gracious," she disputed the assertion made in the report that she and Malone "did not get along" in the time period of 1995. Agent Howard, in her report, claimed that "Malone told Stone to stay out of the operation at HTP" after Stone protested the WNPA's switch to new glossy tags used to label rugs in place of the older cardboard tags. With a measure of annoyance, Stone observed, "That's all wrong. . . . It was WNPA that changed the tickets . . . It had nothing to do with Billy. . . . How she [Howard] got to that I have no idea." Stone again pointed out that it was Cook, not Malone, who instructed Stone to stay out of the WNPA's operations at the trading post. Stone also did not recall or understand Howard's statement that "Stone claimed that she was never intimidated by Malone." Stone clarified, "There was never anything negative about the relationship [with Billy Malone]."

In a general assessment of the accuracy with which Howard had documented her interview, Stone commented, "It's a mischaracterization, whether purposeful or not, of what I said."

▲▼▲

Steve Getzwiller's Sunday, August 8, 2004, interview was documented in a report apparently written that very same day by Chip Davis from the NPS Office of Professional Responsibility.[13]

Getzwiller was first approached for an interview the previous week when Davis spotted him in the rug room at Hubbell Trading Post. Getzwiller was gathering his own rugs and getting ready to leave for Santa Fe that same afternoon to set up for the month-long Indian Market. He told Davis he didn't have time that afternoon but might be able to meet later that week or the next in Santa Fe. When Davis called the following week to schedule the meeting in Santa Fe, he asked Getzwiller if Yee could join them for the interview. Getzwiller bluntly responded "No," telling Davis that if Yee came along "he can plan on waiting in the car, just like he made Bill sit on his couch for eighteen hours during the raid." Davis arrived alone.

Davis's report is noteworthy primarily for its brevity rather than any overt inaccuracies or misrepresentations. In fact, beyond basic introductory material, the one-and-a-half page report contained only five substantive paragraphs that referred to Billy Malone or Hubbell Trading Post.

The first of these few paragraphs simply described Getzwiller's thirty-year background and relationship with Malone, acknowledging that he "had known Billy Malone since he worked for Cliff and Bruce McGhee [sic] at the Pinon [sic]

Trading Post." The report also acknowledged Getzwiller's belief that Malone was "honest and only had the interest of HUTR and the community in mind when he did business." The report contained a little of the history provided by Getzwiller about how the NPS unsuccessfully attempted to recruit him to replace trader Bill Young back in 1978. Getzwiller was not interested in the position, so recommended it hire Al Grieve. Later, after Grieve's retirement, Getzwiller was also instrumental in helping recruit Malone as the replacement.

Davis's report did accurately summarize some of Getzwiller's criticisms of how the WNPA managed Hubbell Trading Post, citing a long list of "bad business decisions" that ultimately drove down its own profits and alienated the community. Meanwhile, as documented in the report, Malone continued to show his commitment to the trading post, often spending "7 days a week . . . trying to secure the business," eventually building sales "from $300,000 to over $1 million annually during his time there."

But when Steve Getzwiller was later shown the report written by Davis and asked to comment, he expressed with annoyance, "*It's not there.*"

I described Getzwiller's reaction to Davis's report, in item 3 of my October 23, 2006, transmittal memorandum to Rob Long:

> You may recall that I have previously shared concerns with you about the omission or reference of any kind, within briefing materials provided me by Agent Yee, to the earlier interviews that were in fact conducted with both Steve Getzwiller and Nancy Stone. You will recall that I became aware of both of these omissions (of prior interviews) only during my own interviews with these individuals. As recently as 9-13-06 you and I again discussed our shared concerns about whether omission of this type may have been deliberate, as opposed to inadvertent.
>
> Thursday morning, 9-14-06, Steve Getzwiller unexpectedly contacted me at my office to inquire about the investigation and to share information he had heard at a recent NPS meeting regarding the future of HTP. I took advantage of this unexpected meeting with Mr. Getzwiller to have him review my own report of his interview for accuracy. He confirmed that my report accurately reflected information he had shared with me on February 12, 2006. Then, in an effort to further explore concerns about the omission of the report documenting his previous interview with Agent C. Davis, I had Mr. Getzwiller read Agent Davis's report (which I now have, and is included within the body of my completed

report). Mr. Getzwiller confirmed that much of the information he had shared with Agent Davis during his August 8, 2004[,] interview was not included in Agent Davis's report. Mr. Getzwiller specifically confirmed that he told Agent Davis about the time, several years ago, when he spent several days helping Billy Malone apply obsolete HTP tags to Malone's own rugs that were stored in his HTP garage. Mr. Getzwiller was quite emphatic that he had told Agent Davis about this entire account, in considerable detail; noting that this had been one of the key points he attempted to share with Agent Davis, in an effort to confirm and explain that Malone personally owned hundreds of rugs that were stored in his house and garage.

Even with the previously omitted reports of interviews now in hand, there was very little reason to take comfort in what I was discovering about the manner in which those interviews with Nancy Stone and Steve Getzwiller had been conducted and documented.

From the earliest stages of my involvement in the investigation, I had been pressured to provide briefings not only to my own supervisors but also to non–law enforcement managers and even WNPA officials. The first of these briefings occurred in a conference call on February 16, 2006, that included Regional Director Mike Snyder. While cautious and reserved about the information I shared, I did alert him to problems detected in the search warrant affidavit and subsequent seizure of unlisted property from Malone's residence, citing the very real prospect that evidence seized under the search warrant could be inadmissible. However, I did not elaborate on the prospect of returning property to Malone. I also did not share information about the credibility problems I was seeing in other previous case activity.

The very next day I placed my own call to RSAC Brian Smith to share my and Long's growing concerns about problems we were detecting in the way Yee had apparently conducted and supervised the investigation to this point. I was somewhat more candid in this conversation, and I outlined most of the discrepancies and other issues I had identified in the case, including legal problems with the search warrant and newly detected omissions of exculpatory information from case reports. I mentioned Long's analogy of the agents who'd been conducting the investigation to "Keystone Kops" and Sukenic's comments about Yee and "another fine mess." I told Smith about the discussions Long and I were now having about possibly returning the seized property to Billy Malone. I also shared my own growing frustrations in obtaining complete and timely answers in response to calls and requests communicated to Yee.

Smith acknowledged that Yee had a reputation for being difficult to supervise and less than forthcoming with information. He told me he was dealing with Yee on several other cases in which this had also been a problem. Smith promised to assist in correcting that situation. He suggested I copy him (electronically) on all requests or orders directed to Yee and have him (Smith) relay any requests that were especially sensitive or urgent. In response to my growing concerns about integrity, Smith reminded me that when all was said and done it was still "our job to put bad guys in jail" but offered that "when this is all over" and Malone had been put away, the NPS might want to conduct its own internal review of the investigation to identify ways in which it could improve how it did business.

This conversation reinforced for me of the need to exercise extreme caution in what I shared with not only regional officials but also other agents and supervisors. Smith's comments reminded me that I had reason to be concerned about the reaction I would receive if it was suspected that I was attempting to conduct my own "internal investigation" (which I was not) or advocating for an outside investigation into NPS conduct and activities. I was familiar enough with how the NPS operated to know that given the chance, NPS management, including my own supervisors, would do everything possible to prevent the documentation of serious and potentially embarrassing deficiencies within the organization, no matter what the consequences for Billy Malone and the integrity of the investigation.

I knew it would not be tolerated if it was even suspected that I had detected the need for an outside review or investigation, raising the very real prospect that I would then be removed from the case and replaced by someone else far less critical in their approach. Documentation of the issues and case deficiencies I was seeing was critical to fulfilling my own legal obligations to a fair and impartial investigation, but crossing the line into the realm of an internal investigation into the conduct of other NPS agents and officials would not be countenanced. I had no doubt that I would be ordered to remove any particularly damning information I might try to include in my own reports. I would be walking a very fine line in my efforts to conduct a fair and thorough investigation into the allegations made against Billy Malone while simultaneously documenting the ever-growing list of issues and concerns I detected in how the NPS had previously conducted the investigation.

The week of February 20, 2006, I headed to Denver to attend a seminar sponsored by the NPS on Indian law and policy. While there I hoped to interview at least two more potential witnesses I had identified living in the area: former SPMA executive director Tim Priehs and former SPMA accountant Kris Medina. The trip would also provide another opportunity to meet with Yee.

In spite of what Yee had told me about the difficulties in locating Tim Priehs, I found it easy enough. Both his telephone number and address were listed in the telephone directory. I called and left a message indicating who I was and my desire to conduct an interview.

Tuesday evening, February 21, 2006, Tim Priehs called me back. He was more than happy to talk.

Priehs confirmed that he was the one who actually hired Billy Malone back in 1981 after the NPS asked him to apply. He described Malone as a very good trader who had a real connection with the local artists. He added that Malone was indispensable as a trader and at the same time difficult to supervise and reticent to comply with directions handed down from the SPMA.

Acknowledging that he'd heard about Malone being fired and the NPS investigation, Priehs volunteered that "I have no reason to believe that Bill ever did anything improper." And in direct response to all the rugs and jewelry found in his home, and allegations that Malone had stolen from the trading post, Priehs said, "I wouldn't believe it. . . . His wife was a jeweler. . . . Bill was a collector." As a point of comparison, Priehs added, "Let me tell you about [former NPS managers] Art White and John Cook. All of them had great stuff, and a lot of it." Then, referring back to Malone, he said, "I would guess he did have a lot of [his own] stuff."

In attempting to explain the challenges the SPMA faced in supervising Malone, Priehs said, "There were people like Jim Babbitt. . . . We did a really comprehensive review of Hubbell. Babbitt was involved. . . . We put some more restrictive policies on Bill." But, he added, within the new policies there was a clear "omission of anything saying Bill couldn't do private trading on his own." Priehs didn't claim any specific or firsthand knowledge of Malone engaging in his own private trading, selling, or purchasing while at Hubbell but added, "I know he was selling his own wife's jewelry. . . . Given the atmosphere[,] . . . given the culture, we did what we could."

Priehs continued, observing that "John Pearson had a very high frustration level with Bill as he tried to bring him" into the twentieth century. But, he noted, "Bill was dedicated and honest. He wasn't living the high life." It was in this part of our conversation that Priehs told me that "he fought hard for the weavers," acknowledging that Malone's insistence on purchasing less-than-desirable rugs from young Navajo weavers was a major point of conflict. Priehs attempted to limit the outlay of cash on inventory, but Malone continued to advocate for the young weavers and to note the benefits of keeping them employed and learning the art.

When I asked Priehs about Malone writing and endorsing WNPA checks, he explained that "part of Navajo trading is people wanting cash." When Malone started at Hubbell back in 1981, "There were a lot of weavers at that point that didn't have checking accounts." The SPMA later initiated a policy requiring the issuance of a check, instead of cash, to pay weavers and other artists. Then, according to Priehs, "They would have to endorse it. . . . [T]hey would endorse it and cash it [at the same time]. . . . Especially the elderly weavers who were illiterate. . . . [T]hey would at least make a mark."

Priehs speculated that the market for Navajo rugs has been shrinking and that Navajo weavers more and more know what their product is worth. "Navajo textiles" have been pricing "themselves out of the market . . . since the 1980s." Then he added, "Hubbell, if not already, will become economically unviable." As far back as the Hubbell Task Force, Jim Babbitt was saying, "This business is fatal." But when I asked if Malone might be responsible for a drop in the WNPA's profits at Hubbell Trading Post, Priehs bluntly responded, "A drop in profit relating to Bill screwing up? That's ridiculous."[14]

While not providing any new insights, my conversation with Tim Priehs did serve to corroborate much of what John Pearson had already said, as well as a great many of the things Nancy Stone, Steve Getzwiller, Clifton and Bruce McGee, and Bruce Burnham had told me about Billy Malone. It was clear that among the people who had known and worked with Malone for a long time, he was widely respected. It was also clear that none of those people believed he had done any of things alleged by LeAnn Simpson and the WNPA. They all believed that any suspicions about Malone were more likely the result of some misunderstanding or a reluctance to accept the way he did business.

The one final interview I hoped to accomplish while in the Denver area was with Kris Medina, who had been a full-time accountant for SPMA from 1987 to 1994. Steve Getzwiller provided me with her name and phone number. She, too, was easily located at her office just two or three miles east of Yee's own office building on the very same street. I met with her the next day, Wednesday, February 22.

Medina explained that her duties at the SPMA included periodically traveling to Hubbell Trading Post to conduct audits and inventories. She acknowledged that in performing those duties she always encountered a general comingling of Malone's personal property that was stored at the trading post alongside WNPA property. She knew that Malone commonly traded his own rugs, jewelry, and other items "on the side" at the trading post. Both of these practices, tolerated but not encouraged, led to some difficulty in conducting inventories.

To accomplish her inventories, Medina would have Malone point out which of the rugs, jewelry, and other items were his, which items belonged to his wife, Minnie, which were on consignment for friends and other traders, and which belonged to the SPMA. Medina added that "his paperwork wasn't the greatest," but she excused or at least put up with that because she knew he'd been a trader and a collector for decades and that that was a part of who he was and how he'd always done things.

Medina went into great detail about the procedures used to track inventory, distinguishing consignment from SPMA property. She outlined the process the SMPA used to monitor operations and maintain accountability while simultaneously allowing Malone to conduct his business in a traditional manner. Medina described the enormous challenge the SPMA faced in reconciling these two interests, but she saw the effort as being worthwhile.

Medina subsequently also provided me with a five-page outline detailing all of the procedures the SPMA used and the safeguards it had put in place to conduct audits and inventories at Hubbell Trading Post while she was employed as accountant. Attached to her outline were additional comments about some of the complaints the SPMA periodically received:

> Twice, that I am aware of, in the seven years I worked with SPMA, an HTP employee voiced concerns regarding incorrect sales practices at HTP. These concerns were taken most seriously by the Tucson office, and under the direction of John Pearson and Tim Priehs, an internal unannounced review was conducted of sales practices. During one review, (I believe it was in late 1991 or early 1992) HTP [*sic*] three sales clerks were terminated for theft. The trader had no involvement in this incident. On a second occasion, a sales staff member voiced concerns to me that the trader was not recording all sales and purchasing transactions. No physical proof was provided to me or to the Tucson office of fraudulent transactions. An unannounced internal review and physical inventory occurred and no fraudulent activity was found. There were no unexplained variances in the cost of goods sold or sales margin or cash flows. There were no

missing checks, unrecorded deposits and the outside public accounting firm found no major discrepancies.

A week or two later Medina sent me the following message:

Mr. Berkowitz,

I used to exchange Christmas cards and occasional correspondence with [one of the HTP employees]. I do not remember the specific date, but in 2004 I received a note from [her] regarding the arrest of Bill Malone, Trader at Hubbell Trading Post. I was disturbed and dismayed by the card and did not keep it. However, I remember the gist of the content well.

[The employee] expressed she was pleased that Bill had been "finally" arrested for illegal activities, including theft of trading post inventory and was no longer the trader. She stated that I could not discuss this information with anyone as she was not supposed to discuss it. The tone of her note was vengefully gleeful, especially regarding Bill being detained by officers. She stated she and another staff member were acting as interim trader or supervisory sales person at the post.[15]

Medina's recollections about her experiences at Hubbell Trading Post seemed to also confirm much of what the other past employees had told me, not only about Billy Malone and the way he operated as an old-time trader but also about the politics and rivalries that existed in that workplace. And while I had not uncovered any information that would prove Malone was innocent of the allegations, there was certainly a growing body of evidence to suggest there might be some other explanation for what had occurred at Hubbell Trading Post.

Later that same day I stopped by the NPS offices in Lakewood to see if Yee had yet submitted a request to the U.S. Attorney's Office for subpoenas to obtain Malone's bank records. He had not.[16] I again told him to make that a priority, so we could determine if there'd been any unusual activity reflecting the deposit of potentially stolen funds or revenues from the sale of stolen property.

It was this same week I received word from Long with very good news. Noted criminal defense attorney Mike Kimerer had contacted Long to say that his client, Billy Malone, was willing to come in for an interview. Our efforts had been successful, and both Malone and his attorney were scheduled to meet with us at the U.S. Attorney's Office in Phoenix the following Tuesday, February 28, 2006.

The Simple Truth
(Yoo ch'ííd t'áá gééd)

Securing an interview with Billy Malone was a major step forward in the investigation and long, long overdue. And while Malone's participation in the interview was subject to conditions of a "free-talk agreement," meaning that truthful statements made by Malone could not be used directly against him, it still meant we would have the opportunity to question him about the alleged check forgeries as well as all the other allegations that had been made. We hoped to obtain a real understanding of what he had been up to and how he conducted business at the trading post.

Even under the terms of the free-talk agreement that Long had negotiated, the peril Malone faced in coming forward to talk and answer questions should not be understated. First, of course, if he lied to us he risked a prosecution for violation of 18 USC 1001 (false statements), a felony. But beyond that, we would also be able to make derivative use of whatever statements he made, as leads to pursue independent sources of confirmation for that same information, all of which could be used in a prospective prosecution. What's more, if we *were* able to independently verify any incriminating statements he made, we *would* be able to use his statements to discredit him if he later tried to challenge or dispute our independent findings. That meant, for example, if he admitted to us that he had forged some or all of the checks, and we independently used a forensic handwriting examiner to establish that he had made the forgeries, we (the government) *could* use Malone's admissions against him if he later offered testimony challenging the findings of the handwriting examiner.[1] Most significantly, the provisions of the free-talk agreement in no way amounted to a grant of immunity against prosecution for any offenses, past or present, we could independently support. In our own minds (i.e., my mind and that of Long) as well as for Malone and his attorney, the prospect of a prosecution was still very much a reality and on the table.

By all accounts from the people with whom I'd spoken and asked for help in arranging an interview, Malone was eager to tell his story to someone who would really listen with an open mind and give him a fair shake. He wanted to move forward and get on with his life.

I arrived at the U.S. Attorney's Office an hour or so before the scheduled meeting, both to review my own findings from interviews conducted over the past week or so and to discuss the strategy for the interview with Long. I brought copies, front and back, of all the checks on which we believed Malone had applied forged endorsement signatures. That would be a central area of questioning. But we also wanted to learn more about claims that Malone had stolen money as well as rugs and jewelry from the trading post, since no real evidence supporting those allegations had been uncovered in the year and a half since the NPS had begun its investigation. Finally, we wanted to identify a way to verify whatever account and explanation Malone might provide. That would be important not only because we could not use his true statements directly against him in a prosecution but also because, again, it would still constitute a prosecutable offense if we could prove that Malone lied to us. One option I wanted to keep open was the ability to request that Malone submit to a polygraph examination in an attempt to assess the truthfulness of his statements. I had close friends and contacts in both the FBI and the U.S. Secret Service, and knew they would assist in administering a polygraph examination for the asking. Long agreed.

I was quite surprised when I first saw Billy Malone. His appearance and demeanor were not at all as I had imagined, based on Yee's descriptions and characterizations and those of others that had participated in the investigation. He was a slight, slender figure, tired looking and with a pale complexion. His voice was soft with a slight quiver. While it looked as if he had tried to dress up for the occasion, his worn baseball cap, thin button-tab western shirt, and pressed jeans suggested he was a little out of his normal environment. Perhaps most notable was his completely flat facial expression and tone of voice.

In comparison, his attorney, Mike Kimerer, was gregarious and comfortable, greeting the many attorneys he met in the hallway, whom he had obviously done business with in the past.

We sat down in a small conference room. Rob Long and I sat on one side of the conference table, while Malone and his attorney sat facing us on the other side. There was surprisingly little overture, other than a brief discussion about the conditions of the free-talk agreement. Both Long and I emphasized our desire to proceed in a conversational manner rather than an interrogative one. We wanted Malone to take the lead in explaining what had really happened at the trading post. Both he and his attorney agreed with that approach.

Both Long and I took notes throughout the interview, which we later compared during preparation of my final report.

In our preliminary discussions, we supplied an explanation to Malone and his attorney about the general allegations that had generated the investigation back in 2004. This was the first formal notice ever provided to Malone concerning the allegations of check forgery as well as theft of SPMA/WNPA money and property.

Malone matter-of-factly acknowledged that he had forged the endorsement signatures on a number of checks over the past few years in an effort to circumvent restrictions on the acquisition of inventory at the trading post. But he adamantly denied he had ever stolen from the SPMA/WNPA, his clients, or anyone else.

It began when the WNPA started restricting Malone in his use of corporate funds to purchase rugs, jewelry, and other artwork and simultaneously pressured him to reduce the volume of inventory, overall, at the trading post. Malone strongly disagreed with this strategy. He believed that he needed to keep a large inventory of quality rugs and jewelry on hand in order to maintain Hubbell's reputation and standing in the art world and the trading community. He also feared that if he was restricted in his ability to purchase rugs and jewelry, many of the more talented artists in the area who had been loyal to him and the trading post over the years would start taking their work to other trading posts or stores in town. To circumvent those restrictions, he started paying for artwork out of his own pocket, using his own money.

When an artist or local resident came in with a rug or piece of jewelry too valuable to purchase with WNPA funds, or when inventories were already at their limit, Malone would buy the item with his own money, at an agreed-on price. At this phase of the transaction, the artist probably wouldn't realize that the money for the purchase was coming from Malone's own pocket rather than from the WNPA. Then Malone would tag the item for consignment, using the name of the artist rather than his own, as the owner/consigner. That made it appear as though the item had been placed on consignment by the artist. And since most of the artists needed money right away and couldn't afford to place their own items on consignment and wait for a sale, Malone didn't tell them what he was doing or even ask them to place the items on consignment themselves.

Malone admitted that he was afraid the current management in Tucson wouldn't let him place his own property on consignment at the trading post, even though many WNPA managers, including current and former directors and board members, had done so themselves. Malone simply didn't think he would be permitted to do this or that he would be permitted to place the volume of merchandise on consignment that he wanted. That was also why he kept so much consignment merchandise stored at his residence, rotating items in and out of Hubbell's and other trading posts. That enabled him to maintain a large volume of quality artwork at Hubbell's, far beyond what WNPA wanted to pay for. But equally important, according to Malone, was finding a way to keep the local artists and other residents employed and with steady stream of cash in their pockets and to keep those artists coming into Hubbell Trading Post.

As for the check forgeries themselves, Malone's explanation was stunningly simple.

When the consignment item sold, Malone would then—and only then— issue a WNPA check. But instead of making the check out to himself, he issued it in the name of the actual artist from whom he had purchased the item. He usually issued the check in an amount reflecting a slight (10–15%) increase or commission over what he actually paid. Then, he would forge the endorsement signature on the check and cash it to pay himself back.

Malone acknowledged that he had been friends with Russ Griswold Sr. for years and did most of his check cashing at Griswold's Trading Post in Tse Bonito, New Mexico. But neither Griswold nor his family knew about the signatures.

Malone almost always used the money from the forged checks, including his commission or markup, to buy more artwork from that same or another local artist rather than pocketing the money. That way he was as able to keep the local artists employed; he was able to buy from them time after time, increasingly paying them more money. He would purchase more, better, or more expensive artwork, thereby maintaining the quantity and quality of inventory he desired for the trading post.

Malone estimated that at one point as much of 70% of the total inventory at Hubbell Trading Post was from consignment, and that a significant percentage belonged to him. His ability to purchase more and better consignment inventory grew as he turned over consignment items and realized a slight profit from each sale and then reinvested that profit in the same or another artist rather than keeping the profit for himself. Most of the other consignment inventory came from other traders like Bruce Burnham or Steve Getzwiller, along with a handful of his own relatives and other local residents.

Malone explained that when a consignment item sold, the WNPA still realized its standard profit, whether it was a piece from Burnham or Getzwiller or something for which he had fronted the money. The WNPA still made its profit because the sale price of the item would always reflect a markup between 50–100% over the wholesale purchase price paid by Malone. That markup went to the WNPA.

As an example, if Malone paid a weaver $500, her rug might sell for anywhere from $750 to $1000. After the sale, Malone would issue a check in the weaver's name for $575 (reflecting the amount Malone paid the weaver out of his own pocket, plus a markup or commission). Then he'd endorse and cash the check and reinvest the entire amount in another rug from that same or another weaver. That way, according to Malone, the WNPA still realized a profit of between $250 and $500 on the transaction without any WNPA funds having been expended, a $250 to $500 profit for WNPA that would not otherwise have been made. Finally, the end customer always knew or negotiated the purchase price as they would for any other item purchased at the trading post.

Malone provided the names of several artists and residents whose work he had purchased and placed on consignment and whose signatures he had forged. Included were his daughter Karen Jean Jackson and his son-in-law Perry Shorty. Malone acknowledged that there may have been others, but he could not readily recall their names.

After listening to Malone's explanation, I showed him the stack of a hundred or so photocopied WNPA checks that Yee had provided, displaying both the front and back sides. Malone examined each check and the endorsement signature on the back. He acknowledged and noted, with his mark, that eighty-eight of the checks bore his forged endorsement signature. But he stated that twelve did not. He added, however, that he wasn't entirely certain about many of the signatures, since the checks spanned a period of several years, and he was basing his account on the appearance of the handwriting rather than on specific recollection of having made the forgery.

When I asked Malone to provide an explanation for the losses claimed by the WNPA in Hubbell Trading Post profits, he speculated that it might have resulted from its own efforts to reduce the quantity and quality of inventory by cutting back on wholesale purchases. He also pointed out that when the WNPA began doing audits on a quarterly basis, the audits started to show what appeared to be missing inventory. That was because he sometimes forgot about rugs that were at his house or on loan to another trading post or museum show. Malone recalled one occasion when there initially appeared to be approximately $70,000 in inventory missing, simply because it was off-site and not readily available for inspection.

Malone also questioned whether the current managers at the WNPA really even knew what *they* were doing. He cited at least one audit when they altogether forgot to check accounts receivable, amounting to $200,000. They had to return that amount to Hubbell Trading Post to finish their audit.

Malone also speculated that profits at the trading post might have declined in recent years with the general decline in traffic through the area resulting from elevated gas prices, as well as the recent fires impacting much of the Four Corners region.

According to Malone, all of the property found at his residence and seized by NPS agents was either his or had been in his lawful care and custody. None of it was stolen. He explained that he had been collecting and acquiring Indian art for years, well before coming to work at Hubbell Trading Post. Both at Hubbell's and before, he openly traded and purchased rugs and jewelry for himself, on the side. Most of the other jewelry, rugs, and baskets seized during the raid were the work product of his wife, his son-in-law, and other family members who stored items at his house.

Malone acknowledged that there might have been some Hubbell Trading Post property at his house. But that was only because he frequently brought things home from the trading post to re-tag or store, in between off-site exhibits or loans to other trading posts. He also explained that he used old, obsolete Hubbell Trading Post tags, along with regular blank tags, to mark and identify many of the rugs in his own collection.

As credible as Malone's explanations seemed to both Long and me, there was still the matter of how to verify his account. I asked Malone. He speculated that if he had access to his consignment ledgers (seized by the NPS during the search warrant) he might be able to cross reference at least some of his transactions. But he never kept a record of the cash amount he paid for a rug or piece of jewelry before placing it on consignment. He never kept a record of the difference between the amount he paid and the amount for which he subsequently wrote a check. Still, we all agreed that I would provide Malone with a copy of his consignment ledgers on the off chance they would help him to verify his account.

Then, after receiving an affirming nod from Long, I asked Malone if he would submit to a polygraph examination, administered by either the FBI or the U.S. Secret Service. Malone immediately agreed. I redirected the question to Malone's attorney to obtain his approval. After a brief discussion in which I assured him that only a certified FBI or Secret Service polygraph examiner would be used, he, too, consented.

In anticipation of the exam, I asked if Malone would cooperate by accompanying me to Tucson where the seized rugs, jewelry, and other property were being stored. I wanted him to examine all the property that had been seized and try to identify the owner of every single piece. His truthfulness in that identification process would constitute at least part of the area addressed during polygraph examination. Again, with concurrence of his attorney, Malone readily agreed to cooperate.

As our meeting neared an end, I asked Malone something that had been on my mind for some time. I asked if he would have submitted to an interview and provided essentially the same account of events and activities two years earlier, had he been asked prior to execution of the search warrant and termination from his position with the WNPA. Malone answered, "Sure."

At one point during a short break, when only Malone and I were in the room, I asked how he was doing. He appeared sad and tired. He acknowledged that it had been a mistake to forge the endorsement signatures. In a soft voice, he said, "I guess I crossed the line." After a few more quiet moments he said, "I guess I'll get whatever I've got coming." He added that before the investigation and being fired, he had always thought he might be buried at Hubbell Trading Post when he died. But he guessed that wouldn't happen now.

Before we all stood to gather our things and depart, I asked Malone's attorney if he wanted me to check with him, first, before future contact and questioning with his client, including for the proposed examination of the property at the WACC and the polygraph examination. He said that wouldn't be necessary. If Malone was comfortable with it, I could contact and speak with him directly, with the understanding that such discussions would continue to fall under the provisions of the free-talk agreement.[2]

One thing that struck me throughout the interview was that Malone's attorney seemed to know no more about what Malone had done than we did. In fact, periodically throughout our conversation, Kimerer chimed in with his own questions, trying to better understand what Malone was saying about how business was conducted at the trading post and about how and why he had forged the checks. When I later asked Malone about this, he acknowledged that he had spent only a limited amount of time briefing Mr. Kimerer, not only because he did not actually know why he was being investigated but also because he was afraid to run up bills or exceed the amount of the loan made by his friends to help him retain an attorney.

On reflection, the interview with Malone was remarkable for the very simplicity of the explanations he provided, which stood in stark contrast to the complex and convoluted scheme and conspiracy envisioned in earlier reports and case projections. There was a surprising familiarity in the simple candor and resignation of his account. His explanations made perfect sense, especially from the perspective of someone who had lived nearly his entire life on the reservation, where nearly everyone just muddles along in the face of obstacles and adversity and finds the simplest and shortest way to get between two points. With allowances made for potential inaccuracies in the claims made by the WNPA about its own financial status, the account Malone provided explained virtually everything that had been observed. It reminded me of Occam's razor, that when all is said and done, the simplest explanation of the facts is the most likely.

There was one final point that both Long and I noted about the account provided by Malone. If true, no actual theft had occurred or been contemplated in committing the forgeries. The federal offense of check forgery (18 USC 513) requires only that the forgeries are committed with the intent to deceive another person, organization, or government. But arguably, there might not be a victim to the crime, since according to Malone, the WNPA made a profit with every transaction Malone completed with his forged endorsement signature. And none of the individuals whose names had been used by Malone had voiced any complaint. In fact, much later, several of those individuals would actively express no objection whatsoever to Malone having forged their signatures, seeing it as being much like the way that a husband might forge his wife's signature to cash a check written as a gift to both of them. Malone had their permission. Little, if any, court guidance could be found in existing case law to assist in determining if this unusual scenario was even contemplated under the statute.[3]

Rugs, Jewelry, and Kitchen Utensils

*(Diyogí dóó Bééshłigaii dóó dootł'izhii bee áda' alyaa,
áádóó, naalyéhí da' adą́ą́ góne' chodaa ínígíí)*

EVEN BEFORE OUR interview with Billy Malone, Long and I had agreed that barring any unforeseen developments, we would eventually need to return all of the property seized during the June 9, 2004, raid. The affidavit submitted and search warrant obtained by Yee was so completely fraught with false statements and errors that we would face an uphill battle to get any of the seized items, including listed receipts, ledgers, and other documents, admitted into evidence.[1] Added to that was the fact that none of the rugs, jewelry, or other personal property taken from Malone's home had even been listed on the search warrant, making seizure of those items well beyond the scope of what was authorized, never mind all the subsequent problems related to chain of custody.

Since we now had a credible explanation for all the property being lawfully in Malone's home in the first place (now corroborated by several witnesses), there was no legal justification left for keeping it in government custody. Even if we ended up charging Malone with check forgery, the property illegally seized would need to be returned to the place or person from which it was taken. Attempting to further corroborate Malone's account with a polygraph examination would be the final step before making that move. But the affidavit and application for search warrant prepared by Yee were still sealed under court order, and we had not yet shared any of that information with Malone or his attorney.

The next day (March 1) on my way home I stopped in the Flagstaff office of the FBI to arrange for one of their agents to administer a polygraph examination to Billy Malone. Unlike the depiction of polygraphs in most television cop shows, competent polygraph examinations take a considerable amount of planning and preparation, and their area(s) of focus are extremely narrow. I needed to meet with the examiner to discuss details of the investigation and a strategy for questioning before we brought Malone in to be tested. The FBI would need to open up a file for an "assist" on my investigation, and assign one of their agents certified as an examiner to the case. We made preliminary contact in a March 6, 2006, telephone call, briefly discussed the case, and agreed to meet in person within the next month or so to finalize plans for an examination.

In the following weeks I was busy working on other cases that took me out of state to Texas and New Mexico. But in between my travels I did find time for one other interview that was on my list of things to do in the Hubbell investigation.

On March 16, 2006, I drove down to Tse Bonito, New Mexico, just across the state line from Arizona at Window Rock. That's where Russell Griswold Sr. ran his trading post and pawn operation, just beyond the boundary of the reservation.

Walking in, it was apparent that Griswold's was more a pawn and check-cashing operation than a trading post. In fact, Griswold's is today one of the largest pawn operations in the region. Because Griswold has a reputation as an old trader with whom treasured pieces of jewelry and other family possessions can be entrusted, Navajo clients from the far reaches of the reservation travel there. Both his staff and clientele were almost entirely Navajo, but there were no grocery items or hardware to be found. Instead, the display cases were sparsely stocked with weaving accessories and pawn jewelry, and only a dozen or so rugs were hanging from the walls and ceiling.

I asked one of the staff if Griswold was in. She poked her head inside an adjoining office and an older white man came out to greet me. He appeared to be in his seventies, was neatly dressed in khaki slacks and a pressed, button-down shirt. I identified myself, and he confirmed that he was the owner, Russell Griswold Sr. I explained that I was the newly assigned investigator in the Hubbell investigation, and wanted to speak with him about his friend Billy Malone. Griswold said he was aware of the events at Hubbell and was happy to share whatever information he could. He escorted me back into his office.

Also present in the office was Griswold's wife, who sat at her desk, laboriously breathing through a nasal cannula connected to an oxygen tank. Throughout our conversation the Griswold's twin sons (but *not* the third son who had been targeted as Malone's "coconspirator") both came in and out of the office. Griswold explained that he and his wife had been traders in the Four Corners area of reservation for many years, principally at a trading post near Red Mesa. They were once robbed there and left tied up by bandits until Navajo neighbors rescued them. That incident, along with increasing restrictions on pawn operations and their own advancing years, prompted them to relocate closer to town and establish their current business in Tse Bonito.

Griswold said he had known Billy Malone for years as both a friend and business client. Malone frequently came in to cash checks from Hubbell Trading Post. Griswold directed my attention to a desk where Malone would usually sit (instead of the front counter) and tabulate the checks and count out money. Malone typically prepared his paperwork, checks, and cash on his own and presented his bundle to Griswold or his wife when he was finished. They never monitored Malone or assisted him until he had completed his paperwork and handed the checks to them to be counted and cashed. They seldom if ever examined or double-checked Malone's paperwork. Griswold's twin sons did sometimes assist Malone, but he typically did his business with either Griswold or his wife.

Griswold said he'd never actually seen Malone sign or endorse someone else's name or signature on a check, but he acknowledged the common practice of signing on the back of a check to witness someone else's fingerprint or "mark." Both Griswold and his wife added their assurance that Billy Malone would never have stolen money from anyone. They considered him to be a completely honest and honorable person. They observed, however, that as an old-time trader, many people might not understand how he conducted business.

Griswold then took me on a tour his operation, escorting me into an extensive network of back rooms (actually vaults) that housed the literally thousands on thousands of articles being held as pawn. Each of the separate rooms, not visible to the public from the front counters, was stocked with similar items: jewelry, rugs, saddles, or guns, depending on the particular room. Each item had its own tag denoting the owner and information relating to their loan. The sheer volume of items and the meticulous order with which they were maintained was impressive. Griswold explained that the vast majority of these items were eventually claimed by their owner. Those pawned items that did go dead were typically sold in bulk to stores in Gallup or Albuquerque. In addition to the pawn, Griswold showed me his own extensive personal collection of rugs and jewelry that he'd collected over the years.[2]

▲▼▲

The following week (March 22, 2006) I contacted the agent from the Criminal Investigations Division of the IRS who had reviewed Billy and Minnie Malone's tax records. He had found nothing unusual, other than one or two late tax filings. His review of Malone's assets, including both real property and financial accounts, was consistent with his known income. The IRS had no interest in pursuing an investigation.

Just a few days later, on Saturday, March 25, I received a disturbing telephone call from Brian Smith. Pat Buccello's promise that I would be left alone to work Indian country crimes out of my office in Chinle was being rescinded. Now, according to Smith, unless I could come up with my own funding source, I was being ordered to return to Grand Canyon to resume my supervisory position there. I would continue work on the Hubbell investigation from that location but would otherwise be restricted in my ability to investigate other Indian country crimes or participate in activities related to Indian country law enforcement, such as cooperative efforts with the FBI and tribal law enforcement officials. Instead, I was expected to focus on activities at the Grand Canyon and on improving my relations with the superintendent and his chief ranger. I acknowledged his instructions without voicing my own suspicions about the reasons behind this change in our agreement.

As luck would have it, I already had an idea for a way to continue living and working on the reservation. I had been working another case involving the illegal sale of hundreds of fake Navajo rugs in communities throughout Arizona and Colorado. Without either of us knowing it, an FBI agent out of Albuquerque was investigating the same suspect for similar activities in New Mexico. We eventually found out about each other and merged our respective investigations into one case. That resulted in the very first successful prosecution (and conviction) under the provisions of 18 USC 1159, otherwise known as the Indian Arts and Crafts Act.[3] That little-known statute addresses the production and sale of counterfeit Indian arts and crafts, criminalizing the display or sale of arts and crafts falsely represented as Indian-made. Federal interest arises from the devastating economic effect that counterfeit works have on legitimate Indian artisans and communities who try to earn a living by making and selling their unique works.

While working with the FBI agent, I learned that the Indian Arts and Crafts Board (IACB) was interested in funding an agent to focus on violations of the Indian Arts and Crafts Act. The IACB is a little-known federal agency within the

DOI. Its small but incredibly dedicated staff advocates for Native American arti-sans and receives complaints alleging violation of the Indian Arts and Crafts Act. But the IACB has no law enforcement authority of its own. They rely on other agencies to enforce the act. The FBI rejected the proposal that it dedicate one of its agents to these types of cases. I figured it would be worth a try to see if I could fill that role instead. My inquiries to the IACB were well received. Efforts were initiated to develop a cooperative agreement with the NPS for the IACB to fund all or a part of my ongoing work in Indian country.

Meanwhile, on April 12, 2006, I drove to the Crystal Forest Gift Shop, located just beyond the most southern boundary of Petrified Forest National Park, to meet again with Billy Malone. One of Malone's friends had given him a job managing the remote gift shop, where he and Minnie lived part time in the small apartment located in the attic above the store. He provided me with a list of the various codes he'd used to identify pieces sold at Hubbell Trading Post as consignment.

Just one week later I again met with Malone, this time in Tucson at the Park Service's massive WACC. Also present to help me out was Susan Morton.

For the next three full days, April 19–21, 2006, Malone examined and iden-tified every single piece of property from the investigation, now stored at the WACC. That included between five and six hundred rugs and nearly six thou-sand pieces of jewelry. Without our even knowing it, Malone also examined and identified additional consignment items found at Hubbell Trading Post that the WNPA had independently surrendered to Yee a month or two after the raid. In addition to their consignment tags, these latter items bore labels, recently affixed, with the initials "BB," denoting the Bally Building (a commercially made, climate-controlled storage facility), where the items had been stored at the trading post.

Malone identified the items through his own memory and familiarity with items and/or by deciphering the code or number on a tag or sticker. The rugs and baskets were then placed in distinct stacks, according to who owned them. Malone examined the several thousand pieces of jewelry and other small items according to the plastic tub or box within which they had been stored. These pieces of jewelry were generally packaged in smaller bags inside the tub or box. A piece of paper was then placed in each plastic bag, denoting the name of the identified owner. Finally, Morton generated a log of all these items, identifying their respective owner.

There were a few items whose owner Malone wasn't sure about. Those items were duly noted. But overall, Malone very effectively demonstrated that LeAnn

22. Jewelry spread out during Malone's examination and identification process (*author's collection*).

Simpson had been wrong in her January 10, 2006, interview when she speculated that no one "would ever be able to account for property ownership, particularly with respect to consignment property."[4] It was clear that Billy Malone, in his own inimitable way, was intimately familiar with the entire inventory. He was readily able, as well as willing, to account for virtually every rug, basket, and piece of jewelry.

Throughout this intensive three-day process, Malone was completely cordial and cooperative, assisting in every possible way. I made sure that Malone understood and acknowledged that his polygraph examination would, at least in part, attempt to evaluate if he was honestly identifying who really owned each piece of property.[5]

23. One of the rugs from Billy Malone's collection, seized by NPS agents as "suspected stolen property" (*author's collection*).

Both Morton and I were impressed not only by Malone's level of cooperation but also by the excessive amount and random nature of the property that had been seized during the raid. Included among the articles in NPS custody were family photos, old books, calendars, and even kitchen utensils. Among the rugs seized under the guise of "suspected stolen property" were custom pieces with Billy Malone's own name conspicuously woven into the design by the original weaver.

Also, as Morton later documented,

> the inventory of 554 Navajo rugs revealed that 162 of the rugs bore tags from Hubbell Trading Post. A majority of the remainder of the rugs bore no tags. A few rugs bore tags from other trading posts.
>
> None of the thousands of pieces of jewelry bore tags indicating Hubbell Trading Post ownership.[6]

Notably, none of the tags on any of the rugs were of the newer, modern style used by WNPA to replace the older, cardboard ones. Also, even after examining the hundreds of rugs and thousands of pieces of jewelry, Malone was able to tell that at least one item was missing. He had not seen a treasured Pendleton wedding blanket that he had been keeping for his daughter. Records indicated the blanket was taken by NPS agents when they executed the search warrant on Malone's storage lockers in Gallup. But the blanket was not now among the other rugs and blankets in the vault.

Before heading home at the end of the third day, Morton and I stood in the lobby and shared our thoughts. We were both troubled, Morton perhaps more so than I, by the growing realization that this sort of thing could happen in the NPS. I'd seen behavior like this and had already been through this type of ordeal before, in Yosemite National Park back in the 1980s. But we were both now equally convinced that the OIG needed to be notified. Morton had several more years to go before she could retire. I was already eligible and had far less to lose. Plus, I already had contacts in the OIG. I knew I could withstand the stress and inevitable retaliatory fallout better than Morton. We both knew and acknowledged that I would make the report.

Polygraph (No Lies Detected)

(Yoo ch'ííd bąąh ádin)

BOTH ROB LONG and I were fully aware of the limited value of having Billy Malone submit to polygraph examination. Polygraph can be an extremely useful investigative tool, especially in helping to either include or exclude individuals from suspicion. But the results of a polygraph examination, however competently administered, cannot be introduced as evidence in federal court. The findings and opinions of the examiner must be independently corroborated. Also, the results of Malone's examination would probably not influence our decision to return the property seized from his residence. Even if he failed miserably, we would very likely be obligated to return to him everything that had been illegally seized. What we were looking for, however, was a measure of added comfort with that decision and the ability to honestly say that we had pursued every possible means to verify Malone's account.

The polygraph exam was scheduled for Thursday, June 15, 2006.

Malone showed up right on time. I flagged him down as he approached the unmarked entrance to the Gallup offices of the FBI, and escorted him into the building. Once inside, I introduced him to the agent who would be conducting the examination.

In our preliminary discussions, the examiner had suggested that we attempt to combine two distinct issues into one line of questioning. We knew this was a risky approach.

Polygraph examination works by detecting slight physiological variations—specifically in pulse, respiration, blood pressure, and perspiration (galvanic skin response)—in response to questions and answers. As stress is presumed to be associated with deception (or lying), marked variations in physiological response are interpreted in terms of their association with deceptive answers. The experience of the examination itself may be stressful, and so a variety of techniques are employed to determine a baseline for the subject against which responses to relevant questions are compared.

Key to the successful administration of a polygraph examination is the elimination of as many variables, surprises, and distractions as possible, which could by themselves cause stress responses. The examiner and the subject sit alone, in isolation from others and distracting influences. The examiner and the subject review the area of questioning and cooperatively develop specific, simple questions that will be asked. Questions are developed in cooperation with the subject in order to zero in on a very specific point and eliminate ambiguity. By the time the subject is tested, he or she knows what the questions will be. This is done to eliminate surprise and so that the subject can answer (presumably truthfully) with a simple "yes" or "no" or other definitive response. Complex questions, or questions probing more than a single topic and point, are generally avoided because they, too, may create hesitation, confusion, anxiety, or ambiguity that could yield physiological responses indicative of stress.

Nevertheless, in an attempt to expedite matters, the examiner wanted to first attempt simultaneously questioning about two specific areas of concern: the issue of the property found at Malone's home and the circumstances under which he had issued WPNA checks and then forged endorsement signatures on them. As we had feared, there was too much ground being covered in the area of inquiry, with predictable results in his readings.

After a break to discuss how the exam was proceeding and reevaluate strategy, two more exams were initiated. This time, however, questions about the property and the checks were not combined. The first of those exams probed whether Malone had honestly and accurately stated who owned the rugs, jewelry, and other property found and seized at his house (i.e., the property was either his own or in his lawful care and custody as consignment or awaiting repair). The other exam probed the honesty of Malone's explanation about when and why he had forged checks (i.e., solely after the sale of consignment inventory to reimburse himself for out-of-pocket expenses to acquire those items and to generate a small commission that was reinvested in other consignment).

Now, however, we encountered another problem.

The weather in Gallup can be unpredictable, and the town is subject to violent storms and intense winds. As the afternoon progressed, we experienced strong winds that caused the lights to flicker on and off and fluctuations in the power to the polygraph equipment. This produced notable spikes in the charts, both from the power fluctuations and also possibly from distraction of the lights flickering on and off.

By the time we finished, Malone had submitted to examination and been wired up for nearly four hours.

A letter summarized the FBI polygraph report:

It is the opinion of the examiner that the recorded responses to both of these examinations, that is series two and series three, were inconclusive. It should be noted that during the entire time of the examination, the lights were flickering and there appeared to be electrical surges which did have an effect on the polygraph instrument, contributing to the inconclusive results. Therefore, no conclusive determination could be made.[1]

Nevertheless, expressing his personal opinion, the examiner told me that "this guy's telling the truth." He believed Malone had been completely truthful in his answers regarding his issuing checks and then forging signatures on them and also in his account of who owned the property found at his residence.

The letter continued:

It should also be noted that Billy Malone was very cooperative during the entire interview and provided additional information as indicated in the attached report. Malone advised that Hubbell Trading Post was always paid from the sale of merchandise prior to any of the checks being written. Malone forged the checks generally for reimbursement for cash he had taken out of his own pocket to pay the artisans for their work as Hubbell would not do that. He may have added a small commission for himself which he then used to turn around and buy more inventory to be sold. He admitted he probably made a little commission on every forged check, but turned around and put that back in the inventory by purchasing more product to be sold.

Following our initial discussion of these examination results, the FBI agent and I arranged a conference call with Long to share and discuss our findings. We told him that we both believed Billy Malone was and had been telling the truth.[2]

Just before leaving the building I explained to Malone that the electrical problems experienced during the polygraph examination had caused fluctuations resulting in inconclusive readings. I asked Malone if he would be willing, if necessary, to come back later for another polygraph examination. With what was now becoming a predictable display of cooperation, he answered, "Yeah, I guess so."

I Thought We Were Supposed to Be the Good Guys

(Shá hinii nihíjígo yá ʼániitʼééh nih)

THE WEEK OF June 5, 2006, I was in Washington, D.C., to participate in meetings related to the development of an agreement with the IACB. While there, I took the opportunity to track down my contact in the OIG.

We met in his office on June 7, 2006. I provided him with more background on the Hubbell investigation, and shared with him my growing concerns about what I was discovering about how the investigation had been conducted during the first year and a half. I also alerted him to the possibility that the credibility of one of his own agents, Jamie Howard, might have been compromised by her participation in the case and the discovery that one of her own reports appeared to contain false or misleading information. A few weeks later I followed up by sending him a very preliminary draft report, more extensively documenting some of the issues I had already identified in the investigation. I suggested that his office might want to initiate its own investigation of the Park Service's Hubbell investigation after my case was finished.

I spent most of the following month working on my report. I was simultaneously immersed in the politics of negotiating and crafting an agreement between the NPS and the IACB to fund my position in Indian country. That process was made all the more difficult when Pat Buccello introduced the new condition that I "voluntarily" accept a demotion through a reduction in grade before her office would agree to the detail. Obviously, that did not sit well with me. Not only was it an entirely new condition thrown into the mix after I had already come up with a solution to Buccello's latest demand for an outside funding source but it would also result in a reduction in pay as well as my eventual retirement pension.

Things were once again getting very ugly, very fast. It appeared to me that Buccello, along with her own supervisors even higher in the food chain, were again set on making my life difficult and driving me out of the agency altogether, now that the Hubbell investigation was not going as they desired. Once again, my requests to speak directly with Buccello's own supervisors to discuss her actions were met with delays and refusals.

I ultimately circumvented the demand to accept the demotion, but only with outside intervention. In an effort to salvage the agreement, the folks at the IACB independently sought the assistance of even more highly placed human resources specialists within the DOI itself. Those officials determined that the demotion Buccello and her supervisors were pressuring me to accept was illegal and was transparently politically motivated.

More than one colleague with whom I'd discussed this matter had already warned me about the political consequence of returning the property to Malone. But the political fallout was something I'd already considered and rejected as a basis on which to make my decision. There had been no legal basis for its seizure, and there was no legal basis to hold onto it. I wasn't willing to play a part in perpetuating what increasingly appeared to be an unlawful deprivation of property. That made my decision easy. Fortunately, Long agreed with me. He also expressed the opinion that there was no reason to have Billy Malone submit to yet another polygraph examination.

I arranged to again meet with Malone at the WACC in Tucson, this time to return all of his property. Morton would again be assisting me. Malone indicated he'd be bringing his friend Steve Getzwiller to help load and transport the property to a storage facility of his own.

Return of the property was complicated by a number of factors. First was whether to return to Malone all of the property seized from his residence, including that which had merely been in his lawful care and custody but did not actually belong to him.

Next was the problem that Malone had never been provided with an itemized receipt and inventory of property taken from him during the June 9, 2004, raid. Therefore, none of us could confirm that the items in storage and now being returned precisely correlated to the items that had actually been seized. Neither Morton nor I could attest to the accuracy of the inventory, much less the chain of custody. Certainly, Malone had no way to verify that he was receiving back everything that had been taken, and he was not obliged to take anyone's word for it.

Finally, the sheer volume of property now being returned made the preparation and use of an itemized piece-by-piece property receipt impractical. It might literally take weeks or months to have Malone confirm with his initial each of the more than six thousand items now listed on the 548-page spreadsheet inventory of jewelry and the 11-page rug inventory that had been prepared in the months following the actual seizure.

With these concerns in mind, in late June and again in early July 2006, I once again contacted Rob Eaton of the DOI Solicitor's Office. From our earlier conversation in January, Eaton was already aware of the many problems that existed with the case. That included investigator misconduct, false statements in the affidavits for search warrants, seizures exceeding the scope of search warrants, concerns relating to the omission of exculpatory evidence and witness statements, break in the chain of custody, and so forth. Eaton acknowledged his own concerns over the liability faced by Yee and the government arising from how the investigation had been conducted and the very real prospect of a lawsuit alleging civil rights violations and other misconduct.

Now I was seeking Eaton's guidance in the preparation of receipts that would be used to document the return of property to Malone.

The first issue discussed and resolved was whether to limit the return of property to that which Malone actually owned or return to him all of the property that had been in his care and custody.

After discussing the matter with Long, Eaton counseled me to return all of the rugs, jewelry, baskets, pots, and other property directly to Malone (excluding documents needed for further investigation). That was intended to restore the conditions of possession and/or custody that had existed prior to seizure by NPS agents. Responsibility for the ultimate return of property to the rightful owners would be borne by Malone rather than the NPS. That would relieve the NPS of the burden of selectively returning seized property to the individual owners, known or otherwise. In receiving the property back, Malone would resume responsibility for its care and custody.[1]

The matter of how to document the volumes of property being transferred back to Malone was far more complicated. That dilemma would not be fully resolved until late in the afternoon of July 13, 2006, the very day the return was scheduled to take place.

In anticipation of that meeting, on July 11 Morton and I again met at the WACC in Tucson. We spent that day and the next examining and organizing the property, conducting a cursory review and comparison of the property in NPS custody against the detailed inventory of property we now had. That led us to yet another problem. Even just our random and less-than-comprehensive sampling revealed discrepancies and errors in the 548-page spreadsheet jewelry inventory and 11-page rug inventory, including serious inaccuracies in descriptions of property.

I again placed a series of telephone calls to Eaton in search of legal guidance.

As one possible solution, I suggested a property receipt that incorporated, by reference, the detailed inventories we now possessed. I also suggested the simultaneous use of broad language acknowledging that Susan Morton and I, in returning the property, and Billy Malone, in receiving it, were merely acting in good faith and to the best of our knowledge in the belief that the referenced inventory did document, with reasonable accuracy, property that had been seized from Malone's residence on June 9, 2004. Eaton agreed. Under the circumstances, it would be appropriate and sufficient to craft a property receipt in this manner.

That afternoon and evening I crafted a draft receipt attempting to satisfy those unique conditions. I faxed that initial version to Eaton for his review the next morning, on July 12, 2006, the day before our scheduled meeting with Malone.

While all this was going on I received a call on my cell phone from LeAnn Simpson. She was inquiring about progress with the investigation and rumors she'd heard that I would be returning property to Malone. I told Simpson that things were proceeding in consultation with both the U.S. Attorney's Office and the DOI Solicitor's Office. I also acknowledged that I was, in fact, in Tucson at the WACC, preparing to return property to Malone the next day.

The prospect that I would be returning to Malone the rugs and jewelry seized from his residence seemed to really alarm Simpson. She was also concerned that Malone might be given the property that Yee seized separately from the trading post. Simpson was referring to additional property (rugs, jewelry, and baskets) that was stored in the Bally Building, behind the Hubbell Trading Post wareroom, that Yee assumed custody of several months after the raid.

Simpson somehow knew that this property was distinguished by tags bearing the initials "BB." That property was co-stored at the WACC in the same facility with property from the raid. I wasn't sure how Simpson knew these details, but I had my suspicions.

Simpson was adamant that the property the WNPA had surrendered to the NPS not be turned over to Malone. She asked for time to dispatch Scott Aldridge of her office down to the WACC to provide me with a copy of the inventory and receipt for this property. Naturally, I agreed, and met with Aldridge later in the WACC lobby.

Aldridge provided me with a copy of a property inventory and receipt listing items turned over to Yee by the WNPA from the Bally Building. I had not previously seen this document. These items were believed to have been on consignment through the trading post, but no one at WNPA knew who in fact owned the items or had placed them on consignment. Regardless, the one thing Simpson did know was that she did not want any of that property turned over to Malone.

I again contacted Eaton, suggesting more changes in the evolving property receipt, to reflect the distinction between property seized from Malone's residence and property seized later on from the WNPA. Even though he had helped in identifying who owned *all* the property, Malone would be given only those items taken from his residence. Even those rugs and baskets from the Bally Building that Malone said were his would not be returned to him, at least not now. Copies of various draft property receipts were faxed back and forth to Eaton's office, and by the end of the day we had what I thought would be the final version.

Malone and his friend, Steve Getzwiller, showed up right on time the next morning. Getzwiller had a large, enclosed horse trailer attached to his truck in which to haul the property away.

The process of loading and returning the property to Malone went relatively smoothly and was uneventful. With Morton and me helping, it took only three or four hours. However, when it came to finalizing the transaction and securing Malone's signature on the receipt to document the return of property, it was another matter entirely, raising an altogether new area of concern for me about the manner in which senior government officials were attempting to direct the case.

In the course of the morning, Eaton had consulted again with Long. Out of that discussion came the decision to include new language in the receipt. That language was specifically designed to protect the government from liability arising from the manner in which the property had been seized from Malone and the manner in which the investigation against him had been conducted. Eaton called to advise he was transmitting another version of the property receipt for me to present to Malone. That version now included, for the first time, the following phrase:

In consideration of the NPS returning these items to me . . . I agree to release and indemnify and hold harmless the United States of America and its officers and employees from and against any and all claims, demands, or causes of action arising out of or resulting from the NPS's seizure or return to me of the above-described items.

And yet immediately preceding the signature line for Malone was the statement:

I am under no duress and am signing this receipt voluntarily and without threat or coercion.

I immediately called Eaton back to express my concerns over the new language. I told him I wouldn't sign such a receipt if I was Malone and that I thought it was unfair to ask Malone to do so, particularly since he and his attorney were completely unaware of any of the issues and problems surrounding the investigation.

I argued at some length, expressing my belief that by presenting Malone with this new language, we most certainly *were* applying unfair coercion, effectively holding his property ransom and using it to extort by way of trickery a release of liability/hold harmless agreement from him.

Eaton countered that he needed to look out for the government's interests and protect against a possible lawsuit. If Malone objected and refused to sign the current document, we could make changes to the receipt or remove the offending clauses. But Eaton wanted me to present the receipt to Malone in its revised form to see if he would sign it and then to let him know what happened.

I went back to where Malone, Getzwiller, and Morton were waiting. Malone was seated at a table. I handed him the receipt, asking him to read it very carefully. I did not offer him my pen. After reading the receipt he said, with now-characteristic resignation, "Well, I guess I should go ahead and sign this, right?"

It was clear that Malone was resigned to whatever fate was cast on him. In his present state of mind he would have signed the receipt in its current form or just about any other document or confession that had been presented to him. All he wanted to do was end his ordeal and get back from the government whatever of his property he could, so he could get on with his life.

I was disgusted, angry, and torn at having been placed in this extremely awkward position, forced to either follow Eaton's instructions or follow my own conscience and sense of what was right, and caution Malone. If I followed the instructions I had been given, I would be taking unfair advantage of Malone's state of mind as well as his ignorance about any details surrounding the investigation. If I didn't, I would probably be accused of insubordination later on.

Choosing my words carefully, I reminded Malone that he had rights and could exercise those rights and that he could take all the time he wanted to consider the matter. With absolutely no hint of sarcasm, Malone responded that he was under the impression he didn't have any rights. I assured him that he did and that among my responsibilities as a law enforcement officer was the duty to respect and protect his rights. I reminded him that among his rights was the ability to talk to his attorney before he signed anything.

After listening to me talk in the same type of circles a few more minutes, Malone acknowledged that maybe it would be a good idea for him to talk to his attorney first. I assured him that I supported that decision. I facilitated a phone call for him to Mr. Kimerer.

At one point, Malone put me on the phone with his attorney, asking me to explain what was going on. Kimerer was initially inclined to have Malone proceed. In response, I asked if he was familiar with details of the investigation, the search warrant, and the seizure of property, and if he had seen the prepared receipt and was comfortable with its full legal implications. Kimerer acknowledged that he had not seen the receipt and simply assumed that everything in the investigation had been properly handled by the NPS. He had assumed the receipt was in order. But, apparently picking up the hint, he requested I fax a copy of the receipt for him to review. I did so and then had a brief follow-up conversation with him, in which I suggested that further dialogue concerning the receipt be held directly between him (Kimerer) and Eaton.

In the following hours, several more versions were sent back and forth between Eaton and Malone's attorney and eventually me, as it underwent a series of revisions and, ultimately, elimination of the most offending language. When I received the last revision, I called Eaton to confirm that it was the version we were going to use. Eaton acknowledged it was, noting that he had been unsuccessful in retaining the comprehensive hold harmless and release of liability clause in the receipt. Now the only insulation from liability for the government or its agents would be from any claims of damage to property incurred during its return to Malone. Stated another way, Malone wouldn't be able to sue or file a claim for physical damage to any of the rugs, jewelry, or other property if that damage resulted from handling while being returned! In acknowledging his failure to secure broader insulation from liability for civil rights or other violations, Eaton spontaneously exclaimed, "Sorry, Clyde."[2]

The process was completed by the end of the day. Malone signed the property receipt, acknowledging return of the hundreds of rugs and thousands of pieces of jewelry and other property listed on the attached inventory. I also signed as the official authorizing and facilitating the return and Morton signed as witness.

Malone and Getzwiller took off with the property in tow, relieved that at least this phase of the investigation and Malone's ordeal was over. Morton and I closed up the vault where the rest of the property was still stored and signed out of the building.

Morton and I both felt a measure of satisfaction in having done the right thing. Witnessing the return of Malone's property was the first step in making him whole. I also felt good about the steps I had taken to keep Malone from being tricked into signing away his legal rights. Unfortunately, that did not offset my disappointment over the conduct of the Office of the Solicitor and my ever-diminishing confidence in the organization for which I worked. It also did very little to relieve the anxiety I now felt about what the reaction would be to my having returned the "millions of dollars" in property to Malone.

The entire process was a big deal and a major, if controversial, turning point in the case. I subsequently expressed my thoughts about the experience in a series of memorandums to the OIG. My first written comments appeared in the October 24, 2006, cover memorandum accompanying submission of my final report:

> I also want to voice concern about conduct of the field solicitor's office in crafting the receipt for property that was initially presented to Billy Malone at the time his property was being returned to him. As I mentioned to you on the telephone, I was quite taken aback by attempts made to pressure (actually, to trick) Mr. Malone into signing a comprehensive "hold harmless and release of liability" provision when he was completely unaware of any details (or even generalities) relating to the Service's conduct during the course of the investigation. Recall that at the time of this meeting, virtually all of the records relating to this case were still under seal, and neither Mr. Malone nor his counsel had even a chance to review any of the case reports or even the affidavit filed in support of the search warrant. But we (the Government) already knew there were huge issues with the case, with indications of serious governmental negligence and/ or misconduct. I felt as though I was being asked to behave like a used car

salesman, trying, through coercion (the return of his property) to trick a customer into signing away his rights before he even had a chance to understand what was happening or what he was being asked to do.

We, the government (and especially law enforcement), expect others (like Bill Malone) to accept responsibility for their actions when they do something wrong or make a mistake. Shouldn't we (the National Park Service) also accept responsibility for our own mistakes, and not try to escape responsibility or liability through coercion, misrepresentations, and trickery? After more than thirty years in law enforcement you can still call me overly idealistic and naïve, but I thought we were supposed to be "the good guys."[3]

Revelations (The Last Straw)

(Ééhoozin)

T HE POLITICAL FALLOUT resulting from the return of property to Billy
Malone was even greater than I had anticipated. Criticism was directed my
way from both the NPS and the WNPA, alleging that I had switched sides and
turned on my own colleagues. I was able to deal with that easily enough, not
only because I was confident I had done the right thing but also because, from
a purely legal standpoint, there had simply been no alternative. The original seizure of property from Malone had been improper, and the retention of it would
only aggravate the harm done to Malone and compound liability for the government. Nevertheless, I heard one very credible account that regional director
Mike Snyder was openly questioning and criticizing my approach to the investigation and my decision to return the property.

Perhaps nowhere was the impact of returning the property to Malone more
greatly felt than within the senior levels of the WNPA. There, my actions had
apparently caused a near panic, accompanied by resounding criticism and con-
demnation. As it turns out, however, the level of anxiety I had created within the
WNPA did lead to even more revelations about behind-the-scenes politics and
negotiations between the NPS and the WNPA.

Contained within the letter that Scott Aldridge hastily delivered to me at the
WACC documenting Simpson's wish that property seized from the WNPA not
be turned over to Malone was the following request:

WNPA seeks your assistance in returning minimally a copy of the consignment ledger books recovered by investigators. As we understand it, the primary purpose of the warrant served to Mr. Malone was as to [*sic*] recover these important records that belong to WNPA. It is our understanding that the books were found in the WNPA owned van Bill Malone drove. Clyde once mentioned they were marked with a "V" evidence code for the WNPA van location they were found in. Since the start of the investigation in June of 2004 we have continuously asked for these records from Clyde Yee. He promised copies to us on numerous occasions but we have yet to receive them. It is difficult to document every instance we requested these records but it has been a topic of discussion in most of our interactions with Clyde Yee since June of 2004. I am attaching e-mail documentation of one such promise from Clyde for the consignment records dating May 23, 2005.

I received a number of telephone calls from LeAnn Simpson following her calls to the WACC on July 11 and 12. Discussions centered on the balance of property in NPS custody that needed to be returned to the WNPA. Also, as indicated in her letter, Simpson's attentions were refocused on obtaining copies of the consignment ledgers seized during the raid at Malone's residence, which had actually been the original reasons for the warrant. During those same conversations I, in turn, asked Simpson to provide me with copies of additional documents and correspondence between the WNPA, DeVries, Carpenter, and Associates, and the NPS related to activities that took place early in the investigation. I was particularly interested in the letter dated March 24, 2005, from IMR director Steve Martin to LeAnn Simpson *authorizing* the WNPA to terminate its contract with DeVries for the forensic audit. Simpson requested that letter from the NPS after the WNPA had already expended nearly $25,000 of the $75,000 contract. By then, according to Simpson, there was "no indication from Mari DeVries or Clyde that anything was happening," and DeVries "was not being given direction from Clyde and did not know how to proceed with the forensic audit." The $25,000 that the WNPA had already paid out was "mostly for a lot of shuffling and organizing of boxes and papers that DeVries finally received in fall 2004 from Clyde."[1]

I received several more telephone calls and one visit from Simpson in the month or so following receipt of her letter. All of these conversations were independently initiated by Simpson in apparent efforts to voice concerns and frustrations about developments in the investigation. Though it was probably not her purpose, as it turned out much of the information Simpson inadvertently provided during these phone calls and meetings revealed even more significant issues related to the NPS request for the WNPA to help fund the investigation and about the overall relationship between the NPS and WNPA. Because of their significance, I made a point of promptly briefing both Long and the OIG about the conversations. I later included detailed documentation in my final report.[2]

In the first of these calls, on July 31, 2006, Simpson was upset about rumors circulating in Flagstaff and relayed to her by new Hubbell Trading Post manager Steve Pickle. Simpson learned that a group of Malone's friends wanted to hold a fund-raising rug auction for his legal expenses. Word was also circulating that all of the rugs and jewelry originally seized by the NPS had been returned to Malone (which Simpson already knew was true) and that Malone had been completely exonerated. Worse yet, for Simpson, was the rumor that she (Simpson) had sent a letter of apology to Malone.

That rumor particularly upset Simpson, as she emphatically told me there was "no way in hell" she had ever written Malone an apology letter and that she'd "be damned if" she would "ever write him an apology letter." She clearly took these rumors personally and was very angered. She wanted to know if I or the NPS had written Malone a letter of apology (my answer was "No").

During that same July 31 call Simpson said she might not return any of Malone's property that the WNPA still had at the trading post. That idea seemed to have arisen out of her anger and a desire to defy the notion that she in any way felt apologetic toward Malone.

I received another call from Simpson on August 23, 2006. She repeated many of the same things she had said before but expanded significantly on the topic of her own expectations of support and cooperation from the NPS. She shared her belief that the NPS was obligated to keep her informed about progress and developments with the investigation.

Simpson said she'd be in the area (Chinle) in the next day or so and wanted to know if I'd be available to meet. She inquired about access to consignment ledgers seized from Malone during execution of the search warrant, wanting to know when she could get them back. I had finally obtained copies of the ledgers from Yee just the week before this conversation. I told her she could certainly have a copy, possibly when she came up. She seemed pleased with that development, saying she wanted to use them to figure out who owned the consignment property still in WNPA custody at the trading post.

Then things got interesting.

Simpson next went into a virtual monologue, complaining that the investigation had taken far longer than she and the WPNA had been promised and not gone at all as they had expected. She said that when the case began back in 2004, she viewed herself and the WNPA as "partners" in the investigation with the NPS. She had received extensive access to updated case information from Yee. Simpson observed that I seemed to "play my cards much closer to my chest" than Yee had. She claimed to understand that was just my style. But Simpson added that she and the board had been frustrated and disappointed by the reduced flow of information and other recent developments, particularly the return to Malone of millions of dollars in property.

Simpson expressed frustration in not being able to explain to her board and particularly Chairman Babbitt why that had occurred. That was especially disturbing in light of all the money the WNPA contributed to the investigation and assurances it had been given about how the investigation was expected to develop.

Expanding on that subject, Simpson told me about a recent conversation she had with Mike Snyder. Simpson said she had tried to pressure Snyder to get the investigation moving more quickly and provide her and her board with more information. Simpson even acknowledged (bragged?) that when Snyder told her he didn't think he had the influence to do that, she told him to figure who did have that clout and get them to speed things up and get more information for her and the board.

Simpson went on and on about her frustration and anger over rumors that Malone had been exonerated and received a letter of apology from her. She blamed Malone, personally, for spreading that rumor, exclaiming again "I'll be damned if I'll ever apologize to Malone." She reiterated that she might not return any of Malone's property to him that was mixed in with the other consignment inventory at the trading post. When I challenged that, reminding her of the WNPA's responsibility to make a reasonable effort to return any property to its rightful owner, including Malone, she responded, "I'll have to think about that."

Simpson justified her prospectively keeping property that belonged to Malone. She explained that when this case began, all that she and the WNPA had wanted was for the NPS to obtain the consignment ledgers they believed Malone had at his residence, so that the WNPA could use them to conduct its audit. She thought that was the purpose behind obtaining and serving the search warrants.

But after the warrants were served and the NPS found and then seized the vast quantities of property from Malone's residence, Clyde Yee, Chip Davis, Mike

Snyder, and Steve Martin had all variously approached her and the WNPA board requesting financial support for the investigation. According to Simpson, she had been told "it would be to WNPA's benefit" to financially assist the NPS with the investigation. If the WPNA helped to fund the investigation, its relationship with the NPS would improve, and it would gain access to case information ("partnering" with the NPS in the investigation). There was also the prospect that it would recover its costs through disposition of the rugs and jewelry seized from Malone in the raid.[3]

Simpson made it clear that representations made by the NPS led the WNPA to view its contribution to the investigation as a financial investment through which it would be granted privileged access to information, as well as the ability to ultimately recover its costs via property seized from Malone's residence. But with that property now returned to Malone, Simpson viewed it as the WNPA's prerogative to keep the rest of the property it had that might belong to Malone, if that's what it took to compensate for its investment. Simpson claimed she could do that because she doubted anyone would have receipts to prove the property was theirs.

Simpson showed up at Canyon de Chelly on August 25, 2006, to participate in anniversary ceremonies for the national monument. She called me at my office and asked if I could meet her at park headquarters and give her a copy of the consignment ledgers. I drove up and found Simpson waiting for me in the visitor center lobby. I gave her a copy of the ledgers.

Simpson seemed less agitated than she had on the phone. We met in private and talked for approximately two hours. Among other topics, we again discussed the disposition of property.

Simpson related to me a recent conversation she had with Snyder about Hubbell Trading Post consignment property. That conversation had taken place just a few weeks earlier. According to Simpson, Snyder asked why she was even thinking about giving *any* of the consignment property back to anyone. Snyder suggested that the WNPA keep it all and not just the property that might belong to Malone and his family. Simpson said she'd answered Snyder by pointing out that it was important for the WNPA to maintain good relations with the park and the rest of the community (not counting Malone).

As bizarre and twisted as the investigation already was, I was still more than a little surprised at what Simpson was now telling me. I responded that it had been inappropriate for Snyder to make such a suggestion.

Apparently, to this point, Simpson had perceived me as yet another loyal member of the NPS "family" and part of the investigative team with which she and the WNPA were in partnership. Now, however, she seemed to realize the awkward and compromising position she had put herself in by sharing that information with me. She hastily followed up, asking me to consider her comments "off the record" and to "keep it to yourself."

As our conversation continued, I tried to reinforce the need for the WNPA to make every reasonable effort to return *all* of the property to its rightful owners, including Billy Malone. That meant using the best information available, and that probably meant relying on Malone's own account of who did own what consignment property. Otherwise, if the WNPA was going to demand actual receipts or other proof, no one would ever be able to claim their property.

I reminded Simpson that both the FBI and I had interviewed Malone about the property and that to the best of our knowledge Malone had been completely truthful in identifying who owned what. Simpson acknowledged this and seemed to understand the logic in the WNPA working with Malone and accepting his assistance in identifying and returning all of consignment property to its rightful owners, including him and his family.

Toward the end of our meeting, Simpson expressed her concerns about potential liability arising from the case. Apparently to comfort herself, she claimed that firing Billy Malone had been totally unrelated to the NPS investigation. Simpson asked about the statute of limitations on civil liability, noting it had been over two years since she and Babbitt fired Malone. I answered that in claims against the government it was usually two years from the time a party suffered a loss or learned of damages or other basis for tort action. But, I cautioned, I couldn't speak to the WNPA's exposure, particularly as "a partner in the investigation."

Then Simpson asked one more question that demonstrated that she still expected to receive deference and special accommodation and revealed to me the extent to which she did not grasp my own standing and position in the NPS or the investigation. Her question also revealed the concern and anxiety she and the WNPA were experiencing in the face of the unexpected developments in the Hubbell investigation. She asked if the U.S. Attorney's Office might negotiate with Malone over potential WNPA liability, in effect, using that as a bargaining chip in its decision whether to prosecute the Indian trader. I responded with a blunt "No." Growing concerns over potential liability for the WNPA did not end there.

Several months later, in December 2006, outgoing WNPA board chairman Jim Babbitt reportedly called in the big guns, contacting his brother, former secretary of the interior Bruce Babbitt. Jim Babbitt briefed his brother on developments in the Hubbell investigation, seeking a recommendation for legal counsel.

Bruce Babbitt reportedly told his brother he didn't think anyone in the federal government "would come after WNPA," but he nevertheless provided "the name of a lawyer in Phoenix who is a former U.S. Attorney" who was "very familiar with the working [*sic*] of the NPS and the Inspector General's Office."[4]

I received one more call from Simpson the following week, on Monday, August 28, 2006. I was driving to Tucson to meet with Scott Aldridge to return the balance of property to the WNPA. Simpson said she'd spoken with Malone at a Hubbell rug auction the previous Saturday (August 25). She told me she'd decided to work with Malone, if he was willing to work with the WNPA, to help return property to its rightful owners. She was going to accept Malone's claim to whatever property he identified as his or that of a family member.[5]

The disclosures made by LeAnn Simpson about the deal that had been struck between the NPS and WNPA were more than troubling. It didn't even matter if she was telling the entire truth or just blowing smoke in an attempt to impress or influence me. The statements she made could not go away. Not only did they suggest an entirely new level of misconduct at the highest levels of both NPS and WNPA management in their investigation against Billy Malone but also an entirely new and perplexing level of political complexity I faced in completing the investigation and submitting my report.

It was at this point that I knew I would *not* be submitting my report to my own supervisors or sharing its content with anyone else in the NPS other than Susan Morton. It was also at this point I resolved to continue working for the NPS only until I had finalized my report and seen the investigation to its conclusion. Then I would retire.

I commemorated these thoughts in a second memorandum to the OIG, dated July 26, 2007:

> I want to reiterate that these events, along with other disturbing discoveries made throughout the course of my investigation, were central in my own realization that the entire organization for which I worked—from top to bottom and to whom I was reporting, had crossed the line with respect to ethical conduct and respect for Constitutional rights, principles, and procedures. It was at this juncture that I knew I would ultimately need to refer this case to the OIG, and that I knew I could no longer work for or within the NPS or DOI organization.
>
> Also, of course, this transfer of property to Mr. Malone seems to have precipitated the subsequent barrage of phone calls and complaints

I later received from Ms. Simpson wherein she exposed and elaborated about the deal she claimed had been made between her (WNPA) and the National Park Service (Yee, Davis, Martin, Snyder, etc.) for WNPA to provide funding for the investigation in exchange for the promise that they (WNPA) would eventually get all of the property seized from Malone. This experience and the prospect of living through another nightmare like I'd endured back in the 1980s in Yosemite National Park ultimately affected my decision to take an early retirement, when the case was eventually closed. In effect, the lines between "the good guys" and "the bad guys" had become blurred, and I just decided I didn't want to work for the bad guys.[6]

Rush to the Finish
and a Few Loose Ends

(Tsxííłgo ałtsxo ályaago,
ła´ t´áá bighaadígi ályaa dooleeł)

T HE REVELATIONS COMING out of my conversations with LeAnn Simpson and the alarms that set off for me about the role my own supervisors and other senior NPS managers had played in the investigation gave rise to a new sense of urgency to complete the investigation and finalize my report. My biggest concern was that I'd be directed to submit a draft to my own supervisors for review and then ordered to change it before I could submit it to the United States Attorney's Office. Fortunately, the court order sealing Yee's affidavit and application for the search warrant was still in effect. Also, none of my supervisors had been added to the grand jury "6(e)" list, which they were supposed to be on before they could have access to documents contained or referenced within my report.[1] Remarkably, I was repeatedly able to cite both of these factors, without challenge, as a basis for delaying submission of draft versions of my report.

Meanwhile, I now had the final report documenting the forensic handwriting analysis completed by the questioned document examiner from the Jefferson County Sheriff's Department. She finished her examination in June after finally obtaining handwriting samples provided by Billy Malone for comparison against the endorsement signatures on the suspect WNPA checks. Her findings as to supportable suspicions of forgery were mixed, ranging from "highly probable" to "probable" to "not Malone's handwriting." Adding to the ambiguity of findings were conclusions of "not Malone's handwriting" on signatures previously acknowledged by Malone as his (forgery) and findings of "highly probable" for signatures which Malone denied were his.

I also now had a one-page summary (dated July 20, 2006) from the OIG's own team of forensic auditors. That office had assumed responsibility for the investigative audit on March 22, 2005, subsequent to Steve Martin's authorizing the WNPA to terminate the contract with DeVries, Carpenter.[2] The OIG summary was finally generated in response to my request for a report of its findings, necessary to complete the investigation.

The OIG report documented efforts to "trace the HTP and WNPA records and trace the flow of funds and merchandise to assist in identifying the ownership of the seized inventory, second determine whether Bill Malone had sufficient financial resources to purchase the amount of inventory seized." The scope of the OIG's review "included 50 evidence boxes, financial documents provided from the WNPA, and documents provided through Grand Jury Subpoena" and "consisted of the analysis of WNPA audited financial statements, bank records, payroll records, sales receipts, purchase vouchers, credit card statements, cash register tapes, and other business documents provided by WNPA . . . [and Billy Malone's] credit card statements, a few Federal tax returns, mortgage and personal loans, retirement and savings information, credit reports, and other misc. financial records."

Listed in the OIG audit summary were the following results:

We were unable to determine the ownership of the inventory because:
- WNPA did not maintain accurate and complete accounting records for HTP.
- Internal controls were weak or not maintained at HTP and WNPA.
- In particular there was no accountability over cash or inventory, mostly due to lack of segregation of duties, i.e., Malone had control over everything at HTP.

The OIG summary continued:

This type of accounting and control deficiencies had been identified by WNPA's auditors in the company's financial statements, also in two task force reports, and reports from Price Waterhouse, CPA, titled Recommendation to Improve Internal Accounting Control and Administrative Efficiency, September 30, 1986. Based on seven audit reports provided by WNPA for the period 1990 to 2003, the CPA's [*sic*] identified problems with inventory control, protection of inventory, reconciliation of bank accounts, cash counts, point-of-sale processing, segregation of duties, cash advances, and many others. In 2003 the CPA's [*sic*] reported five material weaknesses, three reportable conditions, and made three comments. In 2004 the CPA's [*sic*] reported 11 material weaknesses, nine reportable conditions, and made four comments. The WNPA had been given advance warning of potential problems at HTP[;] however[,] it appears that the situation did not improve over time. It should be note [*sic*] that the HTP operation is quite different from WNPA's normal business of operating book stores at National Parks and developing publications.

Finally, the OIG summary concluded:

We were unable to determine Malone's financial resources, because:

- We could not determine Mr. Malone's net worth due to lack of financial information.
- Mr. Malone did not maintain normal bank accounts for personal or business use.
- It appears that Malone operated his personal and business operations on a cash basis without maintaining a normal accounting system for his business.
- Insufficient tax returns to determine Malone's financial resources and liabilities.
- In addition, the tax returns should have identified the results of operations from Malone's personal business that generated the seized inventory. By not identifying the results of his personal business and the inventory on his Federal tax return Malone could be liable for taxes on the profits earned during the accumulation of the inventory or indicate that the inventory may not be his legitimate property. However, the IRS was contacted by NPS and the IRS did not pursue the case.[3]

The irony in the audit report was inescapable. It had taken more than two years for the government to figure out at least some of what most everyone else on the Navajo Reservation already knew, that Billy Malone lived and operated as an old-time Indian trader, steeped in the traditions and practices of another time and place, far removed from the modern world. As so many others had already pointed out, he most certainly did *not* operate according to the rules of "Business 101."

Even then, government officials didn't seem to understand what that really meant. The situation was reminiscent of the famous Navajo code talkers of World War II confounding the enemy by transmitting messages in their native language. Without even trying, Billy Malone, it seems, had left the government's own highly trained forensic auditors utterly baffled by the seemingly indecipherable manner in which he lived his life and conducted his affairs as an old-time "trader to the Navajo." When everything was said and done, the government auditors were apparently unable to recognize the distinction between Malone's income and his personal, life-long acquisitions and collections or the artistic work products of his own family. They instead clung to the notion that the only possible explanation for all of the rugs and jewelry seized from Billy's residence was that they were either stolen property or disguised profits from his private business dealings.

The head of the inspector general's audit team, Ray Macy, later acknowledged that their task was made all the more difficult by the WNPA's refusal to share additional internal financial records needed for the audit and a general lack of cooperation in the very audit and larger financial crimes investigation the WNPA had generated.[4] The OIG's findings corroborated those made previously by DeVries, Carpenter. None of those audits revealed significant declines in revenue generated at Hubbell Trading Post. They instead suggested that the WNPA's own broader financial practices and accounting systems left a great deal to be desired, raising serious questions about the credibility of the initial claims that Hubbell Trading Post was losing money at all and that Billy Malone must be responsible for those losses.[5]

That conclusion was confirmed in annual reports subsequently released by the WNPA, citing audits conducted by both DeVries and an entirely separate accounting firm, newly contracted in 2005. Those documents indicated no significant variance in revenues throughout the years both preceding and then following the raid and termination of Billy Malone. Individually and collectively, all of those audits and reports further supported the conclusion that the theft of millions of dollars publicly attributed to Billy Malone by officials from the both WNPA and the NPS, and referenced by Yee in his sworn affidavit, *had never even occurred.*[6]

Receipt of the OIG report documenting findings from the forensic audit and the Jefferson County Sheriff's Department report documenting the forensic handwriting analysis provided me with the materials I needed to complete my investigation and finalize my report, which I would then submit to Long for him to evaluate and consider in his determination of whether or not to file charges against Billy Malone.

As a practical matter the only charge now under consideration was 18 USC 513 (forgery of securities). That determination would be based principally on evidence obtained prior to execution of the search warrant at Billy Malone's home, along with the forensic handwriting analysis. That very same case could have been prepared and submitted all the way back in the summer of 2004, without any of the time, expense, or hassle of the past three years. Ironically, prosecution now, if desired, would be all the more difficult because of the enormous credibility problems created in the interim period through the actions of officials from the NPS, the WNPA, the United States Attorney's Office, and the Office of the Solicitor. Putting any one of these officials on the witness stand in a case against Billy Malone would be disastrous for the prosecution and would leave a jury to likely wonder if the right person was really on trial.

I set about the task of completing my report as quickly as possible, hoping I'd be able to submit it directly to Long before my own supervisors would have a chance to request it for review. I also determined to send a copy, simultaneously, to the OIG under the provisions of the Whistleblower Protection Act, requesting that its office undertake a separate investigation into the related conduct of officials from both the NPS and WPNA.[7] My contact in the OIG already knew how I was proceeding. He was anticipating my final report and indicated the OIG would very likely use it as the basis for opening its own investigation, at which point he would probably contact NPS director Mary Bomar directly to tell her the OIG was exercising its authority to assume jurisdiction over the investigation. Likewise, Long was aware of my communications with the OIG, and *had* added my contacts there to the list of individuals authorized to view case materials and reports.

I submitted a draft version of my report to Long on September 14. That report documented and summarized the review I had conducted of previous case activity. It included a number of surprising revelations about many issues related to the investigation, interviews (and inadvertent re-interviews I had conducted) with witnesses, correspondence, and other documents I'd obtained from the WNPA, and copies of reports I now had that had been prepared by Yee, Howard, and the other "task force" participants.

After reviewing my draft report, Long offered several useful comments and suggestions which I incorporated, including the tabulation of results from the handwriting analysis. While editing and reviewing my report as well as materials I'd obtained from Yee, I noticed what appeared to be a couple of other key omissions from the record. I brought these to Long's attention in a September 20, 2006, e-mail:

> Rob:
>
> Had a chance to draft some notes for the analysis we discussed yesterday. . . . In the process reviewed info I have on my computer related to the list of forged checks, etc. What I find (apparently) is no record in any of the materials or reports provided to me by Clyde of Karen Jean Jackson and Perry Shorty having ever been interviewed . . . even though they are the ones named in more checks than anyone else. In materials provided to you by Clyde, do you have any indication of these two people being interviewed? I have no reports suggesting they've ever been contacted. . . .
>
> I'll try calling later today before or after court to explore this and a few other questions I have for you.
>
> Paul

Long confirmed that there was no record in his files of any interview attempts with either of these individuals. That constituted an oversight that needed to be addressed before the investigation could be completed.

The majority of reports that Yee *had* provided to me and the U.S. Attorney's Office documented interviews with individuals whose names appeared on the face of WNPA checks—individuals whose endorsement signatures were suspected to have been forged. Those reports reflected questioning to ascertain if the named individual made the endorsement signature. The vast majority confirmed that the signatures were not their own. However of the approximately one hundred checks under scrutiny, more than one-third were issued to either (Karen) Jean Jackson or Perry Shorty, Malone's daughter and son-in-law.

I called Malone seeking his assistance in contacting them. He readily obliged.

Perry Shorty was living in Shiprock, New Mexico, where he was the minister at the Door Christian Fellowship Church. We arranged to meet Friday, October 6, at the McDonald's near the intersection of state highways 491 and 64.

In speaking with Shorty I learned that he had, in fact, been approached for an interview when Yee finally served him with a subpoena for his handwriting samples. Shorty had declined to answer Yee's questions. Now, however, with his father-in-law's consent, he was willing to answer any questions I had to help bring the investigation to a close.

Shorty was raised in Shiprock, on the Navajo Reservation, but around the age of eighteen had moved to Gallup. He became a born-again Christian and also started to learn the art of making jewelry. Over the years he developed and honed his skill to become one of the most recognized and respected Navajo jewelers in the country, creating elaborate and detailed pieces of silver and turquoise, often in the older, more traditional style. Shorty relies on the sale of his highly coveted jewelry at the larger Indian markets to supplement his meager salary as a Pentecostal minister.

It was in Gallup that Shorty met his wife, Carol, who he learned was the daughter of the famous Indian trader at Hubbell Trading Post. Shorty spoke affectionately but candidly about his father-in-law, explaining how Malone had helped him over the years to develop his own reputation as a silversmith.

Malone had also helped Shorty and his wife invest in Navajo rugs, which he bought on their behalf from local weavers and placed on consignment at Hubbell Trading Post as an investment. Shorty initially gave Malone money to buy some rugs, and Malone probably supplemented those funds with some of his own money to help out. Details of what to buy, how much to spend, and how much to ask were left to Malone. Shorty simply provided his father-in-law with some cash to buy a few rugs, and whenever a rug sold, that money was reinvested directly back into the purchase of more rugs, to again be placed on consignment. Shorty usually didn't even see the rugs that were purchased and placed on consignment for him. He left it all up to Malone, including endorsing and cashing the checks made out to him when a rug sold. Shorty said that he had not yet even realized a cash profit or received a cash return. Instead, he characterized the process as equivalent (and as an alternative) to investing his money into a regular bank or other interest-bearing or money market account and leaving it alone and waiting to see if his investment would appreciate in the long run, over time.

I showed Shorty photocopies of a number of WNPA checks made out to his name and bearing endorsement signatures also in his name on the back. Shorty acknowledged that he had never seen any of the checks, and that none of the endorsement signatures on the back of those checks were his. Again, however, he said that his father-in-law had his permission to make endorsement signatures for him, since he was family.

I pointed out that Shorty had only made reference to his father-in-law buying rugs on his behalf for consignment, but not jewelry. He acknowledged that this was the case and that he couldn't recall ever having placed any of his own jewelry on consignment. He explained, however, that over the years his father-in-law had personally purchased a large number of his own pieces. His father-in-law probably had hundreds of his bracelets, necklaces, and other pieces in his private collection, along with hundreds if not thousands of pieces from other silversmiths.

Shorty described his father-in-law as "old school," using his own money to purchase jewelry and other Indian works whenever he could both because he just liked it and also to help out the local artists and provide them with an income. "He loves the work. . . . It's in his nature to trade and help people." Shorty added, "There's nothing else for him," speculating that Malone would have worked as a trader forever, if he could have.

"Bill was always more than fair with folks," Shorty told me. Because of that, some people were able to take unfair advantage of him. He added, "Bill trusts people too much." Shorty acknowledged that his father-in-law may have crossed the line to help others. When Shorty was himself getting started as a jeweler, even before he had married Carol, Malone had gone out of his way to help him out by purchasing Shorty's jewelry out of his own pocket and by working with him to develop his reputation as an artist. Shorty had seen Malone do the same thing for any number of other Navajo artists, related or not.

Revealing his own confusion over who his father-in-law had worked for and who ran Hubbell Trading Post, Shorty said he had sensed that the NPS was planning to fire his father-in-law because Malone was so different and insisted on doing things his own, old-fashioned way. New rules about how to run the trading post were always being imposed on his father-in-law. But, according to Shorty, "He just worked with what he had and made the business work."[8]

The last interview I needed to conduct was with Billy Malone's oldest daughter, Karen Jean Botello. I met with her the following Wednesday, October 11, at the Gallup High School where she was a full-time English teacher.

Botello told me that she had been approached twice for an interview by Yee. The first time was in late 2004, following execution of the search warrants at her father's residence at Hubbell Trading Post. The second was in late 2005 or early 2006 when she was served with a subpoena for handwriting samples. On both occasions, Botello refused to be interviewed. Now, however, at her father's request, she agreed to speak with me and answer questions.

Botello explained that her full given name is Karen Jean Malone, and that her father sometimes refers to her as Karen, Jean, or Karen Jean. From 1981 through 1995 she was married to Vernon Jackson, during which time she assumed her husband's last name. Following her divorce, she reverted back to Karen Jean Malone, although many people still referred to her as Jackson. In 2000 she married Jarrell Botello and legally assumed her new husband's name, becoming Karen Jean Botello.[9]

Botello said it was her idea to invest in consignment rugs, jewelry, and baskets through her father. Around the time she was attending the University of New Mexico (while she was Karen Jean Jackson) she approached her father for assistance in purchasing a few items that could be placed on consignment at Hubbell Trading Post, as a way to invest her money. She never even considered putting her money into a bank or savings account, because growing up with her family at both Piñon and later Ganado in the remote regions of the Navajo Reservation, there were no banks around. No one had a bank or checking account. It was just normal to keep one's life earnings in rugs, jewelry, or baskets and to treat them "like savings." Botello explained, "We didn't really use banks; it was just rugs and jewelry." Her father even helped pay for her college tuition by selling some of his old rugs and jewelry.

Botello acknowledged that she used the name of Jean Jackson on all items she held in consignment through her father at Hubbell Trading Post, both to avoid name changes and, admittedly, to reduce the visibility of her involvement in consignment interests at Hubbell, which her father's employer might view as a conflict of interest. She periodically gave her father money to purchase rugs, jewelry, or baskets for her and had him place those items on consignment at the trading post in her name (Jean Jackson). Her father usually made the purchases for her, so she might not even know or see the items that were hers. Only when she came to visit her father would she help him pick out items. Botello knew that she had several old baskets on consignment and that those, like all the items she had on consignment at Hubbell Trading Post, were denoted with the initials "J," "JJ," or some similar variation. Those items had now been tied up in government custody for years because of the investigation.

Botello explained that when an item she had on consignment sold, her father would usually call and tell her to come and pick up the check he had waiting for her. She would then typically tell her father to just go ahead and sign the check for her and cash it and use the money to buy more jewelry, rugs, or baskets. She acknowledged that on rare occasions she would pick up the check and endorse it herself but otherwise had her father sign for her.

I asked Botello to examine a number of WNPA checks issued in her name (Jean Jackson), bearing endorsement signatures also in her name. She did not recognize any of the checks and speculated that she'd probably not ever seen them before. She also didn't think any of the endorsement signatures on the checks were her own, but couldn't be certain because her father's handwriting was very similar to her own. Once again, however, she explained that if the endorsement signatures were made by her father rather than herself, that was done with her permission.[10]

▲▼▲

The interviews with Malone's daughter and his son-in-law were remarkable mainly for the added insight they provided about the circumstances under which Malone forged the endorsement signatures. In both cases, whether technically proper or not, he had their authorization and consent to sign checks on their behalf, just as a husband and wife might for one another. Their respective statements were the only ones that (now) addressed the issue of whether Malone might have been authorized or had permission to sign signatures on behalf of others. As far as I could tell, none of the other interviews previously conducted had explored that possibility. But I would later learn that other witnesses, including Malone's predecessor at Hubbell Trading Post, Al Grieve, had offered that same explanation. He, too, had authorized Malone to sign checks for him. Checks made out to Grieve were among those bearing endorsement signatures believed to have been forged by Malone.

Though I was never provided with a documenting report, Grieve much later approached me to confirm that he had, in fact, been interviewed in the early stages of the investigation. He said that he had tried to explain to investigators that he had several of his own rugs, jewelry, baskets, and other items consigned through Malone at Hubbell Trading Post. He simultaneously had a number of open accounts on lay-away items for which he owed money. According to Grieve, when Malone would call to advise that an item had sold, Grieve would try to get in to town (Ganado) to pick up the check. But if he was too busy with the ranch or other business and could not get away, he simply asked Malone to endorse the check for him and apply the money to pay off his account.[11] But none of that was reflected in any of the reports I had seen.

Yet another sidebar to the interview with Karen Jean was the matter of her former husband, Vernon Jackson.

Jackson was formerly a supervisor with the Navajo Police Department and then with the Hopi tribal law enforcement program. He later joined the Criminal Investigations Division of the Environmental Protection Agency. Over the years Jackson had developed skills and acquired experience supervising and managing complex criminal investigations and had risen through the ranks to his current position as a senior special agent.

Jackson had, in fact, been interviewed in the course of the investigation conducted by Yee and his task force. A report documenting *that* interview actually *was* included in the materials Yee had provided.

The interview with Jackson took place August 10, 2004, at the Albuquerque airport. The entire report documenting his interview is only a half-page long. It cites Jackson's occupation, the year he and Malone's daughter, Karen Jean, were divorced, and the address of the small house in Gallup where they lived together while married. Beyond that, the only substantive information cited was that Jackson had known Malone since 1980 and knew Malone was a collector while living in Piñon. He said that Malone "had a lot of stuff at his house including consignment items with tags." The report finally acknowledged that "Jackson was under the impression that Malone was going to open his own trading post [in Gallup] some day and seemed to know how to be a business man."[12]

I spoke with Jackson nearly four years later to learn how he had been approached and to ask what he knew about the NPS investigation.

Jackson first heard about the Hubbell investigation in June 2004 when his children called to tell him their grandma was very sick and upset about the FBI raiding their home at the trading post. Jackson then called Malone and learned it had actually been the NPS that raided their home.

A little while later Jackson received a call from NPS agent Christopher Smith asking to meet for an interview. Jackson was on his way out of town on business but agreed to meet with Smith at the Albuquerque airport. Jackson met there with both Smith and a female officer. They told Jackson they were involved in an investigation at Hubbell Trading Post and wanted to find out what he knew about his former father-in-law.

Jackson told the agents that Malone was one of the most honest people he knew. Jackson tried to explain the long history of internal rivalries and the incessant backstabbing that had gone on at the trading post for years, resulting in any number of personnel complaints between the sales staff jockeying for position. These challenges for Malone, according to Jackson, were aggravated by off-site WNPA supervisors trying to tell Malone how to run things.

The agents asked about the "wads of money" and large quantities of jewelry Malone had at his home. Jackson explained that Malone always carried a lot of cash because most of his clients on the reservation dealt in cash only. He also told them Malone had an enormous collection of handcrafted Navajo jewelry and had been collecting since back in the days when he lived in Piñon.

During the brief airport interview, Jackson took the opportunity to quiz the NPS agents about the agency's strategies in carrying out the Hubbell investigation. They told him about the search warrant executed at Malone's residence and the resulting seizure of enormous quantities of "incriminating evidence." They also told Jackson that "numerous interviews" had been conducted implicating Malone in "serious wrongdoing."

Relying on his own considerable experience as a federal investigator, as well as his history interacting with his former father-in-law, Jackson cautioned Smith and his partner to proceed with great care in drawing any conclusions about Malone. He pointed out that because of Malone's many years as a collector and a trader, it would be very difficult to distinguish and determine what property in his house was his own and part of his private collection versus what was legitimately there as part of the consignment inventory he rotated through the trading post. Jackson told Smith and his partner that regardless of what they believed or had heard, he suspected that most of the property found in Malone's residence probably belonged to him personally. Jackson told the investigators he thought they were going down the "wrong trail" in their assessment of his former father-in-law. He doubted they would be able to establish that Malone had ever acted with any real criminal intent.

There was one particularly unusual thing that Jackson recalled about his brief 2004 airport interview. During the middle of their conversation, the female agent seemed to develop an "attitude" and simply walked away. Jackson concluded that she refused to believe what he had to say and didn't even want to hear it. Only Smith remained to finish the interview. Jackson said he found this troubling and that it raised questions in his own mind about the level of objectivity and professionalism being exercised in the investigation.

A couple months later Jackson received a notice from one of the regional intelligence organizations to which he belonged, alerting him that a special agent from the NPS, Clyde Yee, had run a credit check on him. Jackson called Yee to find out what he was up to and why he had needed to generate a credit report on him. Yee reportedly explained that he was conducting official business and just checking things out as part of the investigation into the activities of Billy

Malone. Jackson was incredulous and pointed out that he had not even seen Malone in nearly ten years. Yee told Jackson that "everyone who has had contact with Malone is a suspect."[13]

Reflecting on this incident, Jackson reiterated his belief that Yee and the other NPS agents really had been going down the wrong trail and didn't seem to know what they were doing. It seemed to Jackson that the NPS was engaged in more of a "fishing expedition" than a legitimate criminal investigation.

A Whistle-Blower, Again

(Oodzíí' baanáá hóone')

O N SATURDAY, OCTOBER 21, 2006, I sent a two-page e-mail to my contact in OIG, alerting him that my report was nearly completed and would be on its way the following week. I summarized some of the more disturbing things that I had documented, observing that

> this investigation could serve as a case-study in just about everything that's wrong with the NPS law enforcement and investigative program (a perfect storm) including inappropriate influence by management and political interests, raw incompetence, possible civil rights and other criminal violations and other serious misconduct or at least egregiously poor judgment exercised from top-to-bottom within the organization.

I knew there would be serious repercussions from sending a copy of my report directly to the OIG before even my supervisors had a chance to see it. Anticipating that inevitable reprisal, my e-mail was red-flagged and captioned "Heads-up and request for advance intervention." I wanted to make sure the OIG was poised to provide me with a measure of cover *before* my supervisors or other NPS officials had a chance to retaliate again.

My final 230-plus page report (an 83-page narrative report, along with

25 separate attachments or "exhibits") was submitted on October 23, 2006. In addition to materials I'd compiled when I first took on the investigation and the recent interviews with Perry Shorty and Karen Jean Botello, that document now contained a summary of the incredible allegations made against Malone:

- Forgery
- Bank fraud
- Theft of United States government property
- Providing false information to the United States government
- Theft of personal property
- Embezzlement of funds
- Social Security fraud
- Extortion
- Wire fraud
- Tax evasion and Tax fraud

The report also contained an analysis with tables and charts of all the evidence in the case supporting (or not supporting) those charges. Those tables and charts graphically displayed the extent to which Billy Malone had been if not altogether falsely accused then certainly *over*-accused as the case developed and took on a life of its own.

The most *unsubstantiated* of the allegations (theft of personal property, wire fraud, Social Security fraud, and extortion) along with comparisons of Malone to Al Capone, and what were arguably inflated estimates of the value of the property seized from Malone's residence ("more than $5 million dollars"), first appeared in reports supporting funding requests.[1] Because total costs for the investigation (including salaries) eventually approached $1 million, speculation later surfaced that many of the charges had been recklessly and imaginatively listed as a part of a sales pitch designed to pander to the WNPA and impress naïve NPS managers by inflating the apparent magnitude of "the big case" in the pursuit and justification of funding.

One complete copy of my report (along with all the additional materials that had been provided to me by Yee) went to Long. I included an extensive transmittal memorandum reflecting additional concerns affecting prospective prosecution. Within that memorandum I offered the following comments justifying the inclusion of statements made by LeAnn Simpson:

I have included comprehensive documentation about these conversations and statements made by Ms. Simpson in the body of my report in the belief that they have evidentiary value, and may also raise significant issues about the objectivity and impartiality with which the investigation was initially undertaken. I am concerned that if complete documentation about this series of conversations is not contained within the body of my report, we could later be subject to claims of omitting exculpatory information. Given the apparent omissions of key information already detected in the earlier phases of this investigation, the last thing I want to do is aggravate or contribute to that situation by omitting statements made to me by witnesses; particularly by LeAnn Simpson, who as the reporting party for this entire matter, plays a central role in the overall investigation.

I did not independently investigate or attempt to corroborate Ms. Simpson's account, beyond acquiring copies of relevant correspondence and contracts, which are already included as attachments to the body of my report. However, statements made by Ms. Simpson about the manner in which she and WNPA were approached for financial assistance with the NPS investigation, and the various promises and agreements that were reportedly made to WNPA by NPS officials, does account for and provide a measure of insight into the periodic timing of calls I've received from both regional and Washington-level personnel pressuring me to call Simpson and provide her with case briefings and updates.

As you know from our earlier conversations and e-mails, I have shared this and other case information with senior officials of the Department of the Interior's Office of Inspector General, in the belief that their office may have concern and exercise jurisdiction over acts (as well as omissions) committed by officials implicated by Ms. Simpson's statements.[2]

A second complete copy of my report went to the OIG under cover of a separate transmittal memorandum documenting additional issues not reflected in the official report. That cover memorandum closed with the following comments:

The last point I'd like to emphasize is the extraordinarily difficult situation that is created within the current NPS organizational structure (and particularly within the NPS Special Agent and Law Enforcement Program) for individuals like me who may uncover serious improprieties, but have nowhere to turn, and no one to trust within their chain-of-command with sensitive information. I speculate that in a "normal" law enforcement organization (and I have worked in one other organization where this was the case), the majority of supervisors and managers have at least earned a modicum of trust and confidence from subordinates to enable a "whistleblower" to seek out at least *someone* in their chain-of-command who can be trusted with information, and lend support and assistance in addressing or at least referring problems to the right place.

Unfortunately, in my opinion, our organization is so saturated with individuals—particularly at the top—who have been selected for their positions based solely upon their personal friendships or alliances with (other) managers, and the resulting organization is so completely closed and openly "fraternal" in nature, that an employee would be crazy to voice concerns or bring a serious complaint forward. Those who do speak up pay a very high price, serving as clear examples for others to not follow suit. You're already familiar with the large number of fairly serious cases I've dared to refer to your office over the years. Imagine how many similar incidents actually occur on a regular basis within the National Park Service, but do not get reported.

... The result is that in most instances, serious problems are not voiced and, therefore, not addressed. The further result is a series of disastrous decisions and actions (often affecting public safety or the rights of citizens) like those that appear to have unfolded in the Hubbell Investigation.

... As your office or others consider and evaluate everything that went wrong with the Hubbell Investigation, I hope you'll consider, in a historical context, the overall organizational structure and composition that allowed this mess to develop. ... The current situation is nothing new, and you can look back over time within the NPS and find any number of similar examples of investigations unethically and incompetently undertaken, with disastrous—but often concealed—consequences (Yosemite, 1985?).

As I said in an earlier e-mail, this (Hubbell) case stands as another perfect example of the type and magnitude of disaster that can, has, and predictably will continue to occur in an organization so completely politically and fraternally influenced as is the current NPS law enforcement program.

I am fully braced for the grief and harassment that will inevitably follow submission of my report, coming from any number of directions, including LE supervisors[,] . . . peers, WNPA, Mike Snyder, Steve Martin, Jim Babbitt, and others. I don't claim to be the world's greatest investigator, but I offer no apologies for the work I've done on this case, or for the manner in which I've attempted to bring this matter to your attention for an independent review. I'm proud if I've been able to turn a very bad situation around, right a few wrongs to prevent someone (who admittedly did make some serious mistakes) from being completely railroaded by a very bad investigation, and assure a balanced and just outcome.

If nothing else, I genuinely hope the issues identified in how this case was mishandled will be used by your office to finally compel the critical changes and reforms, from top-to-bottom, that are needed to establish a professional law enforcement program in the National Park Service.

Thanks again.

I did not notify anyone in my chain of command that I had completed my investigation and submitted my report. As far as they knew, I was still working on the case, and waiting for the court to unseal Yee's affidavit and application for a search warrant.

Finalizing and submitting my report was a huge relief but not the end of my worries. If anyone demanded that I change my report and omit information damaging to the NPS or the WNPA, I would be able to fully document the changes and omissions, and there would be a record of what had originally been contained in my report. But it would still not be a pleasant experience. So I was extremely relieved to learn that after receiving the final report, the OIG requested that Long not allow any other NPS personnel to see it, including my own supervisors.[3]

Now it was just a matter of time and stress, as I waited for word from Long about his decision on prosecution and word from the OIG about the prospect for an internal investigation. I was just hoping I'd have answers before anyone from my own chain of command demanded an explanation of what was going on.

However, my stress level once again became elevated when, on November 1, 2006, I received the following e-mail from Brian Smith:

Paul—

Reference Hal's request, please make contact with him and get him the information he needs.

Thanks,
Brian

Appearing immediately below Smith's message was the following communication from Hal Grovert, the IMR's associate director for operations:

Brian,

Can I get a final report from Paul Berkowitz on the Hubbell case. Mostly what I need is a final disposition on the property and why. Regional Director Mike Snyder is meeting with the WNPA Board next month, and I would like him to be able to talk to them as to the end of the investigation. . . .

Hal

I could hardly believe it. While I had successfully dodged requests to share my report and brief my own supervisors about the most recent developments, I was now being directed to share that report and provide a briefing to some of the most senior people who were now implicated in my investigation and who were (hopefully) about to become the subject of an internal investigation undertaken by the OIG. The irony was staggering, but it was not without an undercurrent of humorous vindication. If nothing else, this latest e-mail exchange served to reinforce the level to which NPS investigations were compromised and driven by management and political interests.

I immediately followed up with my own e-mail message to the OIG, attached to Brian Smith's and Hal Grovert's request. My message was brief and to the point:

Now would be a good time for intervention.

I simultaneously left a number of voice messages with my OIG contact expressing the urgent need for him to notify NPS director Mary Bomar that the OIG was taking over the investigation.

I reached my OIG contact by telephone around 6:30 the next morning (November 2). He had very welcome news. He had just met with Bomar and told her that his Program Integrity Division was assuming jurisdiction over the Hubbell investigation. With the exception of my transitional support, the NPS was directed to stand down, fully withdraw from the investigation, and not investigate, participate, or insert itself in any way, unless specifically requested. Also, I was now authorized to invoke the OIG's authority to restrict further distribution of my own report and other case information and refuse any inquiries or requests I might receive from my own supervisors.

Later that same day I received another e-mail, this time from Pat Buccello:

Paul,

I have been notified that the OIG is taking over the Hubbell case and we are directed not to do anything further. Obviously, you will be providing the IG with whatever they need as they proceed.

Thanks,
Pat

Once again, my contacts in the OIG had come through for me at the last moment.

I breathed a huge sigh of relief in the recognition that the investigation had successfully transitioned into a new stage and that my own investigative efforts were completed.

Now, I only had to stick it out and endure the inevitable scorn of my colleagues and supervisors until the United States Attorney's Office made its decision as to whether to prosecute. Then, I thought, I'd be able to retire (albeit earlier than I had planned) and walk away from the case and the NPS with a clear conscience and the prospect of a postretirement existence free of the stress I had lived with for too many years.

Job Satisfaction ("It's Over")

(Hojoobá´ ígo índa ííłtsxoh)

BY LATE 2006 the inspector general's multiyear Grand Canyon/PGI Contracting fraud investigation was nearing completion. That entire mess,
accompanied by a flurry of lawsuits and even legislation to compensate the many
subcontractor-victims, had been in the Arizona and Utah press for nearly three
years, leaving the NPS with a huge black eye. It was turning out to be another in
a series of very bad years for the Grand Canyon superintendent who, whether
by coincidence or design, was now being pressured to either accept an expedient
transfer to Washington, D.C., or retire.

That same superintendent secured his assignment at the Grand Canyon in
2000 after a politically laced Colorado River rafting trip with secretary of the
interior Bruce Babbitt. Now, in an attempt to save his position and resist growing pressures to move on and out, the superintendent was calling in favors from
the likes of senators Jon Kyle and John McCain. According to park sources, the
superintendent even went on a camping retreat with McCain to plead his case.
That effort reportedly backfired after McCain surprised the new secretary of the
interior with inquiries on the superintendent's behalf. The secretary was angered
to have been caught off guard and less than fully briefed on the situation at the
Grand Canyon and the political moves afoot. Then, after receiving briefings on the
OIG's various investigative activities at Grand Canyon, McCain reportedly bowed
out and withdrew his support. All of this, for me, explained why the pain I created

for the superintendent had dropped off the radar screen, and he was no longer in a position to influence or oppose my own threatened return to the park.[1]

Like most organizations, in the NPS when one political door closes, another swings open. The growing problems and pending vacancy at Grand Canyon created the opportunity for NPS deputy director Steve Martin to return west to take over as superintendent. In the strange organization of the NPS, that position carries at least as much power, pay, and prestige as does NPS deputy director. Aided by his friend, Mike Snyder, Martin overcame a number of his own political hurdles to leverage the transfer to Grand Canyon. Rumors of his coup and pending arrival as the new superintendent spread like wildfire throughout the NPS several months before his official February 2007 transfer date. Accompanying those rumors was prophetic word that his wife, Cyd Martin, would also be returning to her home base in the IMR to establish an office in Flagstaff. Reflecting her own growing power and influence, her duties and authority were expanded to encompass supervision over all three of the national park sites situated on the Navajo Reservation: Navajo National Monument, Hubbell Trading Post NHS, and Canyon de Chelly National Monument.

Both of these arranged transfers, and particularly the creation of a new "super-superintendent" position for Cyd Martin, signaled what was perceived by many NPS employees as the defining move in the establishment of a new sort of "IMR mafia" under reign of the Martins and Snyder. The less-than-subtle manner in which this regional transformation took place, and the resentment it created with employees excluded from the process, resulted in yet another wave of complaints and demands that an investigation be undertaken by the OIG into noncompetitive selection practices.

Mafia or not, Cyd Martin's elevation to superintendent of the newly created Navajo group of parks meant that she would become my wife's new supervisor. With both her husband's and Snyder's names figuring prominently in my investigative report, the prospect of Cyd Martin now assuming a direct supervisory role over my wife was foreboding. My wife needed to quickly "get out of Dodge" (actually, Chinle and the entire IMR hierarchy) before she, too, suffered her own inevitable wave of reprisal for being married to a whistle-blowing bastard like me.

▲▽▲

It didn't take long for the OIG to launch its investigation. Records indicate its case file no. PI-PI-07–0054-I was opened on November 2, 2006, the same day that Bomar was told the OIG was taking over the investigation. Special agent

Paul Okerberg from the OIG's Program Integrity Division was assigned as the OIG's case agent.

The initial purpose of the OIG investigation was

> to examine the investigative agent's conduct, the partnership with a non–law enforcement entity, any pressure to reach a predetermined conclusion by the Regional Director, and NPS management oversight.

That examination included a specific inquiry into whether

> NPS agents cited false information on a search warrant affidavit; exceeded the scope of the warrant; . . . committed breaches to the chain of custody for property seized . . . and excluded information from investigative reports and failed to follow leads.

But the scope of the OIG investigation soon expanded when it

> became aware of additional concerns regarding the confidentiality of the criminal investigation; the potential release of Criminal Procedure, Rule 6(e) [Grand Jury] information; and the appearance of an inappropriate relationship between NPS and WNPA.

Listed as "possible subjects" of the new OIG investigation were Clyde Yee, Steve Martin, Mike Snyder, LeAnn Simpson, and Jim Babbitt.

Under the heading of "Potential Statutes Violated" was 18 USC 1001 (false statements), one of the federal crimes of which Billy Malone had been accused nearly two and a half years before.[2]

▲▼▲

I received notice about the new case assignment on Monday, November 6, in a telephone call from the OIG. I was given Okerberg's name and number and requested to make contact to set up a meeting. We connected shortly thereafter, made brief telephone introductions, and agreed to stay in touch as our respective schedules around the upcoming holidays firmed up to see if we could arrange a meeting before the end of the year.

Monday, November 13, I was in Albuquerque attending the National Native American Law Enforcement Association conference, where I was scheduled to make a presentation on enforcement of the Indian Arts and Crafts Act and related crimes. That same day, before the session I was hosting, I received a call from Okerberg to finalize plans for a meeting later that month in Phoenix, where we also hoped to meet with Rob Long for introductions and case briefings.

That very same morning, around 11:30 a.m., I received a phone call from Brian Smith. He was seeking information about the OIG's new role in the Hubbell case, explaining that he needed to brief IMR deputy director Hal Grovert so that Grovert could brief Snyder, so that Snyder could, in turn, brief Jim Babbitt, LeAnn Simpson, and other WNPA officials about the OIG investigation at an upcoming WNPA board meeting. Remarkably, Smith was still seeking the same information I had been requested to provide in the earlier e-mail that sent me scrambling to the OIG for emergency intervention!

I respectfully declined to share any significant information. I offered only that the OIG had assumed control of the investigation and that I was scheduled to meet with their agents to provide a case briefing but said I could not tell him anything else. I, on the other hand, had gleaned a key piece of information in my conversation with Smith. It was almost certain, now, that virtually everyone in the NPS special agent organization, the IMR and Washington offices, the WNPA, and beyond now knew that I had already finished my investigation and turned the case directly over to the OIG.

I managed to take some time off for the Thanksgiving holiday with only minor interruptions from work. The following Monday (November 27) I drove down to Phoenix where I was scheduled to meet the next morning with Okerberg. I arrived at Okerberg's hotel lobby around 8:30 a.m. and easily spotted him. He was tall and slender, wore a trimmed beard and had a runner's physique, and was conspicuous by his neatly pressed black business suit and tie. I was dressed in my usual jeans and Hawaii shirt. We introduced ourselves and then went into the dining room where his partner was still eating breakfast.

We talked briefly at the breakfast table. Both Okerberg and his partner had read my report, and they expressed amazement at the incredible series of events in the investigation. Then we piled into my vehicle and headed over to the United States Attorney's Office downtown.

Our meeting with Long lasted only an hour or two. The two OIG agents seemed a little surprised that Long was still evaluating the case against Malone and had not yet made a decision to decline prosecution. Okerberg's partner, in particular, seemed impatient, speculating that whatever Billy Malone might have done, the case had been trashed by the conduct of the people who had initially led and conducted the investigation against him. Long seemed a little taken aback by that evaluation. Still, to his credit, Long indicated he wanted to be thorough in his case review and take his time with a decision. Okerberg, too (who was the lead agent on the new case), expressed support for taking a cautious and methodical approach.

Part of the reason for meeting with Long was to make sure he and his supervisors were aware that the OIG was now looking into the conduct of both NPS and WNPA officials rather than that of Billy Malone. We focused on the question of whether Long and his office would handle any prospective criminal allegations arising from the OIG's case or instead have the matter reviewed by officials in the public corruption section in Washington, D.C. We also went over the matter of which office would issue any subpoenas that might be needed in the OIG's investigation. Most of these questions were left unresolved until the OIG investigation was further underway.

Okerberg and his partner flew out later that afternoon. I drove north up the Grand Canyon, for the first time in over a year, to participate in a shoot for *Court TV*, covering the Robert Spangler serial murder investigation (which stands as an example of some of the really good investigative work that *can* be done in the NPS). One of the agents assigned to my office initiated that investigation as a cold case in 1999, along with the FBI and Arapahoe County, Colorado, Sheriff's Office. The team eventually secured a confession to four murders going back to 1978, a guilty plea in federal court, and a life sentence.[3]

I spent the following week (December 4) in Salt Lake City attending a mandatory gathering of NPS special agents from around the country. I was dreading the meeting, not only because I generally detested the predictable cheerleading, empty speeches, and marginal training presented by our leadership at such events but also because I knew I would encounter most of the individuals who were now the focus of the OIG investigation, including my own supervisors who I had sidestepped to file my report.

The conference was a predictably uncomfortable experience for me. I was conspicuously excluded from certain conversations and even ceremonies recognizing seniority and tenure and also received the occasional stare and disparaging comment about me "switching sides" and "tubing" Clyde Yee. I told myself I didn't much care. Susan Morton, too, was challenged, questioned, and given the cold shoulder for having documented her own concerns about Yee and having allied herself with me. I think it bothered her more. I survived the week without any major bruises. I'm not so sure about Susan.

▲▼▲

The subpoenas for Malone's bank records were never served. In fact much later, while closing out his case files, Long discovered that similar subpoenas had been issued all the way back in 2004, but those, too, had never been served. Now, instead, without need of a subpoena, Malone had his bank provide certified copies of his wife's and his bank records going back to early 2004, before the NPS raid. These were among the last items Long wanted to review. Uncovering absolutely no anomalies or anything suspicious indicated in those records, Long reached his decision. He recommended that the U.S. Attorney's Office close its case file and not prosecute Billy Gene Malone. Long shared that news with me on December 12, indicating that he'd forward a copy of the official letter documenting that decision when that was approved and finalized. That would take nearly three weeks. Then, if I liked, I could hand deliver a copy of the letter to Malone.

The investigation being conducted by the OIG was another matter. That new case would continue for another full year before it was officially closed. Even then, it would take several more years and a series of separate legal actions before the inspector general's report would be made public.

Okerberg flew back in to Albuquerque by himself on Monday, January 8, 2007. I picked him up at the airport and we headed to Santa Fe. We had scheduled a road trip to tie up a few loose ends with remaining evidence, to continue discussions about his transition as the new case agent, and perhaps most importantly, to allow me to introduce him to some of the people involved in the case. Given the level of distrust generated by the NPS in the first phase of its investigation, that would be essential before many of the witnesses both within and outside of the Navajo community would agree to cooperate with yet another government agent who was "there to help."

Most of the paper evidence involved in the original case (items listed for seizure in the warrant) was supposed to be stored in the Santa Fe office of NPS internal affairs agent Chip Davis. Davis was out of town that week but had made arrangements for Okerberg and me to access the lockers where the documents were stored so that we could take a look, assume custody, and return the boxes full of documents taken from Malone as well as the WNPA. Okerberg was reluctant to assume custody of evidence and other property from the old case, so I agreed to take on that role and facilitate its return.

We went to Davis's office the next day (Tuesday, January 9) to take a look. There was clearly far more material than we could fit in my vehicle. Fortunately, we were able to distinguish material taken from Malone's residence from documents obtained directly from the WNPA. That brought the load down to a manageable level.

Using inventory sheets left for us by Davis, we determined that at least one box of records and other property seized from Malone's residence, identified as R26 (the letter "R" identifying the contents as coming from Malone's residence), was missing. That box was supposed to contain an unspecified amount of money, including checks and cash, which were also missing. The inventory sheet indicated both of these "items" (R26 as well as the cash) were still in Santa Fe, in the lockers now before us, but neither was there. I signed for the boxes of Malone's property that were present and loaded them into the back of my vehicle. We left instructions for Davis to ship the balance of property directly to LeAnn Simpson in Tucson.

The next day (Wednesday, January 10) we met with former Hubbell superintendent Nancy Stone, who was now retired and living outside of Albuquerque. I had arranged this meeting hoping that Stone could provide Okerberg with background on the management of Hubbell Trading Post NHS as well as her impressions of how the investigation had been handled. She did this quite effectively, citing for Okerberg "the inherent contradictions that exist for Hubbell Trading Post," how "its statutory mandate to operate as a real trading post, rather than as a gift shop or museum, contrasts with the desire in some circles to see it operate as a money-making venture applying modern business practices."

Stone also shared her opinion that both the NPS and the WNPA made a "rush to judgment," failing to look for plausible explanations for what had occurred, never talking to Malone, or even attempting to learn anything about the history of Hubbell Trading Post or the art of old-world trading. Okerberg had Stone review the report OIG agent Jamie Howard had written documenting her August 2, 2004, interview. It was then that Stone first identified the many errors and mischaracterizations reflected in that report.[4]

Later that afternoon Okerberg and I drove to Gallup, where we were scheduled to meet with Malone at his residence and return the property we now had.

Malone and his wife, along with one of their daughters and her husband and their two children, were all living together in their tiny two bedroom adobe bungalow located just a few blocks south of the main drag (Route 66) running through town. This was the first time Okerberg had met Malone. He, too, seemed struck by Malone's mild and almost meek stature and demeanor. We were introduced to Malone's wife, Minnie, as well as their daughter and her children, who were obediently playing in the adjacent kitchen. We carried the boxes inside and stacked them in the tiny living room. We asked Malone to go through the contents so that he'd be comfortable signing the new property receipt I had prepared. That receipt acknowledged that at least one box of seized property, including an unknown quantity of cash, was still missing.

Before leaving, I opened my brief case and pulled out the letter I had received a few days earlier from Long, dated January 4, 2007. More than a year after I'd inherited the Hubbell case, and more than two and a half years after the NPS had launched its investigation targeting Billy Malone, the U.S. Attorney's Office had finalized its decision. Based on all of the evidence, good and bad, it had decided to close its case files and not pursue a prosecution.

After expenditure of nearly a million dollars, not a single charge would be filed against Malone in the Hubbell investigation. I felt that I had done my job, but it was most certainly not the outcome my own supervisors had anticipated or desired when they assigned me to take over the investigation. It was equally certain I would not be receiving any accolades, awards, or even thanks from the NPS for my work.

I pulled Malone aside, handed him the letter, and told him, "It's over." The NPS investigation and the government's case against him was closed.

Malone's eyes welled up as he read the letter. He reached out to shake my hand, quietly saying "thank you," and then gave me a hug. It was one of the most remarkable and gratifying moments I had experienced in my entire thirty-three-year career.

Nothing Is Ever Easy
(or, It's Hard to Say Good-bye)
(T'áá ałtsogóó nanitł'ah)
(hagooínee' hodi dóó' niiłígi nanitł'ah)

THE NEXT MORNING Okerberg and I headed west for a meeting I'd sched-uled later that afternoon with AUSA Joe Lodge in Flagstaff. We detoured on the way for a stop in Ganado, giving Okerberg his first real opportunity to see a part of the reservation and look around at Hubbell Trading Post.

I had set up the January 11 meeting with the U.S. Attorney's Office in Flagstaff so that Okerberg could hear the account of Yee's prior run-in with that office and the resultant dismissal of theft charges against the other employee at Hubbell Trading Post. Lodge was reportedly not at all pleased to be drawn into the OIG's investigation. He was likely not pleased that the inspector general was involved at all and now scrutinizing the manner in which the original NPS investigation had been conducted. Lodge had assisted in the investigation by authorizing several of the subpoenas used by Yee to secure various records. But I wanted Okerberg to hear, firsthand, about the issues that had led to the complete dismissal of charges, even after acceptance of a guilty plea from the defendant in that other case.

Okerberg flew out that same evening. I stayed the night in Flagstaff and headed back to Chinle the next morning. I was eastbound on I-40 when I received yet another phone call from LeAnn Simpson. She wanted to know if there were any new developments in the investigation. She also wanted to know if I was avail-able to witness and mediate a meeting at Hubbell Trading Post, where she now intended to return most of the remaining property to Malone. I agreed to meet her and Malone the following week at the trading post, with the understanding that my role would be limited to serving as a witness and helping to keep the peace. I would have no direct part in negotiations over property. I was willing to play this limited role solely to help reach a final resolution on the property that had been tied up since the investigation began.

I also told Simpson that the U.S. Attorney's Office had decided not to pursue prosecution and had closed the case against Malone. She was obviously not pleased about that decision. She asked if she could obtain a copy of my report. I told her it was not yet available, since the case had now been taken over by the OIG. My report had been incorporated into its ongoing internal investigation.

Just minutes after hanging up the phone, Simpson received a call from Okerberg, attempting to schedule his own interview with her. Simpson was upset over that prospect and called me right back. She was concerned about the WNPA becoming entangled in an OIG internal investigation and speculated about the need for her own lawyer. She also questioned whether she should go ahead with the meeting next week at Hubbell's to return the balance of property to Malone.

Just as Simpson had entreated Yee, asking him to call and brief Babbitt on the status of the investigation, Simpson now asked me if I could speak with the new WNPA board chair, Christine Szuter. I agreed to make the call, which seemed a great relief to Simpson.

I hung up with Simpson and called Okerberg. He confirmed that he, too, had just spoken with Simpson to arrange an interview and was surprised that she was so alarmed over that prospect. He had no objection to me either calling the new WNPA board chair or participating in the scheduled meeting the following week at Hubbell Trading Post.

When I spoke with Szuter a few minutes later, I confirmed that the OIG had indeed taken over the case as an internal investigation. I added, however, that I didn't think there was any reason to cancel next week's meeting with Malone, particularly in light of how long it had taken and how difficult it had been to schedule. This seemed to assure her. She agreed that the property return could proceed as scheduled.

The following Wednesday morning, January 17, I made the short drive from Chinle back down to Hubbell Trading Post. Simpson, Scott Aldridge, and Steve Pickle were already there, set up in the old wareroom with what resembled a makeshift but well-organized and imposing-looking command center. The scene was anachronistic: the tables, chairs, telephones, computer, printer, and fax machine clashed with the dusty old barnlike facility, complete with warped plank-wood flooring and light peeking through the cracks in the joints where old wooden rafters joined the worn adobe walls. Simpson and her staff were arranging property in preparation for the meeting with Malone.

Malone, dressed in his usual button-tab western shirt, faded jeans, and moccasins, arrived a short time later. He was accompanied by two of his Navajo daughters, Karen Jean and B.J., as well as friend and fellow Indian trader Hank Blair from Totsoh Trading Post in Lukachukai. Blair is an enormous and powerful looking cowboy figure, intimidating by his very presence if not for the huge grin he constantly wears underneath his bushy moustache. Adding to the novelty of the scene, Malone's daughters were equipped with their own notepads as well as still and tripod-mounted video cameras to document the exchange. It was like a scene from a spaghetti western, where two warring factions, ever cautious, were meeting at high noon for an exchange of hostages, each trying to keep the other from getting the upper hand.

Overall, in spite of apparent expectations, the transfer of property went very smoothly. Malone's own strategy for the exchange and dealing with Simpson must have worked, as she eventually turned over everything he identified as his own or a relative's. Malone even spent considerable time helping Simpson identify who owned the property he was not claiming.

More significant for me were a series of comments Simpson made just prior to Malone's arrival, once again expressing her frustrations about the investigation's change in course. Her comments were significant enough that I documented them for Okerberg three days later in a January 20 e-mail:

> Forgot to mention that the other day (Wed. 1/17) right before Malone arrived at HTP for the property exchange, LeAnn was going on at length again about how none of this had turned out the way they'd been told to expect, etc. . . . and again, made clear that she and WNPA would never have contributed money to the investigation if Martin had not personally made the request and told her that "It would be in our best interests" to help pay for the investigation. She noted that all the others (Clyde, Chip Davis, etc.) made the first overtures, but she made clear to them that before WNPA would contribute its funds, then Regional Director Steve Martin would need to make the request. She has been very consistent with this, including her use of the phrase about contributing "being in our best interests." To the extent that she believes it will divert responsibility to

Martin, Snyder, Yee, and others, I suspect she will be fairly "forthcoming" when she eventually does talk . . . unless her lawyer tells her to shut up or you end up having to subpoena her. It is clear to me that she is both angry and nervous about how things are transpiring. She clearly still maintains that Malone was a major crook . . . and she is visibly angry that he's not going to jail[,] is not being charged, got all of the property back, and seems to still be embraced by Navajos and other traders in the community (several older Navajo ladies came up to him throughout the course of the day to greet him and give him hugs. You could almost see LeAnn grimacing when this happened).

With this final phase of my own investigation completed, and what I thought was the last of the property from the case returned to its rightful owners, I put my mind to crafting my retirement notice. I gave my D.C. contact with the OIG a heads-up, along with a request to monitor potential acts of reprisal that might now be directed at my wife. By this time, both of the Martins had returned to the IMR, and Cyd Martin had assumed her role as my wife's supervisor. Though she had no prior experiences with her, Martin was already sending strong and explicit signals to my wife to move on and not waste her time applying for any other positions in the region. In communicating that message, Martin had even referenced my name and my inflexible and "heavy-handed" approach to law enforcement as a major part of my wife's "problem."

Sunday evening, January 21, 2007, I completed my official retirement notice. I faxed the letter that same night and mailed a signed copy the next morning. The letter was addressed to Pat Buccello and her own supervisor, NPS chief ranger Don Coelho. It was less than one page long and to the point. I explained my decision by noting that

I only recently completed work on a very complex and sensitive case that has consumed a major portion of my time and energy over the past year; often at the expense of other priorities and commitments. My investigation was completed last fall. My investigative report was finalized and submitted to the Office of the United States Attorney and other appropriate entities as the year came to an end. Just this past January 4, 2007, the United States Attorney for the District of Arizona closed out their case file on this matter through declination. No doubt this decision, along with the return of millions of dollars in seized property to the target of the

（OR, IT'S HARD TO SAY GOOD-BYE）

investigation[,] has upset a number of people who desired and expected a radically different case outcome. However[,] I consider these decisions to be reasonable, fair, legally supportable, and arguably unavoidable in light of the facts and many disturbing and complicating issues identified through the course of my investigation. I therefore consider my work on this investigation to have been a success. The controversial resolution and distribution of property and evidence related to that case was completed just last week, on Wednesday, January 17. This brings the need for my direct involvement in other continuing aspects of this case to a close. In consideration of the reaction my decisions and recent efforts have received, along with other changing circumstances, priorities, and demands on my time, it also signals for me that after nearly 32 years of federal service, the time is right to retire.

I proposed an effective date of March 1, 2007. That would be ample time to attend a retirement seminar, process my paperwork, and check out before things got really ugly as the OIG investigation got fully underway.

▲▼▲

The following week, on January 24, Okerberg and his partner arrived in Lakewood to inspect Yee's office and the "war room" he'd established for the case, complete with enlarged photos of Malone and his suspected coconspirators posted on the walls and hundreds of thousands of documents amassed in boxes and notebooks. Okerberg had made the decision to not formally interview Yee on this occasion, delaying that until he was better acquainted with details of the case.

Okerberg set up in the war room, where he spent that day and part of the next (January 25) examining the contents of all the case files, evidence, and other records that were present. His partner was increasingly impatient and wanted to hastily wrap up the investigation and move on. But Okerberg persisted. He repeatedly directed Yee to bring him *everything*—"any single thing that you have on Hubbell," including all the boxes of evidence and files related to the case that he might have stored in his office or anywhere else. Okerberg inspected the files and asked Yee questions about materials that seemed to be missing and where they might be. Yee said he wasn't sure, explaining that it had been a long time since he had been actively involved in the case. When Okerberg pressed the issue, Yee at least twice acknowledged that he might still have additional files in his office, which he only then produced. As Okerberg continued his inspection, he discovered several boxes containing undocumented evidence, property, and even checks and cash that had been seized from Malone back in June 2004. Still, when Okerberg asked about specific items such as Malone's long-lost wedding blanket and box R26, Yee was unable to produce those items or explain where they were.

Among the more disturbing files Okerberg *did* locate was one labeled "Not Subject to Discovery." In spite of what Sukenic had told Yee more than a year and half earlier, back in June 2005, the label on that file seemed to suggest that its contents would be kept secret from Malone and his attorney had the case ever been prosecuted and gone to trial. Among the records contained within that file was an October 25, 2004, memorandum prepared by Yee, attempting to justify his handling of evidence and responding to Morton's own memorandum that documented the September 2004 break in the chain of custody.

24. Yee's "Not Subject to Discovery" file, containing reports documenting problems in the early phases of the NPS's Hubbell Trading Post investigation (*photograph courtesy of the OIG*).

On the morning of January 25, before returning to Yee's office, Okerberg and his partner drove to the nearby offices of the OIG to interview the government auditor, Ray Macy. Macy had assisted in the NPS investigation by taking over the forensic audit of Hubbell Trading Post financial records. He told Okerberg that he had spent nearly five months reviewing boxes full of documents that were provided to him by the NPS and the WPNA. Included in those boxes were many originals documents as opposed to copies. That, from the beginning, violated established procedures, since those original documents should have been retained as evidence. Audits were supposed to be conducted using strictly copies. In the process of opening envelopes and examining many of those original documents, Macy located checks and quantities of cash that had not previously been counted, much less even inventoried or identified in evidence records. All of those materials were eventually returned to Yee and were among the boxes that still had not been inventoried or logged into evidence that Okerberg found during his inspection at the war room.

Macy also said that the enormous database the NPS had created for the investigation "was worthless." According to Macy, it was obvious that whoever had generated that database didn't know what they were doing and clearly had no experience in financial fraud investigations.

Macy cited a long list of problems in the WNPA's own accounting procedures, not just at Hubbell but across the board. Those same problems had been repeatedly documented over literally decades, in reports prepared by a number of different accounting firms contracted by the SPMA/WNPA to perform independent audits.

Macy said he encountered incredible resistance from the WNPA in response to his requests for needed financial records. He found the WNPA to be less cooperative than any other entity or organization with whom he had worked in his twenty-five years of federal service. He claimed that Simpson had actually refused to provide him with the WNPA records he specifically requested for use in support of his audit. He found that level of resistance extremely significant, raising red flags. He wondered if the WNPA might have broader financial problems that were being blamed on the operation at Hubbell Trading Post. He added that because of inadequate source documentation and the many other accounting problems at the WNPA, he had been unable to determine if Malone or anyone else had actually embezzled or stolen from Hubbell Trading Post or the WNPA.[1]

Okerberg returned to Yee's office later that morning. After examining everything that Yee had produced, Okerberg collected his things and headed to the airport. But while preparing to board the plane, he received a call from Yee, claiming to have found still more records and evidence in his office. Okerberg did not cancel his flight and head back. He had already seen enough.

▲▼▲

At the very same time Okerberg was launching his investigation, I was trying to extricate myself from that case as well as from the organization to which I had devoted more than half of my life by making preparations for my retirement.

The week of January 28, 2007, I drove to Lake Mead National Recreation Area, near Las Vegas, to attend an NPS retirement seminar. As luck would have it, Pat Buccello was also attending. If that wasn't enough, the registration list showed Clyde Yee was also scheduled to attend. Fortunately for me, he never showed, although several of his friends who had participated in his task force were there, making for a generally uncomfortable mix.

Buccello made some particularly strange comments to me during a couple of breaks. The first was in response to my observation that I'd not heard anything back from the human resources department about processing my retirement papers. Buccello acknowledged deficiencies in that office. But instead of offering to raise the issue on my behalf, she urged me to independently seek out a private contractor and pay him to prepare and process my retirement papers!

The second of her comments, during another break on January 30, was even stranger. Without any overture, Buccello cautiously pulled me aside and bluntly asked in a hushed tone, "Do we need to fire Clyde?"

I was surprised and not quite sure how to respond. I doubted Buccello was genuinely interested in my opinion. Instead, I guessed she had somehow heard about some of the issues being investigated by the OIG and was fishing for more information. She echoed what Smith had told me in February 2006, telling me "confidentially" that they were already dealing with serious problems Yee had created in several other cases. From her expanded description, it sounded like many of the same types of issues I had encountered in the Hubbell investigation dogged those cases as well. In light of the new OIG investigation, she was now wondering if the combination of problems might warrant Yee's removal.

What I didn't know at that moment was that almost immediately after his encounter with Okerberg in the Lakewood office, Yee had placed an emergency call to Brian Smith to alert him about the problems discovered in the handling of evidence, property, and secret files. That generated a defensive response on Yee's behalf from both Smith and Buccello. They were planning an emergency trip to Lakewood to meet with Yee to conduct an "intervention" and attempt to "rehabilitate" the chain of custody for the newly discovered evidence. That plan was formulated in spite of Bomar's explicit instructions that everyone in the NPS keep "out" of the investigation altogether unless specifically requested otherwise by the OIG.

I hedged in my response to Buccello. I told her I couldn't comment and said that she should stand down and wait for the OIG to finish its investigation and offer its findings. But I did tell her about an e-mail I received that very morning from Okerberg notifying me about some of the findings from his recent visit to Yee's office and the discovery of additional property that needed to be returned to Malone.

Included in Okerberg's comments was the following observation:

> The chain of custody on property seized from Malone did not reflect the proper transfer or disposition of the items found and what records were reviewed showed that the location should have been in Santa Fe and not Lakewood. What is of concern is that the items found also contained cash and numerous checks made out to Mr. Malone and Hubbell Trading Post (one for $3,750 and another for approximately $1,000). While these checks may not be negotiable now, they were current when seized and should be immediately returned so that Mr. Malone and Hubbell Trading Post can ascertain whether they can be reissued. SA Yee was not aware that original evidence was still located in the Hubbell Investigation Room adjacent to his office.
>
> In addition, also contact SA Yee as to the location for seized evidence item #R-26. It was not properly documented on the chain of custody as cash and its location according to case records should be in Santa Fe. When SA Yee was asked where the cash (R-26) was located, SA Yee stated that he believed he still has it. Please make a full determination as to amounts, denominations and forward that information back to me. Please consult with AUSA Long and myself should there be any concerns or questions.[2]

Okerberg left additional instructions for Yee to ship those boxes of property to me. Okerberg was asking for my assistance in delivering the property to Malone. I told Buccello I would forward Okerberg's e-mail instructions. She, in turn, promised that Yee would cooperate, fully. She also asked if I wanted

Chip Davis to help out. I told her I didn't think that would be necessary. I forwarded the same e-mail to Brian Smith that same day (January 30), reiterating the OIG's instructions to have Yee ship all of the property directly to me, including at least five boxes of property seized from Malone, so I could arrange its proper return.

Smith called me the next day (January 31), also promising Yee's cooperation. It was during this conversation that Smith first told me about the trip he and Buccello were planning to Lakewood. I cautioned Smith, just as I had Buccello, to be very careful about inserting himself into the OIG investigation or tampering with evidence. I suggested he let Okerberg and his colleagues do their job without any real or perceived interference. Smith dismissed this warning with the rationale that he still had every right to review the investigation with Yee and address any performance issues he might have, since he was still his direct subordinate. In fact, just the next day after our conversation, Smith sent Yee a long list of questions about the investigation and his handling of evidence. I made a point of calling Okerberg to let him know about my conversations with both Smith and Buccello.

The following week, Smith met with Yee in Lakewood. Smith called me again, on Tuesday, February 6, this time with Yee on the line. Smith said that he and Yee spent most of the day going through files and boxes in an attempt to resurrect evidence logs and other documentation. They had located the original evidence sheets corresponding to each box of evidence and explained that Okerberg might not have been able to locate them when he was there the week before because the sheets were stored inside the boxes themselves instead of separately filed. Now, according to Smith, they could fully account for all of the evidence remaining in Yee's custody. That reportedly included all of the cash Yee still had, although there might be problems with the denominations of currency, since the money had been mixed up during counting. It seemed that Smith was attempting to make the case that all of the property, including cash and checks, could now be properly accounted for, even though it had not been available or in proper order to show Okerberg during his inspection the previous week.

I pointed out to Smith that he didn't need to explain any of this to me or for my benefit but should instead make the information available for Okerberg when he came out there again. However Smith seemed to want me to know all the details, including that they had discovered the original inventories/evidence sheets, apparently so I could assure Malone that everything was in order when the property was finally returned to him.

Smith did ask me if I knew where the "original reports" all were. I asked him to clarify if he was referring to all the reports other than those I had prepared. He confirmed that was what he meant. That seemed a particularly odd question considering Yee was actually there with Smith and participating in the phone call. I told Smith I assumed all of the task force reports, including Yee's, were still there with Yee in Lakewood. The only original reports I had were those I had written myself. That seemed to satisfy Smith.

Finally, Smith told me, they had also located three rifles and an antique shotgun from Hubbell Trading Post. Though not seized under the warrants, Yee had assumed custody of the guns as property that might somehow be related to the case. No one at the park or trading post knew who the guns belonged to, so Yee took them under the scope of his investigation. Smith said they'd be shipping me copies of property receipts for the guns. He wanted me to ask Malone if he knew anything about them. I later determined that the three rifles were, in fact, Malone's. The antique shotgun belonged to the National Park Service and was part of the trading post's historic collection.

Smith said they'd be shipping me a total of seven (as opposed to the five Yee had produced for Okerberg) file boxes of materials to be returned to Malone. Among the seven boxes would be the long-lost R26 box, now somehow located, containing more cash and checks. They'd also send a separate envelope containing inventories and receipts to use to document the property when I returned it to Malone.

Almost immediately following my call with Smith, I crafted yet another e-mail to Okerberg, documenting the entire strange conversation.[3]

Odd as Smith's most recent call had been, things continued to get even more bizarre.

On Monday, February 12, I received one final message from Buccello, attached to an e-mail related to the processing of my retirement papers. She said,

> I know you have said you don't trust me. I still feel that is not fair but I can't change what you feel. I have not broadcasted this but I will be gone within 4 months. Been beat up enough by Cam and KTG. I only wish the IG asked me for info on those two!
>
> I want to take care of people as much as I can before I leave, thus I'm keeping my retirement very, very quiet. But please let me know what you need help with and I will try to get it done. You deserve this and much more. I wish you would trust me as I feel my track record deserves that!
>
> Regards, Pat[4]

Aside from merely being strange, this message would later prove insight-ful into events unfolding behind the scene. I was probably the last person Buccello would ever confide in personally, but this was not the first time she'd openly displayed insecurities about my opinion of her. Just six months earlier, in August 2006, she called me out of the blue, ranting and demanding to know why I didn't trust her. In retrospect that call, too, probably signaled something else going on behind the scenes, resulting in her attempts to pressure me into divulging what I knew and might have reported. Suspecting an ulterior motive, I passed along her latest e-mail to the OIG with my own questions about its real meaning and purpose.

My initial thought was that Buccello and Smith had gotten in trouble for meddling in the OIG's investigation and attempting to "rehabilitate" the mess of evidence found (and previously not found) in Yee's possession. A few days later, when I shared Buccello's e-mail with the OIG, I learned that there had in fact been some backlash from the inspector general in response to her and Smith meddling in the OIG investigation by meeting with Yee and sorting through evidence.

But I would also later learn there was more to Buccello's message. Her note apparently anticipated the beginning of the inspector general's long overdue criminal investigation into her own activities. By the end of the year my direct supervisor would herself finally be prosecuted for and convicted of theft of gov-ernment funds. Her bizarre appeal for compassion and her offer to share incrimi-nating information about her own supervisors were more likely an indirect way to reach out to the OIG in a last ditch effort to cut a deal, or at least bring down some of her former compatriots.

Jim Reilly and I had submitted our whistle-blower complaint on Buccello back in 2003, documenting "irregularities" in her personnel records and travel practices. Those practices had, in fact, not stopped, and Buccello may have sensed that yet another investigation was about to be launched.

The OIG received another complaint in April 2007, from yet another NPS agent, "alleging that Buccello failed to perform her assigned duties in order to obtain a free round trip airline ticket." The OIG investigation confirmed that "in March 2007 Buccello failed to appear as a representative of the Director of the NPS at a ceremony honoring fallen NPS officers. . . . When asked why she failed to attend the ceremony, Buccello informed several individuals . . . that her connecting flight had been cancelled. . . . However, the investigation revealed that the flight in question departed only minutes late and that Buccello had voluntarily given up her seat in return for a free round trip airline ticket." The investigation documented yet another incident "in July 2006 [when] Buccello failed to travel to St. Louis, MO to deliver a fatality report to the widow of a fallen NPS special agent." Finally, "the investigation revealed that between April 2005 and March 2007, Buccello charged to the government all or a portion of the airfare associated with nine different personal trips between Washington, D.C., and Maine."[5]

Buccello was charged and then pleaded guilty to one count of 18 USC 641 (theft of public money). She was placed on two years' probation, ordered to perform fifty hours of community service and pay a $10,000 fine, and pay restitution. She received no jail time or home confinement. She was allowed to retire with her full law enforcement pension, nearly $100,000 per year.

But that outcome came far too late to provide me with any relief. Even minimal gratification would not be realized until well after I was out of the picture, six months after my own retirement. The OIG and the U.S. Attorney's Office finally announced the filing of charges against Buccello on October 26, 2007. She appeared in federal court to enter a negotiated guilty plea on October 31, 2007. She was sentenced the following year, on January 23, 2008.[6]

True to form, at the very same time the OIG was conducting its latest investigation into Buccello's travel activities and getting ready to file charges, the NPS was figuring out new ways to reward her. Even though she had been caught once before, her supervisors continued to shower her with a permanent "quality" pay raise, along with thousands of dollars in cash awards the very same year. Then, on March 28, 2007, one of Buccello's supervisors spearheaded efforts to nominate her for one of the Federal Law Enforcement Officers' Association "Outstanding Women in Federal Law Enforcement" awards.[7]

Ironically, the single negotiated count to which Buccello pleaded guilty and received her sentence, theft of public money, is one of the very same offenses falsely alleged in the affidavit submitted in support of the search warrant for Billy Malone's residence at Hubbell Trading Post. That was one of the charges I had been expected to bring against Malone in exchange for being allowed to continue my Indian country assignment and make Buccello's threats to move me back to the Grand Canyon "go away."

The balance of my time waiting for retirement was relatively uneventful.

On February 20, Long called me to advise that the court records related to the case, including the affidavit and application for search warrants on Malone's residence, had finally been "unsealed."

On March 1, I met one last time with Billy Malone to return the balance of his property that Okerberg had discovered still stored in the Lakewood offices and the rest that Yee had subsequently produced. I transported those boxes in their sealed condition, unopened, just as I had received them from Yee and Smith. Included in that property, we now found, was the wedding blanket Malone had been waiting to recover for more than two years. Malone was happy just to get that back. He made no claim that anything else was missing, taking it on faith that everything had finally been returned. In truth, he (and even I) really had no way of knowing if that was true, since he had never been provided with a comprehensive itemized list of all the money and other property that had been taken from him.

The NPS never did get its act together in time to process my paperwork by the scheduled March retirement date. Instead, after voicing my own protests, *it* paid for an independent contractor to process my papers. My new effective retirement date was pushed back to April 1, 2007.

In the meanwhile, my wife had been busy submitting job applications to get out from under Cyd Martin and the greater IMR hierarchy. She secured a new position in Ft. Collins, Colorado, four hundred miles away from the home we'd recently purchased in southwest Colorado.

When April 1 finally rolled around, I woke up a civilian, no longer working in law enforcement or for the government for the first time in more than thirty-three years. Retirement celebration was limited to a card and a present from my wife, who called to congratulate me that same morning from the apartment we were also now renting in Ft. Collins.

The OIG Investigation
(T' áá bikék' eh nínáa' diil káá')

THE OIG INTERNAL investigation continued for another full year. Its find-ings largely corroborated what I had uncovered in my own investigation. But along the way, a handful of equally disturbing new facts about the original investigation came to light, particularly concerning the relationship between the NPS and the WNPA.

▲▼▲

Okerberg re-interviewed a number of witnesses from the original case, includ-ing Nancy Stone as well as Steve Getzwiller, confirming that their statements had been misrepresented or omitted entirely in initial case reports.[1] Chip Davis told Okerberg that he would never intentionally omit information, but he acknowl-edged deficiencies in his own interviews and the reports he had filed. Davis did not refute Getzwiller's claims that he had shared extensive details about Malone using discarded Hubbell Trading Post tags to mark his own rugs. Davis simply could not recall that part of the conversation. Reexamining his own notes from those interviews, Davis acknowledged they were less than comprehensive and complete and that they contained no mention of Getzwiller's statement.

Davis said that the Hubbell investigation could have been handled better. He disagreed with Yee's instructions to use "aggressive interviewing techniques" with witnesses from the Navajo community. But perhaps the most revealing piece of information Davis shared was that LeAnn Simpson had assisted in the investigation by setting up and coordinating most of the interviews with the WNPA's Hubbell Trading Post employees. Simpson was present when many of those interviews took place and was permitted to monitor and participate in them. Okerberg flagged this comment in his notes out of concern that her presence may have intimidated those employees, thus affecting their statements. Indeed, the prospect was dim that any of them would have been candid enough to tell NPS investigators anything that contradicted Simpson or shed a poor light on the WNPA.[2]

Jim Reilly acknowledged that the NPS was "a little out of their element on the Hubbell Trading Post investigation." But Yee also became overly aggressive in pursuing the case and difficult to supervise. Reilly observed that "some exculpatory information was being excluded from the investigation and a sense of arrogance or short-sightedness developed." Reilly told Okerberg about the unrelated incident where he was compelled to issue Yee a letter of insubordination. Reilly also acknowledged that during their 2005 meeting with Sukenic, Yee had to be "prodded" into telling the federal prosecutor about breaking into the evidence vault at the WACC and Morton's memorandum documenting problems with the chain of custody.[3]

Mark Foust, the IMR's ranger activities branch chief when the Hubbell Investigation began, was present during the planning meeting and throughout the raid on Malone's Hubbell Trading Post residence. But by the time of his interview in April 2007, he had been made chief ranger of Glacier National Park.

Foust recalled there was little if any discussion about a plan or strategy during the meeting the night before the raid. He thought it was odd for Simpson and other WNPA staff to be there participating in the operation and receiving investigative briefings and then to be given updates in the months that followed. But Yee was in charge, and Foust was there in a support capacity. Still, Foust said that he did question Yee about his instructions as to what property to seize. Foust understood that the search warrant had been granted principally to secure ledgers and other financial records needed to investigate alleged embezzlement. Also, he was not particularly surprised by the volume of rugs, jewelry, and baskets in Malone's house and garage, because he knew that Malone was an Indian trader. Foust voiced concern on at least two occasions when Yee said that Aspey's instructions were to seize entire stacks of rugs and boxes of jewelry, even if just "one out of ten" of the items in those stacks or boxes had what looked like a Hubbell Trading Post tag or any other sort of tag or marking.

After the search, when the team was assembled back at their hotel, Foust wanted to unload the vans and bring all the seized property into their room for safe keeping. But he was overruled. Instead, Foust got up periodically throughout the night to check on the security of the government and WNPA vehicles and the millions of dollars in property they contained.[4]

Okerberg also interviewed John Wessels, the Park Service's own regional budget chief.[5] Wessels had been present at some of the first meetings with NPS and WNPA officials, during discussions about how to fund the ever-expanding Hubbell Trading Post investigation. He acknowledged that prior to the Hubbell investigation, the NPS had never really scrutinized the funds the WNPA donated to the NPS or how the WNPA managed its operations at Hubbell Trading Post. Wessels speculated that one factor that may have contributed to hundreds of thousands of dollars being misspent on the investigation was that NPS investigators had "no real financial fraud training, and were way over their heads." But he added, "We screwed ourselves by putting the cart before the horse," noting that "Malone was convicted before the investigation began."[6]

The IMR's coordinator for cooperating associations, Kim Sikoryak, was interviewed on April 17, 2007. That interview took place in Sikoryak's office, located on the same floor and almost directly across the hall from Yee's office. Sikoryak confirmed the legal relationship that exists between the NPS and all of its cooperating associations, including the WNPA. He verified that WNPA funds are not government funds and that there is no stipulated level of support, financial or otherwise, that WNPA must provide to the NPS. In fact, Sikoryak pointed out that WNPA can withhold donations altogether if it chooses. Sikoryak told Okerberg that the cooperative agreements between the NPS and WNPA would have been available for review by Yee and anyone else involved in the investigation for the asking, but no one ever made such a request.[7]

Steve Martin was interviewed at his South Rim office. He recalled meeting with LeAnn Simpson and Jim Babbitt in Scottsdale in the spring of 2004 and discussing their suspicions about an alleged forgery and embezzlement scheme. Martin told Okerberg about the series of events leading to his authorization to shut down Hubbell Trading Post for the WNPA audit and the concurrent criminal investigation launched by the NPS.

Martin claimed to have had reservations from the very beginning about the NPS conducting the investigation and about the entire new special agent organization that had been stove-piped out from under the parks and regional offices. But he was assured by both the associate director for visitor and resource

CHAPTER TWENTY-TWO

protection, Karen Taylor-Goodrich, and her deputy, Cam Sholly, that this type of investigation was precisely why the NPS had special agents. He, in turn, had relied on those agents to "do it right." Martin denied that he or the NPS made any agreements with the WNPA to share information about the criminal investigation. But he saw no problem or conflict in the WNPA paying to have its own accounting firm conduct the forensic audit, so long as those accountants were working under the supervision of NPS agents.[8]

The WNPA's Scott Aldridge acknowledged that WNPA headquarters in Oro Valley had more than its own share of problems (beyond those at Hubbell Trading Post), including "a lot of disarray in Accounting." He told Okerberg that the WNPA's accounting troubles stemmed from a failing accounting system along with a lot of turnover in staff and a loss of institutional knowledge. To emphasize that point, Aldridge noted that the WNPA was behind in its financial statements and that the WNPA's 2005 annual report was just being completed at the time of the interview (February 8, 2007).[9]

Marianne DeVries and Jennifer Phillips were interviewed together. DeVries took the lead, but they both confirmed the audits they conducted of Hubbell Trading Post did *not* reveal significant declines in revenue, as had been alleged by the WNPA and subsequently cited as a basis for the NPS criminal investigation. Their statements once again corroborated the independent conclusions of the OIG's own forensic auditor, Ray Macy, and even what Scott Aldridge had said. The WNPA had serious accounting problems of its own, beyond those at Hubbell Trading Post. Gross profits were not accurately reported and accounting totals were buried in the way the WNPA was allocating its costs, including administrative office expenses, cost of the new WNPA headquarters building in Oro Valley, and WNPA salaries.

DeVries readily acknowledged the potential for errors in any audit, especially when they rely on random sampling techniques and, more significantly, information and records provided by the client. But she felt certain Hubbell Trading Post revenues at the time of the raid were not substantially different from previous years. She disputed Simpson's claim that she and her staff had missed fraud indicators at Hubbell Trading Post. To the contrary, DeVries had repeatedly provided the WNPA with documentation about serious problems in its internal controls and system of accounting. She had also provided the WNPA with a number of recommendations for how that situation could be improved, even allowing for the unique challenges encountered at Hubbell Trading Post. But even after Malone was fired and replaced with a temporary (acting) manager, nothing really changed at the trading post. According to DeVries, none of the identified deficiencies were corrected, even the ones the WNPA had cited as a basis for firing Malone. It did not appear that the WNPA implemented any of the recommendations she had made to augment internal controls or correct any of the obvious weaknesses in the Hubbell Trading Post or overall WNPA accounting system.

DeVries felt that the WNPA had suffered from a large turnover in staff over recent years. She bluntly described several recent members of WNPA's accounting staff as "incompetent," including the former Hubbell Trading Post employee (since fired) who first told Simpson that Malone was stealing money.

DeVries and Phillips described the entire Hubbell investigation and their participation in the raid as "a strange situation." They were both "scared out of their wits" when they found themselves drawn into the search of Malone's residence, particularly when they came on several unsecured firearms in the closets they opened. They were also apprehensive about Yee's instructions to seize entire stacks of rugs or boxes of jewelry, even if those stacks or boxes contained just a single item bearing what might be a Hubbell Trading Post tag. In fact, both women were so uncomfortable with the entire experience that they each prepared a letter for their own use to document what they had seen and what they experienced. Still later, they were unable to complete the forensic audit they'd been contracted to perform for the NPS investigation because they were never provided with adequate support documentation.[10]

Aspey was interviewed by Okerberg on April 18, 2007. The former federal prosecutor claimed vague recollection about details of the Hubbell investigation and his conversations with Yee. But he still believed the property seized by Yee under the search warrant might have been salvageable as evidence if the case had gone forward. He believed that issues related to seizure of property exceeding the scope of the warrant and chain of custody could have been resolved. But when Okerberg pointed out the false statements contained in Yee's affidavit — that WNPA funds actually are *not* government funds and that there is absolutely no obligation for the WNPA to contribute *any* percentage of its funds to NPS — Aspey paused. He acknowledged that there might have been a problem with the underlying allegations related to the theft of government funds. Aspey also seemed concerned when Okerberg reminded him that only a small portion of the thousands of pieces of property seized by Yee displayed any sort of tag or "indicia" to suggest they might belong to Hubbell Trading Post. Aspey was adamant that he did *not* direct Yee to seize *all* items, nor did he direct Yee to seize unidentified property. He also acknowledged that whatever the rationale for its seizure if the property was not confirmed as stolen from the WNPA, then it should certainly have been expeditiously returned to Malone instead of remaining in government custody for years. He said he didn't know that had occurred or that there had been any discussion between the NPS and the WNPA about keeping some of Malone's property as a way to recover costs.[11]

Okerberg subsequently provided Aspey with a copy of the report I had written documenting my own interview with him back on January 11, 2006. Perhaps he did not recall that he'd personally reviewed and then extensively edited that report into its final form, deleting entire sentences and adding others, including phrases about what might constitute "indicia." But Aspey questioned whether that final version (his version) accurately reflected what he had said (and written). He responded to Okerberg with a one-page memorandum written on U.S. District Court stationary, dated June 1, 2007. Included were the following comments:

> I do not remember mentioning "reference to ledgers or inventories on scene." I suspect Paul brought that up as one possible way to confirm the "indicia" of ownership and I merely agreed that it would be one possible way. The search scene, in light of the hour, was so fluid I can't imagine limiting the "indicia" to such a specific and limited category of proof.
>
> . . . My personal opinion is Clyde Yee did as professional a job as was possible under the circumstances particularly in light of the less than adequate support received from the agency.[12]

LeAnn Simpson's interview took place February 7, 2007, at WNPA headquarters in Oro Valley. The WNPA's legal counsel along with a senior WNPA board member who was also an attorney were both present throughout the interview.

Simpson said she first learned about problems in the operation at Hubbell Trading Post during her own job interview. Then, after being appointed executive director in August 2003, one of her priority assignments was to focus on Hubbell Trading Post and fix those problems. She personally monitored operations and audited inventory and accounts at the trading post, taking remedial steps early on to address problems she identified. Several employees were fired in the process. Along the way she saw and heard things from other trading post staff that reinforced her growing suspicions that Billy Malone was engaged in a forgery and embezzlement scheme. Simpson shared her suspicions with the WNPA board of directors in mid-April 2004. Just a week or two later Simpson shared those same suspicions with Steve Martin while they were both attending an NPS superintendent's conference in Scottsdale. She asked Martin for permission to shut down the national historic site for several days to conduct a surprise audit. That led the NPS to open a full-blown criminal investigation and raid on the home of the old Indian trader. Simpson emphasized, however, that she never asked the NPS to undertake a criminal investigation. She had simply wanted assistance in securing the consignment ledgers for use in the audit. Still, once the investigation was underway, she was provided with key inside information, including the proposed date that NPS officials would execute their search warrant. Simpson, in turn, shared that information with her board chairman, Jim Babbitt.

Simpson repeated her account of the pre-raid meeting, where she first learned about Yee's plan to use Marianne DeVries and her employee Jennifer Phillips during execution of the search warrant. Simpson said she was uncomfortable with that decision from the very start, not only because it diverted the accountants from participation in the WNPA audit but also because she believed the accounting firm had previously "missed the fraud indicators and potential forged checks on previous audits at HTP." But Simpson time and again yielded to pressure from NPS officials, who by July 2004 were telling her that "no doubt a crime has been committed, and it may be as much as five million dollars." That same account would subsequently be repeated throughout the region by both NPS and WNPA officials. So when Steve Martin personally asked her, Simpson apprehensively authorized up to $75,000 in WNPA funds for a new contract with DeVries to perform the forensic audit for the NPS investigation.

One of the more ironic and certainly conflicting statements Simpson made to Okerberg was that *she* (now) believed it had been inappropriate for the NPS and Yee to have shared so much information about the investigation with the WNPA! Simpson told Okerberg that Steve Martin had never actually given any specific promises or guarantees about what would happen with the investigation, but there was a clear suggestion that criminal charges would be filed. She certainly never expected all of the property that was seized during the raid to be returned to Malone. Simpson told Okerberg that in May 2006 Snyder told her, "It will be nice when this is all over—since you'll get your property back."

Simpson acknowledged being upset over rumors that Malone received an apology from the NPS. She had called Snyder to find out if that was true. But beyond that, she denied much of what she had told me about conversations and agreements made between the WNPA and the NPS for funding the investigation, the disposition of property, and how the WNPA might recover money it contributed to the investigation. She denied having spoken with Mike Snyder about the WNPA trying to recover those costs by keeping Malone's rugs and jewelry and other consignment property in its possession.[13]

However, when confronted with those same accounts, Snyder flatly contradicted Simpson. He not only acknowledged that the conversation had occurred but also claimed it was *Simpson* who had brought up the idea of the WNPA keeping Malone's property as a way to recover its costs. That interview with Snyder took place more than two months after Simpson's, on April 16, 2007.[14]

Snyder generally denied that he had engaged in misconduct or acted improperly in the Hubbell investigation. He displayed only vague recollections of many of the key events in the case and denied having had any significant communications with Jim Babbitt about the investigation. He denied that the WNPA was promised access to case information and updates in exchange for assistance with funding. He claimed it was Steve Martin who told Simpson that "NPS would shoulder the investigation, but WNPA would need to do the same and pay for the auditors to conduct the forensic audit." Snyder told Okerberg that he was not aware of anyone in the NPS providing the WNPA direct access to information about the ongoing investigation.

Then Okerberg read Snyder portions of my own 2006 interviews with Simpson, where she claimed that Snyder had suggested that the WNPA keep Malone's property to compensate for its contribution. Snyder seemed surprised and angered.

Now Snyder's recollection was vivid. With considerable detail, Snyder recalled having breakfast with Simpson immediately prior to a December 2006 WNPA board meeting. "WNPA was frustrated over the lack of progress [in the investigation] and how the money they provided to the investigation did not culminate in the expected returns of merchandise, etc." The report continues: "Simpson wanted Snyder to tell the board that WNPA should keep the evidence seized from Malone's residence to compensate WNPA for the money they had expended on the investigation. Snyder stated he refused to do that."

But later that same morning at the board meeting, Snyder found himself being "lambasted" by the WNPA for the NPS having mishandled the investigation. Snyder told Okerberg that the "WNPA felt the investigation and the associated results was 'a black eye' for WNPA, they were upset and felt the NPS had turned a check fraud case into something bigger and harder to prove. Snyder felt he 'was called on the carpet.'"

Okerberg seized on Snyder's account of the board meeting to press him about the inverted relationship that seemed to exist between the NPS and the WNPA. How could a cooperating association like the WNPA exercise that kind of control over the NPS and its management? Was it normal in the NPS for a non-profit, support organization like the WNPA to summon a regional director to one of its meetings to be "called on the carpet"? Snyder seemed caught off guard. His response was tentative and indirect but provided even more insight into the political reality of the situation. He told Okerberg that "WNPA is very powerful . . . and have a lot of power over the NPS." According to Okerberg's report, "Snyder also commented on the power and politics that entities such as WNPA have over NPS, and jobs and careers sometimes hang in the balance based upon how those relationships are maintained."[15]

Among the more notable efforts in the OIG investigation was an attempt to secure an interview with former WNPA board chairman Jim Babbitt. That request was first submitted on April 13, 2007, through a variety of channels, including LeAnn Simpson, Scott Aldridge, and even the WNPA's contracted legal counsel. The attorney acknowledged the request, and indicated he would check with Babbitt and get back to the OIG with an answer. But by July 30, 2007, Okerberg still had not received an answer and so followed up with yet another request, directed through counsel, to interview Babbitt. Okerberg received the following answer that same day:

> My client believes it has more than assisted in your investigation. As such, no one associated with WNPA wish to discuss this matter with you now or in the future. Please do not contact my client again.[16]

The first interview attempt with Clyde Yee occurred on April 17, 2007. Accommodations were made for Yee to consult with his Federal Law Enforcement Officers Association attorney ahead of time, and have him remotely participate in the interview by telephone.

But the interview ended almost immediately, right after Okerberg provided Yee with his *Garrity* warning.[17] That advisement, similar to *Miranda*, notifies employee/suspects of their criminal and administrative liability for any statements they make but also informs them of their right to remain silent on any issues that might implicate them in a crime. Before questioning could even begin, Yee's attorney advised that his client would not be participating in a voluntary interview. If the OIG wanted to interview Yee and secure his cooperation in their investigation, it would first need to grant him immunity from criminal prosecution and provide him with a *Kalkines* warning, compelling him to answer questions solely in association with an administrative inquiry.[18] The day's interview was over.

Okerberg subsequently contacted Rob Long, in Phoenix, to discuss the prospect of granting Yee immunity in order to compel him to answer questions about his role in the Hubbell investigation. That decision was reached on April 30, when the U.S. Attorney's Office formally declined to prosecute Yee in favor of "administrative remedies." The decision to decline prosecution was

> based on the lack of significant evidence that SA Yee's conduct was criminal, and there were no claims that any monies or items from the evidence seized during the warrant that were unaccounted for.

With that decision from the U.S. Attorney's Office, the OIG investigation shifted into a purely administrative inquiry. Consulting with Long, Okerberg was able to prepare the required *Kalkines* warning for presentation to Yee, compelling his participation in an interview. The terms of the immunity granted in that advisement were sweeping, going well beyond the mere promise that Yee's truthful statements could not be used against him in a criminal prosecution. The agreement also guaranteed that "Yee would not be prosecuted for any criminal exposure he may have had related to the investigation of Bill Malone."

No criminal prosecution would be pursued against Yee unless he lied during his interview. But if he did lie to Okerberg he could then, and only then, face a prosecution for making those false statements to the OIG (18 USC 1001).

Going through NPS headquarters, Okerberg arranged for Yee to be present for a second interview on May 23, 2007, in Washington, D.C. Yee's attorney was present throughout the interview, including during the issuing of the *Kalkines* warning compelling Yee to truthfully answer any and all questions that Okerberg asked.

Yee's responses were generally vague throughout much of the interview, as he was unable to recall details about many of the dates and events in the investigation. No real new information was obtained about issues ranging from the decision to use the WNPA personnel to transport evidence, to Yee's inexplicable difficulty in locating and delays in producing boxes of evidence, cash, checks, valuable blankets, and even firearms in his custody. But Yee did acknowledge several points that offered insight into his perspective on not only his own investigation of Malone, but also the OIG investigation of which Yee was now the focus.

Yee couldn't recall exactly who first told him about the allegations against Malone. He just remembered that someone told him Malone was suspected of forging company checks and keeping the money. Yee claimed it was LeAnn Simpson who told him the WNPA's contract with the NPS required it to pay the government 6.5% of its revenues, making at least a portion of WNPA revenues government funds. But Yee could not recall when or where she said that, and he was unable to reference any supporting reports that documented that conversation. He acknowledged that "he did not verify this information with any other sources, and no NPS law enforcement personnel checked the specifics of the cooperative agreement." Most significantly, Yee claimed he was genuinely surprised when he later learned that no such financial relationship was specified in agreements between the NPS and the WNPA and that revenues generated by the WNPA were *not* government funds. He told Okerberg he did not even know that Kim Sikoryak's office was located immediately across from his own and that copies of all the IMR's cooperative agreements were available there for inspection.

Yee said he couldn't recall who arranged the meeting in St. Michaels the night before the raid. He couldn't recall who decided to include LeAnn Simpson, Marianne DeVries, Jennifer Phillips, or even Mike Snyder. But Yee justified their presence at the meeting, claiming "it was not an operational briefing, as such."

Yee expressed his belief that he had acted properly and according to Aspey's instructions in the seizure of the vast quantities of property from Malone's residence. He claimed that "those items would be fruits of the crime." But he offered no explanation for why less than a third of all the property seized from Malone had any tags or indicia of any kind suggesting they might be WNPA or Hubbell Trading Post property. When pressed, Yee admitted that at the time of the raid he did not even know there was a distinction between WNPA and consignment property or that Malone often comingled the two along with his own rugs and jewelry.

Yee told Okerberg that he saw no conflict or impropriety in asking the WNPA's own contracted accounting firm to participate in the search and seizure of property from Malone's residence. He had discussed that with Aspey and even mentioned it in his search warrant affidavit. He also saw nothing wrong in having the WNPA pay DeVries to conduct the separate forensic audit for his investigation.

Yee admitted that he spoke with Simpson as many as six to ten times a week when the investigation began. He also called Jim Babbitt on one or two occasions to provide updated case information for him to share with the rest of the board of directors. The WNPA seemed committed in its support and interest in the case, and Yee reciprocated with information to maintain its support and help keep its business going. But Yee said he felt no undue pressure from the WNPA, his own supervisors, or other NPS officials to pursue his investigation in a particular way. He denied sharing any secret grand jury information with either Simpson or Babbitt.

Yee admitted that he did not want to tell Sukenic about his decision to break in to the evidence vault or about Morton's memorandum. He shared that information with Sukenic only after Reilly pressured him. But he believed Morton had acted improperly and maliciously, making a "stink" and only creating problems by documenting the incident. He said that "to put it in a formal memo to my supervisor and her supervisor was not just an attempt on her part to express her displeasure, but was an attempt to get my supervisor to take disciplinary action against me."

Yee said he didn't want to tell Sukenic about the incident because he didn't want to "air dirty laundry" in front of the prosecutor. Yee had also believed Morton's memo would not be subject to discovery and could be kept secret, since it was an internal document. But Sukenic immediately corrected Yee, confirming that Morton's memo and any others like it most certainly were "discoverable." That response prompted Okerberg to ask Yee why, then, he still had the "Not Subject to Discovery" file in his office, containing still more documents about problems encountered in the investigation. Yee said he could not remember why.

Throughout most of his interview, Yee seemed fairly composed and restrained, taking his time before answering questions and choosing his words carefully. But he finally let loose when it came to his feelings about me and Morton:

> Agent Morton from the beginning, without having any connection to this case, was shitting on this case from the beginning to anybody who would listen in the Park Service and outside the Service. The same thing with Mr. Berkowitz. . . .
>
> [Berkowitz and Morton] both have a *long* history of shittin' on the other agents, on the rangers, on any case that isn't theirs.

Justifying his feelings, Yee added,

> There are agents who you trust. There are agents who you don't trust. Morton and Berkowitz are not agents that you trust.

Finally, Yee shared his feelings about the criticism he had received about his handling of the Hubbell investigation:

> I don't continually want to have other people telling me that this case is all fucked up, who have no business in this case.[19]

▲▼▲

Most of the fieldwork in the OIG's investigation was completed by mid-2007. The balance of time was spent going through documents, compiling evidence and official correspondence, and writing and rewriting reports. That process was complicated by the revelation that, contrary to national policies, the NPS claimed it could not produce either electronic or hard copies of e-mails related to the Hubbell investigation that were more than thirty days old. That meant there might never be a way to verify the full extent to which various NPS and WNPA officials actually shared information, coordinated activities, reached agreements, or potentially even conspired with one another as they pursued the investigation against Malone.

Dozens of other interviews were conducted, and investigative activity reports prepared over the course of the OIG investigation. Final edits and reviews of the report were completed as 2007 drew to a close.

Finally, on Monday, January 28, 2008, the OIG's Program Integrity Division chief, Alan Boehm, called me to advise that the OIG had officially concluded its investigation and finalized its report. A copy had been provided to NPS director Mary Bomar on January 23, 2008. The report was transmitted under cover of a signed memo from the assistant inspector general for investigations requiring an NPS response identifying proposed corrective action, within ninety days.

Like Malone and everyone else outside the inner circles of the NPS, it would be years before I actually saw the OIG report. But I had assisted by periodically answering questions, filling gaps in information, and preparing supplemental written statements and reports. I had even foregone anonymity, authorizing citation of my own name within the report as the source of the case referral. I was reasonably confident that the OIG's findings corroborated my own.

The OIG report certainly did confirm the many problems I had identified related to securing and executing the search warrant, seizing and handling evidence and personal property, pursuing interviews, preparing reports, documenting exculpatory evidence, and other glaring investigative deficiencies. The report additionally documented the many contradictory statements and explanations provided by various key players in the initial NPS investigation. Particularly noted were the conflicting accounts provided by Yee and Aspey (about what property to seize), by Yee and Simpson (whether Simpson ever told Yee that the WNPA was obligated to pay the government 6.5% of its revenues), and by Simpson and Snyder (whether the two discussed the WNPA keeping Malone's property and whose idea that was). That latter contradiction was highlighted in an OIG case entry titled "Conflicting Statements from IMR Regional Director Mike Snyder & WNPA Executive Director LeAnn Simpson Regarding Agreements for Funding and Disposition of Property."

But the 2008 report went further, identifying a number of other more systemic problems, many of which were remarkably similar to those that had been identified in the OIG's January 2002 report, "A Disquieting State of Disorder: An Assessment of Department of the Interior Law Enforcement." Special attention was again drawn to failures in supervision and management, improper political influence over investigations, and in the case of the Hubbell investigation, the "inverted relationship" that existed between the NPS and the WPNA, manifested in "an almost open door policy in regard to including WNPA in the investigation."

Finally, on the very first page of the OIG's closing report was the following simple but damning statement:

Our investigation determined that NPS Special Agent Clyde Yee, the case agent assigned to the Hubbell Trading Post Investigation, submitted false information on the search warrant affidavit and did not properly account for cash and evidence seized. The U.S. Attorney's Office declined prosecution of Yee in lieu of administrative remedies.[20]

Reflections

(Á hóó t'įįdígíí nát'ą́ą́' nánél íįgo)

I WOULD LIKE TO think that this investigation—this story—might be applied in the NPS as a reminder of what law enforcement is really all about, that it's not merely a matter of putting bad guys in jail or independently dispensing justice but about pursuing the truth (the whole truth) and about both enforcing *and* abiding by the rule of law. I know that for me, even after more than thirty years in law enforcement and as my final investigation, it was also a good reminder about the true importance of respecting and protecting the rights of the accused, because at least once in a while the accused might, just possibly, be more innocent than not and might not be such a bad guy after all. But this story has more lessons to offer about the perils that exist generally where there is an absence of meaningful systems to assure honesty, integrity, and accountability in government.

▲▼▲

The NPS Response to the Hubbell and OIG Investigation

Immediately prior to my retirement, I submitted a written request through the OIG to NPS director Mary Bomar seeking a meeting to discuss the Hubbell investigation and, particularly, the difficult position in which I had been placed by reporting the matter to the OIG. I repeated that request on several occasions, both in writing and over the telephone. As late as November 15, 2007, while attending a memorial service for a fallen employee at Grand Canyon National Park, I was introduced to Bomar, and identified to her as the NPS agent who had closed the Hubbell investigation. On that occasion both my wife and I reiterated our desire to schedule a meeting with her to discuss the case and share disturbing details of the consequences reporting that matter had for us, personally and professionally. We never received so much as a letter, note, e-mail, or even a telephone call or message in response to any of those requests.

In fact, the NPS response to the OIG investigation accounted, at least in part, for the extensive delays in responding to legitimate requests from Malone and his attorney for copies of both NPS and OIG case reports and files. The NPS stalled for more than a year and a half while it pressured the OIG to change the official report to minimize criticism directed at the agency and its employees and eliminate the more damning language reflected in the findings.

The first formal NPS response to the OIG report came in the form of a fourteen-page memorandum, dated April 25, 2008, submitted by the head of the NPS Office of Professional Responsibility and Pat Buccello's acting replacement. But that correspondence in no way satisfied the inspector general's requirement to outline proposed corrective action. Instead, the agency's two top agents challenged findings contained in the OIG report, protesting that if made public in its in current form, documenting as it did many performance, candor, and credibility issues, the consequences for Clyde Yee's career would be fatal. The authors argued strenuously to have the most damning language in the report changed or deleted, making tortuous and specious arguments in defense of Yee while simultaneously belittling the OIG's own investigation. They even cautioned the OIG to approach my own October 2006 report and case referral with suspicion, based solely on rumors that I was now writing a book about the Hubbell investigation!

True enough, my writing efforts were well underway by the time of that April 25, 2008, letter, prompted mainly by my own frustrations with the NPS response and a growing belief that the events in the Hubbell investigation needed to be exposed. But I had not started or even considered that project until well after my retirement in April 2007, more than six months after submitting my report and nearly a year and a half after first alerting the OIG. Still, the energy expended and the extraordinary lengths to which the NPS went in its attempts to have the OIG modify *its* report, or at least prevent its release, confirmed for me my own early fears about the pressure I would have experienced and the consequences I would have faced had I submitted my report through normal channels and stayed on with the agency.

Much later, the NPS attempted to prevent public release of that embarrassing 2008 memo, claiming a variety of privacy concerns and Freedom of Information Act exemptions and arguing that its transmittal to the OIG did not constitute the official NPS response. The NPS instead claimed a one-page memo dated June 23, 2009 (fourteen months after the due date), as its official reply to the OIG's Hubbell Trading Post investigation.

The memo's author (or at least signatory), the acting NPS director, reluctantly acknowledged only "poor case management," "poor handling of evidence," "insufficient supervision and direction," and "poor judgment and performance." He also claimed that "as soon as the related issues of the agent's performance came to our attention and prior to issuance of your report, we took significant actions to address the agent's performance issues."[1] That suggests a belief that what had occurred could be (or had been) remedied through a poor performance evaluation and implementation of some sort of performance improvement plan. In its effort to subtly define the problem solely in terms of just one employee's performance, the NPS altogether sidestepped more troubling issues related to conduct as well as the institutional deficiencies and culture that had allowed all of this to occur. In combination with the earlier April 2008 memorandum, the NPS's June 2009 reply confirmed the agency's long-standing failure to comprehend the true meaning of professionalism, the difference between performance and conduct issues, and the critical need to promote honesty and integrity and enforce only the highest standards possible, beyond mere performance, for the service's law enforcement personnel and program managers.

Brian Smith reportedly *did* attempt to address performance issues through a number of administrative measures. But the NPS culture ultimately prevailed. Over repeated objections from the OIG, NPS managers used government funds to relocate both Yee and his wife (who at the time was posted at a separate duty station on the other side of the state) in a dual-career move to the Grand Canyon. Yee was duty-stationed as a special agent in my old office, conveniently located next door to the courtroom overseen by his friend (and codefendant in a civil rights lawsuit), U.S. magistrate-judge Mark Aspey.

▲▼▲

Effects of the Investigation on the Future of Hubbell Trading Post

Prior to the summer of 2004, Hubbell Trading Post had been run in manner consistent with the wishes of the Hubbell family and the mandate of Congress. The NPS was obligated to maintain the site as a living, working trading post, serving the needs of the local Navajo community while simultaneously accommodating and educating the visiting public. Operation of the historic trading post remained relatively unaffected for the first forty years of NPS stewardship. That came to an abrupt end on June 9, 2004.

In launching its investigation and removing Billy Malone from his position as Indian trader at the famous trading post, the NPS and the WNPA irreversibly altered the course of history at the national historic site whose story they were obligated to preserve and share. They abandoned their role as caretakers of history and assumed a new and unfortunate role as active participants in the demise of a treasured legacy. They inescapably wrote an entirely new and sad chapter in the story of Hubbell Trading Post.

▲▼▲

Cultural Influences and Effects

Many of the old stereotypes surrounding Indian traders surfaced repeatedly throughout the course of the investigation. Malone's friend Steve Getzwiller was openly and disparagingly labeled an "itinerate rug dealer" during one formal planning meeting held early in the investigation. Malone, himself, was casually referred to as a "dirtbag" by members of the investigative team who had never even met him. In an e-mail to LeAnn Simpson, Yee asked, "Did Malone make any statements that he just didn't use banks for personal accounts, anything like that?" But in the very same inquiry, he mockingly dismissed anything Malone might have said, declaring, "Not that we would trust what he said!"[2] That characterization was followed up with the sweeping generalization by an investigator who had never even worked or lived on (or near) the reservation that "I guess you pretty much have to be a crook to be an Indian trader." These same labels and negative stereotypes were passed along and spread to other peripheral players in the investigation, including the handwriting analyst who, after finally meeting Billy Malone, expressed surprise at his gentlemanly appearance and demeanor. That reality was wholly inconsistent with the derogatory descriptions and characterizations that had previously been shared with her by NPS investigators.

When advised by the OIG that the investigation had failed to identify any victims in the community and that no one claimed to have ever been defrauded

25. A historic gathering of Indian traders at a Friends of Hubbell Trading Post charity rug auction to help raise scholarship funds for Navajo, Hopi, and other Native American college-bound students, just prior to the NPS raid. Left to right: Steve Getzwiller, Al Grieve, Billy Malone, Hank Blair, and Bruce Burnham (*photograph courtesy of Vicky Blair*).

by Malone, one senior NPS law enforcement official dismissed that as a concern. That didn't matter. He steadfastly maintained that Malone still had to be guilty. Malone "had the iron fist" and must have used his position and power (even after he'd been fired and evicted) to intimidate all of his victims, "so naturally, residents would not be likely to complain against someone who ruled the community."[3] That same reasoning and incredible level of vilification seems to have permeated the original NPS investigation, explaining the totally unsupported characterizations of Malone as the "Al Capone" of the Navajo Reservation.

Preconceived notions about the sophistication and credibility of the many Navajo players in the case undoubtedly affected the manner in which the investigation was initially undertaken and the way local residents were treated. Many opportunities were missed that might otherwise have yielded significant insights into what had really occurred and was going on behind the scenes.

The overall lack of familiarity with the subtle (and even not-so-subtle) cultural traits and influences found on the Navajo Reservation undoubtedly factored into the manner in which the NPS investigation was conducted and how conclusions about guilt were drawn. Pressure to use aggressive techniques in even the most basic of interviews with local Navajo witnesses was among the more conspicuous failings. That approach was aggravated by an overall failure to comprehend or even consider the different way social interactions occur on the reservation, particularly among older, more traditional residents, and even more so when sensitive topics are being discussed with an authority figure. Adding to the predictable confusion was a failure to understand the most fundamental cultural factors affecting views on property, trade, and trading posts.

I repeatedly heard other NPS law enforcement personnel speculate that Malone must be guilty. Otherwise why hadn't he more vocally protested his treatment and demanded the return of his property? Why didn't he just come forward and explain what was really going on? In the minds of many, Malone's acquiescence was interpreted as a sure sign of guilt. Meanwhile, after the raid when Malone's friends hired an attorney for him, I heard the same officials declare *that* as an indication of guilt. He couldn't win, first condemned as guilty because he did not protest enough and then because he minimally asserted at least some of his rights. That same trait—the passive demeanor and subordination to authority was likewise apparent when I first presented Malone with the heavily edited property receipt containing the extensive waiver of rights and release of liability crafted by the DOI Solicitor's Office. Reflecting his own state of resignation, Malone was fully prepared to go along with the ill-advised waiver of his rights ("Well, I guess I should go ahead and sign this, right?"). All of these behaviors offered clues into the cultural background and thought processes of the Indian trader who had become the focus of such enormous interest and suspicion.

Malone's cooperative response when finally confronted with criminal allegations stands in stark contrast to the posture assumed by Yee and officials from the WNPA, who respectively either demanded immunity and the presence of counsel before consenting to be interviewed by the OIG or who required extensive pre-interview briefings and the presence of their attorney during all of their own interviews with Okerberg. Still others, such as Jim Babbitt, refused to be interviewed, altogether. Several key officials interviewed by the OIG seemed to suffer from inexplicable lapses in memory and were able to offer only vague and inconsistent recollections of key events and conversations. Many, such as Snyder and Simpson, seemed to turn on one another, flatly challenging and contradicting the accounts provided by their respective NPS and WNPA "partners." In contrast, when finally approached for an interview by Long and me, Malone was completely forthcoming and had his attorney present only during our first meeting. Thereafter, he freely participated in every requested interview and meeting, including his FBI polygraph examination, without any further consultation with legal counsel.

Some skeptics within NPS circles have incorrectly claimed that Malone consented to be interviewed and "confessed" to his activities only after being granted immunity. But that's not true. Neither Malone nor his attorney knew, and for that matter even I did not know, if Malone would face prosecution until well after his initial interview and subsequent polygraph examination. None of us knew what the outcome would be until January 4, 2007, when the U.S. Attorney's Office formalized the decision to decline prosecution and close the case against Malone. In fact, throughout the course of both my own criminal investigation and Okerberg's subsequent internal investigation, only one person ever requested (actually, demanded) or was granted immunity from prosecution as a condition of speaking with investigators.[4] That person was *not* Billy Malone. Malone consented to be interviewed and even polygraphed without any such assurance. Only time will tell if anyone from the WPNA, the NPS, or from any other government agency will ever display that same level of candor and courage by stepping up to the plate, acknowledging mistakes, and taking responsibility for *their* own actions or the actions of their respective organizations.

The culture of the NPS was evident from the very start of the investigation, and even before it began. The selection of Pat Buccello as NSAC was a bad omen indeed. Her appointment as head of the newly established Investigative Services Unit confirmed that the NPS had successfully resisted the implementation of meaningful reforms, especially when her supervisors awarded her with an in-grade pay raise *and* a cash bonus, at the very same time the OIG was conducting its *second* investigation into allegations of travel fraud. Then, even after Buccello was convicted for theft of public money and forced to retire, the NPS continued to include her in its peer counselor activities, placing her in touch with the family of yet another fallen employee!

But more conspicuous was the level of favor shown to powerful officials from the WNPA and the extraordinary extent to which NPS officials obligated funds, personnel, and other resources to the investigation. NPS investigators and other officials readily provided the WNPA with unprecedented levels of access to case information and activities through participation in pre-raid meetings, witness interviews, and as many as six to ten calls a week with LeAnn Simpson and multiple case briefings to Jim Babbitt.

The expenditure of nearly \$1 million over the first year and a half of the investigation, along with the commitment of more than a dozen law enforcement personnel, was without precedent for a case of this kind. It also casts serious doubt on Aspey's claim that "Clyde Yee did as professional a job as was possible under the circumstances particularly in light of the less than adequate support received from the agency." In spite of these enormous resources, little or no scrutiny was given to the WNPA's claim of losses attributed to Billy Malone. In a very real sense, there was initially *no* investigation into the allegations made by the WNPA. Instead, in the early stages of the case, the NPS merely investigated— or more accurately targeted—Billy Malone. Even the preliminary allegation of check forgery was not fully investigated during the first year and half of the investigation. And even then it was only pursued after Yee and his team were instructed to secure handwriting samples for analysis and when Malone was finally interviewed. During the first year and half, absolutely no effort was made to scrutinize the claims made by the WNPA that it had suffered losses from theft in the millions of dollars.

The level of deference shown toward the WNPA was also evident in the radical changes made by Cyd Martin's office to the operating guidelines for Hubbell Trading Post. Standards for ensuring the authenticity of the post were abandoned. Criticisms that had once been listed, acknowledging that Malone's removal had adversely affected the community, were altogether deleted. It was this level of pandering and accommodation to the wishes of the WNPA that prompted the OIG to characterize the relationship between the NPS and WNPA as "inverted." That characterization was further supported when Snyder admitted that he was "called on the carpet" by WNPA officials and when he repeatedly yielded to pressures to obtain restricted information so he could provide case briefings at their board meetings.

The extraordinary levels of political control that groups like the WNPA continue to assert over the NPS was, perhaps, best revealed in the statements Snyder made while attempting to justify his own role in the unfolding scandal. It was like a flashback to events of 1990 when the Arizona State Attorney General's Office conducted its criminal probe into illegal battery dumping at Glen Canyon. During that investigation nearly fifteen years earlier, the IMR concessions chief turned deputy regional director had admitted that it would be "political suicide" for a superintendent to document violations committed by powerful corporations, adding that "all of the concessions have strong political friends in government."

Now, as part of the OIG's probe into the Hubbell investigation, Snyder echoed that same excuse, using disturbingly similar language to justify his own actions. Though he denied any specific wrongdoing and claimed only vague recollections of many specific events in the Hubbell investigation, he noted "the power and politics that entities such as WNPA have over NPS[,] and jobs and careers sometimes hang in the balance based upon how those relationships with WNPA are maintained."

A list of other examples showing how the culture of the NPS affected the investigation could fill pages, from pressures to reach a predetermined outcome, to resistance in acknowledging and addressing ongoing conduct issues, to attempts to conceal exculpatory evidence and serious case deficiencies. Throughout all of these incredible events, Morton and I were apparently the only ones who thought there was anything seriously wrong. Even after case deficiencies were independently corroborated and confirmed, those of us who first documented and reported those problems were vilified and subjected to more agency scorn, ridicule, and harassment than were the individuals engaged in misconduct. The very suggestion that Susan Morton had documented problems with the chain of custody only to get Yee in trouble or because she was "jealous of Clyde's big case" or that my report to the OIG was suspect because two years later I was writing a book reveals serious problems in the underlying mindset and psychology of the NPS organization.

That culture and psychology is pervasive. Elements extend well beyond the boundaries of just the NPS and into organizations like the WNPA. That's not all that surprising, considering how those organizations are formed and staffed and how closely they partner with NPS officials. That explains how, even late in the game after the case was unraveling, LeAnn Simpson could actually have thought that I would keep her incriminating statements to myself and not document them in my report. Weren't we all members of the same NPS family? But in all the case briefings and other information that Yee shared with Simpson, he apparently failed to mention, as he had to the OIG, that "there are agents who you trust; there are agents who you don't trust. Morton and Berkowitz are not agents that you trust."

▲▼▲

The Reports
Early efforts by Malone to merely obtain copies of both the application and affidavit for the search warrant, listing just the basic allegations and offenses of

which he was initially suspected, were unsuccessful, even after those documents were unsealed by the court on January 30, 2007. Apparently no one in the NPS, the DOI, the OIG, or even the Department of Justice felt obliged to explain to Malone why he had been targeted, had his home raided, had his property seized, been fired from his job, and kicked out of his home. None of those officials believed that Malone had a right to know what had really happened or why his life had been turned upside down. Copies of the once-secret court documents used to launch the investigation in June 2004 were not provided to Malone until October 2008, in response to a lawsuit filed at the urging of his friends and colleagues.

Consequently, when Malone did succumb to friendly pressure to file his own lawsuit, he did so under an enormous handicap, without access to *any* of the official documents that supported and documented the investigation against him. Instead, the basic allegations contained in his lawsuit (wrongful termination, defamation of character, and multiple violations of his civil rights) were pieced together based solely on accounts and information shared by Malone's friends and various supporters. It was only through that costly legal action that Malone was finally able to obtain copies of the application and affidavit in October 2008, attached to the government's preliminary response to his lawsuit.

It would take nearly three more years for Malone to acquire copies of both the NPS and OIG investigative reports and related documents. Attempts by his attorney to obtain those reports through four separate Freedom of Information Act (FOIA) requests were inexplicably thwarted until late 2010, as the OIG resorted to its familiar tactic of withholding public records by simply ignoring legitimate requests. The documents were obtained only after the watchdog and whistleblower advocacy group PEER joined in the effort by filing its own (the fifth) FOIA request for the reports, citing the public's right to know about "incompetence, misconduct, and corruption within NPS law enforcement" and related "instances of official malfeasance."[5] That FOIA request, also ignored, was followed by separate legal action against the OIG, itself for failing to comply with the FOIA. The records were obtained only after PEER filed its own lawsuit in federal court, compelling their release.[6]

There is ample room for speculation about what was going on behind the scenes to create such enormous resistance to releasing any of the reports. The simplest explanation is that the OIG was merely acting with typical bureaucratic recalcitrance. Its record of responding (or *not* responding) to FOIA requests is, quite simply, terrible. Often as not, FOIA requests are simply ignored, either because of neglect or inadequate staffing, left to gather dust at the top of a heap of other long-forgotten requests. This institutional failure undoubtedly contributed to delays.

Less forgivable is the prospect that the OIG actually did not want the reports to be made public, for a number of plausible but inexcusable reasons. In spite of its purported independence and oversight role, the OIG is as much a political entity as any agency in government. It has on more than one occasion used its enormous power, influence, and discretion to selectively withhold or alternatively publish reports for maximum political benefit. That record supports the theory that the OIG was playing politics by yielding to pressures from the NPS and its allies to withhold the facts and findings documented in both my own and the OIG report. The extent to which NPS officials fought to have the report altered in an effort to limit damage and embarrassment is well documented within their own correspondence to the OIG.

Yet another political explanation is that the OIG was showing deference to other government officials implicated in the reports. Law enforcement agencies (including the OIG) are always reluctant to document poor judgment or misconduct by colleagues in other agencies, particularly prosecutors or judicial officials. It is easily conceivable that the OIG did not want to openly embarrass a federal prosecutor turned federal judge or an attorney on the staff of the Office of the Solicitor.

Adding to speculation about political influences is the very real prospect that the OIG was reluctant to document and expose problems and dissent within its own ranks. I had first alerted OIG officials in D.C. about those problems early in my investigation. Questions were raised about Jamie Howard's role in the Hubbell investigation and about the accuracy and credibility of the report she prepared documenting her interview with Nancy Stone. That reportedly gave rise to a separate inquiry, though that report was not included within the larger OIG report prepared by Okerberg.

Turmoil within the OIG did not stop there. Thereafter and throughout the preparation of his final report, Okerberg reportedly engaged in a series of heated arguments with his own supervisors over edits and deletions they were demanding and making without his knowledge or approval, as they questioned whether some of the information he had documented and included in his drafts should ultimately be included.[7] Additionally, Okerberg had included a formal proposal for the OIG to subsequently undertake its own separate audit of the WNPA's overall financial records and practices in his initial case submission. That proposal was authorized at the highest levels of the OIG and was scheduled to occur shortly after Okerberg's investigation was completed. But support for that separate investigation was inexplicably withdrawn, and the audit never occurred. That change in posture raised the specter of even higher levels of political influence. Speculation was fueled by the revelation that the WNPA consulted with former interior secretary Bruce Babbitt about the Hubbell investigation. Babbitt knew and worked with Earl Devaney, the inspector general, during the Clinton administration. They were both appointed by President Clinton. And as the WNPA's own records document, the former secretary of the interior reportedly told his brother Jim Babbitt that he didn't "think anyone in the federal government would come after WNPA."[8]

Both NPS *and* OIG efforts to prevent or delay release of the reports spanned two separate administrations, that of President George W. Bush and that of President Barack Obama. FOIA policy during the Bush administration was predictably restrictive, relying heavily on post-9/11 national security interests to disclose information only after considering all possible reasons to withhold it.

But the day after his January 20, 2009, inauguration, President Obama proclaimed a new era of ethics and transparency in government, issuing an executive order directing agencies to "act under a presumption of favor" in response to requests for documents under the FOIA. He declared that

> the Freedom of Information Act should be administered with a clear presumption: In the face of doubt, openness prevails. The Government should not keep information confidential merely because public officials might be embarrassed by disclosure, because errors and failures might be revealed, or because of speculative or abstract fears. Nondisclosure should never be based on an effort to protect the personal interests of Government officials at the expense of those they are supposed to serve. In responding to requests under the FOIA, executive branch agencies should act promptly and in a spirit of cooperation, recognizing that such agencies are servants of the public.[9]

But even that proclamation seems to have had no effect whatsoever on the NPS or the OIG. Whatever the explanation, their response in delaying release of the reports for nearly three years most certainly did not reflect compliance with either the spirit or the letter of the law as spelled out in the FOIA. Those delays led to the observation by PEER executive director Jeff Ruch that "the Inspector General is supposed to be part of the solution to government malfeasance, but in this case the IG is a part of the problem."[10]

▲▼▲

The Lawsuit

Malone v. Yee was filed in United States District Court of Arizona on February 28, 2008, two years to the day after my own first meeting and interview with Malone at the U.S. Attorney's Office in Phoenix.[11] The lawsuit was filed as a "*Bivens* claim," alleging a conspiracy to violate Malone's civil rights under color of law.[12] Filing a *Bivens* claim, a challenging process, is one of the few legal remedies available to citizens seeking redress for harm caused by government officials. Named as defendants were:

Clyde Yee
Steve Martin
Cyd (Cydny) Martin
Michael "Mike" Snyder
Carl "Chip" Davis
Patricia "Pat" Buccello
Brian Smith
Mark Aspey
Rob Eaton
LeAnn Simpson
Jim Babbitt
Western National Parks Association

A certain amount of tactical maneuvering can be expected in any form of litigation. Certainly, Malone and his attorney never expected the government (or the WNPA) to concede to all of the allegations without a fight. Still, it's worth recalling the testimony of Richard L. Delonis in his 2003 presentation on ethics legislation before the Senate Subcommittee on Criminal Justice Oversight, in which he quoted the opinion of John Sutherland in *Berger v. United States*, 295 U.S. 88 (1935), that it is the U.S. attorney's interest "that justice shall be done" and that "it is as much [a U.S. attorney's] duty to refrain from improper methods calculated to produce a wrongful conviction as it is to use every legitimate means to bring about a just one."[13] Though Malone's civil suit is still not settled, motions filed by attorneys for both the government and the WNPA provide insight into the mindset of the defense.

All nine of the named government defendants, including the convicted NPS special agent-in-charge Patricia Buccello, were represented at government expense by the U.S. Attorney's Office. The AUSA representing those current and retired employees from the NPS, the U.S. Attorney's Office, and the Office of the Solicitor, filed a motion for dismissal, arguing the following:

- Malone missed his opportunity to file a lawsuit because the statute of limitations for civil recourse expired two years after NPS and WNPA officials raided his home. The government argued that *if* Malone's rights were violated, such violation commenced on June 9, 2004. Therefore, Malone's right to sue for such violation expired on June 9, 2006, even though his property was still in government custody, the investigation was still on-going, and all case files and other information regarding the investigation were still being kept secret and would remain secret for at least another two-and-a-half years *after* the statute of limitations had purportedly lapsed.
- Malone's rights were never really violated because, ultimately, he was not prosecuted. In effect, according to the government, since Malone was never arrested and none of the government's actions and none of the property taken from Malone had been used in a prosecution, no violation of his civil rights had occurred. Even if some officials acted improperly and in a manner that *might* have violated his rights, it didn't matter since their efforts and actions did not result in an arrest and prosecution.
- Even if Malone's rights were violated, the nine federal defendants were protected under sovereign immunity and could not, therefore, be sued.

A second AUSA who inherited the civil case in the middle of 2009 reportedly boasted more succinctly that the NPS and other government employees would probably "get off" because their actions merely demonstrated gross incompetence, as opposed to the necessary mens rea, or a mental state demonstrating malice, needed for Malone to prevail in his *Bivens* claim. Stated another way, however improper or harmful their collective actions were, the government defendants could not be held liable unless Malone could produce evidence of an orchestrated or coordinated effort (i.e., "a meeting of the minds" demonstrating a conspiracy) to violate his civil rights. Harm caused through a simple series of blunders, disconnected acts of malfeasance, or even a tidal wave of incompetence and cover-up would not rise to the level necessary for Malone to prevail. Given the manner in which the original Hubbell investigation was initiated and pursued, *that* requirement would present the biggest challenge to Malone in the pursuit of his civil claim.

Meanwhile, the attorney for the WNPA representing the association as well as LeAnn Simpson and Jim Babbitt individually argued that:

- All of the claims, representations, and allegations presented by WNPA to the National Park Service, true or not, were privileged, and could not be cited as slanderous or defamatory. Not acknowledged were statements allegedly made to parties not involved in the investigation, including Nancy Stone and at least one other individual.
- Participation in the investigation by WNPA employees and agents occurred as private parties and employees of a non-profit organization, rather than as state agents; and solely at the request of the NPS. Therefore, the National Park Service, alone, was responsible for their actions and any resulting harm suffered by Billy Malone.
- WNPA's decision to fire Malone was based solely upon his "gross negligence," and was entirely unrelated to the concurrent criminal investigation.

Included in materials submitted by the defense was a letter dated February 27, 2007, from the attorney for the WNPA (a former federal prosecutor), flatly contradicting former federal prosecutor (and now federal judge) Mark Aspey's later assessment of Yee.

In his written statement dated June 1, 2007, Aspey had defended the NPS case agent, proclaiming that "Clyde Yee did as professional a job as was possible under the circumstances particularly in light of the less than adequate support received from the agency."

But in his own letter, counsel for WNPA lashed out, declaring that the federal criminal investigation was "dead after the incompetent manner in which Special Agent Yee executed the search warrant on Mr. Malone's residence" and repeatedly used non–law enforcement (i.e., WNPA) personnel in the investigation. The WNPA further argued that

> Whatever mistakes were made in the course of the investigation . . . [those mistakes] . . . were made by NPS Special Agents and not by WNPA. My client has enjoyed a long and highly cooperative and distinguished

association with the NPS, and the failings of Special Agent Yee and others must not be allowed to besmirch WNPA's good name and services to the NPS.[14]

Finger pointing aside, if taken at face value, the collective arguments presented both by the government and the WNPA seem to suggest that Billy Malone suffered no real harm, no wrongdoing had occurred, and there was no legal remedy available to Malone in any event. Stated more simply, nobody did anything wrong, nothing wrong occurred, and nobody was responsible for whatever *had* occurred and whatever harm Malone might have suffered!

That defensive posture stands in contrast to the reaction displayed throughout the investigation by Billy Malone, even after his life had been nearly destroyed by the raid at his home, the very public firing from his job, and the illegal seizure of most of his life savings in property. When he was finally confronted with the only supported allegation against him (forgery), Billy Malone not only admitted to his actions ("I guess I crossed the line") but openly accepted his fate ("I guess I'll get whatever I've got coming").

Processing of Malone's federal lawsuit was delayed and made all the more complicated by apparent conflicts of interest presented by the judges assigned to hear the matter. One after another, three separate federal judges assigned to the case were forced to recuse themselves because of their own relationships with named defendants.[15] The case was finally assigned to a visiting Federal District Court judge from Alaska!

The old saying that "wheels of justice turn slowly" is an optimistic cliché, at best. It would take nearly two years just for Malone's lawsuit to proceed to the first hearings before the presiding judge who would rule on the government's and WNPA's preliminary motions for dismissal, even before he was given access to any of the government reports! In the interim, Malone very nearly died, spending more than three months hospitalized in an intensive care unit, sustained by a ventilator and other artificial life support. He somehow survived that episode, as did his lawsuit, which is still making its way through the system.

In the meanwhile, little or nothing has really occurred in the NPS to prevent a recurrence of the kind of events that took place in that investigation. No one has been held accountable and no meaningful reforms have been implemented. Billy Malone has yet to be made whole, much less receive anything resembling an apology for the ordeal he suffered at the hands of officials from the NPS and the WPNA.

▲▼▲

Final Thoughts

With details about the Hubbell investigation slowly gaining attention, some people have attempted to place blame upon the Republican administration that was
in power at the time. This is cited as more than a mere coincidence in the belief
and perhaps even the hope that it both explains and excuses the disturbing series
of events that occurred in this story. However, when it comes to the Hubbell
investigation and the NPS law enforcement program, I reject that theory or the
notion that the fault lies with any one political party or administration. I reject
it not only because it is wrong, but also because it diverts attention and distracts
from the more basic integrity issues that exist within the NPS, transcending partisan politics. No single administration has really had all that much influence
or affect, good or bad, on the day-to-day (or year-to-year) operations of any
government institution, especially culturally entrenched agencies like the NPS.
A careful evaluation of other incidents and investigations over time reinforces
the argument that NPS management is fully capable of its own misconduct and
scandal, including political manipulation and censorship, without the influence
or assistance of any given administration.

Some senior officials in the NPS have opportunistically claimed that the
disastrous events in this story resulted principally from the mandated law
enforcement program reforms and 2003 realignment of the NPS special agent
program. Others blame the special agent program altogether or the management of the IMR at the time. Variations on this theme have been voiced on
the Internet and internally within the NPS; just about anything and anyone
who might be responsible for changes over the decades in the way the NPS has
approached law enforcement have been blamed. Surely we did things better
back in the good old days (whenever *that* was!). Still others have cited the events
in this case as justification for relieving the federal government and the NPS
of law enforcement responsibilities in national parks altogether. The NPS law
enforcement program, they argue, was pressed beyond its capabilities. The NPS
law enforcement program is broken and fatally flawed. Instead, responsibilities
should be transferred to state or local law enforcement authorities. I reject all
of these conclusions as well.

The NPS has never even tried to manage its law enforcement program with
anything approaching uniformity, leaving it vulnerable to all manner of abuse
and neglect. The inconsistent levels of professionalism exhibited in different
locales and different specialized operations were an unfortunate reality for as

long as I was in the agency, and certainly well before, and remain so in the present. I have personally witnessed and attempted to expose this same sort of conduct and management approach to law enforcement and investigations, going back literally decades. And the NPS certainly never implemented or succumbed to meaningful reform of the law enforcement program it does have. The so-called reforms that did result from the OIG's 2002 report were nothing but a shell game, a mix of smoke and mirrors creating the illusion of change on an organizational chart and in policy documents while preserving the status quo in the real world of NPS culture, politics, and operations.

Likewise, claims that NPS law enforcement personnel lacked experience or expertise in conducting financial fraud investigations, that they lacked proper policies and procedures, that investigators demonstrated poor performance or were incompetent are—true or not—nothing but diversion techniques and false excuses. The same can be said for Aspey's dubious assertion that Yee was somehow handicapped by a lack of agency support.

It was not hard to see that huge problems existed in the case and that serious and even fatal errors had been made in the most preliminary stages of the investigation. I discovered this within the first week or two of my own case review and after the first few interviews I conducted. Those problems were not so much a reflection of any particular lack of experience or expertise, the absence of written policies and procedures, poor performance, or even incompetence. They instead reveal a systemic failure to address glaring integrity issues within the organization. They are a reflection of the absence of a genuine commitment to honesty, integrity, and the fair and impartial enforcement of the law.

It's neither fair nor accurate to characterize the law enforcement program of the NPS as broken. That's because the present program was actually designed to be this way. Depending on the political significance of a given incident or case, and the luck of the draw or even deliberate manipulations in who is assigned to an investigation, there is simply no assurance that a fair, impartial, and competent job will be done. It's not that the agency is *incapable* of good objective work. Great work is done all the time. But within the culture and organization of the NPS, a deliberate effort has been made to assure that investigations *can be* manipulated to satisfy the needs and wishes of politicians and powerful managers. That is unfair not only to the victims of crime (or the target of an investigation) but also to the many honest and extraordinarily talented rangers and special agents who *do* work for the agency and individually strive for high standards. It's a classic case of bad apples spoiling the barrel, where the acceptance of bad behavior and dishonest employees compromises or destroys the credibility of the entire organization. The uncertainty of that situation and the inconsistency in how investigations are conducted is a direct result of how the NPS manages its law enforcement program.

In its approach to law enforcement as something other than a distinct profession, the NPS has failed to accept and apply the requisite high standards for ethics and integrity that are demanded of true professionals. Rather than applying a hard and fast litmus test for honesty and integrity, the agency approaches standards for delegating and retaining law enforcement authority as a balancing act between an employee's loyalty, obedience, and the good he or she accomplishes for the agency, and the amount of harm or damage done along the way. Under that model, given the right political conditions, raw incompetence, fatally poor judgment, and even persistently egregious misconduct can be excused and tolerated. But in professional law enforcement, no amount of dishonesty is acceptable, and no amount of loyalty or even good work can justify or excuse the abuse of authority or disregard for the rule of law and constitutional rights. Any other approach is not just bad law enforcement; it's bad *for* law enforcement and bad for the NPS.

Congress itself has contributed to the perpetuation of this condition by repeatedly turning a blind eye to known problems and protecting highly placed friends within NPS management. Decades of inbreeding, resistance to change, and a tolerance for misconduct and incompetence has intentionally resulted in a law enforcement program that is more vested in satisfying the desires of politicians and local managers and shielding incapable or unscrupulous employees than in the fair and effective enforcement of the law.

The historic lack of adequate attention to park law enforcement needs is the principal reason Congress, in 1976, reinforced law enforcement authority for the NPS through passage of the General Authorities Act, noting that

> effective law enforcement in the Park System has been severely hampered by the remoteness of many areas, coupled with the need for clarification of law enforcement authorities for National Park Service personnel. The isolation of those areas from conventional federal, state, and local law enforcement agencies has made law enforcement dependent primarily on employees of the National Park Service.[16]

Nothing has really changed since that time, and there is no reason to believe that local law enforcement is any more willing or prepared to provide to parks or the millions of American and international tourists the kind of law enforcement services they deserve. Besides, our national parks belong to *all* of the American people. Crimes that occur in parks are crimes against us all. From a legal as well as philosophical standpoint, it is entirely appropriate for our national parks to be uniformly protected and policed by a professional, federal law enforcement organization.

There is no reason why the NPS, under sufficient pressure and imposition of a credible and independent system of oversight and accountability, could not turn itself around and reform its law enforcement program into one that is uniformly professional and free of political influences. Given the enormously talented and idealistic people drawn to careers in the NPS, its corps of rangers and special agents could easily be transformed into one of the best law enforcement organizations in the country, a truly elite force of law enforcement professionals. That goal could be accomplished over the course of just a few years. But that will take a new attitude and a new crop of mentors and leaders whose own record demonstrates both the experience and the credibility necessary to effectively promote a renewed emphasis on ethics, integrity, and accountability. And before that can happen, the agency must purge itself, from the top down, of the current crop of managers and supervisors whose loyalty lies with the status quo and who gained admission to the NPS fraternity by growing up into the old culture or through special favors from those who did.

Another point missed in the argument for dismantling the NPS law enforcement program is how all of the issues contributing to failures in law enforcement are also issues that come up in virtually every other program administered in the agency. The direct impact of those deficiencies may not be as graphic or visible, but they are no less real. The same actions required to fix the NPS law enforcement program—that is, the abandonment of a decrepit agency culture and the adoption of rigid new standards for integrity and conduct—are needed in these other program areas as well. The many good NPS employees working hard every day to serve the visiting public and preserve park resources "for future generations" deserve to work in an organization free from corrupting political influences (both internal and external) as much as anyone.

It's worth restating a key point presented early in the introduction to this book.

More than a story just about Billy Malone, the Hubbell investigation, and NPS law enforcement, this has been a story about the NPS itself. It has been a story about political influence, incompetence, corruption, and the absence of meaningful safeguards to assure honesty, integrity, and accountability in government. There are other stories waiting to be told about other incidents affecting NPS program areas far removed from law enforcement. Examples include maintenance workers unnecessarily exposed to toxic chemicals or instructed to improperly dispose of refuse because it was too expensive to do the job right; fire personnel encouraged to proceed with dangerous prescription fires "out of prescription" in order to achieve annual goals and assure future funding (i.e., "burning for dollars"); clerical personnel ordered to manipulate records to conceal overexpenditures or the illegal diversion of funds; and even resource managers and scientists prohibited from performing mandated environmental compliance evaluations or ordered to manipulate scientific studies and reports to keep from delaying a pet construction project or "obstructing" a competing program initiative.

None of this is new, and the NPS has been put on notice more than once about serious integrity issues within its operations and particularly within its law enforcement program. Many of these same types of problems were exposed as far back as 1985, when I made my first feeble effort to expose serious corruption and raise issues like these in my testimony before a subcommittee of the House Committee on Interior and Insular Affairs.

The NPS's, the OIG's, and even Congress's failure to acknowledge and confront those issues back then laid the groundwork for how the agency manages its law enforcement program today. That failure, in turn, has served to promote the growth of an agency culture accepting of the types of abuses perpetrated against Billy Malone in the Hubbell investigation. The events described in this book were a foreseeable outcome of that culture.

The underlying culture of the NPS has never been properly challenged. Costly program reviews conducted in the past by the National Academy of Public Administration, the International Association of Chiefs of Police, Booz, Allen, and Hamilton, and others have all failed to address this issue. This is a key area where the OIG, in particular, has repeatedly failed in its program review and oversight role. With every successive change in administration, the OIG mistakenly allies itself with a new group of NPS managers at the top of the agency, as they pledge their support and cooperation in the implementation of needed changes. But those new NPS managers inevitably come from and are loyal to the very same culture that created the problems in the first place. Before real change can occur, the NPS needs to reevaluate the concept of agency loyalty and redefine for its workforce what it means to be a trusted employee.

With that in mind, we can say that Inspector General Devaney most certainly failed to achieve his goal of bringing meaningful reform to the law enforcement program of the NPS. What happened to Billy Malone and the manner in which the Hubbell investigation was conducted is clear proof of that. The OIG's January 2002 report, "A Disquieting State of Disorder: An Assessment of Department of the Interior Law Enforcement," has, regrettably, become just another in a long list of critical reports gathering dust on a shelf.

In his February 2007 testimony before the House Natural Resources Committee, Inspector General Devaney once again addressed the magnitude of ethics and integrity deficiencies permeating DOI agencies like the NPS. Devaney cited "a culture that lacks accountability," observing that supervisors generally received lighter punishments than lower-ranked employees and that senior executive service members were "remarkably immune to any adverse action greater than a reprimand." He also highlighted problems with the DOI's efforts to reform law enforcement operations, reiterating that only a fraction of the reforms directed by the secretary of the interior have been fully implemented. Devaney acknowledged, however, that the vast majority of DOI employees are "hard working, ethical, and well-intentioned."[17]

Most of those same points were articulated more than twenty-five years earlier, in my own testimony before the House Subcommittee on National Parks, Forests, and Public Lands. I closed that testimony with the following statement:

> The National Park Service as a whole . . . has some of the most dedicated and motivated employees in the entire federal workforce. They consistently demonstrate that they are among the most highly trained and highly skilled law enforcement and public safety officials to be found anywhere. As a group, we are immensely proud of the work we do. All I ask is that you make it possible for us to be equally proud of the agency for which we work. The expertise is there. The longing for professionalism is there. All that is needed is your firm guidance to bring us to that end.[18]

More than twenty-five years later, with the National Park Service centennial in sight, the many honest and hard-working employees of that agency are still waiting for an answer to that call.[19]

Afterword

ONE OF THE challenges in writing a book like this is deciding when it's really finished. Events in this story have continued to unfold years after my own and Paul Okerberg's investigations were completed. I struggled with the decision of when to wrap things up, finalize the manuscript, and submit it for publication.

Malone's civil rights lawsuit may not be resolved for years. Like his health, it has suffered both setbacks and recoveries. It's impossible to forecast the long-term outcome and affect of Malone's *Bivens* claim, particularly in light of appeals that will inevitably be filed by whichever side initially wins or loses. I certainly believe that what happened to Malone was wrong and that he was treated unfairly. But given his burden in taking on powerful institutions like the NPS and the WNPA and proving a government conspiracy, I am not optimistic that his lawsuit will ever provide him with the sense of vindication and justice he is seeking. Delaying publication of this book until that matter was resolved was not an option. Besides, the final outcome of Malone's lawsuit will not change the facts or alter the disturbing nature of what really occurred. That is all the more reason to move ahead now. I want this story to be told before too much time passes, and too many more people pass from the scene. I want to help set things right.

Meanwhile, the NPS and the WNPA seem to have moved on, unchanged by these events. The OIG continues to play silly games in its attempt to prevent the release of incriminating reports and documents. But efforts on multiple fronts, including the PEER FOIA lawsuit and subpoenas and discovery finally authorized in Malone's *Bivens* lawsuit, have yielded a sufficient number of documents and other sources of information to fill critical gaps and complete the account of what happened.

The single most tragic event in this story did not occur until the spring of 2010, when Susan Morton took her own life. I've investigated enough suicides over the course of my career to know that there is seldom any one thing, person, or event that bears the blame. We will never know all the things that factored into Susan's decision. But I know, and Susan's family and other friends know, that she was troubled and stressed by her job. That undoubtedly contributed to her decision, even though the NPS was quick to determine that hers was not a work-related death.

I kept in close contact with Susan up until the very end. We spoke and exchanged e-mails often. I know she was disappointed with the NPS and even angered by what she had seen on the job. She felt isolated and alienated from most of her colleagues; there were few if any people she could confide in about work. She made a point of calling me from home and exchanging e-mails only on her personal computer. We did talk about work, and I did my best to offer suggestions for how to deal with her stress and the frustrations of her job.

I trusted Susan absolutely to tell the truth and do the right thing. She was one of the few people with whom I could share and discuss details of the Hubbell investigation. She was the only person in the NPS who I trusted enough to allow to review and comment on draft versions of my report. The last time Susan and I got together in person, I let her look at the manuscript for this book. She seemed encouraged. She wanted this story to be told.

It seems that some of Susan's NPS colleagues resented her. Yee said she couldn't be trusted. That says more about Yee and his associates than it does about Susan. Susan wouldn't just stand by and keep quiet when bad things were happening. When someone screwed up, Susan would say so. If someone did something wrong, she would report it. That was how Susan lived and worked. And that's precisely why I did trust and respect Susan, both as a friend and a colleague. She had integrity and was honest to a fault. She was one of the good guys, one of the really good employees in the NPS. That made her tops in my book—in this book.

This book is for Susan.

Appendix

Selected Federal Statutes, Regulations,
Policies, and Court Opinions (i.e., Case Law)
Affecting Honesty and Integrity in Government

O UR SOCIETY TEACHES that we're supposed to be honest and tell the truth. Government officials, in particular, are expected to adhere to a higher standard of honesty and integrity. This is especially so for individuals who work in law enforcement and the criminal justice arena: the police, the prosecutors, and the courts. They are supposed to be "the good guys" and do what's right. As the oath prescribes, they are supposed to "tell the truth, the whole truth, and nothing but the truth."

More than mere platitudes, in the world of government these concepts are backed up by a hierarchy of court decisions, statutes, regulations, and policies enacted to ensure that we tell the truth and that government officials, and especially those in law enforcement, do what's right and look out for and protect the rights of others.

Most federal employees are disturbingly unfamiliar with these laws, regulations, and even policies. This is no mere coincidence, especially in those agencies where reporting or disclosing misconduct to outside or independent authorities is actively or passively discouraged. Instead, instruction in ethics focuses on the recitation of the literally hundreds of rules listed in personnel manuals to regulate specific employee conduct and activities (e.g., duty to follow orders, restrictions on the personal use of government equipment, etc.), as opposed to the broader topics of overall honesty, integrity, and respect for constitutional principles.

The following is a compilation of some of the laws, regulations, policies, and court decisions affecting honesty and the duty to report misconduct. Descriptions accompanying each citation are my own. I don't offer scholarly legal definitions and analysis so much as make a lay effort to capture their essential meaning and application in daily government life. They are presented not just because they're a good thing to know but also because they help in understanding the level of misconduct that occurred in the Hubbell investigation.

▲▼▲

Applicable Statutes, Regulations, and Policies

Statutes and regulations are presented under their abbreviated heading, with the term "USC" denoting U.S. Code, and the term "CFR" denoting Code of Federal Regulations. The number preceding either USC or CFR indicates the respective title number or chapter number, while the number following either USC or CFR indicates the specific section of the USC or CFR.

▲▼▲

18 USC 1001 (False Statements)

Whoever, in any matter within the jurisdiction of the executive, legislative, or judicial branch of the Government of the United States, knowingly and willfully—

1) falsifies, conceals, or covers up by any trick, scheme, or device a material fact;
2) makes any materially false, fictitious, or fraudulent statement or representation; or
3) makes or uses any false writing or document knowing the same to contain any materially false, fictitious, or fraudulent statement or entry;

shall be fined under this title or imprisoned not more than 5 years, or both.

This is the principal felony statute addressing "false statements" under federal law. In the context of this statute, a statement is considered to be "materially false" if it might reasonably serve to influence the decisions or activities of the federal government or its agencies or employees in the performance of duties. However, the false statement need not "succeed" in influencing government activities in order to be considered a violation of the statute. A false statement made to (or by) a federal official (or on a federal form or report) that is immediately detected may still be considered a false statement for purposes of the statute. So if someone makes a false statement to a federal agent during an interview, or makes a false entry on an official form but is immediately challenged on the point and "caught" in the lie, the person who made the statement can still be successfully prosecuted for having made a false statement. Likewise, if an employee defrauds the government or steals federal funds (18 USC 641) by making a false claim (such as on a travel or payroll voucher), he or she likely also commits a violation of 18 USC 1001.

In its 1998 decision, *Brogan v. United States*, the Supreme Court extended application of this law to false statements of denial made in response to an inquiry or accusation (previously recognized as the "exculpatory no" exception). So, for example, if a federal employee reflexively but falsely responds "no" to a question from a supervisor about an official matter (such as "Did you use the government car to drive your daughter to school?"), a simple "no" in response can be cited as a false statement and used as the basis for charging a violation of the statute. As the court explained, the answer "no" is a statement within the meaning of the statute, and the misrepresentation conveyed in that response is sufficient to constitute a violation, since it impairs a legitimate governmental function (i.e., to determine if government property is being properly used).

This law and similar statutes relating to perjury committed during judicial proceedings and other statements made under oath (found at 18 USC 1621 et seq.) are arguably the strongest and most important federal laws relating to honesty in government. Unfortunately, 18 USC 1001 is also one of the most commonly violated laws within the federal government. A violation is technically committed every time someone misleads or lies to a federal official or whenever a federal employee makes a false statement in an official document, report, or other official written or verbal communication.

In spite of this, 18 USC 1001 is also one of the most infrequently prosecuted statutes, utilized in only a small fraction of instances where a bona fide violation is determined to have occurred. This is particularly so in the case of violations by federal employees, where a lesser remedy is typically sought in the form of "administrative action" or discipline taken against the employee by their employer; and no report is ever even filed with federal prosecutors or law enforcement personnel. This practice, of course, can lend itself to considerable abuse where the agency is lax or inconsistent in its own administration of sanctions.

18 USC 1621 (Perjury)

Whoever—

1) having taken an oath before a competent tribunal, officer, or person, in any case in which a law of the United States authorizes an oath to be administered, that he will testify, declare, depose, or certify truly, or that any written testimony, declaration, deposition, or certificate by him subscribed, is true, willfully and contrary to such oath states or subscribes any material matter which he does not believe to be true; or
2) in any declaration, certificate, verification, or statement under penalty of perjury as permitted under section 1746 of title 28, United States Code, willfully subscribes as true any material matter which he does not believe to be true;

is guilty of perjury and shall, except as otherwise expressly provided by law, be fined under this title or imprisoned not more than five years, or both. This section is applicable whether the statement or subscription is made within or without the United States.

This is the principal felony statute addressing false statements or statements a speaker makes "under oath," such as sworn testimony presented in court, that the speaker "does not believe to be true." Violation carries the same penalties as violation of the counterpart statute, 18 USC 1001.

18 USC 4 (Misprision of Felony)

Whoever, having knowledge of the actual commission of a felony cognizable by a court of the United States, conceals and does not as soon as possible make known to the same judge or other person in civil or military authority under the United States, shall be fined under this title or imprisoned not more than three years, or both.

This statute obligates citizens (including federal employees) to report felonious misconduct to appropriate federal officials. Application to federal employees, however, is problematic since it necessarily places on them the responsibility to report felonious misconduct even when that misconduct is engaged in by a colleague or supervisor. More than one government employee has struggled with the question of what to do when they have observed a colleague or supervisor misusing government equipment or funds, falsifying a report, or lying about an official matter. Further complicating this is the question of to whom the report should be made, since in many situations, the offending party is the supervisor or official to whom one would normally make the report.

This statute, too, like 18 USC 1001, ranks very high on the list of statues seldom applied and prosecuted. Were this not so, virtually every federal employee (and other individual) who knew of a colleague or supervisor lying in some official capacity, who did not report the same, would themselves be the subject of a federal investigation and prosecution. That said, there are arguably a great many federal employees who have inadvertently committed a crime by merely "keeping their mouths shut" and failing to report colleagues or supervisors they have observed lying or committing other serious violations in their official duties.

28 USC 535(b) (Investigation of Crimes Involving Government Officers and Employees)

> Any information, allegation, matter or complaint witnessed, discovered, or received in a departmcnt or agency of the executive branch of the Government relating to violations of federal criminal law involving Government officers or employees shall be expeditiously reported to the Attorney General by the head of the department or agency or the witness, discoverer or recipient as appropriate.

This is an administrative provision of law and failure to comply carries no criminal penalties. It provides guidance to employees of the executive branch (e.g., employees of the majority of civilian agencies, including the NPS or even the Department of Justice) in deciding their course of action when encountering misconduct. This section is supplemented by regulations that address the same topic.

5 CFR 2635.101 et seq. (subsection 11) (Required Disclosure)

> Employees shall disclose waste, fraud, abuse and corruption to appropriate authorities.

This regulation provides standards of ethical conduct for employees of the executive branch of the government but provides no guidance in identifying "appropriate authorities."

5 USC 3331 (Federal Oath of Office for Executive Employees)

I, [name], do solemnly swear (or affirm) that I will support and defend the Constitution of the United States against all enemies, foreign and domestic; that I will bear true faith and allegiance to the same; that I take this obligation freely, without any mental reservation or purpose of evasion; and that I will well and faithfully discharge the duties of the office on which I am about to enter. So help me God.

28 USC 530B (Citizens' Protection Act of 1998)

(a) An attorney for the Government shall be subject to the state laws and rules, and local Federal court rules, governing attorneys in each State where such attorney engages in that attorney's duties, to the same extent and in the same manner as other attorneys in that State.

(b) The Attorney General shall make and amend rules of the Department of Justice to assure compliance with this section.

The statute continues in section 201, addressing punishable conduct:

(a) VIOLATIONS—The Attorney General shall establish, by plain rule, that it shall be punishable conduct for any Department of Justice employee to—

1) in the absence of probable cause seek the indictment of any person;

2) fail promptly to release information that would exonerate a person under indictment;

3) intentionally mislead a court as to the guilt of any person;

4) intentionally or knowingly misstate evidence;

5) intentionally or knowingly alter evidence;

6) attempt to influence or color a witness' testimony;

7) act to frustrate or impede a defendant's right to discovery;

8) offer or provide sexual activities to any government witness or potential witness;

9) leak or otherwise improperly disseminate information to any person during an investigation; or

10) engage in conduct that discredits the Department

(b) PENALTIES—The Attorney General shall establish penalties for engaging in conduct described in subsection (a) that shall include—

1) probation;

2) demotion;

3) dismissal;

4) referral of ethical charges to the bar;

5) loss of pension or other retirement benefits;

6) suspension from employment; and

7) referral of the allegations, if appropriate, to a grand jury for possible criminal prosecution.

36 CFR 2.32 (False Reports)

(a) The following are prohibited:

3) False Information:
   Knowingly giving a false or fictitious report of other false information: (i) to an authorized person investigating an accident or violation of law or regulation, or (ii) on an application for a permit.

4) False Report:
   Knowingly giving a false report for the purpose of misleading a government employee or agent in the conduct of official duties, or making a false report that causes a response by the United States to a fictitious event.

This is a regulation promulgated by and applicable within areas administered by the NPS. Violation of either section is a class B misdemeanor (criminal) provision, punishable by a fine up to $5,000 or by up to six months in prison or both.

NPS Law Enforcement Directives and Reference Manual (RM-9) (Law Enforcement Code of Ethics)

- I will faithfully abide by all laws, rules, regulations, and policies governing the performance of my duties and I will commit no act that violates these laws or regulations, or the spirit or intent of such laws and regulations while on or off duty.
- In my personal and official activities, I will never knowingly violate any local, state, or federal law or regulation, recognizing that I hold a unique position of public trust that carries an inherent personal commitment to uphold the laws and the integrity of my profession. For these reasons, I understand that this code places special demands on me to preserve the confidence of the public, my peers, my supervisors, and society in general.
- As a commissioned employee of the NPS, I will conduct all investigations and law enforcement functions assigned to me impartially and thoroughly, and report the results thereof, fully, objectively, and with accuracy.
- In the investigative process, I will be judicious at all times and I will release information pertaining to my official duties, orally or in writing, only in accordance with the law and established policy.

Applicable Court Rulings

BRADY V. MARYLAND, 373 U.S. 83 (1963)

In this precedent-setting case the court ruled that prosecutors have a duty to disclose to the defense any material that might be favorable to the defendant on the issues of guilt or punishment. Also, a defendant who is tried and convicted of criminal charges where material exculpatory evidence was not disclosed by the prosecution, *irrespective of the good faith or bad faith of the prosecution*, has been denied due process of law with respect to the fairness of their trial and is entitled to reversal of the judgment if the nondisclosed evidence undermines confidence in the conviction (*United States v. Bagley* 473 U.S. 667 [1985]).

GIGLIO V. UNITED STATES, 405 U.S. 150 (1972)

Giglio is a precedent-setting case where the court ruled that prosecutors are obligated to notify the defense of any issues that might tend to impeach the credibility of government witnesses offering testimony against a criminal defendant.

Petitioner filed a motion for a new trial on the basis of newly discovered evidence contending that the government failed to disclose an alleged promise of leniency made to its key witness in return for his testimony. At a hearing on this motion, the AUSA who presented the case to the grand jury admitted that he promised the witness that he would not be prosecuted if he testified before the grand jury and at trial. The other AUSA who tried the case was unaware of the promise. The court held that "neither the Assistant's lack of authority nor his failure to inform his superiors and associates is controlling, and the prosecution's duty to present all material evidence to the jury was not fulfilled and constitutes a violation of due process."

UNITED STATES V. HENTHORN, 931 F.2D (9TH CIR. 1991)

In this 1991 case, the 9th Circuit Court of Appeals chimed in specifically on the matter of the honesty and integrity of law enforcement officers. The court held that law enforcement agencies must disclose to criminal defendants all impeachment materials contained in a testifying officer's personnel file, official and otherwise. These materials include any and all records that document a credible allegation of misconduct, dishonesty, or bias or any other issue that could reflect on one's truthfulness. In the wake of this decision the U.S. Department of Justice implemented its own *Henthorn* policy, requiring federal prosecutors to direct that a *Henthorn* search be conducted on any testifying agent's official and unofficial personnel files and that the prosecution disclose to the defense any prospective *Henthorn* issues that could be used to discredit or impeach that witness. Ironically, however, the Department of Justice policy does not apply to the federal prosecutors themselves, who are not required to divulge any issues of honesty or integrity that may be documented in their own personnel files. Still, federal prosecutors are subject to a separate administrative law addressing ethical standards (Citizens' Protection Act of 1998).

UNITED STATES V. ZUNO-ACRE, 44 F.3D 1420 (9TH CIR. 1995)

In another case affecting the government's obligation to disclose exculpatory information to the defense, the court emphasized that "exculpatory information cannot be kept out of the hands of the defense just because the prosecutor does not have it, where an investigating agency does. That would undermine *Brady* by allowing the investigating agency to prevent production by keeping a report out of the prosecutor's hands until the agency decided the prosecutor ought to have it, and by allowing the prosecutor to tell the investigators not to give him certain materials unless he asked for them."

Kyles v. Whitley, 514 U.S. 419 (1995)

The court held that "favorable evidence is material, and constitutional error results from its suppression by the government, if there is a 'reasonable probability' that had the evidence been disclosed to the defense, the result of the proceeding would have been different. . . . One does not show a *Brady* violation by demonstrating that some of the inculpatory evidence should have been excluded, but by showing that the favorable evidence could reasonably be taken to put the whole case in such a different light as to undermine confidence in the verdict."

United States v. Blanco, 392 F.3d (9th Cir. 2004)

The court reiterated that the government has a duty to "turn over to the defense in discovery *all* material information casting a shadow on a government witness's credibility." In this case, "the government wrongly suppressed impeachment information about a confidential informant in violation of *Brady* and *Giglio*."

Notes

Introduction

1. Interview with Billy Malone, Aug. 14, 1998, Northern Arizona University, Cline Library, Special Collections and Archives Department, UITA Oral History Project, NAU.OH.75.24.
2. NPS/IMDE case no. 04–008 (AKA "the Hubbell investigation").
3. John Freemuth, "Absolutely American and Absolutely Democratic: National Parks and Policy Change," *George Wright Forum* 16.3 (1999): 66.

Chapter One

1. "Indian country" is a term of law defined at 18 USC 1151, and generally refers to those lands within the limits of any Indian reservation under the jurisdiction of the U.S. government. It is also loosely used to refer to that region of the southwestern United States—and particularly around the Four Corners area of Arizona, New Mexico, Utah, and Colorado—dominated by the presence of a number of large and prominent Indian reservations, including the Navajo, Hopi, Zuni, and various Ute and Apache reservations.
2. In this context the term "chapter" applies to a community of a large enough size within the Navajo Nation to warrant political recognition and status within the tribal government. Chapters were first established under the tribal government in the 1920s (predating the Indian Reorganization Act of 1934) to address community needs and develop community leadership. The chapter houses are where community meetings usually occur and where local residents have the opportunity to raise issues and voice opinions in what can often be a rather free-flowing and unrestrained forum. Chapters can be quite large geographically and typically include residents that reside a considerable distance from the chapter house itself and whatever other development or central community may exist. The trading posts often became the social center of the chapter and assumed the chapter name, as did the particular rug designs created by weavers of the area.

3. Interview with Bruce Burnham, Feb. 13, 2006, NPS/IMDE case no. 04–008.
4. Albert Manchester and Ann Manchester, *Hubbell Trading Post NHS: An Administrative History* (Santa Fe, N.Mex.: Southwest Cultural Resources Center, USNPS, 1993), 56–57.
5. The General Allotment (or Dawes) Act of 1887 (25 USC 331 et seq.) attempted to assimilate Indians into the larger society and to push them to adopt the white man's system of property and ownership by dismantling the reservations. The president was authorized to allocate to any individual Indian not more than 160 acres of reservation lands for his or her grazing or agricultural use. This often resulted in large segments of "surplus" reservation lands, and lands originally assigned to Indians were in many cases resold to non-Indians. Nearly forty-five years later this authorization was effectively ended through the Indian Reorganization Act of 1934 (25 USC 461 et seq.), which permitted the secretary of the interior "to restore to tribal ownership the remaining surplus lands of any Indian reservation opened before June 18, 1934" or to open those lands "to sale, or any other form of disposal. . . . Provided, however, that valid rights or claims of any persons to any lands so withdrawn existing on the date of the withdrawal shall not be affected." The same act authorized the DOI to purchase lands outside of reservations for assignment to individual Indians.
6. Earl Ashcroft, panel discussion, "A Gathering of Traders: A Historic Gathering of Generations of Southwestern Indian Traders," Cortez, Colo., Oct. 27, 2007.
7. Raymond Locke, *The Book of the Navajo* (Los Angeles: Mankind, 1976); Sally Noe, *Gallup, New Mexico, U.S.A.* (Virginia Beach, Va.: Donning, 1997); Sally Noe, unpublished article.
8. "A Gathering of Traders: An Historic Gathering of Generations of Southwestern Indian Traders."
9. *CBS Evening News*, June 14, 1973.
10. "Dead pawn" refers to property taken in pawn for which timely payments have not been made by the owner. The pawnbroker may then legally sell off the property to a third party.
11. Bill Donovan's presentation along with related discussion is documented on the second of the two-disk DVD set, *2007 Gathering of Traders, Cortez, Colorado*, produced and distributed by INTERpark Inc. (www.petroglyphtrail.com).
12. E.g., 2000 census.
13. The term "clan" in Navajo society applies to the system of kinship in which descent is traced through the mother and not the father. A child belongs to his or her mother's clan and is known by that clan name.
14. 43 USC 315–16 et seq.
15. Clyde Kluckhohn and Dorothea Leighton, *The Navaho* (Cambridge, Mass.: Harvard University Press, 1974), 300.
16. The term was first coined by anthropologist George M. Foster (1913–2006).
17. Sam Negri, "Last of the Old Time Traders," *Arizona Highways*, 73.1 (1997): 4–13; interview with Bruce Burnham, Feb. 13, 2006, NPS/IMDE case no. 04–008.
18. Interview with Russell Foutz, 1999, Northern Arizona University, Cline Library, Special Collections and Archives Department, UITA Oral History Project, NAU. OH.75.16.

19. Ledger of licensed Indian traders, U.S. National Archives, Washington, D.C., records of the Bureau of Indian Affairs 75.14.6.
20. Edward T. Hall, *West of the Thirties: Discoveries Among the Navajo and Hopi* (New York: Doubleday, 1994), 147.
21. *Turquoise Rose* (2007) is highly recommended for its accurate depiction of contemporary Navajo life, including the role of Indian traders. The film features an all-Navajo cast in Navajo roles, along with several real-life Anglo characters from the Indian arts and crafts and trading community.
22. Manchester and Manchester, *Hubbell Trading Post NHS*, 21–22.
23. Manchester and Manchester, *Hubbell Trading Post NHS*, 36, 43.
24. Manchester and Manchester, *Hubbell Trading Post NHS*, 37, 39, emphasis in original.
25. Manchester and Manchester, *Hubbell Trading Post NHS*, 40.
26. Manchester and Manchester, *Hubbell Trading Post NHS*, 54.
27. Interview with John Pearson, Jan. 17–18, 2006, NPS/IMDE case no. 04–008.
28. Manchester and Manchester, *Hubbell Trading Post NHS*, 22.
29. Manchester and Manchester, *Hubbell Trading Post NHS*, 43.

Chapter Two

1. Interview with Billy Malone, Aug. 14, 1998, Northern Arizona University, Cline Library, Special Collections and Archives Department, UITA Oral History Project, NAU.OH.75.24.
2. Hugh Lee is himself a noteworthy figure in the history of Indian law for his role as respondent in the 1959 U.S. Supreme Court case of *Williams v. Lee*. This watershed ruling established that "Arizona [state] courts are not free to exercise jurisdiction over civil suit by one who is not an Indian against Indian where cause of action arises on Indian reservation" (358 U.S. 217, 79 S. Ct. 269, 3 L. Ed. 2d 251 [1959]).
3. Interview with Billy Malone, Aug. 14, 1998, Northern Arizona University, Cline Library, Special Collections and Archives Department, UITA Oral History Project, NAU.OH.75.24.
4. Interview with Billy Malone, Aug. 14, 1998, Northern Arizona University, Cline Library, Special Collections and Archives Department, UITA Oral History Project, NAU.OH.75.24.
5. Interview with Billy Malone, Aug. 14, 1998, Northern Arizona University, Cline Library, Special Collections and Archives Department, UITA Oral History Project, NAU.OH.75.24.
6. Interview with Billy Malone, Aug. 14, 1998, Northern Arizona University, Cline Library, Special Collections and Archives Department, UITA Oral History Project, NAU.OH.75.24.
7. Including from Fern and Don Smouse at Borrego Pass Trading Post near Crown Point, New Mexico, Lavonne Palmer's Dunn Mercantile Trading Post at Fort Defiance, Bob French's Rugs in Kirtland, New Mexico, and even from his former employers from the 1960s and 1970s, Cliff McGee at Piñon Trading Post and Al Fritch at Lupton Trading Post.
8. Interview with Clifton McGee, Feb. 9, 2006, NPS/IMDE case no. 04–008.
9. Interview with Bruce McGee, Feb. 10, 2006, NPS/IMDE case no. 04–008.

10. Interview with Nancy Stone, Feb. 2, 2006, NPS/IMDE case no. 04–008.

11. Interview with Kris Medina, Feb. 22, 2006, NPS/IMDE case no. 04–008.

12. Interview with John Pearson, Jan. 17–18, 2006, NPS/IMDE case no. 04–008.

13. Interview with Tim Priehs, Feb. 21, 2006, NPS/IMDE case no. 04–008.

14. Peter Iverson, *Diné: A History of the Navajos* (Albuquerque: University of New Mexico Press, 2002), 281.

15. Interview with Bruce Burnham, Feb. 13, 2006, NPS/IMDE case no. 04–008.

Chapter Three

1. The NPS uniform, worn by employees of all types throughout the agency, is distinguished by its green pants and grey shirt.

2. 5 USC 3331.

3. Andrea Lankford, *Ranger Confidential: Living, Working, and Dying in the National Parks* (Old Guildford, Conn.: Globe Pequot, 2010), is highly recommend for its accurate account of contemporary life working as a ranger in the big parks.

4. http://data.bestplacestowork.org/index.php/bptw/index. A record of poor employee morale within the NPS is reflected in 2009, 2007, and earlier surveys of employee satisfaction conducted by the Partnership for Public Service and the American University's Institute for the Study of Public Policy, consistently ranking the NPS in the bottom third (160) of federal agencies and among the lowest of federal land management agencies for employee job "satisfaction and engagement."

5. See, for example, "Park Service's Top Investigator Pleads Guilty to Theft—Comments," *National Parks Traveler*, Nov. 1, 2007 (http://www.nationalparkstraveler.com/2007/11/park-services-top-investigator-pleads-guilty-theft).

6. John Freemuth "Absolutely American and Absolutely Democratic: National Parks and Policy Change," *George Wright Forum* 16.3 (1999): 66.

7. At least two other NPS rangers had been murdered prior to Ken Patrick: James Carey in 1927 and Karl Jacobsen in 1938. As of 2010, at least ten NPS rangers have been murdered in the history of the agency. Approximately twenty-seven others have been killed in nonassaults during the performance of law enforcement duties. The NPS did not maintain records on these types of incidents until the early 1990s. See Paul Berkowitz, *U.S. Rangers: The Law of the Land* (Redding, Calif.: C.A.T., 1989–95); Paul Berkowitz, "Myths and Misinformation," self-published essay, January 2000.

8. Paul Berkowitz, *U.S. Rangers: The Law of the Land*.

9. Richard West Sellars, *Preserving Nature in the National Parks: A History* (New Haven, Conn.: Yale University Press, 1999), 209.

10. DOI-OIG case no. 4VI090 (Jul. 9, 1985); DOI-OIG case no. 6VI055 (May 9, 1986); *Dan R. Sholly v. DOI*, Merit Systems Protection Board (MSPB) case no. DE-0752–98–0230-I-1 (1998); Heidi Hagemeier, "Yellowstone's Top Ranger Faces Allegations," *Livingston (Mont.) Enterprise*, Oct. 15, 1997; Michael Milstein, "Yellowstone's Chief Ranger Accused of Misconduct," *Billings (Mont.) Gazette*, Oct. 15, 1997; "Ex-Chief Ranger to Offer Defense in Public Hearing," *Billings (Mont.) Gazette*, June 19, 1998; Lorna Thackeray, "Park Worker Testifies in Sex Case against Former Chief Ranger," *Billings (Mont.) Gazette*, June 24, 1998; Associated Press, "Former Chief Ranger at Yellowstone National Park Denies Woman's Allegations," *Billings (Mont.) Gazette*, June 25, 1998;

Lorna Thackeray, "Park Witnesses Disagree on Woman's Character," *Billings (Mont.) Gazette*, June 26, 1998; Scott McMillion, "Yellowstone Ranger Loses Appeal," *Bozeman (Mont.) Daily Chronicle*, Dec. 22, 1998; Lorna Thackeray, "Administrative Law Judge Upholds Action against Yellowstone Chief Ranger," *Billings (Mont.) Gazette*, Dec. 22, 1998; Angus M. Thuermer Jr., "Park Ranger Appeal Nixed," *Jackson Hole (Wyo.) Guide*, Dec. 23, 1998; Scott McMillion, "Appeal Denied: Former Chief Ranger in Yellowstone Can't Clear His Name," *Bozeman (Mont.) Daily Chronicle*, Dec. 23, 1998; *State of California v. Marshal Scott Connelly*, no. F98911279-8 (Consol. Fresno Jud. Dist. Cal. 1998); *United States v. Dane Paul Henry*, no. CR209-0005-001 (D. Ga. 2009).

11. This analogy is reinforced by the NPS's direct descent from the U.S. military, which policed many national parks from 1886 to 1916. Cavalry troops are the direct predecessors to park rangers and, prior to establishment of the NPS in 1916, were stationed in many national parks throughout the West, such as Yellowstone and Yosemite, which were under military command.

12. Midwest Regional Office, "Why NPS Employees Should Join the E&AA."

13. Letter from PEER to NPS director regarding illegal prior restraint of NPS employee speech and related press release, Sept. 23, 2002, responding to NPS IMR, "Employee Ethical Responsibilities and Conduct," P36 (IMR-D), Sept. 16, 2002.

14. E.g., *United States v. Pierson*, no. 6:07-mj-00223-WMW (E. D. Cal. dismissed 2008).

15. Kevin Gilmartin and Jack Harris, "Law Enforcement Ethics: The Continuum of Compromise," *Police Chief Magazine* (Jan. 1998); John Kleining, "Rethinking Noble Cause Corruption," *International Journal of Police Science and Management* 4.4 (2002): 287–314; Thomas Martinelli, "Unconstitutional Policing: The Ethical Challenges in Dealing with Noble Cause Corruption," *Police Chief Magazine* 73.10 (2006): 148–56.

16. John Philbin, *The Law of Nature: Park Rangers in Yosemite Valley* (Philbin Philms, 1986).

17. Statement of Robert O. Binnewies, Feb. 4, 1986, DOI-OIG case no. 6VI 055.

18. E.g., Randy Thompson fatality investigation report, incident date Feb. 26, 1996, Grand Canyon National Park case no. 96-0818 (the park's deputy superintendent ordered NPS investigators to *not* run a toxicology screen, despite the fact that marijuana use was suspected as a contributing factor); "Cerro Grande Prescribed Fire (May 4–8, 2000)," May 18, 2000 (interagency investigation report); interview and e-mail exchange with confidential member of interagency investigation team by Paul Berkowitz, Jul. 21, 2008, Aug. 18, 2008. The Cerro Grande fire began as a "controlled burn" ignited by NPS officials at Bandelier National Monument. That effort, as part of a ten-year prescribed fire schedule, targeted just one thousand acres in the headwaters of Frijoles Creek. The fire almost immediately went "wild" and out of control, forcing the evacuation of more than eighteen thousand residents from the neighboring towns of Los Alamos and White Rock, New Mexico. The blaze ultimately consumed over forty-eight thousand acres, destroying over 235 private homes and damaging nearly as many others. Costs associated with the incident approached one *billion* dollars. In the subsequent interagency investigation, the NPS fire chief reportedly pressured one NPS investigator to skew his findings by saying "Remember who you work for" and "Remember who pays your salary."

19. E.g., "NPS Internal Investigation and Review of Officer-Involved Shooting, Coronado National Memorial," incident date Feb. 6, 2004. NPS investigators assigned to investigate the incident conducted their crime scene documentation and review, shooting walk-through, and reenactment at the wrong location (i.e., *not* where the shooting had actually occurred). Though the error was later confirmed through GPS readings and brought to the attention of senior NPS officials, neither the incident, conflicting statements of involved personnel, nor the performance of internal investigators was reinvestigated.

20. E.g., *Abell v. Department of the Interior*, MSPB no. NY-1221–03–0342-W-1 (2003). See also DOI-OIG, "Investigative Report on Allegations that the National Park Service Improperly Allowed Daniel Snyder to Cut Trees on Government Land," Jan. 19, 2006 (http://www.doioig.gov/images/stories/reports/pdf//Snyder_Investigation.pdf); *United States v. Danno*, no. 3:08CR44 (N.D. W. Va. acquitted Jan. 9, 2008); *Danno v. Department of the Interior*, Office of Special Counsel (OSC) no. MA-07–0702 (2006), *Danno v. Department of the Interior*, OSC no. DI-07–0693 (2007); *Danno v. Department of the Interior*, MSPB no. DC-0752–07–0268-I-1 (2007); Christina Marnick, "Man Claims Park Service Harassment," *(Martinsburg, W.Va.) Journal News*, Feb. 11, 2009 (http://www.journal-news.net/page/content.detail/id/515639.thml?nav=5006).

21. DOI-OIG, "A Disquieting State of Disorder: An Assessment of DOI Law Enforcement," Jan. 2002.

22. The NPS Organic Act refers to the act of August 25, 1916, codified as 16 USC 1–4, establishing the NPS as a federal agency that would jointly administer the country's national parks, monuments, lakeshores, recreation areas, and historic sites.

23. State of Arizona, Office of Attorney General, Special Investigations Section, AGI case no. 90–0250.

24. On payment of the fine the offense was redesignated a class 1 misdemeanor.

25. Interviews with Ron Everhart, 1990, AGI case no. 90–0250.

26. The Law Enforcement (Ranger Image) task force was commissioned by NPS director Gary Everhardt on August 13, 1976. The task force submitted its report on March 15, 1977. Everhardt approved it on April 18, 1977.

27. 122 Cong. Rec. (1976).

28. Harrisonburg, Va. Police Department case no. 871463 (1987); Shenandoah National Park case nos. 87–1516 (1987) and 87–1518 (1987); "Locker Room Peeping Case Goes to Trial," *Northwest Indiana Times*, Jul. 7, 2000; Grand Canyon National Park case no. 01–3576 (2001).

29. Studies and reports going back decades have yielded similar results. See DOI, Office of the Secretary, "Secretary's Task Force on Law Enforcement," 1973.

30. Earl E. Devaney, "Assessment of the Department of the Interior's Law Enforcement Activities," no. 2002–1–0014, Jan. 4, 2002.

Chapter Four

1. "NPS Director's Order #32: Cooperating Associations," sec. 1.
2. "NPS Director's Order #32: Cooperating Associations," sec. 3.5.1.
3. "Cooperative Agreement between WNPA and the NPS," art. 8, sec. E.

4. NPS, "National Park Service Cooperating Associations," 2003.

5. WNPA *2004 Annual Report*; WNPA, *Strategic Plan, 2004–2007*.

6. Interview with Marianne DeVries, Feb. 8, 2007, DOI-OIG case no. PI-PI-07-0054-I; interview with John Pearson conducted by Paul Berkowitz, Jan. 16, 2008.

7. Edward T. Hall, *West of the Thirties: Discoveries Among the Navajo and Hopi* (New York: Doubleday, 1994), 147.

8. Interview with Jim Babbitt, Jul. 21, 1999, Northern Arizona University, Cline Library, Special Collections and Archives Department, UITA Oral History Project, NAU. OH.75.37.

9. Interview with Jim Babbitt, Jul. 21, 1999, Northern Arizona University, Cline Library, Special Collections and Archives Department, UITA Oral History Project, NAU. OH.75.37.

10. Interview with Jim Babbitt, Jul. 21, 1999, Northern Arizona University, Cline Library, Special Collections and Archives Department, UITA Oral History Project, NAU. OH.75.37.

11. On November 7, 2003, the WNPA approved its first strategic plan. The subsequent 2004 publication of that document cited authorization to reestablish the "Hubbell task force," whose responsibility would be to "create a plan that focuses on who will eventually succeed the current Manager/Trader."

12. Interview with John Pearson, Jan. 17–18, 2006, and interview with Tim Priehs, Feb. 21, 2006, NPS/IMDE case no. 04–008.

13. Interview with Kris Medina, Feb. 22, 2006, NPS/IMDE case no. 04–008.

14. Albert Manchester and Ann Manchester, *Hubbell Trading Post NHS: An Administrative History* (Santa Fe, N.Mex.: Southwest Cultural Resources Center, USNPS, 1993), 56.

15. Interview with John Pearson, Jan. 17–18, 2006, and interview with Tim Priehs, Feb. 21, 2006, NPS/IMDE case no. 04–008.

16. David R. Wilcox, "The Staff List," MNA catalogue no. 506 N86ch, table 3, Jan. 2006.

17. MNA, "AAM Responds To Former MNA Board Actions," Dec. 2003; MNA, "Settlement Agreement Reached in Museum Lawsuit," Dec. 21, 2005. See also Gary Ghioto, "Asset Sale Averted Shutdown," *Arizona Daily Sun*, June 5, 2003; Gary Ghioto, "MNA Putsew [*sic*] Plan on Hold," *Arizona Daily Sun*, June 7, 2003; Gary Ghioto, "Museum Needs a More Open Relationship with Members," *Arizona Daily Sun*, June 8, 2003; Gary Ghioto, "MNA Art Sale Called Unethical," *Arizona Daily Sun*, June 22, 2003; Gary Ghioto, "MNA Trustees Urged to Resign," *Arizona Daily Sun*, Jul. 10, 2003; Gary Ghioto, "All 16 Museum Trustees Resign," *Arizona Daily Sun*, Jul. 12, 2003; Seth Muller, "New Museum Board Set to Be Chosen," *Arizona Daily Sun*, Jul. 26, 2003; Seth Muller, "Museum Exhibits New Leadership," *Arizona Daily Sun*, Jul. 27, 2003; Seth Muller, "MNA Faces Accreditation Challenge," *Arizona Daily Sun*, Aug. 5, 2003; "What Was Sold?," *Arizona Daily Sun*, Dec. 17, 2003; Seth Muller, "Sale Costs MNA Accreditation," *Arizona Daily Sun*, Dec. 17, 2003; Seth Muller, "MNA Seeks to Restore Reputation," *Arizona Daily Sun*, Dec. 28, 2003; Mark Shaffer, "Museum Files Suit vs. Broker over Proceeds from Art Sale," *Arizona Republic*, Apr. 26, 2005; *Museum of Northern Arizona v. S. Diamant*, no. S-0300-CV-20050199 (Coconino Cty. Sup. Ct. Ariz. filed Apr. 5, 2005).

18. Manchester and Manchester, *Hubbell Trading Post NHS*, 39.

19. Interviews with LeAnn Simpson, May 24, 2004, and Jan. 10, 2006, NPS/IMDE case no. 04–008.
20. Interview with Tim Priehs, Feb. 21, 2006, NPS/IMDE case no. 04–008.
21. Interview with John Pearson, Jan. 17–18, 2006, NPS/IMDE case no. 04–008.
22. Interview with Nancy Stone conducted by Paul Berkowitz, Dec. 5, 2007 ("It was like talking to a brick wall").
23. Interview with LeAnn Simpson, Jan. 10, 2006, NPS/IMDE case no. 04–008.
24. Brian Dominy, e-mail, Oct. 23, 2004, and Clyde Yee, internal memorandum, Oct. 25, 2004, NPS/IMDE case no. 04–008; interview with John Pearson conducted by Paul Berkowitz, Jan. 21, 2008.

Chapter Five

1. John Philbin, *The Law of Nature: Park Rangers in Yosemite Valley* (Philbin Philms, 1986).
2. Charles "Chuck" Cushman was appointed to the NPS Advisory Board by President Ronald Reagan. Cushman was the founder and president of the National Inholders Association (now known as the American Land Rights Association).
3. DOI-OIG case no. 4VI090 (Jul. 9, 1985).
4. E.g., testimony of Paul Berkowitz, Oct. 15, 1985, House Committee on Interior and Insular Affairs, Subcommittee on National Parks, Forests, and Public Land; "Yosemite Ranger Accuses Park Officials," *San Francisco Chronicle*, Oct. 16, 1985.
5. Letters to representatives Tony Coelho and Bruce Vento from Paul Berkowitz, Jan. 15, 1986, Feb. 3, 1986.
6. E.g., "Park Chief Allegedly Made Secret Taping," *Fresno (Calif.) Bee*, Jan. 28, 1986; "Berkowitz Makes Further Allegations," *Mariposa (Calif.) Gazette*, Jan. 30, 1986; "Binnewies Admits Ordering Recording," *Fresno (Calif.) Bee*, May 9, 1986.
7. DOI-OIG case no. 6VI055 (May 9, 1986).
8. Philip Shabecoff, "Washington Talk: Interior Department: Would Freedom Help the NPS?," *New York Times*, May 27, 1988.
9. Letter to Yosemite chief of law enforcement Leland J. Shackelton from Western Regional Office director Howard H. Chapman, Aug. 12, 1986.
10. The OIG and the GAO also failed to investigate the allegations of sexual abuse. Nearly fifteen years later, in 1998, a young boy in Fresno, California, reported that "he was walking in northeast Fresno when [the park prosecutor] Connelly grabbed him, forced him into his pickup, and tied him up." The Fresno Police Department investigation identified at least three other victims, resulting in Connelly's being arrested and charged with fourteen counts ranging from kidnapping to lewd and lascivious acts and oral copulation with juveniles. He pled guilty in state court to four felony counts, one for each of the four identified victims. See *State of California v. Marshal Scott Connelly*, no. F98911279–8 (Consol. Fresno Jud. Dist. Cal. pled Sept. 23, 1998); Pablo Lopez, "Police Hold Yosemite Ranger on Molestation Charges," *Fresno (Calif.) Bee*, Aug. 1, 1998; "Ranger Videotaped Sex Acts, Prosecutor Says," *Fresno (Calif.) Bee*, Aug. 13, 1998; Jerry Beir, "Ex-Ranger Pleads Guilty in Unlawful Sex Case," *Fresno (Calif.) Bee*, Sept. 24, 1998.

11. For example, "The Middle of Nowhere Syndrome," self-published, 1993; "Not All Is Well That Ends Well," *SWAT Magazine*, 1993; *U.S. Rangers: The Law of the Land* (Redding, Calif.: C.A.T., 1989–95); "Enough," *The Protection Ranger*, Vol. XI, no. 1, 2000, pp. 3–4; "A Ranger's Field Guide to Myths and Misinformation," self-published, 2000; "Nothing Seems to Change," *The Protection Ranger*, Vol. XIII, no. 6, 2002, pp. 5–7; "Big News but No Surprise," *The Protection Ranger*, 2003.

12. Interview with LeAnn Simpson, May 25, 2004, NPS/IMDE case no. 04–008.

13. Interview with Michelle Boden, May 28, 2004, NPS/IMDE case no. 04–008.

Chapter Six

1. *Kyles v. Whitley* 514 U.S. 419, 437 (1995).

2. *United States v. Blanco* 392 F.3d 382 (9th Cir. 2004), quoting *Carriger v. Stewart*, 132 F.3d 463, 480 (9th Cir. 1997). In *Brady v. Maryland*, 373 U.S. 83 (1963), the court ruled that prosecutors have a duty to disclose to the defense any material that might be favorable to the defendant on the issues of guilt or punishment. Also, a defendant who is tried and convicted of criminal charges where material exculpatory evidence was not disclosed by the prosecution has been denied due process of law as to the fairness of his trial, and is entitled to reversal of the judgment if the non-disclosed evidence undermines confidence in the conviction (*United States v. Bagley* 473 U.S. 667 [1985]).

3. Testimony of Richard L. Delonis, 2001, Senate Subcommittee on Criminal Justice Oversight hearings on S.250, Federal Prosecutor's Ethics Act.

4. E.g., *United States v. Randy Stephens*, Grand Canyon National Park case no. 04–2337 (OIG case referral of May 27, 2004).

5. *Groh v. Ramirez*, 124 S. Ct. 1284 (2004); *United States v. Bridges*, 344 F.3d 1010 (9th Cir. 2003).

6. IRS, Criminal Investigations Division Manual, sec. 9.4.9.

7. The order sealing both the application and affidavit in support of the search warrant was issued June 8, 2004. The order *unsealing* those same documents was not issued until January 30, 2007.

8. See *United States v. DeLeon*, 979 F.2d 761, 763–64 (9th Cir. 1992); *United States v. Sartin*, 262 F. Supp. 2d 1154 (D. Or. 2003); *United States v. Zimmerman*, 277 F.3d 426, 436 (3rd Cir. 2002).

Chapter Seven

1. "A search warrant may in all cases be served by any of the officers mentioned in its direction or by an officer authorized by law to serve such warrant, but by no other person, except in aid of the officer on his requiring it, he being present and acting in its execution."

2. Interview with LeAnn Simpson, Jan. 10, 2006, NPS/IMDE case no. 04–008.

3. Interview with Nancy Stone, Jan. 10, 2007, DOI-OIG case no. PI-PI-07–0054-I.

4. Interviews with confidential source conducted by Paul Berkowitz, Mar. 24, 2008, and Aug. 19, 2009. Friends of Hubbell Trading Post National Historic Site, Inc., raises funds from Native American arts and crafts auctions to provide scholarships to Navajo and Hopi college students.

5. Memorandum submitted by Mark A Foust, June 25, 2004, NPS/IMDE case no. 04–008.

6. Clyde Yee, supplement, Sept. 15, 2004, NPS/IMDE case no. 04–008.

7. *Arizona v. Hicks*, 480 U.S. 321 (1987); *Horton v. California*, 496 U.S. 128 (1990). See also *Bond v. United States*, 529 U.S. 334 (2000).

8. Office of the United States Attorney for the District of Arizona (Mark Aspey), *Legal Update*, 2002, 2004.

9. A copy of the draft was faxed to Aspey's office on June 29, 2006. I picked up his handwritten edit approximately two weeks later, on July 10, 2006.

10. Interview with Mark Aspey, Jan. 11, 2006, NPS/IMDE case no. 04–008.

11. E.g., memorandum from Mark Aspey to Paul Okerberg, "Hubbell Trading Post Investigation," June 1, 2007; Guy Whitmer and Russell Roy, "NPS Review, Hubbell Trading Post OIG Investigation," Apr. 25, 2008.

12. Letter from Howard Sukenic to Jim Reilly, Jul. 21, 2005.

13. Clyde Yee, "Preliminary Case Development Plan: Hubbell Investigation," Jul. 19, 2004, NPS/IMDE case no. 04–008.

14. Susan Morton, "Presence of Indicia of Stolen Property on Items Seized from Bill Malone," Aug. 25, 2006, NPS/IMDE case no. 04–008.

15. Clyde Yee, supplement, Sept. 15, 2004, NPS/IMDE case no. 04–008.

16. Clyde Yee, supplement, Sept. 15, 2004, NPS/IMDE case no. 04–008.

17. Interview with LeAnn Simpson, Jan. 10, 2006, NPS/IMDE case no. 04–008.

18. Interview with LeAnn Simpson, Jan. 10, 2006, NPS/IMDE case no. 04–008.

19. LeAnn Simpson and Jim Babbitt to Billy Malone, June 16, 2004, WNPA memorandum regarding employment status. The allegation of sexual abuse was never investigated or confirmed. The referenced individual subsequently quit her own job after an argument with Malone's successor over changes implemented at the trading post.

20. "Notes Prepared by Scott Aldridge," termination meeting, June 16, 2004, signed by Scott Aldridge and LeAnn Simpson.

Chapter Eight

1. Clyde Yee, "Preliminary Case Development Plan: Hubbell Investigation," Jul. 19, 2004, NPS/IMDE case no. 04–008.

2. WNPA, notes for conference call, Jul. 29, 2004.

3. National park sites along the U.S. border with Mexico have been heavily impacted by illegal drug smuggling, which has had a devastating effect on protected resources and the safety of park visitors and employees. The NPS actively participates in interagency efforts to combat those activities through the assignment of NPS agents to the High Intensity Drug Trafficking Area task force.

4. Memorandum from Susan Morton to Jim Reilly, Oct. 4, 2004.

5. Letter from Clyde Yee to Chris Simpson, Aug. 31, 2004, NPS/IMDE case no. 04–008.

6. Susan Morton, "Hubbell Trading Post Investigation Evidence," Oct. 4, 2004, NPS/IMDE case no. 04–008.

7. Susan Morton to Paul Okerberg, "Response to Special Agent Clyde Yee's Memorandum Dated 10/25/04," June 26, 2007.

8. Interview with Clyde Yee, May 23, 2007, DOI-OIG case no. PI-PI-07–0054-I.

9. WNPA, notes for conference call, Jul. 29, 2004.

10. Albert Manchester and Ann Manchester, *Hubbell Trading Post NHS: An Administrative History* (Santa Fe, N.Mex.: Southwest Cultural Resources Center, USNPS, 1993), 37, 43.

11. Conversation between Steve Getzwiller and Cyd Martin, Mar./Apr. 2007. E-mail from Nancy Stone to Paul Berkowitz, Oct. 24, 2007.

12. WNPA/NPS task force, "Task Force Report for the Operation of the Trading Post at Hubbell Trading Post National Historic Site," Apr. 14, 2005, 23.

13. Interview with Navajo weaver Mary Lee Begay (translation by daughter Lenah Henderson) conducted by Paul Berkowitz, Sept. 6, 2007.

14. Letter from Laura Graves to NPS, Sept. 30, 2004.

15. Teresa J. Wilkins, *Patterns of Exchange; Navajo Weavers and Traders* (Tulsa: University of Oklahoma Press, 2008), 41–42.

Chapter Nine

1. Whistle-blower reprisal complaint submitted to DOI-OIG, May 9, 2005.

2. DOI-OIG case report no. CR-07-731-PCT-NVW. That investigation resulted in one twenty-nine-count indictment and another twenty-three-count indictment of senior officials with Pacific General, contracted to perform several multimillion dollar projects under the administration of that same superintendent. In letting the contracts, the park allegedly failed to enforce the Miller Act and federal acquisition regulations that otherwise require posting of performance and payment bonds (Office of the United States Attorney, District of Arizona, "PGI Officials Indicted for Fraudulently Obtaining Federal Construction Contracts in the Grand Canyon," Jul. 5, 2007); testimony of Ron Steed, Nov. 6, 2007, Senate Committee on Energy and Natural Resources, Subcommittee on National Parks; Christopher Smith, "Construction Funds for Grand Canyon Projects Disappear," *Salt Lake (Utah) Tribune*, Jan. 31, 2004; Jackie Brown, "Contractor Default Prompts IG Probe," *Grand Canyon News*, Aug. 11–17, 2004; Cyndy Cole, "Alston Out as Grand Canyon Superintendent," *Arizona Daily Sun*, Jan. 25, 2007; Cyndy Cole, "House Bill to Reimburse Canyon Subcontractors," *Arizona Daily Sun*, Apr. 19, 2007; "Federal Grand Jury Returns Grand Indictments in GCNP Project," *Arizona Daily Sun*, Jul. 6, 2007; "Contractor Pleads Guilty to Canyon Construction Fraud," *Arizona Daily Sun*, Apr. 25, 2008; "Canyon Contractor Fined $2.3M for false claims," *Arizona Daily Sun*, Apr. 22, 2009. The company president pled guilty to six counts of making false statements (18 USC 1001), and his vice president pled guilty to one count of misprision (knowing concealment) of a felony (18 USC 4). The pleas were accompanied by a $2.3 million dollar judgment (Office of the U.S. Attorney, District of Arizona, "U.S. Secures $2.3 Million Judgment against Florida Man for False Claims Related to Federal Construction Contracts at Grand Canyon National Park," Apr. 22, 2009).

3. Interview with Clyde Yee, May 23, 2007, DOI-OIG case no. PI-PI-07–0054-I.

4. Interview with two AUSAs, Flagstaff, Ariz., Jan. 11, 2007, DOI-OIG case no. PI-PI-07–0054-I. This documented interview was not included in the OIG's final (released) report.

5. Letter from Howard Sukenic to Jim Reilly, Jul. 21, 2005.

Chapter Ten

1. Paul Berkowitz, "Completion of Investigative Report," cover memorandum, Oct. 23, 2006, NPS/IMDE case no. 04–008. Both *Giglio v. United States* (405 U.S. 150 [1972]) and *United States v. Henthorn* (931 F.2d [9th Cir. 1991]) are precedent-setting cases in which the courts ruled that prosecutors are obligated to notify the defense of any issues that might tend to impeach the credibility of government witnesses offering testimony against a criminal defendant.
2. Office of the United States Attorney for the District of Arizona (Mark Aspey), *Legal Update*, 2002, 2004.

Chapter Eleven

1. Letter and contract from DeVries, Carpenter, to the WPNA board of directors, Jul. 30, 2004, signed and dated Aug. 2, 2004, by LeAnn Simpson.
2. "NPS Director's Order #32," sec. 3.5.1.
3. "NPS Director's Order #32," sec. 3.5.1. This same restriction had been violated in the early 1980s when the Yosemite Natural History Association helped fund the NPS's undercover drug investigation in Yosemite National Park.
4. SPMA, *Area Handbook* (March 1997), 2:1.
5. Interview with LeAnn Simpson, Jan. 10, 2006, NPS/IMDE case no. 04–008.
6. Transmittal memorandum (whistle-blower complaint), Oct. 24, 2006, NPS/IMDE case no. 04–008.
7. Brian Dominy and David Sandbakken, supplemental report, Nov. 16, 2004, NPS/IMDE case no. 04–008.
8. Interview with John Pearson, Jan. 17–18, 2006, NPS/IMDE case no. 04–008.
9. 18 USC 1152, the so-called Indian Country Crimes Act defines the circumstances under which offenses committed in Indian country fall within the respective jurisdiction of the tribe, the state, or the federal government. Generally, those offenses committed by an Indian against an Indian are considered exclusively tribal offenses. Offenses committed by a non-Indian against a non-Indian are considered state offenses. Offenses committed by an Indian against a non-Indian or by a non-Indian against an Indian are generally considered to be exclusively federal offenses. 18 USC 1153, the Major Crimes Act, identifies fourteen excepted "major" crimes (e.g., murder, rape, robbery, etc.), which, although committed by an Indian against an Indian, are still considered federal offenses, unless occurring in one of the so-called PL 280 states, identified at 18 USC 1162, which extends to Alaska, California, Minnesota, Nebraska, Oregon, and Wisconsin, full jurisdiction over offenses committed by or against Indians on reservations or otherwise. Notwithstanding any of these three statutes, offenses that are federal crimes throughout the United States, such as violation of federal drug laws, federal firearms laws, and federal tax laws, assault on a federal officer, and theft of federal funds or property, remain under federal jurisdiction even when they occur within Indian country, regardless of the tribal standing or affiliation of the offender.
10. Paul Berkowitz to Rob Long, "Completion of Investigative Report," Oct. 23, 2006.

Chapter Twelve

1. Interview with Nancy Stone, Feb. 2, 2006, NPS/IMDE case no. 04–008.
2. Interview with Clifton McGee, Feb. 9, 2006, NPS/IMDE case no. 04–008.
3. Interview with Bruce McGee, Feb. 10, 2006, NPS/IMDE case no. 04–008.
4. Ray Manley and Steve Getzwiller, *The Fine Art of Navajo Weaving* (Tucson, Ariz.: Ray Manley Publications, 1984); Steve Getzwiller, *Treasures of the Navajo Horsemen* (Wickenburg, Ariz.: Desert Caballeros Western Museum, 2003); Peter Iverson, *Diné: A History of the Navajos* (Albuquerque: University of New Mexico Press, 2002), chap. 8.
5. E-mail from Nancy Stone to Paul Berkowitz, Oct. 24, 2007.
6. Hubbell Trading Post, *Guidelines for Preserving Traditional Trading Practices*, draft of August 2004 versus draft of January 2005. E-mail from Nancy Stone to Paul Berkowitz, Oct. 24, 2007.
7. Interview with Steve Getzwiller, Feb. 12, 2006, NPS/IMDE case no. 04–008.
8. Interview with Bruce Burnham, Feb. 13, 2006, NPS/IMDE case no. 04–008.
9. Joseph J. Kolb, "Stephen Paul Wallace: Vet Proudly Recognized as Lone Non-Navajo Code Talker," *New Mexico Magazine*, Jul. 2002, 16–17.
10. Interviews with Keith Wallace conducted by Paul Berkowitz, Aug. 9 and 11, 2009.
11. Transmittal memorandum to Rob Long, Oct. 23, 2006, NPS/IMDE case no. 04–008; interviews with Nancy Stone conducted by Paul Berkowitz, Jan. 10, 2007, Mar. 5, 2008; interviews with Steve Getzwiller conducted by Paul Berkowitz, Feb. 12, 2006, Sept. 14, 2006.
12. Interview with Nancy Stone, Aug. 2, 2004, DOI-OIG case no. OI-CO-04–0453-I.
13. Interview with Steve Getzwiller, Aug. 8, 2004, NPS/IMDE case no. 04–008.
14. Interview with Tim Priehs, Feb. 21, 2006, NPS/IMDE case no. 04–008.
15. Interview with Kris Medina, Feb. 22, 2006, and subsequent correspondence, NPS/IMDE case no. 04–008. The letter writer was the same employee that many colleagues and other members of the community believed was a witch.
16. Request for those subpoenas was not made until Mar. 21, 2006.

Chapter Thirteen

1. Letter from United States Attorney for the District of Arizona to Michael Kimerer, Mar. 15, 2006, NPS/IMDE case no. 04–008.
2. Interview with Billy Malone, Feb. 28, 2006, NPS/IMDE case no. 04–008.
3. *United States v. Blood* 435 F.3d 612 (6th Cir. 2006).

Chapter Fourteen

1. See *Franks v. Delaware*, 438 U.S. 154 (1978). *United States v. Leon*, 468 U.S. 897, 923 (1984): "Affidavits containing reckless or intentional false statements by the affiant are subject to challenge by a motion to controvert. . . . The defendant need not present clear proof that misrepresentations were deliberate or reckless."
2. Interview with Russell Griswold Sr., Mar. 16, 2006, NPS/IMDE case no. 04–008.
3. *United States v. Rose Morris*, no. 1:05–001 CR 1378 JC (D. N.M. 2007).

4. Interview with LeAnn Simpson, Jan. 10, 2006, NPS/IMDE case no. 04–008.
5. Interview with Billy Malone, Apr. 19–21, 2006, NPS/IMDE case no. 04–008.
6. Susan Morton, "Presence of Indicia of Stolen Property on Items Seized from Bill Malone," Sept. 13, 2006, NPS/IMDE case no. 04–008.

Chapter Fifteen
1. FBI FD-498 polygraph report with attachments.
2. Interview with Billy Malone, June 15, 2006, NPS/IMDE case no. 04–008.

Chapter Sixteen
1. Follow-up, Jul. 13, 2006, NPS/IMDE case no. 04–008.
2. Paul Berkowitz, "Preparation of Property Receipts Used in the Return of Rugs and Jewelry to Mr. Billy Malone," Jul. 26, 2007.
3. Cover memorandum, whistle-blower complaint, Oct. 24, 2006, NPS/IMDE case no. 04–008.

Chapter Seventeen
1. Letter from LeAnn Simpson to Paul Berkowitz, Jul. 21, 2006.
2. An e-mail message documenting these same communications was sent to the OIG and copied to Long on August 24, 2006.
3. This "understanding" was documented by the WNPA as early as July 28, 2004, in an internal e-mail from LeAnn Simpson to various WNPA board members. That e-mail contains details of the NPS request to have the WNPA pay for the forensic audit and speculation that "this entire mess could cost the organization $150,000. . . . It may be that in the end the $150,000 could be 'recovered' in some manner. And I'll let Jim [Babbitt] talk about that."
4. E-mail from Christine Szuter to WNPA board members, Jan. 13, 2007.
5. Interviews with LeAnn Simpson, Jul. 31–Aug. 28, 2006, NPS/IMDE case no. 04–008.
6. Paul Berkowitz, "Preparation of Property Receipts Used in the Return of Rugs and Jewelry to Mr. Billy Malone," Jul. 26, 2007, DOI-OIG case no. PI-PI-07-0054-I.

Chapter Eighteen
1. Federal Rules of Criminal Procedure section 6(e) provides that matters occurring before the grand jury may not be disclosed to anyone, except as provided by the rules. Thus, the AUSA and anyone assisting the AUSA are prohibited from disclosing matters occurring before the grand jury, except as otherwise provided in that rule. Individuals assisting in a criminal prosecution may be put on a "6(e) disclosure list" by the AUSA to assist in the investigation and prosecution of the case. Once individuals are on this list, they may be shown grand jury information. However, grand jury information or information derived from it may not be used in any other proceeding without district court authorization.
2. Letter from Steve Martin to LeAnn Simpson, Mar. 24, 2005, NPS/IMDE case no. 04–008.

3. OIG summary report, Jul. 20, 2006, DOI-OIG case no. OI-CO-04–0453-I.
4. Interviews with Ray Macy, Jan. 25, 2007, and Jan. 31, 2007, DOI-OIG case no. PI-PI-07–0054-I.
5. Interviews with Marianne DeVries and Jennifer Phillips, Feb. 8, 2007, DOI-OIG case no. PI-PI-07–0054-I.
6. SPMA/WNPA annual reports, 2001–6.
7. 5 USC 2302. This law purports to offer protection from "prohibited personnel practices" to federal executive branch employees who report "(i) a violation of any law, rule, or regulation, or (ii) gross mismanagement, a gross waste of funds, an abuse of authority, or a substantial and specific danger to public health or safety."
8. Interview with Perry Shorty, Oct. 6, 2006, NPS/IMDE case no. 04–008.
9. Following a second divorce, Botello again reverted to her given name of Karen Jean Malone.
10. Interview with Karen Jean Botello, Oct. 11, 2006, NPS/IMDE case no. 04–008. The official report incorrectly cites the date of this interview as October 6, 2006.
11. Interviews with Al Grieve conducted by Paul Berkowitz, Aug. 9, 2009, and Aug. 10, 2009.
12. Interview with Vernon Jackson, Aug. 10, 2004, NPS/IMDE case no. 04–008.
13. Telephone conversation with Vernon Jackson, May 28, 2008. E-mail exchange between Vernon Jackson and Paul Berkowitz, Jul. 29–Aug. 1, 2008.

Chapter Nineteen

1. Clyde Yee, "Preliminary Case Development Plan: Hubbell Investigation," Jul. 19, 2004, NPS/IMDE case no. 04–008.
2. Cover letter from Paul Berkowitz to Rob Long, Oct. 23, 2006, NPS/IMDE case no. 04–008.
3. E-mail from Paul Berkowitz to Rob Long, Oct. 26, 2006.

Chapter Twenty

1. E-mails from a confidential NPS source to Paul Berkowitz, Dec. 22, 2006, and Jan. 19, 2007. See also Cyndy Cole, "Alston Out as Grand Canyon Superintendent," *Arizona Daily Sun*, Jan. 25, 2007.
2. Case initiation report, Dec. 8, 2006, DOI-OIG case no. PI-PI-07–0054-I; closing report, Jan. 16, 2008, DOI-OIG case no. PI-PI-07–0054-I.
3. NPS case no. GRCA93-0764/GRCA 99-0256; Arapahoe County S.O. case no. 78-10957; FBI case no. 196D-PX-64041. See also Leonard Johns, Gerald F. Downes, and Camille D. Bibles, "Resurrecting Cold Case Serial Homicide Investigations," *FBI Law Enforcement Bulletin* 74.8 (2005): 1–7; Robert Scott, *Married to Murder* (New York: Pinnacle Books, 2004).
4. Interview with Nancy Stone, Jan. 10, 2007, DOI-OIG case no. PI-PI-07–0054-I.

Chapter Twenty-One

1. Interviews with Ray Macy, Jan. 25. 2007, and Jan. 31, 2007, DOI-OIG case no. PI-PI-07–0054-I .

2. E-mail exchange between Paul Okerberg and Paul Berkowitz, Jan. 29, Jan. 30, 2007.

3. E-mail from Paul Berkowitz to Paul Okerberg, Feb. 7, 2007.

4. "Cam" and "KTG" refer to Buccello's supervisors at that time, the NPS associate director for visitor and resource protection (KTG) and her deputy (Cam).

5. Department of Justice, Office of the U.S. Attorney for the District of Columbia, "Former Official for the National Park Service Sentenced for Fraud Involving Theft of Public Money," Jan. 25, 2008.

6. *United States v. Patricia Buccello*, no. 07–517M (D.D.C., 2007).

7. E-mail from Lane Baker to the field, Mar. 28, 2007.

Chapter Twenty-Two

1. Interview with Nancy Stone, Jan. 10, 2007, DOI-OIG case no. PI-PI-07–0054-I; closing report, Jan. 16, 2008, DOI-OIG case no. PI-PI-07–0054-I; interview with Nancy Stone, Aug. 2, 2004, NPS/IMDE case no. 04–008; interview with Steve Getzwiller, Feb. 6, 2007, DOI-OIG case no. PI-PI-07–0054-I; closing report Jan. 16, 2008, DOI-OIG case no. PI-PI-07–0054-I.

2. Interview with Carl "Chip" Davis, Apr. 17, 2007, DOI-OIG case no. PI-PI-07–0054-I; investigative activity report, Nov. 7, 2007, DOI-OIG case no. PI-PI-07–0054-I; closing report, Jan. 16, 2008, DOI-OIG case no. PI-PI-07–0054-I.

3. Interviews with Jim Reilly, Jan. 23–24, 2007, DOI-OIG case no. PI-PI-07–0054-I; closing report, Jan. 16, 2008, DOI-OIG case no. PI-PI-07–0054-I.

4. Interview with Mark Foust, Mar. 12, 2007, DOI-OIG case no. PI-PI-07–0054-I; closing report, Jan. 16, 2008, DOI-OIG case no. PI-PI-07–0054-I.

5. Wessels was promoted to IMR regional director in late 2010, following Snyder's retirement.

6. Interview with John Wessels, Jan. 25, 2007, DOI-OIG case no. PI-PI-07–0054-I; closing report, Jan. 16, 2008, DOI-OIG case no. PI-PI-07–0054-I.

7. Interview with Kim Sikoryak, Apr. 17, 2007, DOI-OIG case no. PI-PI-07–0054-I; closing report, Jan. 16, 2008, DOI-OIG case no. PI-PI-07–0054-I.

8. Interview with Steve Martin, Apr. 19, 2007, DOI-OIG case no. PI-PI-07–0054-I; closing report, Jan. 16, 2008, DOI-OIG case no. PI-PI-07–0054-I.

9. Interview with Scott Aldridge, Feb. 8, 2007, DOI-OIG case no. PI-PI-07–0054-I.

10. Interview with Marianne DeVries and Jennifer Phillips, Feb. 8. 2007, DOI-OIG case no. PI-PI-07–0054-I; closing report, Jan. 16, 2008, DOI-OIG case no. PI-PI-07–0054-I.

11. Interview with Mark Aspey, Apr. 18, 2007, DOI-OIG case no. PI-PI-07–0054-I; closing report, DOI-OIG case no. PI-PI-07–0054-I.

12. Response from Mark Aspey, June 1, 2007, DOI-OIG case no. PI-PI-07–0054-I.

13. Interviews with LeAnn Simpson, Jul. 31–Aug. 28, 2006, NPS/IMDE case no. 04–008.

14. Interview with LeAnn Simpson, Feb. 7, 2007, DOI-OIG case no. PI-PI-07–0054-I; closing report, DOI-OIG case no. PI-PI-07–0054-I; investigative activity report, Nov. 7, 2007, DOI-OIG case no. PI-PI-07–0054-I.

15. Interview with Mike Snyder, Apr. 16, 2007, DOI-OIG case no. PI-PI-07–0054-I; investigative activity report, Nov. 7, 2008, DOI-OIG case no. PI-PI-07–0054-I; closing report, DOI-OIG case no. PI-PI-07–0054-I.

16. E-mail exchange between OIG and WNPA legal counsel, Apr. 13, 2007, Jul. 30, 2007, DOI-OIG case no. PI-PI-07–0054-I.

17. *Garrity v. New Jersey*, 385 U.S. 493, 87 S. Ct. 616 (1967).

18. *Kalkines v. United States* 473 F.2d 1391 (1973). A *Kalkines* warning compels an employee/suspect to make statements or risk termination of their employment but also provides that employee with criminal immunity for their statements and derivative evidence.

19. Interviews with Clyde Yee, Apr. 17, 2007, May 23, 2007, DOI-OIG case no. PI-PI-07–0054-I; closing report, Jan. 16, 2008, DOI-OIG case no. PI-PI-07–0054-I.

20. Closing report, Jan. 16, 2008, DOI-OIG case no. PI-PI-07–0054-I; DOI-IG, "Administrative Investigation (Hubbell Trading Post)," Jan. 23, 2008.

Chapter Twenty-Three

1. Ernest Quintana, "NPS Response to Hubbell Trading Post Investigation," June 23, 2009.

2. E-mail from Clyde Yee to LeAnn Simpson, June 16, 2005.

3. Interview with Kevin Fitzgerald, Mar. 20, 2007, DOI-OIG case no. PI-PI-07–0054-I.

4. Interview attempt (refused) with Clyde Yee, Apr. 17, 2007, DOI-OIG case no. PI-PI-07–0054-I; compelled interview with Clyde Yee, May 23, 2007, DOI-OIG case no. PI-PI-07–0054-I.

5. FOIA request to Sandra Evans from Jeff Ruch, June 15, 2009.

6. *Public Employees for Environmental Responsibility v. U.S. Department of the Interior Office of the Inspector General*, no. 1:09-cv-01862 (D.D.C. 2009). See also PEER, "The Last Indian Trader Ruined by Park Service Incompetence; Lawsuit Filed to Unearth IG Report into Agency Misconduct," Sept. 30, 2009.

7. E-mail exchanges between Paul Okerberg and Alan Boehm, Jan. 4–7, 2008.

8. E-mail from Christine Szuter to WNPA board of directors, Jan. 13, 2007.

9. Executive order and memorandum to heads of executive departments and agencies on FOIA, Jan. 21, 2009.

10. PEER, "The Last Indian Trader Ruined by Park Service Incompetence."

11. *Malone v. Yee*, no. 3:08-cv-08027 (D. Ariz. Feb. 28, 2008).

12. *Bivens v. Six Unknown Named Agents of the Federal Bureau of Narcotics*, 403 U.S. 388, 91 S. Ct., 1999 (1971). The court ruled that federal officials could be sued in federal court in a manner similar to that set forth at 42 USC 1983, which applies to state officials who violate a person's constitutional rights under color of law, so long as that violation occurred as the result of a conspiracy between two or more parties.

13. Testimony of Richard L. Delonis, 2001, Senate Subcommittee on Criminal Justice Oversight hearings on S.250, Federal Prosecutor's Ethics Act.

14. Letter from Lewis and Roca LLP to DOI-OIG, Feb. 22, 2007.

15. The case was initially assigned to Judge James A. Teilborg, then Judge Mary H. Murguia, and then Judge David G. Campbell. The case was finally assigned to visiting Judge H. Russell Holland.
16. 122 Cong. Rec. (1976).
17. Jenny Mandel, "Interior IG: Senior Execs 'Immune' from Punishment," *The Government Executive*, Feb. 16, 2007.
18. Testimony of Paul Berkowitz, Oct. 15, 1985, House Committee on Interior and Insular Affairs, Subcommittee on National Parks, Forests, and Public Lands.
19. The NPS was established August 25, 1916: "There is created in the Department of the Interior a service to be called the NPS, which shall be under the charge of a director. . . . The service thus established shall promote and regulate the use of the Federal areas known as national parks, monuments, and reservations hereinafter specified, except such as are under the jurisdiction of the Secretary of the Army, as provided by law, by such means and measures as conform to the fundamental purpose of the said parks, monuments, and reservations, which purpose is to conserve the scenery and the natural and historic objects and the wild life therein and to provide for the enjoyment of the same in such manner and by such means as will leave them unimpaired for the enjoyment of future generations."

Index

Albright, Horace, 58

Aldridge, Scott, 85, 109, 110, 228, 233, 270, 286

ARA Leisure Services. *See* Glen Canyon Battery Dumping Case

Arizona State Attorney General. *See* Glen Canyon Battery Dumping Case

Ashcroft, Eugene, 14

Ashcroft, Wilford "J. W.," 14

Aspey, Mark, 112, 116, 125–28, 144; Berkowitz interviews, 169–70; Malone sues, 309; OIG interviews, 287–88; OIG letter, 288; and Yee, 296

Assistant United States Attorney (AUSA): role and responsibility, 113–15

Babbitt, Bruce, 74, 261; and Earl Devaney, 308–9; and WNPA, 238–39. *See also* Glen Canyon Battery Dumping Case

Babbitt, Jim, 86–89; and Bruce Babbitt, 238–39, 308; case briefings/involvement, 122, 138–39, 191–92, 264, 289, 290, 293, 303; and Malone, 89–90, 92, 94–96, 140, 184, 200–201, 285; Malone sues, 309, 311; OIG investigates, 263; OIG interview request, 291, 302; and Steve Pickle, 139, 186; and LeAnn Simpson, 236

Berkowitz, Paul, 104–8; Mark Aspey interviewed, 169–70; and Mary Bomar,

297–98; case agent, 156–57; case briefings, 157–60; Karen (Malone) Botello interviewed, 246, 248–50; Buccello retirement e-mail (Feb. 12, 2007), 279–80; Bruce Burnham interviewed, 189–92; Congressional testimony, 318; and Rob Eaton, 172, 226–31; evidence, 166–68; Steve Getzwiller interviewed, 183–89; Russ Griswold Sr. interviewed, 213–14; Indian Country Unit, 147–49; Vernon Jackson interviewed, 250–53; Rob Long meeting, 168–69; Rob Long transmittal, 255–56; Malone interviewed (Feb. 28, 2006), 204–11; Malone interviewed (Apr. 12, 2006), 216; Malone meeting (Apr. 19–21, 2006), 216–19; Malone interviewed/polygraphed (June 15, 2006), 220–23; Malone property, 225–31; Malone meeting (Jan. 10, 2007, case closed), 267–68; Malone property (Jan. 17, 2007), 270–72; Malone property (Mar. 1, 2007), 282; Bruce McGee interviewed, 182–83; Cliff McGee interviewed, 181–82; Kris Medina interviewed, 201–3; OIG complaint, 219, 224; OIG contact, 263–65; OIG meeting, 266–68; OIG transmittal, 256–58; John Pearson interviewed, 173–76; political pressures, 170–71; Tim Priehs interviewed, 200–201;

and Long interview (Feb. 28, 2006), 204–11; Berkowitz interviews (Apr. 12, 2006), 216; Berkowitz and Morton meet with (Apr. 19–21, 2006), 216–19; FBI interviews/polygraphs (June 15, 2006), 220–23; fired by WNPA, 130–31; lawsuit, 309–12; OIG interviews, 267–68; property returned by NPS (Jul. 13, 2006), 225–31; property returned by WNPA (June 17, 2007), 270–72; property returned by NPS (Mar. 1, 2007), 282; raid at home of, 123

Malone, B.J., 271

Malone, Minnie (Goodluck), 38, 43–45, 53, 202, 267

Martin, Cyd, 140, 145, 187, 304; Malone sues, 309; as Navajo group superintendent, 262, 272, 282

Martin, Steve: deputy director, 145; evidence vault, 167; Steve Getzwiller meeting (attempt), 187; Grand Canyon superintendent, 262; Hubbell closure/investigation, 100, 121, 289; Malone sues, 309; OIG investigates, 263; OIG interviews, 285–86; WNPA funding for investigation, 234, 236–37, 240, 242, 289, 290. *See also* Graves, Laura; Martin, Cyd; Simpson, LeAnn; Snyder, Mike

McCain, John, 261

McGee, Bruce: interviewed, 181–83, 192, 201; on Malone, 51

McGee, Clifton: interviewed, 181–82; on Malone, 44, 49–51

McGee's Indian Art Gallery, 7

McKinley County (NM) Sheriff's Office, 172

Medina, Kris: interviewed, 200, 201–3; on Billy Malone, 52–53

Mihalec, Dave, 167–68

Mormons, 16, 30

Morton, Susan, 102, 239, 265, 305; Berkowitz assisted, 163, 166–68; evidence custodian, 134–35; issues with chain-of-custody, 135–36, 152, 161, 169, 265, 274, 284, 294, 305; Malone meeting, 216–19; property return, 225–31; Yee's comments about, 294, 305; suicide, 320

Museum of Northern Arizona (MNA), 32, 89, 96, 139, 191

National Park Service (NPS): culture, 59–74 passim, 76, 79–81, 299, 303–5, 314–18; law enforcement authority, 75; law enforcement program, 64–65, 75, 313–15; law enforcement program review and reforms, 76–80, 102–3; "oath of

office," 59–60; OIG report (responses), 79, 298–99; organic act, 58; political influences, 69–74; ranger image, 75; WNPA influence over, 296, 303–5. *See also* Glen Canyon Battery Dumping Case; noble cause corruption; Office of the Inspector General; Yosemite mafia; Yosemite National Park

Navajo Criminal Investigation Unit, 148

Navajo jewelry. *See* Navajo rugs and jewelry

Navajo rugs and jewelry: history, trading, and value, 7–15 passim, 29, 47, 48, 54, 90–92, 94, 143, 175, 179, 183, 201; and Billy Malone (historical association), 2, 39, 46–47, 49–53, 55–57, 90, 92, 173–75, 180–82, 186, 190–91, 195–96, 198, 202; suspicions regarding/seized as evidence, 90, 109–12, 124–26, 128–31, 133–34, 138–39, 144, 158, 162, 166–67, 170–71, 184–85, 187, 200–201, 205–10, 212, 216–18; returned to Malone, 225–31. *See also* Burnham, Bruce; Getzwiller, Steve; Indian Arts and Crafts Act; Malone, Billy; Shorty, Perry; Simpson, LeAnn; Snyder, Mike; Western National Parks Association

Navajo time, 24–25

Navajo Treaty, 1, 14, 15, 28, 29, 30

noble cause corruption, 68

Northern Arizona University, 192

Notah-Dineh Trading Company. *See* Leighton family

"Not Subject to Discovery" file, 274

Null, Perry. *See* Turpen's (Tobe) Trading Post

Obama, Barack, 308

Office of the Inspector General (OIG), 3, 4, 6, 68, 70, 105–8, 145–46, 149, 261, 262; assessment of NPS law enforcement, 76–80, 102; notified, 170–71, 219, 224, 231–32, 235, 239, 245, 254, 256–58; assume jurisdiction, 258–60, 263; release report, 305–9. *See also* Devaney, Earl; Freedom of Information Act; Howard, Jamie; Macy, Raymond; Okerberg, Paul

Office of Professional Responsibility (NPS), 69, 137, 196, 298

Office of the Solicitor, 6, 172, 231, 245, 302, 307, 310. *See also* Eaton, Rob

Okerberg, Paul, 262–63; Scott Aldridge interviewed, 286; Mark Aspey interviewed (Apr. 18, 2007), 287–88; Mark Aspey submits letter to (Jun. 1, 2007),